Lift-Off for
Early Literacy

D0870936

Lift-Off for Early Literacy

Directed Reading Opportunities for Struggling Students

by

Charlene Iannone-Campbell, M.A., C.A.S.E., NBCT

and

Susan Lloyd Lattimore, Ed.M., M.S.

Baltimore City Public Schools

·P A U L·H·
BROOKES
PUBLISHING Co.®

Baltimore • London • Sydney

Paul H. Brookes Publishing Co.
Post Office Box 10624
Baltimore, Maryland 21285-0624
USA

www.brookespublishing.com

All royalties from the sale of this book will be donated to Project Early ID and its continued efforts to promote pre-K literacy skills.

Typeset by Integrated Publishing Solutions, Grand Rapids, Michigan.
Manufactured in the United States of America by
Versa Press, Inc., East Peoria, Illinois.

The publisher and the authors cannot be held responsible for injury, mishap, or damages incurred during the use of or because of the activities in this book and its accompanying CD-ROM. The publisher and authors recommend appropriate and reasonable supervision at all times based on the age and capability of each child. This book and its accompanying CD-ROM are sold without warranties of any kind, express or implied, and the publisher and authors disclaim any liability, loss, or damage caused by the contents of this book and its accompanying CD-ROM.

All examples in this book are composites. Any similarity to actual individuals or circumstances is coincidental, and no implications should be inferred.

Select contents from Dr. Jean Feldman's cheer cards are used by permission as part of lesson plans in transcripts for dialogue between educators and children in DROPPS 1, 2, 6, 9, and 10 and in the OPT DROPP on the accompanying CD-ROM.

Clip art in this book and on the accompanying CD-ROM © istockphoto.com and © 2011 Jupiterimages Corporation; sound clips on the CD-ROM © 2011 Jupiterimages Corporation.

Every effort has been made to ascertain proper ownership of copyrighted materials and obtain permission for their use. Any omission is unintentional and will be corrected in future printings upon proper notification.

Library of Congress Cataloging-in-Publication Data
Iannone-Campbell, Charlene.
 Lift-off for early literacy : directed reading opportunities for struggling students / by Charlene Iannone-Campbell and Susan Lloyd Lattimore.
  p.   cm.
 Includes bibliographical references and index.
 ISBN-13: 978-1-59857-099-1 (pbk.)
 ISBN-10: 1-59857-099-4 (pbk.)
 1. Reading—Remedial teaching. 2. Reading (Early childhood) I. Title.
LB1050.5.I26 2011
372.43—dc23   2011032668

British Library Cataloguing in Publication data are available from the British Library.

2015   2014   2013   2012   2011
10   9   8   7   6   5   4   3   2   1

Contents

Contents of the
Accompanying CD-ROM

About the Authors

Susan Lloyd Lattimore, Ed.M., M.S., has worked with Baltimore City Public School children since 1975 as a special educator, reading specialist, and early literacy teacher leader. Her concern for the plight of struggling readers led her and a team of dedicated colleagues to launch Project Early ID, a response to intervention pilot program that became the basis for this book. From 2005 to 2010, she served as Director of the project, which identifies and addresses early indicators of reading difficulties.

Inspired by her older brother, who has intellectual challenges, Ms. Lattimore has spent much of her life learning about and implementing best practices in special education and reading resource programs. She holds a master's degree in special education from Temple University and Certificates in Educational Technology and Outdoor Education from the University of Maryland. In 2001, Ms. Lattimore was honored as a Porter Scholar by the American Federation of Teachers, which led to a master of science degree with a concentration in reading from The Johns Hopkins University. She has Advanced Professional Certification as a reading specialist and special educator.

While working as a special educator in Baltimore elementary schools, Ms. Lattimore developed a Story Pals program that recruited and trained parent, community, and university volunteers to read aloud every week to students with reading and language difficulties. In 1991, she founded The Barclay School Clean Team and Eco-Band and has worked with hundreds of students on environmental activities such as installing bird and butterfly gardens, restoring bay grasses, raising oysters, and composting. Ms. Lattimore was a mentor to new teachers in Project Early ID and to special educators in Baltimore City Public Schools, and she is currently an academic coach in the Baltimore Curriculum Project. She teaches part time in The Johns Hopkins Graduate School of Education.

Ms. Lattimore lives in Baltimore with her husband. Their children attended public schools, and two of her daughters are also teachers.

Charlene Iannone-Campbell, M.A., C.A.S.E., NBCT, is Director of Early Learning for Baltimore City Public Schools. She is dedicated to urban education and is passionate about providing excellent preschool resources to Baltimore's youngest learners and their families. She has been an educator for 18 years and has served as a classroom teacher, special educator, department head, reading specialist, and mentor-teacher.

Ms. Iannone-Campbell received her M.A. in leadership in teaching and Certification in Advanced Studies in Education (C.A.S.E.) from the College of Notre Dame of Maryland. She holds Advanced Professional Certification from the Maryland State Department of Education as a reading specialist and is also certified in the areas of early childhood, elementary and special education, and administration. Ms. Iannone-Campbell holds the distinction of certification as an exceptional needs specialist from the National Board of Professional Teaching Standards. She teaches part time in the Graduate Schools of Education at both The Johns Hopkins University and Notre Dame of Maryland University.

Ms. Iannone-Campbell spent the first year of her professional life in a Montessori children's house and then several years as a second grade teacher before deciding to turn to the world of finance. Prior to returning to education in 2000, she built a successful career as a tax manager at The Black & Decker Corporation—although the field of public education continually beckoned to her.

Ms. Iannone-Campbell lives in Baltimore City with her husband, Jim. Her two daughters, Lyndsay and Jordan, attended local public schools before going onto college and graduate school. Lyndsay holds a master's degree in women's studies and is currently completing a master's degree in social work. Jordan is a teacher-intern in Baltimore City schools in pursuit of her master's degree in teaching.

As part of their work in Project Early ID, Ms. Iannone-Campbell and Ms. Lattimore designed a teacher-to-teacher model of professional development entitled Jump Into Reading and created a series of Parent University workshops on early literacy. Their training as Orton-Gillingham reading therapists and Direct Instruction teachers helped to mold the curriculum that they developed and delivered in tiered intervention, resulting in strong student performance. At The Johns Hopkins University, they co-teach Emergent Literacy: Research into Practice, a gateway course into the Reading Specialist Program.

Ms. Lattimore and Ms. Iannone-Campbell work collaboratively to research, develop, and disseminate early literacy best practices. They have presented their strategies and results at professional conferences, including the International Reading Association, The International Dyslexia Association, and the Council for Exceptional Children, Division of Early Childhood. They have drawn on their collective areas of specialty in developing the DROPPS intervention program, which provides the basis for their professional development seminars.

Foreword

It is a pleasure to write the foreword to *Lift-Off for Early Literacy: Directed Reading Opportunities for Struggling Students*. Charlene Iannone-Campbell and Susan Lloyd Lattimore have done a masterful job crafting this curriculum around the lessons they developed for their own prekindergarten students who needed Tier 2 support. My remarks are intended to convey the value of this resource for helping ensure that all children get off to a good start in literacy.

Most, if not all, of the materials for literacy instruction published within the past 5 or so years focus on evidence-based practice, and they encompass to varying degrees the National Reading Panel's five major skill areas of phonemic awareness, phonics, vocabulary, comprehension, and fluency. This book is in the same good company as many others in that regard. In addition, an increasing number of resources are now available that provide lesson plans within a response to intervention (RTI) framework, as does this volume. However, what differentiates this book from the other resources is the focus on *early and differentiated* literacy instruction for students in prekindergarten who show signs of struggling. My quick search of the literature did not turn up any books that are comparable. Several publications are intended for the primary grades, but none is designed with content tailored to prekindergartners.

The primary focus of Directed Reading Opportunities (DROPPS) is the core phonological skills that underlie word reading, an emphasis that is quite appropriate for children who are not readily mastering these skills in the larger classroom context. Carefully sequenced activities develop children's rhyme awareness and discrimination, sentence and compound word segmentation, syllable awareness, blending, and segmentation, and beginning sound alliteration, among other skills. Within the authentic context of the activities, oral language and vocabulary is fostered. A strength of the program is that this important domain of early literacy development is not neglected.

What is particularly appealing about DROPPS is that instruction takes place within an engaging context. This program relies heavily on games, rhymes, songs, and fingerplays to convey essential information about the sound structure of our language. Research has shown that early literacy instruction for young children works best when it resembles play rather than didactic drills. In a study of early literacy development in Baltimore, my colleagues and I found that prekindergarten children who frequently played rhyming games at home with their parents and siblings had better phonemic awareness than those who did not, and that an "entertainment" orientation to literacy fostered more motivation for learning to read than a "skills" orientation (Serpell, Baker, & Sonnenschein, 2005).

In their introductory chapter, Charlene and Susan briefly describe the research component of Project Early ID, the impetus for this book. They show that children participating in the first cohort of the project were more likely to read at grade level on a standardized achievement test by the end of first grade than were Baltimore school children citywide. As part of the external evaluation of the project, my research team administered a variety of early language and literacy assessments across the multiple years of the study. We identified comparison schools with similar demographic and achievement data who were implementing the standard Baltimore curriculum, and we administered assessments to children at these schools as well. Relative to prekindergarten comparison classrooms, Early ID classrooms revealed dramatic improvements in phonological awareness; we attribute this to the fact that children who were struggling with the sound system of the language received Tier 2 lessons like those included in this book.

The Early ID pilot project is now completed, and data are in for all three cohorts of children followed from prekindergarten through first grade. Tier 2 (and 3) interventions were provided if progress assessments indicated they were warranted, in kindergarten and first grade as well as in prekindergarten. The results of the quasi-experiment showed that children in the Early ID classrooms were more likely to be reading at grade level at the end of Grade 1 than children in comparison classrooms. This advantage was not only on phonemic awareness, but also on word identification and other early literacy skills (e.g., alphabet knowledge, conventions of print, meaning). Teachers interested in using DROPPS with their students will be pleased to know that this recent scientific evidence supports the overall effectiveness of the lessons themselves.

Lift-Off for Early Literacy is written in an engaging style and without jargon. The authors have the knowledge and expertise to convey information to teachers that can readily be used. The DROPPS games and activities are clearly described, and the instructions for implementing the lessons are explicit. Teachers can have confidence that they and their paraprofessionals will be able to implement the program successfully in their classrooms. Based on extensive field-testing, Charlene and Susan acquired a good sense of how young children respond to the lessons and what they find captivating. My research assistants and I can attest to the smiles on the faces of the Early ID participants as they sang the rhyming songs that are included in these Tier 2 lessons. I have no doubt that teachers and students alike will benefit from this valuable instructional resource.

Linda Baker, Ph.D.
Professor and Chair
Department of Psychology
University of Maryland, Baltimore County

REFERENCE

Serpell, R., Baker, L., & Sonnenschein, S. (2005). *Becoming literate in the city: The Baltimore Early Childhood Project.* New York: Cambridge University Press.

Preface

We teach struggling readers in Baltimore City Public Schools. In our experience as longtime classroom teachers, special educators, and reading specialists (we are lucky—we have all three areas covered!), we saw many students as far up the grades as middle school who could not match letters with sounds and then blend them into words. These children, many of whom were *not* special education students, expended so much energy in decoding words that they had little energy or motivation left for comprehension of word or story meaning. This fact alone presents a major area of concern for teachers in the content areas such as science and social studies. Many middle and high school content area teachers say that before they can teach effective comprehension strategies to help their students understand and process the content, they must first teach decoding skills. Research shows that when children fall behind early in reading, interventions are not implemented until at least third grade; children at this point have fallen behind their classmates (Snow, Burns, & Griffin, 1998). Good teachers know that is too late.

Conversely, we saw students as young as first grade using good prereading strategies. They participated in class discussions to interpret story pictures, connected their prior experiences to the characters in the story, and made predictions to set the stage for reading; however, when it came time for them to actually *read* the words, they guessed their way to the end of sentences. We saw first hand that guessing became an oft-used strategy in first grade and beyond—students just kept guessing until they got it right!

Of course, these students *rarely got it right*, which led them to incredible feelings of frustration and failure, loss of interest, and acting-out behaviors. What about the larger picture? Research further shows that 75% of third graders who are reading below grade level are the same students who will fail to be promoted from ninth grade (Hall, 2007). Does this affect the high school drop-out rate? Educators, already know the answer, especially if they work with children in urban areas.

So, what do educators know? First, there is a very small window of time to move students from *struggling readers* to *reading stars* because children who are not reading on grade level at the end of first grade rarely catch up (NICHD Early Child Care Research Network, 2005). Second, those working with prekindergarten (pre-K), kindergarten, and first-grade students *must* teach these young learners to read with an unprecedented urgency. The time is now. Gone are the days of the comfort of the spiraling textbook curriculum. How many times have colleagues said, "Oh, if they miss consonant blends now (insert any reading skill), they'll get it again later"? Good, eagle-eye teachers know that is a big fallacy! If students are not reading on grade level by the end of first grade, we are out of time.

Well, then, what should educators do? The response to intervention (RTI) model answered that question for us and, in 2005 Project Early ID was born. With the support of Baltimore City Public Schools and private funders, we launched an intervention project to provide manageable step-by-step early literacy instruction in several early childhood classrooms. As we implemented our pilot and through the 5 subsequent years of our program, our research showed that almost 40% of our students from pre-K through Grade 1 were below benchmarks at one time or another and needed help to prevent further slippage (Baker, Sulivan, & Garrett, 2011).

Where do educators begin? In our pilot, we began by identifying the desired outcome and working backward to the source. We believe that Maria Montessori, Italian physician and educator said it best: "The greatest sign of success for a teacher . . . is to be able to say, 'The children are now working as if I did not exist'" (as cited in Lewis, 2011).

Our desired outcome was to have our students reading. By the end of first grade, we wanted our students to be capable, independent readers who read grade-level texts with understanding and joy and did it without us. How can first grade students read a grade-level text without our help? *They can because they have been well prepared to do so.*

How do educators get students ready? Once we identified the outcome, the source was easy: Start in pre-K. Although many RTI programs began later on in school, we knew from research that good phonological skills are the hallmarks of good readers and that phonological awareness instruction begins in pre-K (National Early Literacy Panel, 2009). It made sense to all of us in Project Early ID to begin our pilot in pre-K, where we could identify problem areas early and intervene with strategic instruction. We geared up for early prevention.

The rest of the story is history, and the successful results of our pilot lie between the pages of this book. We scripted our words as we said them during our small group instruction for use by all individuals working with pre-K students. The words in this curriculum have been tested and used by us and enabled our students to demonstrate grade-level phonemic and oral language skills before they went into kindergarten. The lessons are delightful to teach because they include these key activities that support early literacy: readalouds, talking, listening, music, and storytelling. Fingerplays, rhymes, multisensory activities, alliterative songs, and movement are used to activate the students' awareness that spoken words have qualities and to foster print awareness.

Take and use this curriculum, follow it faithfully, and watch your young learners soar! It is our gift as teachers to you, our fellow teachers.

REFERENCES

Baker, L., Sulivan, C., & Garrett, A. (2011). *An evaluation of the Baltimore City Public School System's Early Identification and Intervention Project: Year five results and final report.* Baltimore: University of Maryland, Baltimore County.

Lewis, J.J. (2011). *Maria Montessori quotes.* Retrieved from http://womenshistory.about.com/od/quotes/a/montessori.htm

National Early Literacy Panel. (2009). *Developing early literacy: Report of the National Early Literacy Panel.* Retrieved from http://lincs.ed.gov/earlychildhood/NELP/NELPreport.html

NICHD Early Child Care Research Network. (2005). Early child care and children's development in the primary grades: Follow-up results from the NICHD Study of Early Child Care. *American Educational Research Journal, 42*(3), 537–570.

Snow, C.E., Burns, M.S., & Griffin, P. (Eds.). (1998). *Preventing reading difficulties in young children.* Washington, DC: National Academies Press.

For the Reader

We wrote *Lift-Off for Early Literacy: Directed Reading Opportunities for Struggling Students* with two main goals in mind:

- To provide an evidence-based intervention curriculum in a teacher-to-teacher format for Tier 2 students within a response to intervention (RTI) framework

- To build a strong foundation for emergent reading skills to develop in struggling prekindergarten (pre-K) students

Because our pilot study, Project Early ID, was cofunded by Baltimore City Public Schools and several private foundations, we had the privilege of working as reading specialists to support pre-K classroom teachers and at-risk students in several schools throughout low-income areas in Baltimore City. We were the only reading specialists dedicated solely to early literacy.

Our instruction was based on the RTI model which, for our purposes, identified pre-K students who were lagging behind their peers in areas of phonological awareness (see Chapter 1 for more information about the DROPPS theoretical framework). Research has shown that early identification of children with poor phonological awareness is critical because these are the students who are at-risk for future reading failure (Adams, 1990).

WHAT MAKES THIS PROGRAM MORE USABLE THAN OTHERS?

When we produced DROPPS, we used a technique called Teacher Talk—that is, we reviewed and compiled our personal lesson plans and wrote down our words in a specially prepared script for teachers, paraeducators (or "paras"), and any consistent adult classroom volunteer to use with students. (Note: The term *para* stands for "paraeducator/classroom assistant" and is used throughout in a more expanded meaning, as it includes any consistent adult who works in the classroom on a daily basis.) The DROPPS program is more usable than other programs because it is specifically scripted for student achievement and success.

By using Teacher Talk, not only can teachers and paras implement the same lesson objectives and formats, materials, and transition activities that led to our project's success, they also can use the words that we used in teaching and watch students grow academically, as we did! Our experience as reading specialists and special educators, plus strong research-based results, has guided us in preparing Teacher Talk.

In fact, we hope that any teacher who needs a strong intervention curriculum and may not have the support of a paraeducator or other classroom assistance will use DROPPS as well. By using Teacher Talk, all classroom personnel (teachers, paraeducators, and consistent adult volunteers alike) are better prepared to maximize their time with students, to support instruction in the most meaningful way, and to obtain the most meaningful results.

Once the scripts are reviewed and practiced before teaching the lesson, the paras will feel comfortable and confident in using them. Classroom personnel also should review and print relevant game instructions and materials from the accompanying CD-ROM prior to presenting lessons. We also highly recommend implementing a schedule of close collaborative consultation and support with the classroom teacher, reading specialist, or other early literacy teacher leader when DROPPS is used by anyone other than a teacher (see Chapter 2 for more information).

HOW WAS THE SUCCESS OF PROJECT EARLY ID MEASURED?

Success was evidenced by our pre-K students reaching benchmarks on their curriculum-based assessments, *Get It! Got It! Go!* (McConnell, 2001), and other ongoing assessments. It also was shown by the strong academic results that were obtained by the evaluation team from the University of Maryland, Baltimore County (UMBC), who were our primary researchers (see Chapter 1 for further details).

HOW DID WE IDENTIFY THE STUDENTS?

We started by helping the classroom teacher with universal screening of all students in late fall and, from these initial assessments, identified small groups of students (no more than 5) who had dipped below generally accepted phonological guidelines (see the pre-K hierarchy of skills information in Chapters 1 and 2 for more information about the universal screening and benchmarks that were used). We met with them for 20 minutes per day and focused on a range of activities termed DROPPS (for "**D**irected **R**eading **OPP**ortunitie**S**"), which supported their classroom reading curriculum (*Open Court Reading*; SRA/McGraw-Hill, 2002). This was known as our Tier 2 instructional group, and the specialized, targeted lessons that we gave form the basis of the DROPPS program.

As we worked with these groupings of four or five students, we also identified students who needed more intensive intervention. These students became our Tier 3 instructional group, and we met with them for an additional 20 minutes per day in groups of one or two students. However, the scope of *Lift-Off for Early Literacy* deals with Tier 2 intervention.

We realize that many schools and school districts do not have reading intervention specialists dedicated to early literacy, so we became determined to share our instructional format and lessons with other pre-K teachers throughout the United States. We hope that they experience the joy, as we did, of seeing an early identification and intervention process produce the blossoms of literacy success with our youngest learners.

WHAT EXACTLY ARE DROPPS?

DROPPS are 20-minute targeted intervention lessons that can be "dropped in" to any pre-K core literacy curriculum at any time that extra skill work is necessary. DROPPS are based on the pre-K hierarchy of phonological awareness skills that students should know before they move into kindergarten. Research supports early acquisition of these emergent literacy skills as hallmark characteristics of subsequent good readers (National Reading Panel, 2001).

We designed the DROPPS lessons to reinforce the very specific phonological skills (e.g., rhyme awareness, syllable blending) that students may not acquire through exposure to the standard reading curriculum the first or second time around.

WHO GIVES THE DROPPS LESSONS?

DROPPS can be "dropped in" by teachers, paraeducators, and consistent adult volunteers and used during the literacy block—preferably during students' independent time, workshop activities, or differentiated instruction. The DROPPS lessons take many interesting and appealing forms, such as board games, fingerplays, card sorts, and well-known rhymes.

DOES THE DROPPS PROGRAM ADDRESS DIFFERENTIATION?

Yes! We believe in the strength and quality of the DROPPS program and advocate its use in any area of literacy instruction and at-risk prevention, from RTI initiatives to differentiated instruction.

The DROPPS program addresses the two differentiation questions that we heard from many teachers:

- Which of my students need to reinforce what skills?

- Once I identify the students who need specialized help, what materials do I use to meet their needs?

We applied a very straightforward concept that comes from our experience as special educators working in the inclusion classroom: group students together who show similar needs and use the DROPPS to reinforce their particular area of weaknesses and firm it up. This is the premise of Tier 2 intervention.

We also found that once the differentiation question is solved, many teachers did not have additional resource materials beyond the standard curriculum for students who needed intervention lessons in phonological awareness. The DROPPS program solves that dilemma. The lessons are **D**irected **R**eading **OPP**ortunitie**S** that can be "dropped in" to any curriculum as follow-up activities without scrambling for materials. Each lesson is detailed in its entirety.

HOW DOES THE TEACHER GROUP THE STUDENTS?

The teacher begins the grouping process by asking the following question: Which of the 3 R's does the student need?

- **R**epeating

- **R**eviewing

- **R**eteaching

Through many years of classroom practice and research, we saw that 100% of new skill instruction in the area of literacy should be *repeated*, usually through the standard classroom curriculum and the recommended multisensory techniques that accompany all research-based reading curricula. Repeating instruction benefits the entire classroom population. No immediate differentiation is necessary during this process, as the teacher repeats the same skill or skill set during group instructional time.

The second R, *reviewing*, forms the basis of this book and its accompanying CD-ROM—that of Tier 2 instruction. The DROPPS program provides targeted skill review to those identified students who need an extra boost to help them reach benchmarks. As a rule of thumb, Tier 2 is comprised of students who usually score below 80% on a curriculum-based assessment but above 40%. For example, based on these criteria, a group of three students who need help with rhyme discrimination can be paired with two students whose rhyme awareness is still emerging to form a differentiated group of five students. These five would be perfectly teamed for learning. The teacher would then find the applicable DROPP (in this case, DROPP 2: Rhyme Discrimination), and the teacher or para would begin the outlined, easily implemented lesson.

The third R is *reteaching*. Reteaching is necessary to those students who need extensive multisensory approaches. In these cases, we have used techniques from programs such as *Orton-Gillingham* or *Project Read* (Gillingham & Stillman, 1997; Language Circle Enterprises, 2006). In Project Early ID, we met with these students and provided one-to-one or one-to-two intensive intervention—known as Tier 3. (Tier 3 is not addressed in this book.)

ARE DROPPS EASY TO IMPLEMENT?

DROPPS are so easy to implement because we provide users with detailed, easy-to-follow flowcharts of skills, transitions in and out of every lesson, and, of course, the lessons themselves. A full lesson, including transitions, takes between 20 and 30 minutes.

The program shows teachers when to use a DROPP and for how many days (usually 10). Each lesson also includes a simple skill assessment checkout to aid in determining whether a student has mastered the specific skill.

Once a skill is mastered, the student moves from Tier 2 back into Tier 1, or full-group (classroom) instruction. If several students need to review the skill again (for another round of 10 days), they (plus any newly identified students) can enter the group to make up another differentiated group of five. The teacher or para can choose another Activity Set of lessons within the same DROPP and start the process again. Because the groupings are flexible, students can move in and out of Tier 2 instruction very easily. This approach allows the most students to be served and individual needs to be met.

Because all DROPPS have Activity Sets of complete lessons, everything you need is included within this book and its accompanying CD-ROM. The teacher is the main guide for the lesson; he or she should consult regularly with the para to identify the students in the Tier 2 group and point the para to the applicable DROPPS selection.

CAN THE SAME RESULTS BE ACHIEVED WITHOUT HAVING A TRAINED READING SPECIALIST IN THE CLASSROOM?

Yes. We prepared *Lift-Off for Early Literacy* and presented the DROPPS lessons using Teacher Talk exactly as though we were giving the lessons ourselves. We used our expertise and experience of almost 50 combined years of classroom practice and developed a hands-on, step-by-step manual explicitly for use by teachers or by paras under the guidance of teachers.

Throughout the years of our ongoing project, we met many adults serving students in the pre-K classrooms and working with teachers. These adults served students on a consistent basis, and many were not paid employees (unlike the classroom assistants or paraprofessionals). Some were either parent or community volunteers, tutors from area churches, or retired adults who worked as members of Experience Corps.

Lack of funding and/or time often meant that these willing classroom adults did not receive sufficient training to enable them to work at their maximum potential and support students in the most meaningful way. Yet, they came into the classrooms day after day and were always eager to lend their capable hands and hearts. Sometimes they cut out materials for the teachers, read selected stories, soothed homesick 4-year-olds, or helped coordinate outdoor and lunchtime activities. Some of these adults previously had been teachers or paraeducators and wanted to give back to their schools and communities. Over time, we saw clearly that they, with some training, support, and the scripted DROPPS program, could be counted on to help students attain academic success.

In collaboration with the teacher, paraeducators and any consistent adults working in the classroom truly will be able to make the scripted lessons their own and apply the numerous teaching approaches, tips, and techniques to their small reading groups. They can indeed provide the intervention and teach the same DROPP targeted lessons that we, as reading intervention specialists taught, with the same strong results.

REFERENCES

Adams, M.J. (1990). *Beginning to read: Thinking and learning about print.* Cambridge, MA: MIT Press.

Gillingham, A., & Stillman, B.W. (1997). *The Gillingham manual.* Cambridge, MA: Educators Publishing Service.

Language Circle Enterprises. (2006). *Project Read.* Bloomington, MN: Author.

McConnell, S. (2001). *Get It-Got It-Go!* The preschool individual growth and development indicator. St. Paul: University of Minnesota, Center for Early Education Development.

National Reading Panel. (2001). *Teaching children to read: An evidence-based assessment of the scientific research literature on reading and its implications for reading instruction.* Bethesda, MD: National Institutes of Health.

SRA/McGraw-Hill. (2002). *Open Court Reading.* Columbus, OH: Author.

Acknowledgments

It is quite a challenge to translate an effective early intervention program into written form that can be envisioned and delivered by others. We could not have done so in this book without the patience, guidance, and encouragement of many people.

It has been wonderful to work with Astrid Pohl Zuckerman at Paul H. Brookes Publishing Company, who constantly shone a clear light down this new path for us.

This intervention curriculum grew out of Project Early ID, an early literacy response to intervention pilot in the Baltimore City Public Schools, and we sincerely thank everyone who has supported the program from its inception. We begin with the project's students, who give us our greatest encouragement by giving their best every day.

Our school-based teams of teachers, paraprofessionals, and the principals at the Barclay School #54, Edgewood #67, Gwynns Falls #60, Windsor Hills #87, Dallas Nicholas # 39, and Calverton #75 receive resounding thanks for the energy, collaboration, scheduling adjustments, and countless other supports that have allowed the project to work. A Cooperative Colleagues "Razzle-Dazzle" goes to Althea Cromer-Pierre, Carole Green, Jenny Heinbaugh, Carmen Holmes, Truemella Horne, Tanya Jackson, Andrea James, Hartavia Johnson, Bonnie McCoy, Iris Murdoch, Joanna Nicolich, Krishnia Rainey-Botaang, Elaine Shugarman, and Keyah Spann. We also issue hearty thanks to our project coordinator, Matt Griffin, for his patient and diligent work.

We are grateful for the generous funding provided to Project Early ID by the Abell Foundation, the Lockhart Vaughan Foundation, the Zanvyl and Isabelle Krieger Fund, the Aaron Straus and Lillie Straus Foundation, the Lois and Philip Macht Family Philanthropic Fund of the Associated Jewish Community Federation of Baltimore, The Shelter Foundation Inc., and the Baltimore City Public Schools. We especially thank Bob Embry, Karen Kreisberg, Betsy Krieger, Bonnie Legro, Amy Macht, and Pete Powell from these foundations for their ongoing guidance that has helped the project grow successfully. Thanks also to the Greater Homewood Community Corporation for fiscal management of grant funds, along with personnel support.

From its first steps, Project Early ID was creatively guided by a team of dedicated individuals who shared their knowledge and experience to help us chart our course through smooth and choppy waters. Our special thanks go to Jane Baker, Linda Baker, Buzzy Hettleman, and Sue Torr for their unswerving support and keen advice. Dr. Linda Baker worked tirelessly with Dr. Adia Garrett and Colleen Sullivan to analyze the abundance of data that informed our literacy lessons, with the help of an enthusiastic team of graduate assistants from the Department of Psychology at University of Maryland, Baltimore County.

We gratefully acknowledge Dr. Andres Alonso and the leadership of Baltimore City Public Schools for supporting the project.

All of these individuals and organizations have our abiding gratitude for helping us spread the word about the importance of early identification and intervention, through Project Early ID and through this book.

Charlene Iannone-Campbell would like to thank two people who played instrumental roles in her development as a reading teacher: Dr. Mariale Hardiman, for setting the bar as high as she did at Roland Park Elementary/Middle School and expecting the faculty to dig deep so our students could fly high, and her first reading coach, Joan Schenkel, for modeling and leading her, as only a Direct Instruction teacher can.

Susan Lloyd Lattimore's greatest debt of gratitude goes to her first teacher—her mother, Virginia Lloyd, who continues to be her steadfast advisor, cheerleader, and role model. Her spirit, patience, wisdom, and good humor, both in the classroom and at home, laid the foundation for Susan's rewarding teaching career. In addition, Susan thanks her sisters, Cathy, Mel, and Lauren, for their unswerving support and all of their contributions, practical and whimsical, to her work and her life.

We derived our courage to even attempt such an endeavor as writing a book from each other: co-authors and colleagues, Hopkins co-teachers and sidekicks, we sustained each other through family crises, personal loss, and writer's block, reminding each other again and again that this work of teaching children to read is the hardest, most important, most rewarding work there is.

Finally, this book could not have come to fruition without the unfailing support of our families. Our husbands and anchors, Jim Campbell and Jack Lattimore, have offered uncompromising love, patience, foresight, and quirky humor that make it possible for us to do what we do. Our daughters Lyndsay, Jordan, Emily, Amara, and Kerry are a constant source of sunshine and happiness, coupled with doses of reality and encouragement. They are our perpetual inspiration.

*This book is dedicated to the hard-working teachers of Baltimore City Public Schools,
whose mission it is to promote and accelerate student academic excellence
in the classroom and in life. In partnership with families,
you are making a profound difference in the lives of Baltimore's children.*

*In loving memory of
John T. Lloyd
and
Charles and Rosella Iannone*

Theoretical Framework and Concept Design of DROPPS

It is certainly exciting to be an educator in the 21st century because technological advances provide amazing information about the processes of learning to read. Research hospitals and universities have sophisticated tools to study the developing child, and many are actively working with schools and communities to translate new information into meaningful practice. Thanks to this process, known as translational research, many parents are aware of the critical link between an infant's earliest language skills and later reading ability. Similarly, early childhood educators are becoming more informed about the essential role of phonological sensitivity in the early literacy development of 3- to 5-year-olds.

Looking a bit further up the educational scale, we see teachers across all grade levels and content areas incorporating science-based reading research into their daily instruction to assist struggling readers. Their efforts are supported by administrators who realize that in order to comply with the No Child Left Behind (NCLB) Act of 2001 (PL 107-110) and the Individuals with Disabilities Education Improvement Act (IDEA) of 2004 (PL 108-446) and its subsequent reauthorization, as well as to meet the rigorous standards of the Race to the Top reforms (U.S. Department of Education, 2011), schools must provide high-quality, differentiated instruction and timely interventions to struggling students, delivered not only by teachers but also by paraeducators and related services providers.

Clearly, educators at every level are striving to translate sound research into instructional practices that effectively support all students. Although this wave of reform is exciting, some of its implications are also daunting. Comprehensive research from the National Institute of Child Health and Human Development (NICHD) branch of the National Institutes of Health (NIH) revealed that reading interventions in fourth grade rather than in late kindergarten take four times as long and are less effective. National Research Council reports (Bowman, Donovan, & Burns, 2000; Shonkoff & Phillips, 2000; Snow, Burns, & Griffin, 1998) showed that students who fall behind in reading in the early grades are at risk of being poor readers throughout their lives. Clearly, early reading intervention is critical. But how can it be provided—consistently, effectively, and economically—in a typical school setting? The Directed Reading Opportunities (DROPPS) curriculum is a research-based intervention program that answers this question.

DROPPS AND PROJECT EARLY ID

The DROPPS curriculum is based on Project Early ID, a successful early identification and intervention pilot program that has been implemented in several Baltimore City Public Schools since 2005. Project Early ID follows a multitiered response to intervention (RTI) framework and has demonstrated that virtually all children can achieve developmentally appropriate language and literacy benchmarks by the end of first grade when provided with targeted supports as needed in a small-group or individualized setting for short periods of time. The design for Project Early ID was based on a thorough review of RTI literature and represented a major step forward for two reasons.

1. While other researchers (Torgesen, 2002; Vaughn & Linan-Thompson, 2003) were considering theoretical models of RTI instruction, Project Early ID was unique in its practical application of RTI for more than 5 years in typical inner-city public schools.

2. Project Early ID begins in prekindergarten (pre-K), unlike many early reading interventions that do not begin until first grade (Clay, 1985; Hall & Moats, 2002; University of Texas at Austin, 2006).

The project's design and implementation have undergone a thorough evaluation by a team of researchers from the Applied Developmental Psychology department at the University of Maryland, Baltimore County, with Dr. Linda Baker as the primary investigator. Strong positive results of the pilot phase of Project Early ID demonstrated the appropriateness of providing brief, targeted phonological and vocabulary supports to children as young as 4 years old. Results of districtwide achievement tests (Stanford Achievement Test, Tenth Edition; Harcourt Educational Measurement, 2002) confirmed that the project is meeting its goal of increasing the percentage of students reading at grade level in first grade to at least 90%. Not surprisingly, students who were part of Project Early ID since pre-K scored measurably higher than students who entered in kindergarten or first grade (see Figure 1.1).

There were 125 4-year-olds in the pilot project's pre-K classes, and almost half of them received Tier 2 small-group supports at some point during their pre-K year, when needs were indicated by universal screening and classroom progress checks. The Tier 2 lessons, described in detail in this book, took only 20 minutes a day to deliver, yet they yielded powerful results in strengthening the foundational literacy skills of our students. Following the hierarchy of phonological skills prescribed by the Academy of Orton-Gillingham Practitioners (2009), the University of Oregon (n.d.), the National Reading Panel (NRP; 2001), and NELP (2009), the DROPPS lessons strengthen students' emergent skills in rhyming, word awareness in sentences, compound words, syllables, and phonemes. At the same time, lesson checkouts support the teacher in determining quickly where skill weaknesses occur.

Project Early ID showed that it is possible to solidify the fundamental reading skills of a greater percentage of students than in the average American classroom. The data illustrate that providing supports in pre-K resulted in more students acquiring the bedrock phonological skills that lead to proficient reading. This is important because reading trajectories are remarkably stable, as the NRP's (2000) meta-analysis of reading research confirmed. Studies conducted by the NICHD (2000) found that 74% of children who are poor readers in early elementary school remain poor readers in ninth grade. Conversely, we can project that students who participated in Project Early ID who are reading well when they leave first grade are more likely to meet with academic success and avoid the pitfalls that plague so many struggling readers in the United States—grade-level retentions; cumbersome special education screening; and the inability to gain access to the wonders of science, literature, and all other areas of learning (Baker, 2006, 2007, 2008).

We believe what we accomplished in Baltimore City Title I schools can be done in other settings using DROPPS as the centerpiece of a straightforward RTI framework.

OVERVIEW OF THE RESPONSE TO INTERVENTION FRAMEWORK

RTI refers to a process that provides instructional supports (*Intervention*) in direct *Response* to the needs of students in general education classrooms at varying levels of intensity (see Figure 1.2). RTI

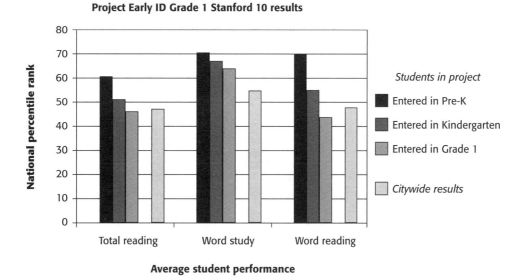

Figure 1.1. A comparison of first-grade standardized test performance in reading on the Stanford Achievement Test, Tenth Edition (Stanford 10; Harcourt Educational Measurement, 2002), relative to onset of intervention.

is based on multiple tiers of instruction and typically includes periodic screening of all pupils (Tier 1), small-group instruction (Tier 2), and more intensive individual supports (Tier 3). Students who persistently fail to achieve benchmark performance over time may be referred for evaluation by a multidisciplinary team to determine if even more intensive interventions are needed, such as special education. It is important to remember, however, that RTI not only identifies students in need of special services, but also focuses on quality reading instruction for all students.

RTI is a positive method of reaching students who are at risk because they do not have to endure repeated failures before receiving appropriate intervention. Assessment data makes it easy to determine appropriate instructional groupings, thereby providing services quickly to every child who falls below grade-level benchmarks. Weak skills are targeted in brief, systematic courses of instruction, and when students master expected benchmarks, they return to Tier 1 status with the ability to succeed alongside their peers. Movement between tiers is fluid and provides brief, timely supports for all struggling learners. This makes RTI more far reaching as well as more cost effective than traditional intervention paradigms.

DROPPS AND THE RESPONSE TO INTERVENTION PROCESS

Tier 1

Tier 1 refers to the core instructional program for the whole classroom. It should consist of high-quality, scientifically based curricula; reasonable class size; and best teaching practices with ongoing professional development to support instructional excellence using the core curricula and curriculum-based assessments. In addition, concise assessment of every student in the class is an essential piece of the RTI framework. With DROPPS, as delivered in Project Early ID, we conducted universal screening of all students in a class four times per year. In pre-K, we recommend starting with informal classroom observations during the first 6–8 weeks of school, while the young students settle in to school routines, before administering any screening assessments.

In Baltimore we supplemented these with the *Get It! Got It! Go!* (McConnell, 2001) fluency screening measures of students' progress in the Individual Growth and Development Indicators (IGDIs; Carta, Greenwood, Walker, & Buzhardt, 2010) of picture naming, rhyming, and alliteration. We

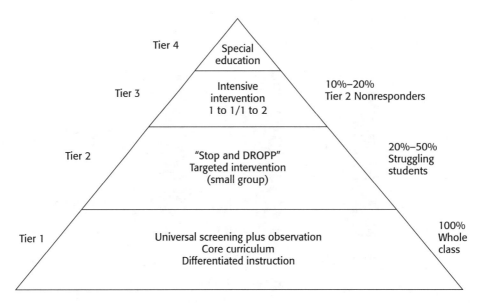

Figure 1.2. Response to intervention pyramid as demonstrated by Project Early ID. (*Key:* DROPP, Directed Reading Opportunity.)

also used the Phonological Awareness Profile (PAP; Robertson & Saltzer, 1995) to monitor student growth in phonological sensitivity and to better inform our in-house curriculum planning.

By analyzing students' scores using the described measures, project teachers saw which students lagged behind benchmarks and formed Tier 2 instructional groups based on the Pre-K Hierarchy of Skills. This quick data analysis helped teachers form instructional groupings for the literacy block. Table 1.1 shows the relationship between concepts and Activity Sets. See the DROPPS scope and sequence chart (see Table 1.1); the Chapter 2 scope and sequence section has details and a sample scenario of how teachers can assess their students and set up Tier 2 small groups throughout the school year.

Tier 2

Tier 2 intervention is the next phase of student support, providing an important step beyond the typical lessons offered within the scope of classroom literacy instruction. Ideally, during the small-group "reading workshop" after the morning message and whole-class instruction, students receive teacher guidance and meaningful independent practice to reinforce skill steps they may have had trouble grasping. There are a number of pitfalls associated with this small-group practice period. As noted in the For the Reader section at the front of the book, we are often approached by teachers who lack resource materials beyond curricular intervention guides consisting primarily of worksheets that are exact replications of the whole-class lesson. Given that the teacher's time is divided between three to five small groups of children, these activities may do little to promote growth in those students who struggled with the skill during the first exposure. These are the students who stand to make important, permanent gains when provided with DROPPS as additional Tier 2 review lessons.

Tier 2 Supports Are Provided Over and Above Tier 1 Instructional Time

Note the important concept of providing Tier 2 DROPPS in addition to the core literacy instruction. Although some RTI demonstrations define *Tier 2* as the standard small-group instruction in a classroom, we have found it best to provide the targeted 20-minute DROPPS over and above the core instruction wherever possible (e.g., 20-minute intervention lessons during morning warm-ups). In this

Table 1.1. Relationship between Directed Reading Opportunity (DROPP) concepts and Activity Sets

DROPP	Concept development	Activity Sets
1	Rhyme awareness	1.1, 1.2, 1.3
2	Rhyme discrimination	2.1, 2.2, 2.3, 2.4
OPT DROPP	Rhyme production (optional DROPP; see the accompanying CD-ROM)	OPT DROPP 1
3	Sentence segmentation	3.1, 3.2
4	Compound word blending	4.1
5	Compound word segmentation	5.1, 5.2
6	Syllable awareness	6.1
7	Syllable blending	7.1, 7.2
8	Syllable segmentation	8.1, 8.2
9	Blending awareness	9.1, 9.2
10	Beginning sound alliteration	10.1, 10.2, 10.3

way, students are given every opportunity to absorb the core instruction, which is then maximized by the targeted DROPPS.

The Tier 2 DROPPS lessons are effective because they address the smallest steps of skill acquisition. In the Rhyming Skill Sets, for example, students are first given ample practice in rhyme awareness and will move to rhyme discrimination before being asked to produce rhymes. This step-by-step coverage assists the Tier 2 instructor in determining where a student's confusion originates while building a solid skill foundation for the child. In the event that a child fails to understand the concepts behind even these basic steps, he or she could be moved to the earliest DROPP activities in which general listening skills and the qualities of words are emphasized.

Such a meticulous instructional process is not necessary for the majority of students in a class. According to The International Dyslexia Association (2000), reading skills are acquired fairly effortlessly in about 80% of the general population, given a sound teaching method incorporating basic and balanced literacy practices. But ample research has confirmed that the other 20% of learners have alternative patterns of learning and are likely to experience persistent reading difficulties if not provided explicit, detailed instruction in the processes of decoding (Foorman, Francis, Fletcher, Schatschneider, & Mehta, 1998; Kame'enui & Carnine, 1998; Shaywitz, 2003). These are the children for whom Tier 2 supports are critical.

Tier 3

Although Tier 3 lessons are not included in DROPPS, a discussion of this tertiary level of instruction is germane to a thorough understanding of the RTI paradigm. Tier 3 services are specialized and individualized supports for students with more persistent, intensive needs. Many RTI models define *Tier 3* as special education. In Project Early ID, however, Tier 3 consisted of pull-out tutoring sessions provided by a reading specialist for 20 additional minutes per day to students who struggled in spite of receiving Tier 2 intervention. We found this design preferable to the Tier 3/special education model for several reasons. For one thing, the Tier 3 students benefited from continuing to work in their Tier 2 DROPPS groups in addition to receiving their individual tutoring under the umbrella of general education. This is noteworthy because children at these young ages develop and respond at widely different rates and for many different reasons. By monitoring students' performance in Tier 3, we were able to get a clearer look at the students' rates of progress within the pre-K educational mainstream. This enabled us to discern which students simply needed *more* practice time, which needed *more and different* skill practice (e.g., relearning with multisensory alternatives), and ultimately, which children were exhibiting more significant cognitive, social-emotional, and/or behavioral impairments over time. Students in the first two categories responded to Tier 3 instruction by gradually returning to Tiers 1 and 2 with a solid grasp of early literacy skills. The few remaining students whose weak rate of acquisition and skill retention warranted further scrutiny still benefited from the specialized instruction; moreover, when called for, the special education screening process was expedited by the comprehensive data and the wide range of strategies that were already in place through the RTI intervention.

PREKINDERGARTEN PHONOLOGICAL SUPPORTS LEAD TO IMPROVED READING BY FIRST GRADE

Figure 1.3 illustrates that Project Early ID's implementation of RTI resulted in a significantly higher percentage of successful readers by first grade. Knowing that our students had been able to master the primary building blocks needed for *learning to read*, we were confident that they were well equipped to handle the upcoming phases of literacy instruction—becoming competent at *reading to learn*. Our students' results corresponded to the researched projections of Torgesen (2004), which indicated that more than 90% of students should be expected to read at grade level when given proper instruction and supports. How gratifying to see our students' performance increase to reflect those ideal percentages! Clearly, there is a road map for effective early intervention. The DROPPS model of RTI shows that there is a straightforward way to provide meaningful reading instruction. Let's take a closer look at the "nuts and bolts" of implementation that led to Project Early ID's success.

DETAILS OF DROPPS IMPLEMENTATION

Number of Students in a Typical Class Who May Need Tier 2 Supports

A review of current RTI literature indicates that 15%–20% of an average class could be expected to qualify for Tier 2 instruction (Haager, Klingner, & Vaugn, 2007). In Project Early ID, the numbers were higher, for interesting but understandable reasons. In our pre-K pilot classes, a total of 56% of the students received Tier 2 instruction at some point during the year; however, more than half attended only one or two sessions. These Tier 2 students were from Title I classrooms with a higher-than-average number of English language learners (ELLs) and included many students who were initially shy about participating in their pre-K classrooms. These students benefited greatly from the small-group attention, and many seemed to need just a short "boost" of oral language and vocabulary support to help them understand and succeed in Tier 1 whole-class instruction for the remainder of the year.

The Tier 2 students who remained in groups throughout most of the pre-K year constituted 27% of the class—about 5 students in each class of 20, which is a greater number than projected for an average RTI implementation. One third of these solidly passed the rhyming alliteration and oral language benchmarks and returned to Tier 1 by the end of pre-K. The final 18% stayed in Tier 2 for all four sessions and continued to qualify for Tier 2 in kindergarten. This figure is aligned with the percentage of students typically at risk for reading difficulty, so it is not surprising that most of these children continued to need individualized supports. By first grade, however, the total number of students needing Tier 2 supports dropped to 13%, or 2 or 3 students per class—all of whom exceeded the national baseline for grade-level performance by the end of the year. This illustrates how far early intervention can go in beating the odds of reading failure.

Length of a DROPPS Session

Each daily skill lesson takes 20 minutes to deliver, and a DROPPS session, or Activity Set, runs for a 10-day span. There are scripted lessons (Teacher Talk) that are repeated over 10 sequential learning days.

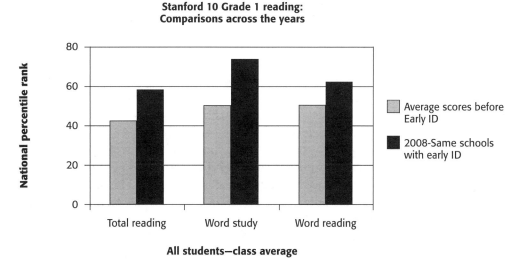

Figure 1.3. Average class scores of project schools before and after Project Early ID intervention. (*Key:* Stanford 10, Stanford Acheivement Test, Tenth Edition [Harcourt Educational Measurement, 2002].)

The Activity Sets are written to address essential skills in short, targeted instructional sessions. Each 10-day set is followed by a quick assessment checkout of the DROPPS skill. The checkout results guide the process of flexible regrouping of students according to skill mastery and student needs (see Chapter 2 for more details).

This frequent, consistent progress monitoring addresses a trend that surfaced in Project Early ID, wherein several students in each group mastered the essential skill more quickly than their Tier 2 counterparts when provided with individualized directions and practice. We adjusted our original project design of 30 daily lessons per session to 10-day Activity Sets in order to allow more fluidity in movement between tiers as students progress at their own rates, according to their unique developmental differences.

Incorporating Newly Enrolled Students into the DROPPS Intervention Model

Students who arrive during the course of the school year can be individually assessed and placed in a DROPPS Tier 2 intervention group as quickly as any needs are identified.

At this point, we would like to mention an enrollment issue that arose in all of our pilot cohorts during the pre-K year—the influx of students without any prior school experience, at various points throughout the year. Under typical circumstances, these inexperienced youngsters can really throw classroom instruction off course; however, with the DROPPS model of RTI in place, these students' needs can be addressed by forming new Tier 2 groups with Activity Sets that are earlier on the hierarchy of skills than the general class emphasis. This ready-made system of supports helps new students make the transition more easily into classroom routines and lessons with no delay in individualized skill instruction.

Determining Placement for Students with Inconsistent Performance

It is best to provide a child with Tier 2 supports if there is any question of need. For example, when a child scored inconsistently on benchmark assessments and/or in the Tier 1 whole-class instruction in our pilot project, we sought the classroom teacher's judgment, and if there was any suspicion of learning difficulty—as opposed to a "bad testing day"—then we provided intervention. Once the child is in the small group, the source of the child's confusion becomes clearer and can be confirmed with intervention data. We believe it is better to err on the side of caution than to withhold needed supports.

How Teachers and Paraeducators or Consistent Volunteers Can Collaborate to Deliver Tier 2 Instruction Effectively and Efficiently

As the classroom planner, the teacher reviews student data and prescribes instructional supports. With DROPPS' scripted lessons, the teacher can confidently guide paraeducators or consistent adult volunteers (jointly referred to as "paras" throughout this curriculum) to implement the 20-minute Activity Sets and the assessment checkouts that will ensure consistent, high-quality intervention supports. Chapter 2 provides a practical scenario on how this can be done.

It is the teacher's responsibility to preview the overall program as well as each Activity Set's detailed overview to become familiar with the activities and teaching tips and provide the materials for each lesson. It is crucial that the teacher guides the process and never relies on paras to make pedagogical decisions. The teacher then schedules the 20-minute Tier 2 lessons at a regular time that does not interfere with any other core instruction. Chapter 2 provides clear instructions on collaborative program implementation.

It is the responsibility of paras and volunteer instructors to familiarize themselves with the 10-Day Planners and the Teacher Talk of each Activity Set they will deliver and to practice the lessons for enjoyable and efficient delivery. As noted in Chapter 2, our motto is "Prepare, prepare, prepare!", with a weekend preview of the five upcoming lessons, songs, and games as well as a daily review that will help all instructors optimize their instructional time with students for truly enhanced learning.

How DROPPS Skills and Lessons Relate to State and National Standards

All DROPPS lessons are aligned with the general reading processes of the Maryland State Curriculum in the areas of phonemic awareness and vocabulary. These foundational skills, which provide the basis for early literacy, will undoubtedly be translated into the Common Core Standards that are currently being developed for prekindergarten (see http://mdk12.org/instruction/curriculum/reading/starndard1/gradePK.html).

SUMMARY

The DROPPS program, as demonstrated by Project Early ID in Baltimore City schools, significantly reduced the number of students who were at risk for reading problems. Thanks to this program, classroom teachers, reading teachers, paras, volunteers, and tutors can gain access to and deliver delightful, research-based intervention activities that will have the same positive and long-lasting impact on their students.

Getting Started with DROPPS

We wrote the DROPPS intervention curriculum as a teacher-to-teacher manual of pre-K instructional support lessons based on our successful RTI pilot—Project Early ID—which took place in several Baltimore city schools. The lessons, which are for Tier 2 intervention support, can be implemented immediately and scaffold any pre-K literacy curriculum because they are based on the hierarchy of pre-K skills, from basic phonological awareness (e.g., rhyming) to phonemic awareness (e.g., alliteration of beginning sounds). We believe in the strength and quality of the DROPPS program and advocate using it in any area of instructional support and at-risk prevention—from RTI initiatives to differentiated instruction.

As noted in the For the Reader section, we produced DROPPS using a technique called Teacher Talk—that is, we reviewed and compiled our personal lesson plans and wrote down our own words in a specially prepared script for teachers and paras to use with students. The result is that every lesson in the DROPPS program is specifically scripted for student achievement and success—teachers and paras are given the precise words to say to the students in their small group. The correct student responses and actions are indicated as well as scaffolded responses that will ensure positive, success-driven responses.

Using Teacher Talk not only allows teachers and paras to use our same lesson objectives and formats, materials, and transition activities—they can actually say the words that we used in teaching our own groups and watch their students grow academically. Our experience as reading specialists and special educators plus strong research-based results have guided us in preparing Teacher Talk.

THE DROPPS PROGRAM

The DROPPS program is a comprehensive intervention curriculum that contains 220 days of intervention lessons, organized by Activity Sets that correlate with all 10 DROPPS (as well as another optional DROPP on the accompanying CD-ROM; see Table 2.1). Within the Activity Sets are the intervention lessons that we used with our Tier 2 students in Project Early ID that resulted in strong student success (see Theoretical Framework and Concept Design).

The DROPPS program was designed for small-group instruction within the classroom—the idea being that the intervention lessons could be "dropped" into any pre-K core curriculum as support for struggling learners. We recommend finding a quiet corner of the classroom with a round table and enough chairs for everyone. If a round table is not available, then seat yourself in the middle of the children, not at the head of the table. Being in the middle of the action is "the best seat in the house" so you can observe each child, make continual eye contact, and spend every moment of your 20-minute lesson fully invested in your students' learning.

Overview

All DROPPS begin with an Overview that encompasses specific concept goals and objectives, lesson duration, and valuable instructional information related to both teaching and learning in the subsequent Activity Sets. Included in the Overview are essentials for student growth and achievement—recommended teaching approaches and techniques, instructional tips for success, game rules and management ideas, literature links with tips for student-centered read-alouds, vocabulary exercises, information on assessment checkouts, and more. It is highly recommended that you review each particular DROPP Overview before beginning the corresponding Activity Sets.

Activity Sets

Each DROPP consists of Activity Sets that contain the scripted, intervention lessons. The Activity Sets are numbered by DROPP; some DROPPS have up to four Activity Sets, and some have only one (based on the complexity of the skill to be acquired; see the DROPPS scope and sequence chart in Table 2.1 and on the CD-ROM). As we taught our Tier 2 groups throughout the Project Early ID years, we realized that some skills were mastered more quickly with moderate review and practice, whereas other skills needed some extra time to emerge (e.g., rhyme discrimination in DROPP 2). We included additional Activity Sets in each DROPP, if applicable, to accommodate all of the young learners in Tier 2 and provide them with enough practice to bring them to concept mastery.

Each Activity Set consists of four distinct Teacher Talk or scripted intervention lessons that are used on 10 sequential learning days. The four lessons are repeated over the 10-day span with a skill assessment checkout given to each student individually shortly after the last lesson on Day 10. The exception is the OPT DROPP (on the accompanying CD-ROM), which is an optional whole group activity and thus does not have four small group lessons.

A convenient 10-Day Planner is presented at the beginning of the Activity Sets and provides the sequence of lessons in a brief format for quick teacher review. Also included is a handy Lesson Descriptions framework, which indicates items such as individual lesson names, the transitions used, and the vocabulary word(s) introduced. In addition, a Materials Needed graphic organizer is provided so that needed materials can be gathered. In some cases, it will be necessary to download and print related materials (e.g., game boards, card decks) from the accompanying CD-ROM. Here and throughout the Activity Sets, text prompts and CD-ROM icons will alert teachers and paras to items that need to be obtained from the CD-ROM.

Lessons

The first of four scripted intervention lessons immediately follows the 10-Day Planner. We recommend that once you begin an Activity Set of four lessons with your students, you continue the lessons every day for 10 days. Daily, consistent, small-group time spent in targeted concept development with the teacher is one powerful component of the Activity Sets (and DROPPS as a whole). Strive to saturate your students in the concepts you are teaching and they are learning.

Using the Scripted Intervention Lessons

The scripted intervention lessons are set up in a specific format for ease of reviewing, understanding, and using with your students. Each lesson takes about 20 minutes in total to complete with moderately paced tasks. The lessons should never drag or become unduly long—be conscious of your time and adjust accordingly. Often, slow-paced lessons cause behavior management problems simply because the students get tired of waiting. The lessons begin with a brief informational table detailing student and teacher objectives that are lesson specific; the names of any songs, rhymes, or

Table 2.1. Directed Reading Opportunities (DROPPS) scope and sequence chart

Pre-K hierarchy of phonological skills	DROPP	Activity sets	Number of lessons	Number of days	Cumulative school days
Word level					
Rhymes					
Awareness	1	1.1, 1.2, 1.3	10/set	10 days/set = 30 days	30
Discrimination	2	2.1, 2.2, 2.3, 2.4	10/set	10 days/set = 40 days	70
Production	OPT DROPP (see accompanying CD-ROM)	OPT DROPP Activity 1	3	—	—
Sentences					
Sentence segmentation	3	3.1, 3.2	10/set	10 days/set = 20 days	100
Compound words					
Blending	4	4.1	10/set	10 days/set = 10 days	110
Segmentation	5	5.1, 5.2	10/set	10 days/set = 20 days	130
Syllable level					
Awareness	6	6.1	10/set	10 days/set = 10 days	140
Blending	7	7.1, 7.2	10/set	10 days/set = 20 days	160
Segmentation	8	8.1, 8.2	10/set	10 days/set = 20 days	180
Phoneme level					
Blending	9	9.1, 9.2	10/set	10 days/set = 20 days	200
Beginning sound alliteration	10	10.1, 10.2, 10.3	10/set	10 days/set = 30 days	220

Note: See the CD-ROM for a printable version of this chart.

fingerplays used; and a list of materials. This section allows you to gather your instructional tools for the day without having to take learning time away from your group.

The detailed and scripted intervention lessons directly follow the informational table. Lessons 1–3 are divided into 3 separate tasks.

- Task 1 introduces the students to the big idea of the lesson and transitions them to their small group to be ready to learn.

- Task 2 focuses on the specifics of the lesson—the main concept presented—and may include songs, movements, games, a literature link with a read-aloud book, and/or a vocabulary building exercise.

- Task 3 marks the end of the lesson and transitions students to leave their small group. Many of the short cheers and songs we used for our transitions are posted on the Dr. Jean Feldman web site (http://www.drjean.org).

Lesson 4 reviews Lessons 1 and 3 and gives students the opportunity to practice the games, songs, read-aloud books, and so forth from the prior 9 days before their skill assessment checkout on Day 10. Because Lesson 4 is a review lesson and may require a little extra time, Task 3 is often eliminated for that day.

Scripted Format of Teacher Talk

The scripted lessons provide specific directions for the teacher to follow. There are three major parts to the lesson—Teacher Talk, directions for the teacher, and the children's response.

- Teacher Talk consists of the actual words the teacher will use during the lesson. This text is shown in regular print within the script. We recommend that you follow the script exactly for optimal student achievement—say every word, do every movement, and be positive and encouraging.

- Additional information for the teacher takes the following forms: 1) general directions about the activity, which appear in the left column, or 2) "stage directions" during an activity, which appear in italic print and accompany relevant Teacher Talk sections. It is important to follow all directions.

- The target spoken response from the children is indicated by bold print.

Unless otherwise indicated, it is a good idea to prompt the students for the correct response. Give them the first sounds or actually say the first few words and have the children say them with you or repeat the word. This procedure keeps your lessons moderately paced and helps you maintain your

20-minute time frame. For an example of Teacher Talk in action, see the following Vocabulary Build and Review lesson.

Vocabulary: Build and Review

We strongly believe in using as many instructional moments as possible throughout your day to help students improve their vocabulary and growth in oral language usage and understanding. Although the main thrust of DROPPS is phonological awareness, we embedded a brief vocabulary component based on student need. The new vocabulary that is addressed for each lesson is indicated by the vocabulary icon ◇ at the beginning of each lesson.

Always explain vocabulary in a direct, simple way that students can understand, internalize, and use. Use a multisensory approach whenever possible to help with vocabulary memory. Children love to act out words and situations, so use exaggerated movements with the students because large muscles have memory. Steps that involve a multisensory approach are indicated by the ✷ icon. Guide the students to use complete sentences whenever appropriate during the vocabulary exercise.

Having the students repeat the new vocabulary word or phrase is another important feature of the exercise. Incorporate the new words throughout the school day and engage the students in two-way conversation to reinforce their vocabulary and oral language growth.

In presenting new vocabulary, follow a basic two-step approach and modify it according to the word and its usage in context. In the example that follows, the vocabulary word is *whack*.

Use instructional moments to improve vocabulary and oral language. Always explain vocabulary in a simple way.

| ◇ **Vocabulary** |

WHACK

Read the book and lead the students in playing the thumb drums. Watch everyone and make sure they are in rhythm. Go slowly. Show the pictures while reading.

If I see a fly buzzing around in my house, then I will probably try to whack it. What do you think I will do to the fly if I whack it? Sit up tall and proud if you know. *Call on one or two children.*

Follow a two-step approach. Step 1: Ask children to describe (or act out) the vocabulary word. Yes, a whack is like a slap. *Slap the air in front of you.* Everyone, what does *whack* mean?

TEACHING TIP: Act it out. Use exaggerated movements with the students. Large muscles have memory. Have them slap the air in front of them.

▶ Children's response: Slap.

Step 2: Give students the description and have them supply the word. Show me a slap with your hands. Yes, a whack is like a slap.

Everyone, what's another way of saying *slap?*

▶ Children's response: Whack.

TEACHING TIP: Use the new word in a sentence using your students' names. This always gets their attention.

Yes, *whack*. Malik gave the fly that was buzzing around his house a whack. Can someone use the word *whack* in a sentence for me? Hold one finger in the air if you can tell me a sentence and use the word *whack*. *Take one or two student responses. Guide the students with their sentences to find success.*

▶ (Children respond with a sentence.)

Nice job using the word *whack*.

Reinforcement Through Multiple Means

See the Reinforcement Through Multiple Means chart on the accompanying CD-ROM for a key to the icons used throughout the Activity Sets.

Skill Assessment Checkouts for Progress Monitoring

After you have completed your review lesson (Lesson 4), it will be necessary to set aside a few minutes during that same day to give each child an individual skill assessment checkout to monitor progress within the intervention. The skill assessment checkouts are available on the accompanying CD-ROM. One skill assessment checkout is provided for every DROPP and is to be given at the end of each 10-day Activity Set (at Lesson 4). A reminder will appear in each lesson as applicable. These short checkouts take about 1–2 minutes per child to administer.

We call the skill assessment a *checkout* because you check out whether each student mastered the skill in the intervention group. At the same time, it provides an instructional tool to guide the future placement of those students who have just completed the Activity Set. Which students are ready to leave the group and return to Tier 1 instruction only, and which students must participate in the next Activity Set?

As some of the group members move back to Tier 1, new members are ready to move in based on classroom benchmarks and other criteria. (See p. 19 for the scope and sequence section on how to select students to participate in Tier 2 small-group intervention.) Current group members should get first preference on those premium slots if they need the additional review and practice. Rotating them out of the group too soon and without the data to support your decision might put students at risk for falling behind and having to repeat/start anew on a particular skill.

The checkout itself is clear and easy to administer. A sample follows in Figure 2.1 as an example to review with the directions that follow. The directions are listed at the top, the Teacher Talk follows the directions, and the scoring information appears directly after the assessment items. Make a copy for each child, date the assessment, and file it in a separate folder for each child as a record of the Tier 2 interventions the student has received, including the assessment checkout results. This data is a valuable resource not only in determining the next step for small-group intervention but also in providing documentation of early literacy growth.

To score the checkout, look for the coding specific to each Activity Set appearing after the assessment items. The coding is based on the number of items the student must complete in the checkout (either 5 items or 10 items) and is as follows.

- *M*: Student knows the skill most of the time and has *mastered* the skill (10 of 10 to 8 of 10 or 5 of 5 to 4 of 5); 80%+

- *E*: Student knows the skill some of the time and the skill is *emerging* (7 of 10 to 6 of 10 or 3 of 5); 60%–70%

- *NH*: Student *needs help* with the skill (5 of 10 and below or 2 of 5 and below); ≤ 50%

The checkout codes are derived from the following assumptions.

- 80%–100%: concept/skill mastery

- 60%–70%: the concept/skill is emerging or still developing, and the student may or may not need some extra practice

- 50% and below: the concept/skill is not emerging or developing, and the student definitely needs more time and practice. These are the students you will want to observe carefully during the next set of intervention lessons. If these students consistently score at 50% and below on most of the checkouts as well as perform poorly during classroom literacy instruction and fall behind core curriculum benchmarks, then they may be learners who are at risk and will need more intensive support—perhaps Tier 3 intervention.

The last section of the checkout is the Assessment Decision Grid, which appears at the bottom of each student's checkout sheet. After all checkouts are scored and ready, it is time to discuss the student's results with all classroom personnel that are involved, preferably at a regularly scheduled meeting. For the most valid results, the Assessment Decision Grid should be completed soon after scoring the checkout because the student's performance will be uppermost in your mind.

Interpreting the Scoring Grid

Interpreting the scoring grid on the skill assessment checkouts is simple and straightforward. Once you complete a few of them, you will feel quite comfortable with the entire assessment process. Refer to the Assessment Decision Grid at the bottom of Figure 2.1 while reading the following material to gain a better understanding of the previously outlined scoring codes.

If you checked the mastery box on the left-hand side, then the student completed 80%–100% of the items correctly. The student mastered the skill and does not need further intervention help. Move him or her out of the intervention group and continue with Tier I core instruction only.

If you checked the needs help box on the right-hand side, then the student completed 50% or less of the items correctly. The student has clearly not mastered the skill and needs continued help with the concepts. He or she will stay in the intervention group and move to the next Activity Set within the same DROPP. It is important to keep a close watch on student progress.

Figure 2.1 shows two "skills are emerging" options. If your student's concept or skill is still emerging or developing because he or she completed 60%–70% of the items correctly, then you must make an assessment decision.

For some children, the emerging score (plus other criteria) may mean they are ready to leave the intervention group and return to Tier 1. The criteria for this group follow: Although a student has not mastered the skill yet, he or she is close to mastery. The student understands most concepts presented in the intervention group *and* also during classroom literacy instruction. Upon observation, the student demonstrates a consistent comfort level with the skill over at least 10 days and is able to meaningfully engage in skill development activities during whole group instruction. This shows that the skill is close to full emergence. If a student fits these criteria, check the box to move the student out of the intervention group and back to Tier 1 instruction. Keep a close watch on the student's continued improvement.

For other students, the emerging score may mean they need more practice and must stay in the small group and complete the next Activity Set. The criteria for this group follow: Although a student has not mastered the skill, he or she is clearly making progress in understanding the concepts in the intervention group. The student is also beginning to participate in skill development activities during whole group literacy instruction. If a student fits these criteria, check the box to stay in the intervention group and move to the next Activity Set within the same DROPP. He or she must complete all lessons in the Activity Set and probably will attain mastery in the next skill assessment checkout.

By having collaborative conversation with all pertinent classroom personnel, you will be able to review and discuss the previously listed guidelines, make a realistic assessment decision, and check the appropriate box on the Assessment Decision Grid.

Praise, Points, and Reward Tokens

One of our foundational beliefs as teachers is that we always motivate our students with words, nods, and smiles as well as reward them with authentic, specific praise—praise that specifically identifies the achievement that is praiseworthy. For example,

- Great job rhyming *pig* and *wig*.
- You are working hard with your compound words.
- Nice work saying *Jack* and *Jill*.
- You are learning many new words.

We highly recommend this method of praise and have many of these affirmations scripted into the lessons. We also scripted focus tips throughout the lessons to keep students engaged in the lessons and fully participating in the learning activity. Check on student focus by asking a question and then giving them an easy direction to follow, such as

- What does *whack* mean? Touch your nose if you know.

- Where is your lap? Put your hands in your lap if you know.

- Have you ever seen a brook? Sit up tall and proud if you have.

Use a new word with a student's name. Children love getting everyone's attention, and this will certainly get their attention. Examples include the following:

- Everyone, use *jig* to show another another way of saying, "Taleaha's sister was dancing a silly, little dance."

- Everyone, I want you all to say, "I held Mekhi's sister on my lap." Get ready.

  - **Children respond: I held Mekhi's sister on my lap.**

  - Everyone, where did I hold Mekhi's sister?

  - **Children respond: I held Mekhi's sister on my lap.**

  - Yes, I held Mekhi's sister on my lap.

Another way of keeping students focused and engaged is to keep colorful chips/tokens on hand in different textures and sizes to give out as points in the various games played throughout this program—large, official poker chips; spongy stars; translucent circles; colored math cubes; and so forth. It is best to hand the earned point to the student and for him or her to place it in a small box in front of him or her (empty mint boxes work great) to minimize the temptation to play with the chip. Keep the box open, though, so you know how many chips each student has earned—this will guide you on who to call on so each child is a winner. At the end of the lesson, students empty their boxes, count their points, and announce their score to the group. All students in the group should always have the same number of points.

It is important to ensure that every child wins every game. Keep playing, bend the rules, or give a point for extra effort—whatever it takes for all students to reach success. One way to add an extra punch to games you have played many times is to offer bonus points after everyone already wins. Children love the idea of an extra bonus, and once you offer them bonus points in one game, the students are hooked and will frequently ask for them. It is a great way to sneak in additional practice without them knowing it.

TRAINING TIPS FOR SUCCESSFUL IMPLEMENTATION OF THE PROGRAM

Before using the scripted lessons, it is essential to prepare by rehearsing them aloud. Because the intervention lesson is only about 20 minutes long, you want to maintain your instruction in a pleasing, smooth flow of Teacher Talk and not have to reread the script as you fumble for words, songs, or movements. Unfortunately, fumbling over words and actions during instruction can cause you to lose confidence in yourself as a teacher. Students instinctively know this and begin to lose focus and interest.

Our motto is "Prepare, prepare, prepare!" We recommend previewing 5 days of lessons on the weekend or during planning periods and then reviewing each one before actually teaching the lesson. Sing the songs, get up and practice the movements, play the games, and preview the storybooks ahead of time in order to optimize instructional time with your students.

As you practice reading the script aloud, pretend the students are actually sitting with you in group and responding to you according to the words and actions in the script. Go through each task

Skill Assessment Checkout for DROPP 2

Student Name: _____ Assessor: _____

Directions: Administer the checkout to each student after completing Lesson 4 of each Activity Set.
- Copy one skill assessment checkout for each student in the group.
- Fill in the date in the designated space under the Activity Set you are testing.
- Two examples are given on each line. Use the first set of words for Activity Set 2.1, the second set for Activity Set 2.2, the third set or Activity 2.3, and the fourth set for Activity Set 2.4.
- Circle Y (Yes) if the student's answer is correct or N (No) if the student's answer is incorrect. Use one test item per line.
- Teacher Talk is in plain, roman print.
- Score the checkout and continue to the assessment decision grid.

Skill Being Assessed: Student can discriminate between words that rhyme and words that do not rhyme

PRACTICE:

Letís see if you know your rhymes. I'm going to say two words and ask you if they rhyme.

Does eight rhyme with skate? Listen: eight, skate *(say each part slowly)*. Do the rhyme? Show me thumbs up if they rhyme or thumbs down if they do not rhyme.

(Child responds with thumbs up).

Yes, they rhyme.

ASSESSMENT:

Begin the assessment. Repeat the directions and start with the words on the rst line below. Circle Y or N. Repeat the directions and continue until the assessment is finished. If the child makes three errors in a row, discontinue testing.

						Activity Set							
						2.1		**2.2**		**2.3**		**2.4**	
	2.1	**2.2**	**2.3**	**2.4**	**Date:**								
1.	then, hen	pen, when	say, way	sing, ring		Y	N	Y	N	Y	N	Y	N
2.	day, may	they, hay	he, me	up, right		Y	N	Y	N	Y	N	Y	N
3.	star, toes	car, nose	at, do	Bill, Will		Y	N	Y	N	Y	N	Y	N
4.	cow, brow	Sue, blue	no, go	mule, school		Y	N	Y	N	Y	N	Y	N
5.	lamb, rule	school, dog	pig, take	rain, main		Y	N	Y	N	Y	N	Y	N
6.	cat, rat	chair, bear	cow, now	can, ran		Y	N	Y	N	Y	N	Y	N
7.	pen, ten	hen, Ben	to, you	like, rake		Y	N	Y	N	Y	N	Y	N
8.	far, bar	tar, star	I, why	Pat, Mike		Y	N	Y	N	Y	N	Y	N
9.	pain, tree	rain, he	lie, try	ten, when		Y	N	Y	N	Y	N	Y	N
10.	soap, hope	chain, train	so, you	pie, take		Y	N	Y	N	Y	N	Y	N
	Count the *Y* (Yes) scores and write over 10.					__/10		__/10		__/10		__/10	
	Scoring: Circle *M, E,* or *NH* for each Activity Set.					M E NH		M E NH		M E NH		M E NH	

Scoring:
- M: Student knows the skill most of the time and has mastered the skill (scored 8/10–10/10)
- E: Student knows the skill some of the time and the skill is emerging (scored 6/10–7/10)
- NH: Student needs help with the skill (scored 5/10 and below)

(continued)

Figure 2.1. Completed skill assessment checkout. (See Interpreting the Scoring Grid on p. 14 for more information.)

Figure 2.1. *(continued)*

Skill Assessment Checkout for DROPP 2 *(continued)*

• •

Student Name: _____ Assessor: _____

Additional Observations:

_____

_____

_____

_____

Assessment Decision Grid

This will be a collaborative decision with the teacher and involved classroom personnel (see Chapter 2).

Check one box below:

The Student Completed Tier 2 Intervention	
❐ **with skill mastery** *Move out of group to Tier 1 core instruction*	❐ **and skills are emerging** *Move to the next Activity Set*
❐ **and skills are emerging** *Move out of group to Tier 1 core instruction*	❐ **and needs help** *Move to the next Activity Set*

in sequence and soon you will develop a rhythm such as the one we conveyed in the script or create a rhythm of your own. Adhere to the script as closely as possible during your practice periods and do not improvise or change it.

When you are first beginning your journey as a reading interventionist using DROPPs, rehearse the lessons several times over so you can look away from the script while in group without getting confused or feeling uneasy. When you are teaching the group lesson, follow the script exactly as you did during your practice sessions, and remember to keep your pace at a moderate speed to maintain student focus and to stay within your 20-minute time frame.

Personal Trainer Tip: Stick to the Script

Repeating our words instead of saying your own may not "fit you" at first, but we recommend that you keep practicing aloud and continue to forge ahead. We know you will be glad you did because your commitment to the children and their literacy growth will pay off in many ways—both now and in the future. After a short while, you will start to own the tasks and the words, become more confident in your work as an early literacy interventionist, and see the tangible results of your hard work and that of your students as they progress on their road to becoming reading rockets that soar!

TRAINING, PREPARATION, AND ONGOING SUPPORT FOR PARAPROFESSIONALS AND VOLUNTEERS

As with any new program, the teacher or a program supervisor must take time to train and practice with paraprofessionals and volunteers ("paras") before they begin using an Activity Set. This may be done in a 30- to 40-minute session during which the teacher models each of the lessons' activities and then involves the paras in role-playing those activities. There are numerous instructional strategies, verbal directions, focus tips, and cheers that repeat throughout the program, and over time these will require little advance practice because instructors can rely on lesson icons to signal their delivery.

Another effective way to prepare paras for Tier 2 instruction is to model the activities during whole-class Tier 1 instruction as warm-ups for other core literacy instruction. In this way, the teacher can demonstrate effective pacing and group response techniques while polishing the ability of the whole class to perform the chosen phonological awareness task. This has the added benefit of familiarizing Tier 2 students with upcoming skills and tasks.

It is essential that teachers provide ongoing support and scaffolding to paras who may need help troubleshooting when problems arise or when new lesson activities are introduced. In addition, they will need help and encouragement to keep on track and adhere to the lesson time lines and activities. Early on in the introduction of a new Activity Set, it may be necessary for the teacher to take a few minutes to model the introduction of new activities to the small group so that the para can repeat them correctly over subsequent days.

Finally, it is critical that the teacher establish a system for effective, ongoing communication with paras. It is ultimately the teacher who guides and provides the time, materials, training, and support that will allow students to receive enhanced and meaningful instruction from paras. The following steps are suggested for successful teacher communication with paras (Causton-Theoharis, Giangreco, Doyle, & Vadasy, 2007, p. 60):

1. Establish a 15-minute meeting time for each day.

2. Set aside a longer (45–60 minutes) meeting time for each week.

3. Determine during noninstructional times to discuss progress of individual students.

4. Meet when students do not need supports (e.g., lunch, recess).

5. Establish a communication notebook to be used by the teacher and paraprofessional.

6. Use e-mail as a way to efficiently check in each day to answer important questions.

DROPPS SCOPE AND SEQUENCE: COVERING ALL OF YOUR EARLY LITERACY BASES

Let's take a look at the RTI components and the literacy skill steps that make up the DROPPS program. Table 2.2 shows the prescribed hierarchy of phonological skills for pre-K. There are five key phonological skill areas for pre-K students that lay a strong foundation for developing later reading skills.

1. Rhyming
2. Word awareness in sentences
3. Compound words
4. Syllables
5. Phonemes

The DROPPS lessons are designed to guide young children to pay attention to the qualities of spoken—not written—words through songs, stories, fingerplays, nursery rhymes, dance, and games. As the children have fun playing with words, they are developing the essential skills that will eventually help them associate sounds with letters and use those sounds to form words in beginning reading.

DESCRIPTION OF THE DROPPS

The scope and sequence chart (see Table 2.1) shows how the DROPPS and their corresponding Activity Sets mirror the pre-K hierarchy of skills. This ensures that all of the necessary phonological steps for pre-K students are specifically and thoroughly addressed in the DROPPS lessons. Take a few minutes to familiarize yourself with the chart, then read the following bulleted items to understand how the DROPPS program works across the school year and how easy it is to implement.

- Column 2 shows the DROPPS' sequential numbers, beginning on the Word Level with rhyme awareness and ending with initial sound awareness.

- In Column 3 you see the Activity Sets with numbers correlating to the specific DROPP with which you are working. This straightforward numbering system makes it easy to find the next step you need for your Tier 2 small-group supports.

- The DROPPS contain varying numbers of Activity Sets, depending on the length of time we observed students typically needing for that skill's mastery. The lessons within each set are structured to spiral upward in a sequential format toward mastery.

- Each Activity Set is designed for 10 days of instruction, with one 20-minute lesson per day. In total, this amounts to 220 days of lessons, ensuring that there are more than enough activities to cover each DROPP skill thoroughly, regardless of the children's rate of progress.

- The rhyme production DROPP is considered an optional DROPP ("OPT DROPP")—that is, an OPT DROPP to use for the whole class. This DROPP, which is available on the accompanying CD-ROM, consists of three lessons that can be delivered over 3 days and will help pre-K students begin to learn the most difficult of the rhyming skills—coming up with their own rhyming words. This skill will become more established in kindergarten.

Table 2.2. Pre-K hierarchy of phonological skills

Word level
Rhymes
Awareness
Discrimination
Production
Sentences
Sentence segmentation
Compound words
Blending
Segmentation
Syllable level
Awareness
Blending
Segmentation
Phoneme level
Awareness
Isolation (beginning sounds)

Key: Pre-K, prekindergarten.
See the CD-ROM for a printable version of this table.

The What and Why of Each DROPPS Phonological Skill

Table 2.3 provides a synopsis of each skill step in the DROPPS program and how it is important to the development of a strong foundation for reading and writing.

RESPONSE TO INTERVENTION COMPONENTS

As noted previously, the focus of this curriculum is Tier 2 small-group intervention. Walking through the full program flow chart (Figure 2.2) will show you how the DROPPS lessons fit into a tiered RTI model and how it can work in your classroom.

Steps for Evaluating Students' Skills

Observation

The first step in implementing RTI is to assess all of the students in a class to see how they are progressing in skills that relate to later reading competence. In pre-K, an observation period of 6–8 weeks is recommended before giving any screening tests because the children need time to adjust to the newness of school. This is a good time to take anecdotal notes on students' skills in the following domains.

- Language: Can the children understand directions, communicate personal experiences, and ask questions to express needs and wants?

- Print awareness: Do children recognize concepts of how books are used, any environmental print (e.g., a store logo), or any letters, including their own names?

Universal Screening

The next step is universal screening—using quick measures that will show you which children have begun to acquire the phonological skills on the pre-K hierarchy. Your core curriculum may have benchmark tests that measure an individual student's performance. We have found that general outcome measures such as *Get It! Got It! Go!* (G3) are quick and effective screening tools for identifying children who would benefit from early intervention.

By November of pre-K, according to the PAP, or about age 4, children can be expected to show the emergence of rhyming awareness in spoken words and word awareness in spoken sentences. These would be the first areas to address in universal screening using the following steps.

- Introduce the whole class to the skill(s) being tested and the materials that will be used. Practice in the testing format—for example, choosing (pointing to or saying) the picture name that rhymes with a given word or clapping out words in short sentences.

- Individually test each child on the targeted skills. For example, giving the G3 Rhyming Subtest and having students clap out the words in 5 short sentences will take 3–4 minutes per student.

- Record all results on a class chart to see how the students compare with standardized performance benchmarks and to others in the class.

- Group students by areas of need and get ready to provide your successful supports.

Universal screening is done three or four times through the year according to the sequence in which the children would be expected to develop the skills on the pre-K hierarchy.

Steps for Tier 2 Small-Group Intervention

Once you have successfully completed universal screening, you will have identified any students in your class who are lacking some important literacy skills. This important information will make it

Table 2.3. Directed Reading Opportunities (DROPPS) scope and sequence: Covering all early literacy bases

DROPPS phonological skill	What it is	Why it is important
1: Rhyme awareness	The ability to tell whether two spoken words rhyme with each other	Students must be able to hear rhymes and enjoy them before they can produce them. Rhyming helps students learn about sounds in words.
2: Rhyme discrimination	The ability to discriminate between words that rhyme and words that do not rhyme	Students must be able to understand the difference between words that rhyme and words that do not rhyme. This is a step to becoming phonologically aware.
OPT DROPP: Rhyme production	The ability to produce a real or nonsense word that rhymes with one that was heard	Students who can produce rhymes on their own are mastering a more advanced step of phoneme sequencing. This is an important precursor to reading.
3: Sentence segmentation	The ability to segment short spoken sentences into individual words	Recognizing that spoken sentences are composed of separate words helps students understand word boundaries in print. This "word awareness" is strongly linked to the ability to read and write.
4: Blending	The ability to hear two short spoken words and blend them into a compound word	Children who can hear and blend together the two segments of compound words develop the awareness that words are made up of parts or segments. This awareness is strongly linked to the ability to decode and spell words.
5: Compound word segmentation	The ability to segment a spoken compound word into two small words	Separating a compound word into its smaller words shows children that a word can be broken into parts. This prepares them for the eventual understanding that word parts correspond to letter symbols, which they will learn to read.
6: Syllable awareness	The ability to detect the separate syllables in spoken words	Through syllable play, young children learn to recognize the larger units of sounds in words, a necessary step toward being able to detect the individual sounds, or phonemes, in words.
7: Syllable blending	The ability to orally blend two to three syllables into a whole word	Practice in syllable blending helps children pronounce longer words by increasing the ability to hold sounds in memory. This prepares young children for the later skill of blending word parts in order to read.
8: Syllable segmentation	The ability to segment the syllables in spoken words	Young learners must learn to manipulate larger units of speech, such as syllables and onset-rime, before they can detect individual sounds in words.
9: Blending awareness	The ability to blend sounds into words using onsets and rimes and words with two to three sounds	As children manipulate the sounds of onset-rimes and then phonemes, they master the finer steps of phonemic awareness, which is a necessary foundation for reading.
10: Beginning sound alliteration	The ability to hear initial sounds in words and to tell if two words begin with the same sound	Understanding that words begin with a particular sound and that certain other words start the same way gently shifts the child into perceiving phonemes—the smallest sounds of language. This leads to understanding the alphabetic principle.

Note: See the CD-ROM for a printable version of this table.

possible for you to deliver the exact instruction each child needs in small groups over a short period of time. The following show the RTI model at work.

- Timely supports provided in the general education setting that prevent the development of most reading problems

- Simple checkouts to monitor students' success

- Flexible movement of students in and out of differentiated groups

- More time for more effective whole-group instruction (Tier 1)

Looking at the next step shown on the program flow chart, students with no identified weaknesses will need only Tier 1 whole-class instruction. Your job is to engage every student in the

When do your students need a Directed Reading Opportunity (DROPP)?

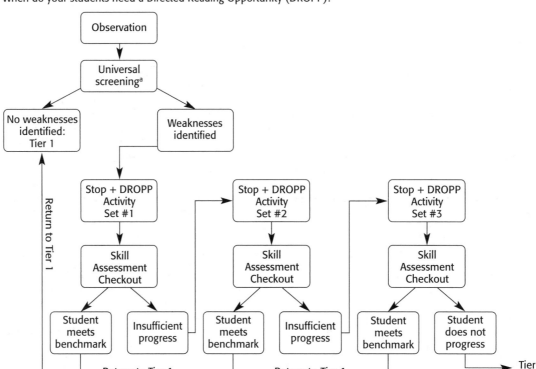

Figure 2.2. Full program flow chart/decision-making process guide. (*Note*: ᵃcurriculum-based measurements: curriculum benchmarks.)

research-based curriculum chosen by your administration. This task is made much easier by knowing that students who need extra practice in these core skills will receive it in Tier 2.

Respond Promptly When Weaknesses Are Identified

The remaining sectors of the flow chart show how to provide the Tier 2 reinforcement using the DROPPS program. Students with identified weaknesses in one of the key phonological skill areas previously mentioned will "Stop and DROPP" into a small group for the skill they need.

HOW A DROPP ACTIVITY SET WORKS: A Classroom Example

Let's examine the specific steps of the first DROPP to see how the Activity Sets are used day by day (see Figure 2.3).

Chris's Prekindergarten Class

Universal Screening and Tier 1 Instruction

Chris has twenty 4-year-olds in his pre-K class. In September and October, during whole-class Tier 1 literacy instruction, he teaches the children the meaning of the word *rhyme* and the similarities in the sounds of rhyming words, incorporating nursery rhymes and stories that he reads for their enjoyment. He observes a wide range of student behaviors when he does the read-alouds, from active enjoyment and repetition of rhymes to disinterest and puzzlement.

In mid-October, Chris familiarizes the students with the format of the G3 Rhyming Subtest by demonstrating and practicing how to recognize rhyming picture names. Chris and his classroom

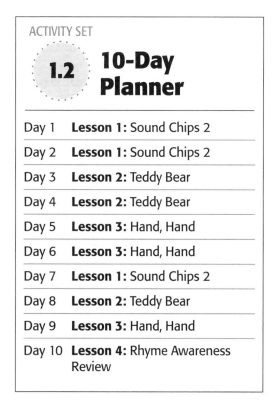

Figure 2.3. Sample: Activity Sets 1.1 and 1.2, day by day.

para, Sue, set aside about an hour during which they give every child the individually administered Rhyming Subtest of the G3 (screening tool). Sue compiles the results of this universal screening. The results, along with any anecdotal information gathered thus far, are then analyzed and discussed.

Determining Tier 2 Placement

Chris observes that four students scored well below the expected aim line in rhyme recognition, and the skill had not emerged at all in three other children. A decision is made that these seven children will receive Tier 2 small-group instruction beginning with rhyme awareness.

Next, Chris and Sue preview DROPP 1 Rhyme Awareness Activity Set 1.1, and determine the materials, work space, and scheduling needs for delivering the activity lessons to the children. They make arrangements for Sue to work with each small group for 20 minutes each day in a quiet corner of the classroom, at "choice" time or the prelunch transition time, so the seven children can receive extra instruction beyond their core literacy instructional time.

Activity Set 1.1: Progress Monitoring and Assessment Decision

The students have completed all of the Rhyme Awareness Activity Set 1.1 lessons by Friday of the second week, after 10 days in a Tier 2 small group, and Sue spends a few minutes giving each child the checkout task of showing "thumbs up" as correct recognition of rhyming pairs. Four of the students are able to recognize all of the rhymes correctly. One child is successful on 6 of 10 checkout items, and the remaining two children scored at 50% or below. Chris and Sue meet to review the checkout results. Placement decision: The four mastery students will return to Tier 1 (large group) only, and the remaining three students will continue to receive Tier 2 services, this time using Rhyme Awareness Activity Set 1.2.

Activity Set 1.2: A New Consideration

Over the weekend, Sue familiarizes herself with the new fingerplays and rhyming books that accompany Rhyme Awareness Activity Set 1.2 so that she can begin the activities on Monday morning. Joe is a new student in class who has no previous school experience. During the Tier 1 whole-class literacy instruction, Chris pays special attention to Joe, who is adjusting well. At break time, Sue takes a few minutes to show Joe the G3 Rhyming Cards and then gives him the Rhyming Subtest, on which he demonstrates inconsistent but emerging rhyme recognition skills. At lunchtime, the two instructors confer and decide that Joe will benefit from being included in the Tier 2 group. Although it is possible that Joe will pick up all the necessary skills in Tier 1, Chris decides to err on the side of caution and provide more individualized supports for the next 2 weeks. Sue welcomes Joe into the newly formed Tier 2 group for the first lesson of Activity Set 1.2.

Activity Set 1.2 Checkouts

On the 10th day, Chris gives the checkouts in order to see for himself how well the children recognize rhyming pictures. Two of the children, including Joe, demonstrate concept mastery with a score of 80% or better. The other 2 children answer several items correctly and although their rhyming awareness seems to be developing after 20 days in Tier 2, they still need more time and practice. These are the students that Chris and Sue will observe more carefully in both Tier 1 and Tier 2. If they perform poorly in their literacy instruction and fall behind core curriculum benchmarks, then they may be at-risk learners who need more intensive support—perhaps Tier 3 intervention.

TIPS FOR SUCCESSFUL IMPLEMENTATION

- **Schedule the 20-minute DROPP activities at a time that does not interfere with core literacy or math instruction.** In the most effective RTI demonstrations, Tier 2 supports are meant to be provided over and above the essential classroom teaching. Be creative in finding little opportunities during the day that will make such a big difference in terms of student success.

- **Look at Tier 1 before implementing Tier 2.** If more than 30% of the class is struggling with an important skill, then you may need to reassess, reteach, and review that skill with the whole class before scheduling small-group supports. You may find that only a few students have thoroughly grasped the skill, in which case a small enrichment group for those mastery students would be a more effective response than numerous small groups to support the struggling students.

- **Use universal screening time to preview upcoming skills.** While you are doing a 1- or 2-minute G3 Subtest with each child, you can use any DROPPS checkout to gauge class readiness for the next step of phonological skill. For example, after matching the G3 rhyming pairs, ask the child to clap out the small words in a few compound words. This is a quick way to obtain valuable information for your instructional planning.

- **Have reasonable expectations for student success.** It may take weeks or even a few months for some children to grasp new skills. Although their growth might not be measurable for awhile, you can be assured these students are benefiting from the meaningful practice opportunities that are provided in the small group. The early provision of Tier 2 supports is the best way to prevent the development of later reading difficulties.

- **Give all students a lot of practice in the "phonology zone."** Do not advance up the skills hierarchy beyond developmental expectations. Hearing the differences in words in pre-K is more important than memorizing words on paper. If your students are meeting all of the expected phonological benchmarks—rhyming, initial sounds, and clapping out words and syllables—then that is great. You might be tempted to "teach ahead" with phonics and word recognition, but your time would be better spent having more fun with phonological skills and enriching the children's vocabulary with plenty of shared reading.

DROPPS: RESPONSE TO INTERVENTION IN ACTION

By now, you have seen how the DROPPS program can enhance the core literacy program in your early childhood class by supporting the development of every student's essential phonological skills in a timely fashion. By implementing the straightforward RTI framework, whole-class instructional time is used more effectively. For students needing individualized, small-group practice, this manual provides exactly what you need in order to deliver proven, step-by-step lessons that will reinforce those emerging skills. If you are fortunate enough to have a para or consistent volunteer to work with a Tier 2 group, then the scripted Teacher Talk will ensure that they can do just what is needed to support emerging skills. It only takes 20 minutes a day to differentiate early literacy instruction for your students by using the systematic DROPPS activities.

Rhyme Awareness

Overview

WHY RHYME AWARENESS IS IMPORTANT

Rhyme awareness is one of the first steps to becoming phonologically aware and is an important precursor to reading. Rhyming helps students learn about sounds in words. Students must first be able to hear rhymes and enjoy them before they can produce them.

HOW DROPP 1 IS STRUCTURED

DROPP 1 has three complete Activity Sets: 1.1–1.3. Each Activity Set consists of four scripted lessons (Teacher Talk) that are used on 10 sequential learning days (the four lessons are repeated over the 10-day span). These intervention lessons are aimed at practicing and reviewing the skill of rhyme awareness. DROPP 1 has 30 days of intervention lessons in all (three Activity Sets of 10 days each). During the first 9 days of each set, students learn the words to rhyming songs and nursery rhymes, learn dance movements and fingerplays, and take part in interactive rhyming stories. On the 10th day, students review the skills to prepare for a short skill assessment checkout. (See the CD-ROM for the DROPP 1 Skill Assessment Checkout.)

Length of Activity Sets and Lessons

Each Activity Set is designed to be delivered across 10 sequential learning days. Each day's intervention lesson, including the transition activities, takes about 20 minutes to complete.

Lessons 1–3 within the Activity Sets are generally divided into 3 tasks.

- Task 1 is the transition into the lesson and lasts about 2–3 minutes.

- Task 2 is the concept/skill portion and lasts for approximately 12–15 minutes.

- Task 3 is the transition out of the lesson and lasts about 2–3 minutes.

Lesson 4 is slightly different because Task 3 has been eliminated to allow more time for review. Lesson 4 is generally divided into 2 tasks.

- Task 1 is the transition into the lesson and lasts about 2–3 minutes.

- Task 2 is the concept/skill portion and may be divided into Task 2A and Task 2B. This task lasts for approximately 15–18 minutes.

Goal and Emphasis of the Rhyme Awareness Lessons

The goal of Activity Sets 1.1–1.3 is to saturate your students in rhyming songs, fingerplays, movement, and rhyming books. The "Rhyming Exercise Song," a short snappy song and large muscle exercise, has become a mainstay of our rhyming instruction and is emphasized in all Activity Sets. Always exaggerate and emphasize the rhyming words—make them as clear as possible for the students to hear. We use a multisensory approach throughout the lessons that is geared to directly reinforcing the concept of rhyme awareness: your students *see* pictures, *sing* rhymes, *hear* rhymes, participate in *large muscle motions*, and use other *body movements*.

TEACHING TIP: **Check for Success**

Maintain eye contact with all students in your group, and ensure they are responding correctly and on cue. By doing this, you are conducting a mini assessment for each child to see who may need additional help.

Student Objectives

- Know how to listen carefully to the sounds of rhyming words and be able to develop an awareness of rhyme by repeating rhyming fingerplays and songs.

- Know how to listen carefully to the sounds of rhyming words and be able to develop an awareness of rhyme in an interactive rhyming book by accurately predicting the rhyming word in the story.

Teacher Objectives

- Emphasize the sounds of words that rhyme so students can clearly hear that the endings of rhyming words are the same.

- Smile and ensure success for all children.

- Hold the book so that each child can see the pictures.

- Lead children to participate in the interactive rhyming book by coaching them to accurately predict the rhyming word in the story.

- Closely observe each student for focus and full participation.

Teaching Approach

Smile often and show the children how happy you are to be with them. All of these lessons are clearly instructional, but the content is fun and your delivery should be easy and happy. Students will want to join you in group and look forward to it. Small-group time allows you to understand your children's instructional needs and how you can meet them. In order for this to happen, the children must feel comfortable and safe—safe to take risks, learn, and grow. You are opening the door to one of the joys of early childhood literacy—rhyming.

How the Rhyme Awareness Activity Set Develops Early Literacy

Multisensory Techniques

In Activity Sets 1.1–1.3, children are using both fine motor skills and large muscle movements to emphasize rhyming words in songs, poems, fingerplays, and games. Students sing rhymes and hear their classmates sing them; listen for, identify, and locate different kinds of sounds (e.g., loud, soft, long, short, everyday, environmental); and participate in full physical responses to rhyming words by moving to and singing the "Rhyming Exercise Song." Throughout the Activity Sets, students continually confirm rhyming word pairs by nodding their heads and giving a thumbs-up to maintain their complete focus on rhyme.

Making Meaning and Building Vocabulary

As students go through Activity Sets 1.1–1.3, they are exposed to new vocabulary words and phrases associated with nursery rhymes, fingerplays, and read-alouds. These new words and phrases are listed at the beginning of each Activity Set and are presented in a two-step approach (see Chapter 2). Although some of these words are not common ones that the children use easily or hear often in everyday speech, we recommend that you use the new words and phrases throughout the day and in different contexts to reinforce student vocabulary and oral language growth. Encourage your students to use the words when talking to each other. Set time aside to give them the opportunity to engage in meaningful conversation with their peers.

- Activity Set 1.1: entire, nursery, fleece, from the top
- Activity Set 1.2: cheer, mischief, skidoo, whack
- Activity Set 1.3: steeple, straight, stout

Print Awareness

Students will have the opportunity to take part in the read-aloud during the Literature Link in Lesson 3 of these Activity Sets and experience the left-to-right progression of word reading and the overall framework of using a book. Also embedded is the awareness that the rhyming words they hear being read to them are actually in printed form on the pages of the books. Although these concepts of print are presented at an awareness level only and are not intended as explicit instruction in word reading, they will support your students' understanding that rhyming words can be translated into print. This is one of the core foundational understandings in learning to read.

General Tips for Implementing Activity Sets 1.1–1.3

- In Activity Set 1.1, as you introduce rhyming words, use your face as a way of guiding the students to become aware of rhyming words. When singing the words "Do they rhyme?" in the "Rhyming Exercise Song" (introduced here in DROPP 1), show "thumbs up," a big smile, and a vigorous head nod as you exclaim, "Yes, they rhyme!" You are modeling the correct response for your students while cuing it for them at the same time.

- A listening game is introduced in each Activity Set to get the students used to listening carefully for everyday sounds, identifying them quickly, and, in some cases, locating sounds within a specified area. This activity prepares them for learning later skills in the area of phonemic awareness. Phonemes are the smallest sounds in words and children will be expected to listen carefully and identify them, as this is the foundation for future phonics instruction.

- In Activity Set 1.2, teach the students to sing and dance to "Teddy Bear, Teddy Bear"—a popular children's song. We had enough classroom bears for each child to hold as they "performed"—if you do not, encourage the children to bring in bears from home.

Literature Link

There are three rhyming books used in DROPP 1 in order for students to hear rhyme in the context of stories. They are all presented in Lesson 3.

- Activity Set 1.1: *Hop on Pop* (LeSieg, 1963)
- Activity Set 1.2: *Hand, Hand, Fingers, Thumb* (Perkins, 1969)
- Activity Set 1.3: *I'll Teach My Dog 100 Words* (Firth, 1973)

While reading books to students in Activity Sets 1.1–1.3, encourage them to anticipate and predict the rhyming words at the end of the sentences. The rhyming words should be read in an overemphasized voice for easy identification by the students. Read the rhyming lines slowly for the children to hear the rhymes and think about the sound-alike qualities of the rhyming words.

Pause and Punch Technique

As you read, pause slightly just before the first rhyming word, and then punch it with your voice to make an impact. Continue reading to its rhyming match, and when you come to it, pause again to cue the students to supply (predict) the rhyming word. An example follows.

A tiny bug went for a walk (*emphasize the last word in the line*).
He met a cat and stopped to . . . talk! (*Pause for the students to say the rhyming word and as they supply the rhyme, nod vigorously, and emphasize the word* talk.)

Choose easy and familiar rhyming words at first (e.g., *bear* and *chair, mouse* and *house, cat* and *hat*) so the students can make accurate choices when predicting or supplying the rhyme. Some students are strong at predicting rhyming words, whereas others are not. Observing this skill in students provides important insight into rhyme development.

Review

On Day 10 of each Activity Set, students get the opportunity to review the rhyme awareness skills by practicing several of the games, songs, read-aloud books, and so forth from the prior 9 days before their skill assessment checkout. The review is taken from Lessons 2 and 3.

Skill Assessment Checkouts

After your review lesson is completed, set aside a few minutes during that same day to give each child an individual rhyme awareness checkout. These take about 2 minutes per child to administer and provide useful information to guide your small-group placements. Based on the checkout and collaborative conversations with all teachers, you will determine which students should continue on in Tier 2 small-group intervention and which students can successfully return to Tier 1 whole-class instruction.

Assessment Outcome: The student is aware that two familiar words rhyme and that two unfamiliar words rhyme.

ACTIVITY SET 1.1

Lesson Descriptions

Lessons	Sequence of daily activities	◇ Vocabulary
Lesson 1: Sound Chips	Fingerplay for "The Itsy-Bitsy Spider" Target: Game—Listening for sounds Fingerplay for "The Itsy-Bitsy Spider"	Entire
Lesson 2: Mary Had a Little Lamb	Fingerplay for "Five Little Ducks" Target: "Mary Had a Little Lamb" Fingerplay for "Five Little Ducks"	Nursery Fleece
Lesson 3: Hop on Pop	Song and movement for "Head, Shoulders, Knees, and Toes" Target: Rhyming book—*Hop on Pop* (LeSieg, 1963) Song and movement for "Head, Shoulders, Knees, and Toes"	From the top
Lesson 4: Rhyme Awareness Review	Song and movement for "Head, Shoulders, Knees, and Toes" Target: "Mary Had a Little Lamb" Rhyming book: *Hop on Pop* (LeSieg, 1963)	

Materials Needed

☑ Book: *Hop on Pop* (LeSieg, 1963)

☑ Large nursery rhyme book with "Mary Had a Little Lamb"

☑ Picture of a baby nursery

☑ Example of fleece for the children to feel (even cotton balls or a fleece jacket work)

☑ Tokens for behavior/participation

☑ DROPP 1 Skill Assessment Checkout (see Appendix B on the CD-ROM)   **CD-ROM**

Sound Chips Game

☑ Sound clips (see Appendix C on the CD-ROM)

☑ Two colored chips/other tokens for each child

ACTIVITY SET

1.1 **10-Day Planner**

Day 1	**Lesson 1:** Sound Chips	
Day 2	**Lesson 1:** Sound Chips	
Day 3	**Lesson 2:** Mary Had a Little Lamb	
Day 4	**Lesson 2:** Mary Had a Little Lamb	
Day 5	**Lesson 3:** Hop on Pop	
Day 6	**Lesson 3:** Hop on Pop	
Day 7	**Lesson 1:** Sound Chips	
Day 8	**Lesson 2:** Mary Had a Little Lamb	
Day 9	**Lesson 3:** Hop on Pop	
Day 10	**Lesson 4:** Rhyme Awareness Review	

LESSON 1: Sound Chips

OBJECTIVES

Student will

- Know how to listen carefully to everyday sounds and be able to identify them
- Know how to listen carefully to the sounds of rhyming words and be able to develop an awareness of rhyme by repeating rhyming fingerplays and songs

Teacher will

- Guide students in identifying common sounds
- Emphasize the sounds of words that rhyme so students can clearly hear that the endings of rhyming words are the same
- Closely observe each student for focus and full participation
- Smile and ensure success for all children

RHYMES, SONGS, AND FINGERPLAYS

"The Itsy-Bitsy Spider"

MATERIALS

Tokens for behavior/participation
Sound Chips

Sound Chips Game

- ☑ Sound clips (see Appendix C on the CD-ROM)
- ☑ Two colored chips/other tokens for each child

 TASK 1 | Transition fingerplay to begin the lesson (approximately 3 minutes)

INTRODUCE the big idea.

Say the following to the group after calling them together at a table.

We are going to learn about sounds. Some of these sounds are the sounds in words. Some words sound like each other and are called rhyming words. You will learn some good rhyming songs and games.

BEGIN the transition.

You are going to learn to sing a rhyming fingerplay. Words that rhyme are words that sound the same. You may know this fingerplay. It is called "The Itsy-Bitsy Spider." What's the name of the fingerplay?

▶ Children's response: "The Itsy-Bitsy Spider."

Use exaggerated, easy, consistent, and space-conscious finger and hand movements that mimic the song.

Start by singing the first two lines of the song until you have sung two rhyming words. Exaggerate the words spout *and* out *to convey that they are rhyming words.*

My turn to sing.
The itsy-bitsy spider went up the waterspout.
Down came the rain and washed the spider out.

Sing the next two lines until you have sung two more rhyming words. Repeat the song with the children and do the movements.

 Multisensory Reinforcement

Your turn to sing.

▶ Children's response:

The Itsy-bitsy spider went up the waterspout.
Down came the rain and washed the spider out.

My turn to sing.
Out came the sun and dried up all the rain.
So the itsy-bitsy spider came up the spout again.

Exaggerate the words rain *and* again *to convey that they are rhyming words.*

Your turn to sing.

▶ Children's response:
Out came the sun and dried up all the rain.

So the itsy-bitsy spider came up the spout again.

Let's start from the beginning and sing our entire rhyming fingerplay together.

The itsy-bitsy spider went up the waterspout.
Down came the rain and washed the spider out.
Out came the sun and dried up all the rain.
So the itsy-bitsy spider came up the spout again.

Nice work using our voices and our rhymes singing "The Itsy-Bitsy Spider."

◇ **Vocabulary**

ENTIRE

When I say let's sing the entire song, I mean let's sing the whole song. *(form a big circle with your arms)* from start to end. We'll start to sing the song and we won't stop until we sing the entire song.

Explain vocabulary in a simple way. Follow a two-step approach. Step 1: Ask the children to describe (or act out) the vocabulary word. Everyone, show me the entire thing with your arms.

▶ **Children respond by forming big circles with their arms.**

Step 2: Give students the description and they supply the word. Everyone, what's another way of saying the whole thing?

▶ **Children's response: The entire thing.**

TEACHING TIP: Use the new word in a sentence using your students' names. This always gets their attention.

Yes, *entire* means the whole thing. Another way of saying Jameel ate the whole ice cream cone is Jameel ate the entire ice cream cone.

Guide students to use a complete sentence.

Everyone, I want you all to say Jameel ate the entire ice cream cone. Get ready.

▶ **Children's response: Jameel ate the entire ice cream cone.**

Yes, Jameel ate the entire ice cream cone. Everyone, how much of the ice cream cone did Jameel eat?

▶ **Children's response: Jameel ate the entire ice cream cone.**

Yes, Jameel ate the entire ice cream cone. Let's pretend to eat the entire ice cream cone. *Pretend to eat and prompt the children to follow.*

 TASK 2   **Play Sound Chips** (approximately 12–14 minutes)

  PLAY the game.   CD-ROM See Appendix D on the CD-ROM for the Sound Chips Game instructions and Appendix C for the sound clips.

TASK 3 Transition song to end the lesson (approximately 3 minutes)

MAKE THE TRANSITION to end the lesson.	You are going to practice the rhyming fingerplay you learned earlier. Can you re-member the name of the fingerplay? Raise your hand if you remember. *Call on a student.*

▶ Child's response: "The Itsy-Bitsy Spider."

Yes, it's called "The Itsy-Bitsy Spider."

If the student response is incorrect, say, The name of our rhyming fingerplay is "The Itsy-Bitsy Spider." Let's get our spiders ready.

Multisensory Reinforcement

Sing the entire song with them and do the movements.

The itsy-bitsy spider went up the waterspout.
Down came the rain and washed the spider out.
Out came the sun and dried up all the rain.
So the itsy-bitsy spider came up the spout again.

Great job singing about your spiders.

TEACH the "Rhyming Exercise Song."

Listen to the "Rhyming Exercise Song," which we can do together. Remember, words that rhyme are words that sound the same. We want to get our rhyme muscles nice and strong so our rhymes are in great shape. Follow me.

Multisensory Reinforcement

Do the movements: Pause and flex your wrists with your palms up. Put your hands in the sky. *On the word hands, stretch one arm up to the sky and then the other arm.* Do the rhyming exercise.

Model the Activity

Spout *(Stretch one arm up as you say the word.)*
Out *(Stretch the other arm up.)*
Spout *(Switch arms.)*
Out *(Switch arms.)*
Spout *(Switch arms.)*
Out *(Switch arms.)*

Do they rhyme? *Pause here and allow them to show thumbs up or thumbs down before you respond. Look around at each student and make eye contact.* Yes. *Nod vigorously.* They rhyme. *Give two thumbs up.*

Yes. Good job. You are working hard learning your rhymes. Clam claps for us. *Hold both hands at neck height out to the side, with elbows bent, and "clap" fingers to thumb in the shape of a clam. Repeat the claps.*

END Lesson 1.

Everyone now gets their winnings for learning your rhymes and for working hard. *Give out token rewards to each child.*

LESSON 2: Mary Had a Little Lamb

OBJECTIVES

Student will

- Know how to listen carefully to the sounds of rhyming words and be able to develop an awareness of rhyme by repeating rhyming fingerplays and songs

Teacher will

- Emphasize the sounds of words that rhyme so students can clearly hear that the endings of rhyming words are the same
- Closely observe each student for focus and full participation
- Smile and ensure success for all children

RHYMES, SONGS, AND FINGERPLAYS

"Mary Had a Little Lamb"

"Five Little Ducks"

MATERIALS

Large nursery rhyme book with "Mary Had a Little Lamb"

Picture of a baby nursery

Example of fleece for the children to feel (even cotton balls or a fleece jacket can work)

Tokens for behavior/participation

🪐 TASK 1   Transition fingerplay to begin the lesson (approximately 3 minutes)

INTRODUCE the big idea.	We are going to listen carefully for rhymes and then practice our rhymes. You will learn some good rhyming songs.
	Think big. Don't forget, words that rhyme are words that sound the same. What do we call words that sound the same?
	▶ Children's response: Words that rhyme.
Model the Activity	Yes, words that rhyme or rhyming words. Like *play* and *away*. Do it with me. *As you say* play, *put your right palm out and tilt your head to the right and then do the same on the left side as you say* away. *Do this three times.*
	▶ (Children respond by doing it with you.)
	Nice job rhyming *play* and *away*.
BEGIN the transition.	You are going to learn to sing a rhyming fingerplay. You may know this one. It's called "Five Little Ducks."
	What's the name of the fingerplay? *Coach the students for the correct response.*
	▶ Children's response: "Five Little Ducks."
👂 Turn On Your Ears	My turn. Listen. *Sing the first two lines of the fingerplay until you have sung two rhyming words.*
Use exaggerated, easy, consistent, and space-conscious finger and hand movements that mimic the song.	Five little ducks went out one day, Over the hill and far away.
	Sing the next two lines until you have sung two more rhyming words.
	Your turn to sing. *Repeat the fingerplay, do it with them, and count down to one little duck.*
	▶ Children's response: **Five little ducks went out one day,** **Over the hill and far away.**
	My turn.
	Mother duck said "quack, quack, quack," But only four little ducks came back.
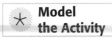 **Model the Activity**	Your turn to sing. *Sing with them and do the finger movements.*

TEACHING TIP: Use drama to increase memory. Look very sad for the mother duck, but get happy quickly when the ducks come back.

▶ Children's response:
Mother duck said "quack, quack, quack,"
But only four little ducks came back.

Let's start from the beginning and sing our rhyming song together.

One little duck…but none of the five little ducks came back.
Let's sing the last verse.
Sad mother duck went out one day,
Over the hill and far away.
The sad mother duck said "quack, quack, quack,"
And all of the five little ducks came back.

Nice job singing "Five Little Ducks." You are working very hard.

Let's give ourselves a round of applause. *Clap hands in a circle for a round of applause.*

 TASK 2   **Learning nursery rhymes** (approximately 12–14 minutes)

INTRODUCE the nursery rhyme.

You are going to learn a nursery rhyme called "Mary Had a Little Lamb." What is a nursery? Touch your nose if you know. *Call on one or two children.*

TEACHING TIP: Check on students' focus by giving them an easy direction to follow.

◇ Vocabulary

NURSERY

Explain vocabulary in a simple way. Follow a two-step approach. Step 1: Show the picture of a nursery and give a brief description of the word.

A nursery is a room where a baby sleeps. What is a nursery? Everyone?

▶ Children's response: A room where a baby sleeps.

Step 2: Give students the description and have them supply the word.

Yes, a nursery is a room where a baby sleeps. Another way of saying a room where a baby sleeps is a nursery.

Everyone, I want you all to say, a nursery is a room where a baby sleeps. Get ready.

▶ Children's response: A nursery is a room where a baby sleeps.

Guide students to use a complete sentence. Yes, a nursery is a room where a baby sleeps. Where does a baby sleep?

▶ Children's response: A nursery is a room where a baby sleeps.

Yes, a nursery is a room where a baby sleeps. We call this a nursery rhyme because some parents and grandparents sing these rhymes to their babies as they fall asleep in their cribs. Let's pretend we are rocking our babies and putting our baby brother or sister in their crib in the nursery. Be gentle.

1.1

TEACHING TIP: Act it out. Use exaggerated movements with the students. Have them rock their babies in their arms and then put them to bed.

Show students the pictures from the nursery rhyme book. The title of our nursery rhyme is "Mary Had a Little Lamb." What is the little girl's name in our rhyme?

Give the correct answer immediately if a student responds incorrectly to a question about the rhyme story. Continue being positive and encouraging.

▶ **Children's response: Mary.**

Yes, the girl's name is Mary. And what did she have in the rhyme?

▶ **Children's response: A little lamb.**

Yes, Mary had a little lamb. Why do you think Mary had a little lamb?

Accept responses from one or two children. Then, guide students toward the concept of a pet. Does anyone here have a little lamb as a pet at home? *Accept responses from one or two children.*

What do you think happens to Mary and her little lamb? *Accept responses from one or two children.*

Let's find out as we listen. *Read the nursery rhyme showing the pictures as you read slowly.*

 Multisensory Reinforcement

Mary had a little lamb,
Whose fleece was white as snow.
And everywhere that Mary went,
the lamb was sure to go.

It followed her to school one day,
That was against the rule.
It made the children laugh and play,
To see a lamb at school.

Should I read it again?

▶ **(Children respond with nods.)**

Reread the nursery rhyme again slowly, showing the pictures. Touch the specific pictures as you read. Okay, listen carefully and repeat after me. Mary had a little lamb. Your turn. Say it.

 Turn On Your Ears

▶ **Children's response: Mary had a little lamb.**

My turn. Whose fleece was white as snow. Your turn. Say it.

▶ **Children's response: Whose fleece was white as snow.**

Fleece is another name for the lamb's fur. Everyone, do you think fleece is soft or hard? *Show your fleece example.*

◇ **Vocabulary**

FLEECE

Explain vocabulary in a simple way.

▶ **Children's response: Soft.**

Yes, a lamb's fleece is soft. Everyone, touch the lamb's fleece.

The children feel the fleece.

TEACHING TIP: Check on students' focus by giving them an easy direction to follow.

Tell me about something else that is soft. Touch your elbow if you know. *Call on several children to respond.*

Let's keep going. My turn. And everywhere that Mary went. Your turn. Say it.

▶ **Children's response: And everywhere that Mary went.**

My turn. The lamb was sure to go. Your turn. Say it.

▶ **Children's response: The lamb was sure to go.**

It followed her to_____ (where?). Everyone?

▶ **Children's response: To school.**

Yes, It followed her to school one day, which was against the rule. What is a rule? Touch your nose if you know. *Call on one child to respond.*

Yes, a rule is something you must do. Tell me about the rules we have at this school. *Guide students to remember some rules.* Can you bring a pet to school?

▶ **Children's response: No.**

Let's find out what happened when Mary's lamb followed her to school. *Show the book.*

It made the children laugh and play to see a lamb at school. Everyone, say it with me.

▶ **Children's response: It made the children laugh and play to see a lamb at school.**

Nice job saying "Mary Had a Little Lamb."

PRACTICE the "Rhyming Exercise Song."

Let's sing the "Rhyming Exercise Song." Let's get our rhyme muscles nice and strong so our rhymes are in great shape. Remember, words that rhyme are words that sound the same, or rhyming words.

 **Multisensory Reinforcement**

Put your hands in the sky. *Stretch one arm up to the sky, then the other arm, on the word hands.* Do the rhyming exercise.

Show *(Stretch one arm up as you say the word.)*
Snow *(Stretch the other arm up.)*
Show *(Switch arms.)*
Snow *(Switch arms.)*
Show *(Switch arms.)*
Snow *(Switch arms.)*

Do they rhyme? *Pause here and allow them to show thumbs up or down before you respond. Look around at each student and make eye contact.* Yes. *Nod vigorously.* They rhyme. *Give two thumbs up.*

Let's try two more words: *rule* and *school. Repeat the song with the new words.*

END the song.

When time is up and before the transition, say, Your rhyming work was so good today. Let's give ourselves the trucker cheer. Do it with me.

(Put your hands on the "wheel" and "steer" it.) Grab your steering wheel.

(Make the sound of a truck.) Rrrrrrr.

(Put your fist in the air and pull the horn.) Honk, honk.

(Talk into your fist.) Grab your CB radio and say, "Good job, good buddy."

TASK 3 Transition fingerplay to end the lesson (approximately 3 minutes)

MAKE THE TRANSITION to end the lesson.	You are going to practice the rhyming fingerplay you learned earlier. Everyone, can you remember the name of the fingerplay? Touch your knee if you remember. *Guide for the correct response.* ▶ Children's response: "Five Little Ducks." Yes, it's called "Five Little Ducks." Eyes on me. Let's sing together. *Repeat the earlier transition.*
END Lesson 2.	Everyone now gets their winnings for learning your rhymes and for working hard. *Give out token rewards to each child.*

LESSON 3: Hop on Pop

OBJECTIVES

Student will

- Know how to listen carefully to the sounds of rhyming words and be able to develop an awareness of rhyme in an interactive rhyming book by accurately predicting the rhyming word in the story

Teacher will

- Emphasize the sounds of words that rhyme so students can clearly hear that the endings of rhyming words are the same
- Hold the book so that each child can see the pictures
- Closely observe each student for focus and full participation
- Lead children to participate in the interactive rhyming book by coaching them to accurately predict the rhyming word in the story
- Smile and ensure success for all children

RHYMES, SONGS, AND FINGERPLAYS

"Head, Shoulders, Knees, and Toes"

MATERIALS

Book: *Hop on Pop* (LeSieg, 1963)

Tokens for behavior/participation

 TASK 1 Transition song to begin the lesson (approximately 3 minutes)

INTRODUCE the big idea.	We are going to listen for words that rhyme and we will practice our rhymes. Remember, rhyming words are words that sound the same. What do we call words that sound the same?
	▶ Children's response: Words that rhyme.
 ✱ **Model the Activity**	Yes, words that rhyme or rhyming words. Like *toes* and *nose.* Do it with me. *Put your right palm out and tilt your head to the right as you say* toes; *then do the same on the left side as you say* nose. ▶ (Children respond by doing it with you.) Nice job rhyming *toes* and *nose.* We will read a story with many rhyming words.
BEGIN the transition. *Before you begin: Students should pull out their chairs so they will be able to touch their toes.*	You are going to sing a rhyming song that you probably already know. It's called "Head, Shoulders, Knees, and Toes." This is a fun song with rhyming words and great movements. Everyone, what's the name of our rhyming song? ▶ Children's response: "Head, Shoulders, Knees, and Toes." Yes. "Head, Shoulders, Knees, and Toes."

**Turn On
Your Ears**

**Model
the Activity**

Listen. Look at me and do what I do. *Exaggerate the movements.*

Head *(Place hands on head.)*
shoulders *(Move hands to shoulders.)*
knees *(Move hands to knees.)*
and toes *(Touch toes.)*

Knees *(Move hands to knees.)*
and toes *(Touch toes.)*

Head *(Place hands on head.)*
shoulders *(Move hands to shoulders.)*
knees *(Move hands to knees.)*
and toes *(Touch toes.)*

Knees *(Move hands to knees.)*
and toes *(Touch toes.)*

Eyes *(Place hands on eyes.)*
and ears *(Move hands to ears.)*
and mouth *(Move hands to mouth.)*
and nose *(Touch nose.)*

Head *(Place hands on head.)*
shoulders *(Move hands to shoulders.)*
knees *(Move hands to knees.)*
and toes *(Touch toes.)*

Knees *(Move hands to knees.)*
and toes *(Touch toes.)*

Vocabulary

FROM THE TOP

*Explain vocabulary in a
simple way.*

Let's take it from the top.

What do you think take it from the top means? Pull your ear lobe if you know.
Guide students to their ear lobes.

Well, I'm glad you know. It means to start. We usually start something at the top,
so *take it from the top* means to start.

Who can think of something we start at the top? *Show an example. Hold up a
book, open to the first page, and point to text at the top of the page.*

▶ Children's response: Reading a book, reading a page.

Follow a two-step approach. Step 1: Give a brief description of the word. Yes, we
start at the top of the page when we read. Or, the top of a book. The top of the
book is called the cover. What does *take it from the top* mean? *Guide students to
use a complete sentence.*

▶ Children's response: Take it from the top means to start.

TEACHING TIP: Act it out. Use exaggerated movements with the students. Large muscles have memory. Have
them pat the tops of their heads.

Step 2: Give students the description, and have them supply the word.

This is usually the thing people do when they want you to start something or
take it from the top. *(Pat the top of your head.)* Do it with me. What's another
way of saying you want to start something? *(Pat the top of your head.)*

▶ **Children's response: Take it from the top.**

Yes, take it from the top. Good job. You are working hard.

Okay. Let's take it from the top *(model the head pat)* and sing the entire rhyming song. That means we will sing the whole song. *Stretch out your arms to show "the whole thing." Sing the song again with movements.*

🪐 **TASK 2**   **Listening to a rhyming book** (approximately 12–14 minutes)

INTRODUCE the lesson.

You are going to read a rhyming story with me and listen for some rhyming words. What about *hop* and *pop?* Do they rhyme? Do they sound the same?

▶ **Children's response: Yes.**

Yes, *hop* and *pop* sound the same. They rhyme. *Give a thumbs up.* What about *pup* and *up?* Do they rhyme? Do they sound the same?

▶ **Children's response: Yes.**

Yes, *pup* and *up* sound the same. They rhyme. *Give a thumbs up.*

This book has many rhyming words. The title of the book is *Hop on Pop. Hold up the book and point to the title as you read.* Take a look at the picture on the cover. Everyone, where is Pop? *Move the book to the children so they can touch it.*

▶ **(Children respond by touching Pop.)**

I wonder who can hop on pop? Can everyone here hop? Very quietly, stand up and hop on one foot. Good job with your hops.

Let's get ready for me to read. See if you can guess some of the rhyming words as I read the book to you. *Read the book aloud.*

> TEACHING TIP: When reading aloud to students, begin to encourage them to anticipate and predict the rhyming words. Pause at the end of a rhyming line for students to orally predict the next word. Over-emphasize the rhymes as you read.

SING the "Rhyming Exercise Song."

 **Multisensory Reinforcement**

Now let's see if we learned some rhyming words. Let's sing the "Rhyming Exercise Song" to check it out. Get ready.

Put your hands in the sky. *Stretch one arm up to the sky, then the other arm, on the word hands.* Do the rhyming exercise.

Wall *(Stretch one arm up as you say the word.)*
Fall *(Stretch the other arm up.)*
Wall *(Switch arms.)*
Fall *(Switch arms.)*
Wall *(Switch arms.)*
Fall *(Switch arms.)*

Do they rhyme? *Pause here and allow them to show thumbs up or down before you respond. Look around at each student and make eye contact.* Yes. *Nod vigorously.* They rhyme. *Give two thumbs up.*

END the song.

Sing the song several times and use the same format. Use the following words, and do as many as time permits: all/ tall; day/play; mouse/house; *and* pup/cup.

You are working very hard. You are the rhyming kings and queens of _____ *(insert name of school).*

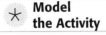

| **TASK 3** | Transition song to end the lesson (approximately 3 minutes) |

MAKE THE TRANSITION to end the lesson.	You are going to sing the rhyming song you learned at the beginning of our lesson. The name of the song is "Head, Shoulders, Knees, and Toes." Everyone, what is our song?
	▶ **Children's response: "Head, Shoulders, Knees, and Toes."**
	Yes, it's called "Head, Shoulders, Knees, and Toes." Eyes on me. Let's sing together. *Repeat the earlier transition.*
	Let's do a sit down cheer for everyone's terrific work today. *Sing to the tune of "Kiss Him Goodbye." Substitute the words "good job."*
END Lesson 3.	Everyone now gets their winnings for learning your rhymes and for working hard. *Give out token rewards to each child.*

LESSON 4: Rhyme Awareness Review

OBJECTIVES

Student will

- Know how to listen carefully to the sounds of rhyming words and be able to develop an awareness of rhyme by repeating rhyming fingerplays and songs
- Know how to listen carefully to the sounds of rhyming words and be able to develop an awareness of rhyme in an interactive rhyming book by accurately predicting the rhyming word in the story

Teacher will

- Emphasize the sounds of words that rhyme so students can clearly hear that the endings of rhyming words are the same
- Smile and ensure success for all children
- Hold the book so that each child can see the pictures
- Lead children to participate in the interactive rhyming book by coaching them to accurately predict the rhyming word in the story
- Closely observe each student for focus and full participation

RHYMES, SONGS, AND FINGERPLAYS

"Head, Shoulders, Knees, and Toes"

MATERIALS

A large nursery rhyme book with "Mary Had a Little Lamb"

Picture of a baby nursery

Example of fleece for the children to feel (even cotton balls or a fleece jacket work)

Tokens for behavior/participation

☑ DROPP 1 Skill Assessment Checkout (see Appendix B on the CD-ROM)

CD-ROM

| **TASK 1** | Transition song to begin the lesson (approximately 2 minutes) |

INTRODUCE the big idea.	We are going to listen carefully for rhymes and then practice our rhymes. You will learn some good rhyming songs. What do we call words that sound the same?
	▶ **Children's response: Words that rhyme.**
✳ **Model the Activity**	Yes, words that rhyme or rhyming words. Like *pup* and *cup.* Do it with me. *Put your right palm out and tilt your head to the right as you say* pup; *then do the same on the left side as you say* cup.
	▶ **(Children respond by doing it with you.)**
	Nice job rhyming *pup* and *cup.* We will read a story with many rhyming words.
BEGIN the transition.	You are going to sing a rhyming song that you already know. It's called "Head, Shoulders, Knees, and Toes." This is a fun rhyming song. Everyone, what's the name of our rhyming song?

Before you begin: Students should pull out their chairs so they will be able to touch their toes.

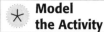

✳ **Model the Activity**

▶ **Children's response: "Head, Shoulders, Knees, and Toes."**

Yes, "Head, Shoulders, Knees, and Toes." Get ready. Let's take it from the top. Look at me and do what I do. *Exaggerate the movements.*

Head *(Place hands on head.)*
shoulders *(Move hands to shoulders.)*
knees *(Move hands to knees.)*
and toes *(Touch toes.)*

Knees *(Move hands to knees.)*
and toes *(Touch toes.)*

Head *(Place hands on head.)*
shoulders *(Move hands to shoulders.)*
knees *(Move hands to knees.)*
and toes *(Touch toes.)*

Knees *(Move hands to knees.)*
and toes *(Touch toes.)*

Eyes *(Place hands on eyes.)*
and ears *(Move hands to ears.)*
and mouth *(Move hands to mouth.)*
and nose *(Touch nose.)*

Head *(Place hands on head.)*
shoulders *(Move hands to shoulders.)*
knees *(Move hands to knees.)*
and toes *(Touch toes.)*

Knees *(Move hands to knees.)*
and toes *(Touch toes.)*

Nice job singing our rhyming song.

 **TASK 2A**   **Reviewing "Mary Had a Little Lamb"** *(approximately 8 minutes)*

REVIEW the nursery rhyme.

The title of our nursery rhyme is "Mary Had a Little Lamb." Let's rock our babies and place them in their cribs in the nursery. If you can tell me what a nursery is, then cover up your baby in his or her crib, put your finger on your lip, and say, "shhh." *Call on one child.*

▶ **Child's response: A nursery is a room where a baby sleeps.**

Yes, a nursery is a room where a baby sleeps. We call this a nursery rhyme because some parents and grandparents sing these rhymes to their babies as they fall asleep in their cribs.

TEACHING TIP: Act it out. Use exaggerated movements with the students. Large muscles have memory. Have them rock their babies in their arms and then put them to bed.

 Turn On Your Ears

Listen first and then we will say it together. *Show pictures from the book.*

Mary had a little lamb,
Whose fleece was white as snow.
And everywhere that Mary went,

the lamb was sure to go.

It followed her to school one day,
That was against the rule.
It made the children laugh and play,
To see a lamb at school.

Everyone, what's another name for the lamb's white fur?

▶ **Children's response: Fleece.**

Yes, a lamb's fleece is his soft fur. Let's start the book again, and everyone say the nursery rhyme with me. *Read the nursery rhyme again, slowly show the pictures, and guide students to repeat the rhyme.*

PRACTICE the "Rhyming Exercise Song."

Let's sing the "Rhyming Exercise Song." Let's get our rhyme muscles nice and firm so our rhymes are in great shape. Remember, words that rhyme are words that sound the same.

 **Multisensory Reinforcement**

Put your hands in the sky. *Stretch one arm up to the sky, then the other arm, on the word hands.* Do the rhyming exercise.

Show *(Stretch one arm up as you say the word.)*
Snow *(Stretch the other arm up.)*
Show *(Switch arms.)*
Snow *(Switch arms.)*
Show *(Switch arms.)*
Snow *(Switch arms.)*

Do they rhyme? *Pause here and allow them to show thumbs up or down before you respond. Look around at each student and make eye contact.* Yes. *Nod vigorously.* They rhyme. *Give two thumbs up.*

🪐 **TASK 2B**   **Reviewing a rhyming book** (approximately 8–9 minutes)

REVIEW the rhyming story.

We are going to read a rhyming story and listen for some rhyming words. What can you tell me about rhyming words? *Give children a hint by tugging on your ear. Pause to allow them to respond.*

▶ **Children's response: They sound the same.**

Yes, rhyming words sound the same. What about *day* and *away*? Do they rhyme? Do they sound the same?

▶ **Children's response: Yes.**

Yes, *day* and *away* sound the same. They rhyme. *Give a thumbs up.* What about *quack* and *back*? Do they rhyme? Do they sound the same?

▶ **Children's response: Yes.**

Yes, *quack* and *back* sound the same. They rhyme. *Give a thumbs up.* What about *house* and *mouse*? Do they rhyme? Do they sound the same?

▶ **Children's response: Yes.**

Yes, *house* and *mouse* sound the same. They rhyme. *Give a thumbs up.* This book has many rhyming words. The title of the book is *Hop on Pop.* *Hold up the book and point to the title as you read.*

I'm ready to read. See if you can guess some of the rhyming words as I read the book to you. Let's say the title of the book together.

▶ **Children's response:** *Hop on Pop.*

(Read slowly and emphasize rhyming words.)

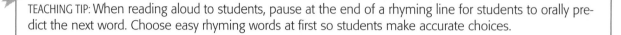

TEACHING TIP: When reading aloud to students, pause at the end of a rhyming line for students to orally predict the next word. Choose easy rhyming words at first so students make accurate choices.

That was fun. Blow the whistle if you liked hearing the rhyming words in this story.

▶ **(Children respond with a "Whoo! Whoo!" as they pull the "whistle.")**

When time is up and before the transition, say, Your rhyming work was so good today. Let's give ourselves the trucker cheer. Do it with me.

(Put your hands on the "wheel" and "steer" it.) Grab your steering wheel.

(Make the sound of a truck.) Rrrrrrr.

(Put your fist in the air and pull the horn.) Honk, honk.

(Talk into your fist.) Grab your CB radio and say, "Good job, good buddy."

END Lesson 4.

Everyone now gets their winnings for learning your rhymes and for working hard. *Give out token rewards to each child.*

CD-ROM

The DROPP 1 Skill Assessment Checkout will be completed for each student following this lesson.

ACTIVITY SET 1.2

Lesson Descriptions

Lessons	Sequence of daily activities	◇ Vocabulary
Lesson 1: Sound Chips 2	Fingerplay for "This Little Boy" Target: Game—Listening for two sounds Fingerplay for "This Little Boy"	
Lesson 2: Teddy Bear	Fingerplay for "Finger Family" Target: Song and movement—"Teddy Bear, Teddy Bear" Fingerplay for "Finger Family"	Cheer Mischief Skidoo
Lesson 3: Hand, Hand	Song and movement for "Head, Shoulders, Knees, and Toes" Target: Rhyming book—*Hand, Hand, Fingers, Thumb* (Perkins, 1969) Fingerplay for "This Little Boy"	Whack
Lesson 4: Rhyme Awareness Review	Fingerplay for "Finger Family" Target: Song and movement—"Teddy Bear, Teddy Bear" Rhyming book: *Hand, Hand, Fingers, Thumb* (Perkins, 1969)	

Materials Needed

☑ Teddy bears for each student, if available

☑ Book: *Hand, Hand, Fingers, Thumb* (Perkins, 1969)

☑ Tokens for behavior/participation

☑ DROPP 1 Skill Assessment Checkout (see Appendix B on the CD-ROM)

Sound Chips 2 Game

☑ Sound clips (see Appendix C on the CD-ROM)

☑ Two colored chips/other tokens for each child

ACTIVITY SET

1.2   10-Day Planner

Day 1	**Lesson 1:** Sound Chips 2
Day 2	**Lesson 1:** Sound Chips 2
Day 3	**Lesson 2:** Teddy Bear
Day 4	**Lesson 2:** Teddy Bear
Day 5	**Lesson 3:** Hand, Hand
Day 6	**Lesson 3:** Hand, Hand
Day 7	**Lesson 1:** Sound Chips 2
Day 8	**Lesson 2:** Teddy Bear
Day 9	**Lesson 3:** Hand, Hand
Day 10	**Lesson 4:** Rhyme Awareness Review

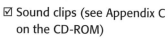

LESSON 1: Sound Chips 2

OBJECTIVES

Student will

- Know how to listen carefully to everyday sounds and be able to identify two of them in sequence
- Know how to listen carefully to the sounds of rhyming words and be able to develop an awareness of rhyme by repeating rhyming fingerplays and songs

Teacher will

- Guide students in identifying common sounds and remind them to hold them in their memory
- Emphasize the sounds of words that rhyme so students can clearly hear that the endings of rhyming words are the same
- Closely observe each student for focus and full participation
- Smile and ensure success for all children

RHYMES, SONGS, AND FINGERPLAYS

"This Little Boy"

MATERIALS

Tokens for behavior/participation

Sound Chips 2 Game

☑ Sound clips (see Appendix C on the CD-ROM)

☑ Two colored chips/other tokens for each child

 TASK 1   Transition fingerplay to begin the lesson (approximately 3 minutes)

INTRODUCE the big idea.

Say the following to the group after calling them together at a table.

We are going to continue to learn about sounds. We know it is fun saying and listening for sounds. Some of these sounds are the sounds in words. Some words sound like each other and are called rhyming words. You will learn some good rhyming songs and play a game.

BEGIN the transition.

You are going to learn a rhyming fingerplay. A fingerplay is a rhyme you say while using your fingers like puppets. You may know this one. It's called "This Little Boy." What's the name of our fingerplay?

▶ Children's response: "This Little Boy"

My turn to say our rhyme. *Say the first two lines of the rhyme until you have said two rhyming words. Exaggerate the words* bed *and* head *to convey that they are rhyming words.*

This little boy is going to bed.
Down on the pillow, he lays his head.

Your turn to say our fingerplay. *Say it with them and do the finger movements. Say the next two lines until you have said two more rhyming words.*

▶ Children's response:
This little boy is going to bed.
Down on the pillow, he lays his head.

Use exaggerated, easy, consistent, and space-conscious finger and hand movements that mimic the song.

My turn. *Repeat the rhyme with them and do the movements.*

Covers himself all up tight.
And falls asleep for the rest of the night.

 Model the Activity

Exaggerate the words tight *and* night *to convey that they are rhyming words.*

Your turn. *Say it with them and do the finger movements.*

TEACHING TIP: Use drama to increase memory. Pretend to fall asleep.

▶ Children's response:
Covers himself all up tight.
And falls asleep for the rest of the night.

My turn.

Morning comes, he opens his eyes.
Throws back the covers with great surprise.
Quickly jumps up and gets himself dressed.
And hurries to school to play with the rest.

Exaggerate the words eyes/surprise *and* dressed/rest *to convey that they are rhyming words.*

Let's start from the beginning and say our fingerplay together. See if you remember the entire rhyme.

This little boy is going to bed.
Down on the pillow, he lays his head.
Covers himself all up tight.
And falls asleep for the rest of the night.

Morning comes, he opens his eyes.
Throws back the covers with great surprise.
Quickly jumps up and gets himself dressed.
And hurries to school to play with the rest.

Nice work using our voices and our rhymes saying "This Little Boy."

 TASK 2   Play Sound Chips (approximately 12–14 minutes)

REVIEW the game: Sound Chips.

 See Appendix D on the CD-ROM for the Sound Chips Game instructions and see Appendix C for the sound clips.

 PLAY the game.

INTRODUCE the game: Sound Chips 2.

See Appendix D on the CD-ROM for the Sound Chips 2 Game instructions and see Appendix C for the sound clips.

PLAY the game.

 TASK 3   Transition song to end the lesson (approximately 3 minutes)

MAKE THE TRANSITION to end the lesson.

You are going to practice the rhyming fingerplay you learned earlier. Can you remember the name? Tap your wrists together if you know.

TEACHING TIP: Check on students' focus by giving them an easy direction to follow.

Call on one student. Guide students in the correct response.

▶ **Child's response: "This Little Boy."**

Yes, it's called "This Little Boy."

Let's start from the beginning and say our fingerplay together. See if you remember the entire rhyme. *Say the rhyme and include movements with your hands.*

▶ **Children's response:**
This little boy is going to bed.
Down on the pillow, he lays his head.
Covers himself all up tight.
And falls asleep for the rest of the night.

Morning comes, he opens his eyes.
Throws back the covers with great surprise.
Quickly jumps up and gets himself dressed.
And hurries to school to play with the rest.

Multisensory Reinforcement

SING the "Rhyming Exercise Song."

Time to do rhyming words. Here's our "Rhyming Exercise Song" that we can do together. We want to get our rhyme muscles nice and firm so our rhymes are in great shape. *Hold your arms up and show your muscles.* Show me your muscles.

▶ **(Children respond by showing their muscles, too.)**

Multisensory Reinforcement

Follow me. Put your hands in the sky. *Stretch one arm up to the sky, then the other arm, on the word hands.* Do the rhyming exercise.

Bed *(Stretch one arm up as you say the word.)*
Head *(Stretch the other arm up.)*
Bed *(Switch arms.)*
Head *(Switch arms.)*
Bed *(Switch arms.)*
Head *(Switch arms.)*

Do they rhyme? *Pause here and allow them to show thumbs up or down before you respond. Look around at each student and make eye contact.* Yes. *Nod vigorously.* They rhyme. *Give two thumbs up.*

Turn On Your Ears

Listen for two more rhyming words.

Sing the song several times and use the same format. Use these words and do as many as time permits: tight/night, eyes/surprise, *and* dressed/rest.

END the song.

You are working hard learning your rhymes. You are a gold star class. You know what that means.
Take out your star box. *(Cup one hand.)*
Get your star. *(Pretend to get a gold star sticker on the pointer finger of the other hand.)*
You are all gold star kids. *(Lick the star and put it on your forehead.)*

END Lesson 1.

Everyone now gets their winnings for learning your rhymes and for working hard. *Give out token rewards to each child.*

LESSON 2: Teddy Bear

OBJECTIVES

Student will

- Know how to listen carefully to the sounds of rhyming words and be able to develop an awareness of rhyme by repeating rhyming fingerplays and songs
- Know how to listen carefully to the sounds of rhyming words and be able to develop an awareness of rhyme by singing rhyming songs and using dance movements

Teacher will

- Emphasize the sounds of words that rhyme so students can clearly hear that the endings of rhyming words are the same
- Closely observe each student for focus and full participation
- Smile and ensure success for all children

RHYMES, SONGS, AND FINGERPLAYS

"Finger Family"

"Teddy Bear, Teddy Bear"

MATERIALS

Teddy bears for each student, if available

Tokens for behavior/participation

 TASK 1　　**Transition fingerplay to begin the lesson** (approximately 3 minutes)

INTRODUCE the big idea.	We are going to listen carefully for rhymes and then practice our rhymes. You will learn some good rhyming fingerplays and songs.
	Words that rhyme are words that sound the same. What do we call words that sound the same?
	▶ Children's response: Words that rhyme.
✷ **Model the Activity**	Yes, words that rhyme or rhyming words. Like *dear* and *cheer*. Do it with me. *Put out your right palm and tilt your head to the right as you say* dear; *then do the same on the left side as you say* cheer. *Do this three times.*
	▶ (Children respond by doing it with you.)
	Nice job rhyming *dear* and *cheer*.
BEGIN the transition.	You are going to learn another rhyming fingerplay. You may know this one. It's called "Finger Family." What's the name of the rhyme?
	▶ Children's response: "Finger Family."
👂 **Turn On Your Ears**	My turn. Listen. *Say the first few lines of the fingerplay until you have said two rhyming words.*
Use exaggerated finger and hand movements that mimic the song, and use exaggerated voice intonation.	This is the Mama, Kind and gentle, Loving all the children dear. This is the Papa, Strong and faithful, His bright smile is full of cheer.
◇ **Vocabulary**	Describe Papa's smile that is full of cheer. *Use your face to show that* cheer *means* happy. Touch your nose if you know. *Call on one or two children; confirm if the answer is correct.*
CHEER	▶ (Children respond with answers.)
Use instructional moments to improve vocabulary and oral language. Explain vocabulary in a simple way.	*Cheer* means happy. What does *cheer* mean? Everyone?
	▶ Children's response: *Cheer* means happy.

Follow a two-step approach. Step 1: Give a brief description of the word. Show an example.

TEACHING TIP: Act it out. Use exaggerated movements with the students. Give a big smile to the students to show that *cheer* means happy. Wait until everyone smiles broadly.

Step 2: Give students the description and have them supply the word. Guide the children to use a complete sentence.

Show me a smile full of cheer. We all have cheerful smiles. Everyone, what's another way of saying we are full of happiness?

▶ **Children's response: We are full of cheer.**

Yes, we are full of cheer. Can one person describe a time when you were full of cheer? *Call on one student.*

▶ **(Child responds appropriately.)**

Yes, you were full of cheer!

★ Model the Activity

Let's take it from the top. *Pat the top of your head.* Your turn. *Say the rhyme with them and lead them to do all movements.*

▶ **Children's response:**
This is the Mama,
Kind and gentle,
Loving all the children dear.
This is the Papa,
Strong and faithful,
His bright smile is full of cheer.

👂 Turn On Your Ears

Let's keep going. My turn. Listen. *Say the next few lines until you have said two more rhyming words.*

This is the brother,
Full of mischief,
Growing up so straight and tall.
This is the sister,
Always happy,
Playing with her favorite doll.

◇ Vocabulary

MISCHIEF

Always explain vocabulary in a simple way.

What does it mean that the brother is full of mischief? Touch the palm of your hand if you know. *Guide them to their palms. Call on one child. Confirm if the answer is correct.*

Follow the same two-step approach as used with previous vocabulary word.

Mischief means doing something you are not supposed to do. What does *mischief* mean? Everyone?

▶ **Children's response: *Mischief* means doing something you are not supposed to do.**

Can one student describe a time when you were full of mischief like the brother in our fingerplay? *Call on one student.*

▶ **(Child responds appropriately.)**

Yes, that is one time when you were full of mischief. Everyone, what's another way of saying we are full of doing something we are not supposed to do?

▶ Children's response: We are full of mischief.

Yes, we are full of mischief. Let's keep learning about our finger family. Your turn to say it. *Say the rhyme with them and do the finger movements emphasizing the rhyming words.*

▶ Children's response:
This is the brother,
Full of mischief,
Growing up so straight and tall.
This is the sister,
Always happy,
Playing with her favorite doll.

TEACHING TIP: At the last verse, use drama to increase memory. Use a baby voice for the baby, and sound earnest and sincere for the last two lines.

My turn.
This wee finger is the baby,
Dearest, sweetest, best of all.
Here you see the happy family,
All its members great and small.

Your turn to say it. *Do the fingerplay with them.*

▶ Children's response:
This wee finger is the baby,
Dearest, sweetest, best of all.
Here you see the happy family,
All its members great and small.

Use exaggerated finger and hand movements that mimic the song, and use exaggerated voice intonation.

Let's start from the beginning and say our whole rhyme together.
This is the Mama,
Kind and gentle,
Loving all the children dear.
This is the Papa,
Strong and faithful,
His bright smile is full of cheer.
This is the brother,
Full of mischief,
Growing up so straight and tall.
This is the sister,
Always happy,
Playing with her favorite doll.
This wee finger is the baby,
Dearest, sweetest, best of all.
Here you see the happy family,
All its members great and small.

Nice job saying "Finger Family." You are working very hard. Kiss your brain. *Kiss your hand and touch your head.*

TASK 2 **Learning rhyming song and movement** (approximately 12–14 minutes)

INTRODUCE the rhyming song.

You are going to learn a rhyming song and dance called "Teddy Bear, Teddy Bear." What's the name of the song and dance?

▶ **Children's response: "Teddy Bear, Teddy Bear."**

 Model the Activity

My turn to sing. Listen and watch me dance. *Stand up and do dance movements that mimic the song.*

Teddy bear, teddy bear turn around.
Teddy bear, teddy bear touch the ground.
Teddy bear, teddy bear go upstairs.
Teddy bear, teddy bear say your prayers.

Each child should have his or her own space. Sing with the children and lead them in their dance movements. Your turn to sing and dance with me.

Everyone stand up.

▶ **Children's response:**
Teddy bear, teddy bear turn around.
Teddy bear, teddy bear touch the ground.
Teddy bear, teddy bear go upstairs.
Teddy bear, teddy bear say your prayers.

Good job singing and dancing. Let's go back and sit in our seats. My turn to sing and dance.

Teddy bear, teddy bear turn out your light.
Teddy bear, teddy bear say good night.
Teddy bear, teddy bear time to wake up.
Teddy bear, teddy bear drink from your cup.
Teddy bear, teddy bear shine your shoe.
Teddy bear, teddy bear skidoo, skidoo.

When you sing skidoo, do two sideways slides. This is not a big movement but a fun one to do with young children, as they should learn to do this developmental movement.

 Vocabulary

SKIDOO

Multisensory Reinforcement

Let's talk about the word *skidoo.*

Explain vocabulary in a simple way. Follow a two-step approach. Step 1: Show an example and give a brief description of the word.

Skidoo is a funny way of saying good-bye and then leaving the room. Watch me. *Do two sideway slides that get you close to an exit.*

TEACHING TIP: Act it out. Use exaggerated movements with the students. If you keep stuffed bears in your classroom, then let each student do the song and dance movements with a bear.

Step 2: Give students the description and have them supply the word. Guide children to use a complete sentence.

Everyone, what's a funny way of saying good-bye and leaving the room?

▶ **Children's response:** *Skidoo* **is a funny way of saying good-bye and leaving the room.**

Yes, *skidoo* is a funny way of saying good-bye and leaving. Let's all stand up and skidoo.

✳ Model the Activity

▶ (Children respond by following you).

Your turn to sing and dance with me. Everyone stand up.

▶ Children's response:
Teddy bear, teddy bear turn out your light.
Teddy bear, teddy bear say good night.
Teddy bear, teddy bear time to wake up.
Teddy bear, teddy bear drink from your cup.
Teddy bear, teddy bear shine your shoe.
Teddy bear, teddy bear skidoo, skidoo.

Let's take it from the top. *Model the head pat.*

Repeat the song and dance with the students.

PRACTICE the "Rhyming Exercise Song."

Let's sing the "Rhyming Exercise Song." Remember, words that rhyme are words that sound the same. We learned lots of new rhymes.

Follow me. Put your hands in the sky. *Stretch one arm up to the sky, then the other arm, on the word hands.* Do the rhyming exercise.

Multisensory Reinforcement

Around *(Stretch one arm up as you say the word.)*
Ground *(Stretch the other arm up.)*
Around *(Switch arms.)*
Ground *(Switch arms.)*
Around *(Switch arms.)*
Ground *(Switch arms.)*

Do they rhyme? *Pause here and allow them to show thumbs up or down before you respond. Look around at each student and make eye contact.* Yes. *Nod vigorously.* They rhyme. *Give two thumbs up.*

Repeat the song with the following word pairs: upstairs/prayers*, and* light/night*.*

END the song.

Your rhyming work was so good today. You deserve fireworks. Watch me first. *Hold palms together in front as if praying.*

Ssssss. *Wiggle your palms up in the air in front of you like a firecracker going off.*

AHHHHHHH! *Clap them above your head. Wiggle your fingers around and down like the sparkles coming from a firecracker.*

Let's give ourselves fireworks together. Do it with me. *Repeat.*

🪐 TASK 3   Transition fingerplay to end the lesson *(approximately 3 minutes)*

BEGIN the transition.

You are going to practice the rhyming fingerplay you learned earlier. Everyone, can you remember the name of the fingerplay? Touch your knee if you remember. Everyone, tell me the name. *Guide for the correct response.*

▶ Children's response: "Finger Family."

Use exaggerated finger and hand movements that mimic the song, and use exaggerated voice intonation.

Yes, it's called "Finger Family." Eyes on me. Let's say our rhyme together.
This is the Mama,
Kind and gentle,
Loving all the children dear.
This is the Papa,

Strong and faithful,
His bright smile is full of cheer.
This is the brother,
Full of mischief,
Growing up so straight and tall.
This is the sister,
Always happy,
Playing with her favorite doll.
This wee finger is the baby,
Dearest, sweetest, best of all.
Here you see the happy family,
All its members great and small.

Nice job saying "Finger Family." You are working very hard learning your rhymes. Let's do our good job dance. *Sing to the tune of "Stayin' Alive," and substitute the words "we did a good job, we did a good job." Extend your right index finger in the air to the left of your body. Put your left hand on your hip. Move your right finger from the air to your side as you sing. Extend your right index finger in the air to the left of your body. Put your left hand on your hip. Move your right finger from the air to your side as you sing.*

END Lesson 2.

Everyone now gets their winnings for learning your rhymes and for working hard. *Give out token rewards to each child.*

LESSON 3: Hand, Hand

OBJECTIVES

Student will

- Know how to listen carefully to the sounds of rhyming words and be able to develop an awareness of rhyme in an interactive rhyming book by using movement with rhyme
- Know how to listen carefully to the sounds of rhyming words and be able to develop an awareness of rhyme in an interactive rhyming book by accurately predicting the rhyming word in the story

Teacher will

- Emphasize the sounds of words that rhyme so students can clearly hear that the endings of rhyming words are the same
- Hold the book so that each child can see the pictures
- Closely observe each student for focus, rhythm, and full participation
- Lead children to participate in the interactive rhyming book by coaching them to use thumb drums and to predict the rhyming word in the story
- Smile and ensure success for all children

RHYMES, SONGS, AND FINGERPLAYS

"Head, Shoulders, Knees, and Toes"

MATERIALS

Book: *Hand, Hand, Fingers, Thumb* (Perkins, 1969)
Tokens for behavior/participation

TASK 1   Transition song to begin the lesson *(approximately 3 minutes)*

INTRODUCE the big idea.

We are going to listen for words that rhyme and we will practice our rhymes. Remember, rhyming words are words that sound the same. What do we call words that sound the same?

▶ **Children's response: Rhyming words.**

Yes, rhyming words. Like *toes* and *nose.* Do it with me. *As you say toes, put your right palm out and tilt your head to the right, and then do the same on the left side as you say* nose.

▶ **(Children respond by doing it with you.)**

Nice job rhyming *toes* and *nose.* We will read a story with many rhyming words.

You are going to sing a rhyming song that you already know. It's called "Head, Shoulders, Knees, and Toes." This is a fun song with rhyming words and great movements. Everyone, what's the name of our rhyming song?

▶ **Children's response: "Head, Shoulders, Knees, and Toes."**

Yes, "Head, Shoulders, Knees, and Toes."

BEGIN the transition.

Before you begin: Students should pull out their chairs so they will be able to touch their toes.

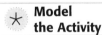
★ **Model the Activity**

You are ready to look at me and do what I do. *Exaggerate the movements.*

Head *(Place hands on head.)*
shoulders *(Move hands to shoulders.)*
knees *(Move hands to knees.)*
and toes *(Touch toes.)*

Knees *(Move hands to knees.)*
and toes *(Touch toes.)*

Head *(Place hands on head.)*
shoulders *(Move hands to shoulders.)*
knees *(Move hands to knees.)*
and toes *(Touch toes.)*

Knees *(Move hands to knees.)*
and toes *(Touch toes.)*

Eyes *(Place hands on eyes.)*
and ears *(Move hands to ears.)*
and mouth *(Move hands to mouth.)*
and nose *(Touch nose.)*

Head *(Place hands on head.)*
shoulders *(Move hands to shoulders.)*
knees *(Move hands to knees.)*
and toes *(Touch toes.)*

Knees *(Move hands to knees.)*
and toes *(Touch toes.)*

Let's take it from the top. *Pat your head.* What's another way of saying you want to start something?

▶ **Children's response: Take it from the top.**

Okay. Let's take it from the top *(model the head pat)* and sing the entire rhyming song. That means we will sing the whole song. *Stretch out hands to show "the whole thing." Sing the song again with movements.*

TASK 2   **Listening to a rhyming book** (approximately 12–14 minutes)

INTRODUCE the lesson.

You are going to read a rhyming story with me and listen for some rhyming words. What about *thumb* and *drum?* Do they rhyme? Do they sound the same? *Put out your right palm and tilt your head to the right as you say thumb; then do the same on the left side as you say* drum.

▶ **Children's response: Yes.**

Yes, *thumb* and *drum* sound the same. They rhyme. *Give a thumbs up.*

What about *Jake* and *shake?* Do they rhyme? Do they sound the same? *Repeat the hand motions.*

▶ **Children's response: Yes.**

Yes, *Jake* and *shake* sound the same. They rhyme. *Give a thumbs up.*

TEACHING TIP: When reading aloud to students, encourage them to anticipate and predict the rhyming words. Read clearly to emphasize the rhymes. Pause at the end of a rhyming line for students to orally predict the next word. Choose easy rhyming words at first so students make accurate choices. Observing this skill in students provides important insight into their rhyme development.

TEACHING TIP: Preview the book before reading to be familiar with the rhyming words—which should always be overemphasized as you read. Read slowly for students to hear and process the rhymes. Show them the pictures as you read.

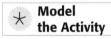 **Turn On Your Ears**

This book has many rhyming words. You are going to read the story with me and learn some hand movements to do as we read. Look at me and listen. This is one of my favorite rhyming books. The title of the book is *Hand, Hand, Fingers, Thumb.* What kind of animal is in the story?

▶ **Children's response: A monkey.**

Yes, a monkey. What parts of his body will the story tell us about? I'll read the title again: *Hand, Hand, Fingers, Thumb. Guide children's response by pointing to the parts of the monkey's hand.* Yes, his hand, his finger, and his thumb. *Hold up your right thumb. Hold up your left thumb.* Good job answering my questions about our book.

Model the Activity

Before we begin to read, I'm going to show you how to use a thumb drum. My turn. Every time I say "dum ditty, dum ditty, dum, dum, dum," you will use your thumb drum to drum out the words on the table.

We have a right thumb drum and a left thumb drum.
When we sing "dum ditty," drum your right thumb. *Tap your right thumb on the table.*
When we sing "dum ditty" a second time, drum your left thumb. *Tap your left thumb on the table.*
Drum them both together on "dum, dum, dum." *Tap both together.*

Now sing with me and play your thumb drums.

Dum ditty, dum ditty, dum, dum, dum.

▶ **Children's response: Dum ditty, dum ditty, dum, dum, dum.**

Repeat the movement and practice several times. Yes. Good job using your thumb drums and listening for rhymes. You are working hard.

 Turn On Your Ears

Okay. Stop your thumb drums and keep them quiet. Get ready to listen to our story. Every time I use my thumb drum, you will use yours too.

Use instructional moments to improve vocabulary and oral language. Always explain vocabulary in a simple way.

Read the book and lead the students in playing the thumb drums. Watch everyone and make sure they are in rhythm. Go slowly. Show the pictures while reading.

If I see a fly buzzing around in my house, then I will probably try to whack it. What do you think I will do to the fly if I whack it? Sit up tall and proud if you know. *Call on one or two children.*

◇ **Vocabulary**

WHACK

Follow a two-step approach. Step 1: Ask children to describe (or act out) the vocabulary word. Yes, a whack is like a slap. *Slap the air in front of you.* Everyone, what does *whack* mean?

TEACHING TIP: Act it out. Use exaggerated movements with the students. Large muscles have memory. Have them slap the air in front of them.

▶ **Children's response: Slap.**

Step 2: Give students the description and have them supply the word. Show me a slap with your hands. Yes, a whack is like a slap.

Everyone, what's another way of saying *slap?*

▶ **Children's response: Whack.**

TEACHING TIP: Use the new word in a sentence using your students' names. This always gets their attention.

Yes, *whack*. Malik gave the fly that was buzzing around his house a whack. Can someone use the word *whack* in a sentence for me? Hold one finger in the air if you can tell me a sentence and use the word *whack*. *Take one or two student responses. Guide the students with their sentences to find success.*

▶ **(Children respond with a sentence.)**

Nice job using the word *whack*.

Let's start all over and read the whole book again.

Reread the book and continue to lead the students in playing the thumb drums. Students will love the words and the drumming sounds as they rhyme. This is great fun—keep the lesson light and fun.

That was fun. Hold up your thumb drums *(give two thumbs up)* if you love playing them as you rhyme.

 **TASK 3**   Transition song to end the lesson *(approximately 3 minutes)*

MAKE THE TRANSITION to end the lesson.

You are going to sing the rhyming song you learned at the beginning of our lesson. The name of the song is "Head, Shoulders, Knees, and Toes." Everyone, what is our song?

▶ **Children's response: "Head, Shoulders, Knees, and Toes."**

Yes, it's called "Head, Shoulders, Knees, and Toes." Eyes on me. Let's sing together. *Repeat the song and movements with the students.*

Let's do a sit down cheer for everyone's terrific work today. *Sing to the tune of "Kiss Him Goodbye." Substitute the words "good job."*

END Lesson 3.

Everyone now gets their winnings for learning your rhymes and for working hard. *Give out token rewards to each child.*

LESSON 4: Rhyme Awareness Review

OBJECTIVES

Student will

- Know how to listen carefully to the sounds of rhyming words and be able to develop an awareness of rhyme by repeating rhyming fingerplays and songs
- Know how to listen carefully to the sounds of rhyming words and be able to develop an awareness of rhyme by singing rhyming songs and using dance movements
- Know how to listen carefully to the sounds of rhyming words and be able to develop an awareness of rhyme in an interactive rhyming book by using movement with rhyme
- Know how to listen carefully to the sounds of rhyming words and be able to develop an awareness of rhyme in an interactive rhyming book by accurately predicting the rhyming word in the story

Teacher will

- Emphasize the sounds of words that rhyme so students can clearly hear that the endings of rhyming words are the same
- Smile and ensure success for all children
- Hold the book so that each child can see the pictures
- Lead children to participate in the interactive rhyming book by coaching them to use thumb drums and to predict the rhyming word in the story
- Closely observe each student for focus and full participation

RHYMES, SONGS, AND FINGERPLAYS

"Finger Family"

"Teddy Bear, Teddy Bear"

MATERIALS

Teddy bears for each student, if available

Book: *Hand, Hand, Fingers, Thumb* (Perkins, 1969)

☑ DROPP 1 Skill Assessment Checkout (see Appendix B on the CD-ROM)　 CD-ROM

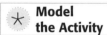 **TASK 1**　Transition fingerplay to begin the lesson (approximately 2 minutes)

INTRODUCE the big idea.

We are going to listen carefully for rhymes and then practice our rhymes. You will practice some good rhyming fingerplays and songs.

Words that rhyme are words that sound the same. What do we call words that sound the same?

▶ Children's response: Words that rhyme.

✳ Model the Activity

Yes, words that rhyme or rhyming words. Like *dear* and *cheer*. Do it with me. *As you say* dear, *put out your right palm and tilt your head to the right, and then do the same on the left side as you say* cheer. *Do this three times.*

▶ (Children respond by doing it with you.)

Nice job rhyming *dear* and *cheer*.

BEGIN the transition.

You are going to practice the "Finger Family."

What's the name of the song?

▶ Children's response: "Finger Family."

✋ Multisensory Reinforcement

Let's start from the beginning and say our rhyme together. *Say the rhyme with them and do the finger movements emphasizing the rhyming words.*

This is the Mama,

Kind and gentle,

Loving all the children dear.

This is the Papa,

Strong and faithful,

His bright smile is full of cheer.

This is the brother,
Full of mischief,
Growing up so straight and tall.
This is the sister,
Always happy,
Playing with her favorite doll.
This wee finger is the baby,
Dearest, sweetest, best of all.
Here you see the happy family,
All its members great and small.

TEACHING TIP: Use drama to increase memory of the rhyme. Use a variety of voices for all of the family members.

Excellent rhyming. Let's give ourselves a snap, crackle, pop cheer. Do it with me.

Snap! *(Snap fingers once.)*

Crackle! *(Rub hands together quickly.)*

Pop! *(Clap hands once hard and quickly. Jet out hands with palms forward and fingers splayed.)*

 **TASK 2A** **Reviewing Teddy Bear, Teddy Bear** (approximately 8 minutes)

REVIEW the rhyming song.

You are going to sing our rhyming song and do our dance to "Teddy Bear, Teddy Bear." What's the name of the song and dance?

▶ **Children's response: "Teddy Bear, Teddy Bear."**

Get ready to sing and dance. Everyone, what's a funny way of saying good-bye and leaving the room?

▶ **Children's response: Skidoo.**

Yes, *skidoo* is a funny way of saying good-bye and leaving. Let's all stand up and get ready to dance and skidoo. *Students should have their own small space to dance. Stand up and do dance movements with the students that mimic the song.*

Teddy bear, teddy bear turn around.
Teddy bear, teddy bear touch the ground.
Teddy bear, teddy bear go upstairs.
Teddy bear, teddy bear say your prayers.
Teddy bear, teddy bear turn out your light.
Teddy bear, teddy bear say good night.
Teddy bear, teddy bear time to wake up.
Teddy bear, teddy bear drink from your cup.
Teddy bear, teddy bear shine your shoe.
Teddy bear, teddy bear skidoo, skidoo.

PRACTICE the "Rhyming Exercise Song."

Let's sing the "Rhyming Exercise Song." Let's get our rhyme muscles nice and firm so our rhymes are in great shape.

Remember, words that rhyme are words that sound the same—or rhyming words.

1.2

 Multisensory Reinforcement

Put your hands in the sky. *Stretch one arm up to the sky, then the other arm, on the word* hands. Do the Rhyming Exercise.

Up *(Stretch one arm up as you say the word.)*
Cup *(Stretch the other arm up.)*
Up *(Switch arms.)*
Cup *(Switch arms.)*
Up *(Switch arms.)*
Cup *(Switch arms.)*

Do they rhyme? *Pause here and allow them to show thumbs up or down before you respond. Look around at each student and make eye contact.* Yes. *Nod vigorously.* They rhyme. *Give two thumbs up.*

TASK 2B   **Reviewing a rhyming book** (approximately 8–9 minutes)

REVIEW the rhyming story.

We're going to read a rhyming story and listen for some rhyming words. What can you tell me about rhyming words? *Give the children a hint by tugging on your ear. Pause to allow them to respond.*

▶ **Children's response: They sound the same.**

This book has many rhyming words. You are going to read the story with me and we'll use our thumb drums. The title of the book is *Hand, Hand, Fingers, Thumb.* What kind of animal is in the story? *Hold up the book and point to the title as you read. This will allow the children to see the cover so they can respond to the question about the type of animal in the story.*

▶ **Children's response: A monkey.**

Describe the parts of the monkey's body the story tells us about. *Call on a student for a response.*

I'm ready to read. See if you can guess some of the rhyming words as I read the book to you. Let's say the title of the book together.

▶ **Children's response: *Hand, Hand, Fingers, Thumb.***

Before we begin to read, let's practice playing our thumb drums.

Sing with me and play your thumb drums.

Dum ditty, dum ditty, dum, dum, dum.

▶ **Children's response: Dum ditty, dum ditty, dum, dum, dum.**

Repeat the movement and practice several times.

Turn On Your Ears

Yes. Good job using your thumb drums and listening for rhymes. You are working hard. Okay. Stop your thumb drums and keep them quiet. Get ready to listen to our story. Every time I use my thumb drum, you will use yours too.

Read the book slowly and emphasize the rhythm and the rhyming words. Lead the students in playing the thumb drums. Watch everyone and make sure they are in rhythm. Go slowly. Show the pictures while reading.

Nice job using your thumb drums. You are learning rhyming words. Let's give ourselves the trucker cheer. Do it with me.

Grab your steering wheel. *(Put your hands on the "wheel" and "steer" it.)*
Rrrrrr. *(Make the sound of a truck.)*
Honk, honk. *(Put your fist in the air and pull the horn.)*

END Lesson 4.

Grab your CB radio and say, "Good job, good buddy." *(Talk into your fist.)*

Everyone now gets their winnings for learning your rhymes and for working hard. *Give out token rewards to each child.*

 CD-ROM The DROPP 1 Skill Assessment Checkout will be completed for each student following this lesson.

ACTIVITY SET 1.3

Lesson Descriptions

Lessons	Sequence of daily activities	✧ Vocabulary
Lesson 1: Find the Timer	Fingerplay for "The Church" Target: Game—Find the Timer Fingerplay for "The Church"	Steeple
Lesson 2: Little Teapot	Song for "One, Two, Buckle My Shoe" Target: Song and movement—"I'm a Little Teapot" Fingerplay for "One, Two, Buckle My Shoe"	Straight Stout
Lesson 3: 100 Words	Song for "Itsy-Bitsy Spider" Target: Rhyming book—*I'll Teach My Dog 100 Words* (Firth,1973) Fingerplay for "The Church"	
Lesson 4: Rhyme Awareness Review	Song for "One, Two, Buckle My Shoe" Target: Song and movement—"I'm a Little Teapot" Rhyming book: *I'll Teach My Dog 100 Words* (Firth,1973)	

Materials Needed

☑ Book containing "One, Two, Buckle My Shoe" with pictures (e.g., Baker, 1994)

☑ Book: *I'll Teach My Dog 100 Words* (Firth, 1973)

☑ Picture of a church steeple

☑ A real teapot or a picture of a teapot

☑ Tokens for behavior/participation

> ☑ DROPP 1 Skill Assessment Checkout (see Appendix B on the CD-ROM)   **CD-ROM**
>
> **Find the Timer Game**
>
> ☑ Timer

ACTIVITY SET

1.3 **10-Day Planner**

Day 1	**Lesson 1:** Find the Timer
Day 2	**Lesson 1:** Find the Timer
Day 3	**Lesson 2:** Little Teapot
Day 4	**Lesson 2:** Little Teapot
Day 5	**Lesson 3:** 100 Words
Day 6	**Lesson 3:** 100 Words
Day 7	**Lesson 1:** Find the Timer
Day 8	**Lesson 2:** Little Teapot
Day 9	**Lesson 3:** 100 Words
Day 10	**Lesson 4:** Rhyme Awareness Review

LESSON 1: Find the Timer

OBJECTIVES

Student will

- Know how to listen carefully to the sound of a hidden timer and be able to locate it in 1 minute
- Know how to listen carefully to the sounds of rhyming words and be able to develop an awareness of rhyme by repeating rhyming fingerplays and songs

Teacher will

- Guide students to listen for the sound of a timer and locate it in a specified area within 1 minute to emphasize prolonged focus on sounds
- Emphasize the sounds of words that rhyme so students can clearly hear that the endings of rhyming words are the same
- Closely observe each student for focus and full participation
- Smile and ensure success for all children

RHYMES, SONGS, AND FINGERPLAYS

"The Church"

MATERIALS

Picture of a church steeple

Tokens for behavior/participation

Find the Timer Game

☑ Timer

CD-ROM

🪐 **TASK 1** | **Transition fingerplay to begin the lesson** (approximately 3 minutes)

INTRODUCE the big idea.

Say the following to the group after calling the children together at a table.

We will continue learning about sounds. It's fun saying and listening for sounds. Some sounds are the sounds in words. Some words sound like each other and are called rhyming words. You will learn some good rhyming songs and play a game.

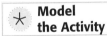
BEGIN the transition.

⭐ **Model the Activity**

Use exaggerated, easy, consistent, and space-conscious finger and hand movements that mimic the song.

You're going to learn a rhyming fingerplay. A fingerplay is a rhyme you say while using your fingers like puppets. You may know this one. It's called "The Church." What's the name of our fingerplay?

▶ Children's response: "The Church."

Yes, "The Church." My turn to say "The Church." Watch what I do with my hands.

Here is the church and here's the steeple. *Turn your hands inside out for the church, then put your index fingers together for the steeple.*

Open up the door and see all the people. *Open both thumbs, then turn your hands over to reveal your fingers as people.*

TEACHING TIP: Use drama and humor to increase memory.

See anybody you know? *Wiggle your fingers as pretend people. Go around and ask students to name one person they might "see" in church.*

Let's do "The Church" together. Get ready and make your church. *Help students turn their hands inside out to make the church—this may take some extra time.*

Your turn to say our fingerplay. *Say the fingerplay with them and do the movements.*

▶ Children's response:
Here is the church and here's the steeple.
Open up the door and see all the people.

See anyone you know? *Ask a few students to name a person.*

Nice job saying "The Church."

1.3

 Vocabulary

STEEPLE

Use instructional moments to improve vocabulary and oral language. Explain vocabulary in a simple way, and have the students repeat back the word or phrase.

 Multisensory Reinforcement

What is a steeple? Put your pinkie in the air if you know. *Call on one or two children; confirm if the answer is correct.*

A steeple is the pointed roof at the top of a church, just like in the rhyming fingerplay we just said. I have a picture of one here, too. *Show children the picture.*

Follow a two-step approach. Step 1: Ask children to describe (or act out) the vocabulary word.

Let's build a steeple again. You build one with me. *Show them with your fingers.* A steeple is the pointed roof at the top of a church. Everyone, show me a steeple with your fingers.

▶ **(Children respond by showing a steeple with their fingers.)**

Yes, that is a steeple.

Step 2: Give students the description and have them supply the word. Guide the students for a complete sentence. Everyone, what's another way of saying a pointed roof at the top of a church?

▶ **Children's response: A steeple is a pointed roof.**

TEACHING TIP: Use the new word in a sentence using your students' names. This always gets their attention.

Yes, steeple. Aninah goes to a church that has a steeple. Everyone, I want you all to say, "Aninah goes to a church that has a steeple." Get ready.

▶ **Children's response: Aninah goes to a church that has a steeple.**

Everyone, what did Aninah's church have?

▶ **Children's response: A steeple.**

Yes, a steeple. Good job learning the word *steeple*.

 TASK 2   Find the Timer *(approximately 12–14 minutes)*

 PLAY the game.

 See Appendix D on the CD-ROM for the Find the Timer Game instructions.

 TASK 3   Transition song to end the lesson *(approximately 3 minutes)*

MAKE THE TRANSITION to end the lesson.

You are going to practice the rhyming fingerplay you learned earlier. Can you remember the name? Tap the middle of your forehead if you know.

TEACHING TIP: Check on students' focus by giving them an easy direction to follow.

Call on a student. Guide students in the correct response.

▶ **Child's response: "The Church."**

Yes, it's called "The Church."

 Multisensory Reinforcement

Eyes on me. Let's start from the beginning and say our fingerplay together. See if you remember the entire rhyme. Let's first build our church. *Make the church first with your hands.* Now we can begin.

Say it with me. *Say the rhyme and include movements with your hands.*

▶ **Children's response:**
Here is the church and here's the steeple.
Open up the door and see all the people.

Time to do rhyming words. Here's our "Rhyming Exercise Song" that we can do together. We want to get our rhyme muscles nice and firm so our rhymes are in great shape. *Hold your arms up and show your muscles.* Show me your muscles.

SING the "Rhyming Exercise Song."

✋ **Multisensory Reinforcement**

▶ **(Children respond by showing their muscles, too.)**

Follow me. Put your hands in the sky. *Stretch one arm up to the sky, then the other arm, on the word hands.* Do the rhyming exercise.

People *(Stretch one arm up as you say the word.)*
Steeple *(Stretch the other arm up.)*
People *(Switch arms.)*
Steeple *(Switch arms.)*
People *(Switch arms.)*
Steeple *(Switch arms.)*

Do they rhyme? *Pause here and allow them to show thumbs up or down before you respond. Look around at each student and make eye contact.* Yes. *Nod vigorously.* They rhyme. *Give two thumbs up.*

END the song.

Nice job everyone. Let's get out our cameras. *(Make a camera with your hands and click with your tongue as you take some pictures of students. They do the same.)*
Click. Click. Click. Looking good. *(Thumbs up. Big smile. Nod.)*

END Lesson 1.

Everyone now gets their winnings for learning your rhymes and for working hard. *Give out token rewards to each child.*

LESSON 2: Little Teapot

OBJECTIVES

Student will

- Know how to listen carefully to the sounds of rhyming words and be able to develop an awareness of rhyme by repeating rhyming fingerplays and songs
- Know how to listen carefully to the sounds of rhyming words and be able to develop an awareness of rhyme by singing rhyming songs and using dance movements

Teacher will

- Emphasize the sounds of words that rhyme so students can clearly hear that the endings of rhyming words are the same
- Closely observe each student for focus and full participation
- Smile and ensure success for all children

RHYMES, SONGS, AND FINGERPLAYS

"One, Two, Buckle My Shoe"

"I'm a Little Teapot"

MATERIALS

Book containing "One, Two, Buckle My Shoe" with pictures (e.g., Baker, 1994)

A real teapot or a picture of a teapot

Tokens for behavior/participation

🌑 **TASK 1**   **Transition song to begin the lesson** (approximately 3 minutes)

INTRODUCE the big idea.

We are going to listen carefully for rhymes and then practice our rhymes. You will learn some good rhyming fingerplays and songs.

Words that rhyme are words that sound the same. What do we call words that sound the same?

▶ **Children's response: Words that rhyme.**

✳ **Model the Activity**

Yes, words that rhyme or rhyming words. Like *two* and *shoe.* Do it with me. *As you say two, put your right palm out and tilt your head to the right. Do the same on the left side as you say shoe. Do this three times.*

▶ **(Children respond by doing it with you.)**

Nice job rhyming *two* and *shoe.*

BEGIN the transition.

You are going to learn another rhyme. You may know this one. It's called "One, Two, Buckle My Shoe." Everyone, what's the name of our rhyme?

▶ **Children's response: "One, Two, Buckle My Shoe."**

 Multisensory Reinforcement

Yes, "One, Two, Buckle My Shoe." Let's look at the pictures as I say the rhyme. We will practice saying our numbers, too. *Show children the book, pointing to the pictures as you go along.*

My turn to say the rhyme.
One, two,
Buckle my shoe;
Three, four,
Shut the door;
Five, six,
Pick up sticks;
Seven, eight,
Lay them straight;
Nine, ten,
A big fat hen.

◈ **Vocabulary**

STRAIGHT

What does it mean when we lay something straight? Touch your nose if you know. *Call on one or two children; confirm if the answer is correct.*

Straight means not crooked and in a row. *Show with your hand what is straight and what is crooked.* Let's get in a straight line. *Line up the children in a straight row.*

Now, let's make our line crooked. *Line up children so that they are not in a straight line.*

Okay, everyone get back into a straight line.

▶ **(Children respond by lining up in a straight row.)**

Yes, you are in a straight line. Everyone, say "We are in a straight line and we are wonderful students."

▶ **Children's response: We are in a straight line and we are wonderful students.**

Nice job learning the word *straight.* Let's say our rhyme again and this time try to guess the rhyme. I think you can do it.

My turn to say the rhyme.
One, two,
Buckle my…

Pause when you reach the rhyming word and have the students say it.

▶ Children's response: Shoe.

Three, four,
Shut the…

▶ Children's response: Door.

Five, six,
Pick up…

▶ Children's response: Sticks.

Seven, eight,
Lay them…

▶ Children's response: Straight.

Nine, ten,
A big fat…

▶ Children's response: Hen.

END the rhyme.

Nice job saying "One, Two, Buckle My Shoe." You are learning rhyming words. Let's give ourselves the trucker cheer. Do it with me.

Grab your steering wheel. *(Put your hands on the "wheel" and "steer" it.)*

Rrrrrr. *(Make the sound of a truck.)*

Honk, honk. *(Put your fist in the air and pull the horn.)*

Grab your CB radio and say, "Good job, good buddy." *(Talk into your fist.)*

TASK 2   **Learning rhyming song and movement** (approximately 12–14 minutes)

INTRODUCE the rhyming song.

You are going to learn a rhyming song and dance called "I'm a Little Teapot." We are all going to be teapots. Here's a teapot. *Show them a teapot or a picture of one.* What do you think is in a teapot? Sit up tall and proud if you know. *Call on one child.*

▶ Child's response: Tea.

Yes, tea is in a teapot. Everyone, touch your cheeks if you like tea. Can someone tell me about a time that you or someone you knew had tea? *Call on one child.* What's the name of the song and dance we will learn today?

▶ Children's response: "I'm a Little Teapot."

 Multisensory Reinforcement

Use exaggerated, easy, consistent, and space-conscious movements that mimic the song.

Yes, "I'm a Little Teapot." My turn to sing. Watch me dance. *Stand up and do dance movements that mimic the song.*

I'm a little teapot, short and stout.
Here is my handle, here is my spout.
When I get all steamed up, then I shout.
Just tip me over and pour me out.

Your turn to sing and dance with me. Everyone stand up. *Each child should have his or her own space. Sing with them and lead them in their dance movements.*

▶ Children's response:
I'm a little teapot, short and stout.

Here is my handle, here is my spout.
When I get all steamed up, then I shout.
Just tip me over and pour me out.

Let's everyone sing and dance one more time. *Repeat the song and dance.*
Now go back to your seats. Nice job being teapots.

 Vocabulary

STOUT

Explain vocabulary in a simple way.

Let's talk about the word *stout.*

Follow a two-step approach. Step 1: Show an example and give a brief description of the word.

Stout means chubby or tubby or fat. *Take out the teapot or the picture of the teapot again and show them the roundness of the teapot.* Teapots are usually little and fat or little and chubby or little and stout.

TEACHING TIP: Act it out. Use exaggerated movements with the students. Show really chubby by gesturing around your middle.

Show me with your hands how stout you are when you sing "I'm a Little Teapot."

▶ **(Children place hands at the same position as in the song—around their bodies but larger.)**

Step 2: Give students the description, and have them supply the word. Guide the students for a complete sentence. Everyone, what's another way of saying our little teapot is chubby or fat?

▶ **Children's response: Our little teapot is stout.**

Yes, our little teapot is stout. Let's take it from the top *(model the head pat)* and do it again. Everyone stand up. *Repeat the song and dance with the students.*

▶ **Children's response:**
I'm a little teapot, short and stout.
Here is my handle, here is my spout.
When I get all steamed up, then I shout.
Just tip me over and pour me out.

End the song and dance.

PRACTICE the "Rhyming Exercise Song."

Let's sing the "Rhyming Exercise Song." Remember, words that rhyme are words that sound the same. We learned lots of new rhymes.

 Multisensory Reinforcement

Follow me. Put your hands in the sky. *Stretch one arm up to the sky, then the other arm, on the word hands.* Do the rhyming exercise.

Stout *(Stretch one arm up as you say the word.)*
Spout *(Stretch the other arm up.)*
Stout *(Switch arms.)*
Spout *(Switch arms.)*
Stout *(Switch arms.)*
Spout *(Switch arms.)*

Do they rhyme? *Pause here and allow them to show thumbs up or down before you respond. Look around at each student and make eye contact.* Yes. *Nod vigorously.* They rhyme. *Give two thumbs up.*

Let's try two more words: *shout* and *out.*

Repeat the song with the new words.

| **END** the song. | Great job with rhyming words. Let's give ourselves ghost waves. *Extend both arms and cross them over as you wave them in the air and go "Oooooo!"*

Let's do it again. *Repeat.* |

🪐 **TASK 3** Transition song to end the lesson *(approximately 3 minutes)*

| **MAKE THE TRANSITION** to end the lesson. | You are going to practice the rhyme you learned earlier. Everyone, can you re-member the name of the rhyme? Touch your ear if you remember. *Guide for the correct response.*

▶ Children's response: "One, Two, Buckle My Shoe."

Yes, it's called "One, Two, Buckle My Shoe." Let's say our rhyme together. *Repeat the rhyme and show each picture in the book as you say that part of the rhyme.*

One, two,
Buckle my shoe;
Three, four,
Shut the door;
Five, six,
Pick up sticks;
Seven, eight,
Lay them straight;
Nine, ten,
A big fat hen. |
| **END** Lesson 2. | Nice job saying "One, Two, Buckle My Shoe." You are working hard learning your rhymes.

Everyone now gets their winnings for learning your rhymes and for working hard. *Give out token rewards to each child.* |

LESSON 3: 100 Words

OBJECTIVES

Student will

- Know how to listen carefully to the sounds of rhyming words and be able to develop an aware-ness of rhyme in an interactive rhyming book by ac-curately predicting the rhyming word in the story

Teacher will

- Emphasize the sounds of words that rhyme so stu-dents can clearly hear that the endings of rhyming words are the same
- Hold the book so that each child can see the pictures
- Closely observe each student for focus, rhythm, and full participation
- Lead children to participate in the interactive rhyming book by coaching them to predict the rhyming word in the story
- Smile and ensure success for all children

RHYMES, SONGS, AND FINGERPLAYS

"The Itsy-Bitsy Spider"

"The Church"

MATERIALS

Book: *I'll Teach My Dog 100 Words* (Firth, 1973)

Tokens for behavior/participation

TASK 1   **Transition fingerplay to begin the lesson** (approximately 3 minutes)

INTRODUCE the big idea.

We are going to listen carefully for rhymes and then practice our rhymes. Think big today. Don't forget, words that rhyme are words that sound the same. What do we call words that sound the same?

▶ Children's response: Words that rhyme.

Yes, words that rhyme or . . . *Prompt for the words rhyming words.*

▶ Children's response: Rhyming words.

Yes, rhyming words. Like *spout* and *out.* Do it with me. *As you say* spout, *put your right palm out and tilt your head to the right. Do the same on the left side as you say* out.

▶ (Children respond by doing it with you.)

Nice job rhyming *spout* and *out.* You are going to practice the rhyming song you know and love. It's called "The Itsy-Bitsy Spider." Everyone, what's the name of our song?

BEGIN the transition.

▶ Children's response: "The Itsy-Bitsy Spider."

Yes, the name of our rhyming song is "The Itsy-Bitsy Spider."

Let's get our spiders ready and sing the song. *Sing the song and include movements with your hands.*

The itsy-bitsy spider went up the water spout.
Down came the rain and washed the spider out.
Out came the sun and dried up all the rain.
So the itsy-bitsy spider came up the spout again.

Great job singing about your spiders.

TASK 2   **Listening to a rhyming book** (approximately 12–14 minutes)

INTRODUCE the lesson.

You are going to read a rhyming story with me and listen for some rhyming words. What about *brown* and *town?* Do they rhyme? Do they sound the same? *As you say* brown, *put your right palm out and tilt your head to the right. Do the same on the left side as you say* town.

▶ Children's response: Yes.

Yes, *brown* and *town* sound the same. *Repeat hand motions.* They rhyme. *Give a thumbs up.*

What about *tall* and *small? Repeat hand motions.* Do they rhyme? Do they sound the same?

▶ Children's response: Yes.

Yes, *tall* and *small* sound the same. They rhyme. *Give a thumbs up.*

This book has many rhyming words. All set? *Snap two times. Guide the students' response.*

▶ Children's response: You bet. *Snap two times.*

  Turn On Your Ears

You are ready to look at me and listen. This is a fun rhyming book. The title of the book is *I'll Teach My Dog 100 Words. Hold up the book and point to the title as you read it.* What kind of animal is in the story?

▶ Children's response: A dog.

Yes, a dog. Who do you think will teach the dog 100 words? *Guide children's response by pointing to the arm on the cover that is holding the stick and let them guess who may be holding it.*

Yes, that could be a boy or a girl or a man or a woman. Let's read to find out. Good job trying to decide who will teach the dog 100 words.

TEACHING TIP: When reading aloud to students, begin to encourage them to anticipate and predict the rhyming words. Pause at the end of a rhyming line for students to orally predict the next word. Also, overemphasize the rhymes as you read.

Read the book aloud. Revisit the prediction.

PRACTICE the "Rhyming Exercise Song."

 **Multisensory Reinforcement**

Let's sing the "Rhyming Exercise Song." Remember, words that rhyme are words that sound the same. We learned lots of new rhymes.

Follow me. Put your hands in the sky. *Stretch one arm up to the sky, then the other arm, on the word hands.* Do the rhyming exercise.

Then *(Stretch one arm up as you say the word.)*
Ten *(Stretch the other arm up.)*
Then *(Switch arms.)*
Ten *(Switch arms.)*
Then *(Switch arms.)*
Ten *(Switch arms.)*

Do they rhyme? *Pause here and allow them to show thumbs up or down before you respond. Look around at each student and make eye contact.* Yes. *Nod vigorously.* They rhyme. *Give two thumbs up.*

Repeat the song for each new word pair.
Let's try two more words: *door* and *more*.
Here are two more rhymes: *nose* and *toes*.
Let's try again: *tree* and *me*.

END the song.

Nice job singing the "Rhyming Exercise Song." You are really learning your rhymes.

 TASK 3

Transition song to end the lesson (approximately 3 minutes)

MAKE THE TRANSITION to end the lesson.

You are going to say and do a fingerplay you learned before. The name of our fingerplay is "The Church." Everyone, what is the name of our fingerplay?

▶ Children's response: "The Church."

Yes, it's called "The Church." Everyone, touch your chin if you are ready to build your church.

TEACHING TIP: Check on students' focus by giving them an easy direction to follow.

Say the rhyme and include movements with your hands.

Let's build our church with our hands. *Build with your hands.* Now we can begin. Say it with me.

Here is the church and here's the steeple.

	Open up the door and see all the people.
	Great job building and saying "The Church." You are a gold star class. You know what that means.
	Take out your star box. *(Cup one hand.)*
	Get your star. *(Pretend to get a star on the pointer finger of the other hand.)*
	You are all gold star kids. *(Lick it and put it on your forehead.)*
END Lesson 3.	Everyone now gets their winnings for learning your rhymes and for working hard. *Give out token rewards to each child.*

LESSON 4: Rhyme Awareness Review

OBJECTIVES

Student will

- Know how to listen carefully to the sounds of rhyming words and be able to develop an awareness of rhyme by repeating rhyming fingerplays and songs
- Know how to listen carefully to the sounds of rhyming words and be able to develop an awareness of rhyme by singing rhyming songs and using dance movements
- Know how to listen carefully to the sounds of rhyming words and be able to develop an awareness of rhyme in an interactive rhyming book by accurately predicting the rhyming word in the story

Teacher will

- Emphasize the sounds of words that rhyme so students can clearly hear that the endings of rhyming words are the same
- Smile and ensure success for all children
- Hold the book so that each child can see the pictures
- Lead children to participate in the interactive rhyming book by coaching them to predict the rhyming word in the story
- Closely observe each student for focus and full participation

RHYMES, SONGS, AND FINGERPLAYS

"One, Two, Buckle My Shoe"

"I'm a Little Teapot"

MATERIALS

Book containing "One, Two, Buckle My Shoe" with pictures (e.g., Baker, 1994)

Book: *I'll Teach My Dog 100 Words* (Firth, 1973)

Tokens for behavior/participation

☑ DROPP 1 Skill Assessment Checkout (see Appendix B on the CD-ROM)   **CD-ROM**

 TASK 1   Transition song to begin the lesson *(approximately 2 minutes)*

INTRODUCE the big idea.

We are going to listen carefully for rhymes and then practice our rhymes. You will practice some good rhyming songs and movements. Words that rhyme are words that sound the same. What do we call words that sound the same?

▶ Children's response: Rhyming words.

Yes, rhyming words. Like *four* and *door.* Do it with me. *As you say* four, *put your right palm out and tilt your head to the right. Do the same on the left side as you say* door. *Do this three times.*

▶ (Children respond by doing it with you.)

Nice job rhyming *four* and *door.*

Let's try another rhyme. Like *eight* and *straight.* Do it with me. *Repeat previous action.*

▶ **(Children respond by doing it with you.)**

Nice job saying our rhymes. You are excellent rhymers.

You are going to practice another rhyme. You know this one. It's called "One, Two, Buckle My Shoe." Everyone, what's the name of our rhyme?

▶ **Children's response: "One, Two, Buckle My Shoe."**

Yes, "One, Two, Buckle My Shoe." Let's look at the pictures as I say the rhyme. We will practice saying our numbers, too.

My turn to say the rhyme:
One, two,
Buckle my shoe;
Three, four,
Shut the door;
Five, six,
Pick up sticks;
Seven, eight,
Lay them straight;
Nine, ten,
A big fat hen.

Let's say our rhyme again and this time try to guess what comes at the end of the line. I think you can do it. *Sing with them, show each picture, and pause for a few moments so they can look at the picture and say the rhyme.*

One, two,
Buckle my . . .
▶ **Children's response: Shoe.**

Three, four,
Shut the . . .
▶ **Children's response: Door.**

Five, six,
Pick up…
▶ **Children's response: Sticks.**

Seven, eight,
Lay them . . .
▶ **Children's response: Straight.**

Nine, ten,
A big fat . . .
▶ **Children's response: Hen.**

Your rhyming work was so good today. Let's give ourselves the trucker cheer. Do it with me.
Grab your steering wheel. *(Put your hands on the "wheel" and "steer" it.)*
Rrrrrr. *(Make the sound of a truck.)*
Honk, honk. *(Put your fist in the air and pull the horn.)*
Grab your CB radio and say, "Good job, good buddy." *(Talk into your fist.)*

BEGIN the transition.

TASK 2A   Reviewing "I'm a Little Teapot" (approximately 8 minutes)

REVIEW the rhyming song.	You are going to practice a rhyming song and dance called "I'm a Little Teapot." We are all going to be teapots again. Here's a teapot. *Show them a teapot or a picture of one.*

What's the name of the song and dance we will do today?

▶ **Children's response: "I'm a Little Teapot."**

Yes, "I'm a Little Teapot." Get ready to sing and dance. Everyone stand up. *Stand up and do dance movements with the students that mimic the song.*

Multisensory Reinforcement

I'm a little teapot, short and stout.
Here is my handle, here is my spout.
When I get all steamed up, then I shout.
Just tip me over and pour me out.

Let's everyone sing and dance one more time. *Repeat the song and dance.*

Nice job being teapots.

Turn On Your Ears

My turn. Listen to our "Have a Seat Song" as you go back to your seat.
Sing to the tune of "Shortnin' Bread."
Everybody have a seat, have a seat, have a seat.
Everybody have a seat on your chair.
Not on the ceiling.
Not in the air.
Everybody have a seat on your chair.

▶ **(Children respond by going back to their seats.)**

Your turn to sing with me. *Sing with them as students are in their seats.*

▶ **Children's response:**
Everybody have a seat, have a seat, have a seat.
Everybody have a seat on your chair.
Not on the ceiling.
Not in the air.
Everybody have a seat on your chair.

TASK 2B   Reviewing a rhyming book (approximately 8–9 minutes)

REVIEW the rhyming song.	We're going to read a rhyming story and listen for some rhyming words. What can you tell me about rhyming words? *Give them a hint by tugging on your ear. Pause to allow them to respond.*

▶ **Children's response: They sound the same.**

Turn On Your Ears

This book has many rhyming words. Get ready to look at me and listen.

This is a fun rhyming book that you all know and love. The title of the book is *I'll Teach My Dog 100 Words. Hold up the book and point to the title as you read.* Explain how a dog can learn words. *Call on one or two children.*

Let's read about this terrific dog who learns 100 words.

TEACHING TIP: When reading aloud to students, pause at the end of a rhyming line for students to orally predict the next word. Choose easy rhyming words at first so students make accurate choices.

PRACTICE the "Rhyming Exercise Song."

Multisensory Reinforcement

Let's sing the "Rhyming Exercise Song." Remember, words that rhyme are words that sound the same. We learned lots of new rhymes.

Follow me. Put your hands in the sky. *Stretch one arm up to the sky, then the other arm, on the word hands.* Do the rhyming exercise.

Green *(Stretch one arm up as you say the word.)*
Seen *(Stretch the other arm up.)*
Green *(Switch arms.)*
Seen *(Switch arms.)*
Green *(Switch arms.)*
Seen *(Switch arms.)*

Do they rhyme? *Pause here and allow them to show thumbs up or down before you respond. Look around at each student and make eye contact.* Yes. *Nod vigorously.* They rhyme. *Give two thumbs up.*

Repeat the song for each new word pair.
Let's try two more words: *pink* and *think.*
Now try these: *chair* and *there.*
Here are two more rhymes: *stone* and *bone.*

Your rhyming work was so good today. We are going to sing the "Give Me a Snap" song. *Sing to the tune of* The Addams Family *theme song.*

Give me a snap. *(Snap twice.)*
Give me a snap. *(Snap twice.)*
Give me a snap, give me a snap, give me a snap. *(Snap twice.)*

Repeat the tune but say, "Give me a cheer."
Give me a cheer. "Hooray!" *(Say "Hooray!" once instead of snapping twice.)*

END Lesson 4.

Everyone now gets their winnings for learning your rhymes and for working hard. *Give out token rewards to each child.*

CD-ROM

The DROPP 1 Skill Assessment Checkout will be completed for each student following this lesson.

Rhyme Discrimination

Overview

WHY RHYME DISCRIMINATION IS IMPORTANT

Rhyme discrimination is important because students must be able to understand the difference between words that rhyme and words that do not rhyme. This is a step to becoming phonologically aware and is a precursor to reading.

HOW DROPP 2 IS STRUCTURED

DROPP 2 has four complete Activity Sets: 2.1–2.4. Each Activity Set consists of four scripted lessons (Teacher Talk) that are used on 10 sequential learning days (the four lessons are repeated over the 10-day span). These intervention lessons are aimed at practicing and reviewing the skill of rhyme discrimination. DROPP 2 has 40 days of intervention lessons in all (four Activity Sets of 10 days each). During the first 9 days of each set, students learn the words to rhyming songs, learn movements to fingerplays, play a game, and take part in interactive rhyming stories by accurately predicting the rhyming word in the story. On the 10th day, students review the skills to prepare for a short skill assessment checkout. (See the CD-ROM for the DROPP 2 Skill Assessment Checkout.)

Length of Activity Sets and Lessons

Each Activity Set is designed to be delivered across 10 sequential learning days. Each day's intervention lesson, including the transition activities, takes about 20 minutes to complete.

Lessons 1–3 within the Activity Sets are generally divided into 3 tasks.

- Task 1 is the transition into the lesson and lasts about 2–3 minutes.

- Task 2 is the concept/skill portion and lasts for approximately 12–15 minutes.

- Task 3 is the transition out of the lesson and lasts about 2–3 minutes.

Lesson 4 is slightly different because Task 3 has been eliminated to allow more time for review. Lesson 4 is generally divided into 2 tasks.

- Task 1 is the transition into the lesson and lasts about 2–3 minutes.

- Task 2 is the concept/skill portion and may be divided into Task 2A and Task 2B. This task lasts for approximately 15–18 minutes.

Goal and Emphasis of the Rhyme Discrimination Lessons

The goal of Activity Sets 2.1–2.4 is to saturate your students in rhyme and emphasize the difference between words that rhyme and words that do not rhyme. The "Rhyming Exercise Song" is used again throughout these lessons as it was in DROPP 1 because the multisensory approach directly reinforces rhyming. The song is also used as a correction procedure when any student has trouble with rhyme discrimination while playing the Rhyming Card Sort Game.

> TEACHING TIP: **Check for Success**
> Maintain eye contact with all students in your group, and ensure they are responding correctly and on cue. By doing this, you are conducting a mini assessment for each child to see who may need additional help.

Student Objectives

- Know how to listen for rhyming words and be able to discriminate between rhyming and non-rhyming words in a card game.

- Know how to listen for rhyming words and be able to discriminate between rhyming and non-rhyming words in an interactive rhyming book by accurately predicting the rhyming word in the story.

Teacher Objectives

- Emphasize the sounds of words that rhyme so students can clearly hear that the endings of rhyming words are the same.

- Hold the cards so that each child can see every card sort.

- Ensure that all children win the game.

- Hold the book so that each child can see the pictures.

- Lead children to participate in the interactive rhyming book by coaching them to predict accurately the rhyming word in the story.

- Closely observe each student for focus and full participation.

Teaching Approach

Continually smile and nod affirmations to your students. Your time with them is clearly instructional, but the content is fun and the goal is always success for all students. Rhyming lessons should feel good to our young learners, and you should hear them rhyming throughout the day. This helps them to remember the rhymes and get used to the sound of rhyming words.

How Rhyme Discrimination Activity Sets Develop Early Literacy

Multisensory Techniques

In Activity Sets 2.1–2.4, children are using both fine motor skills and large muscle movements to emphasize rhyming words in songs, poems, fingerplays, and games. Students sing rhymes and hear their classmates sing them, see and choose rhyming picture cards, and participate in full physical responses to whether or not words rhyme by moving to and singing the "Rhyming Exercise Song." Students also continually confirm rhyming word pairs by nodding their heads and giving a thumbs-up. In this way, they maintain their complete focus on rhyme.

Making Meaning and Building Vocabulary

As students go through Activity Sets 2.1–2.4, they are exposed to new vocabulary words and phrases associated with nursery rhymes and read-alouds. These new words and phrases are listed at the beginning of each Activity Set and are presented in a two-step approach (see Chapter 2). We recommend that you use the new words and phrases throughout the day and in different contexts to reinforce student vocabulary and oral language growth.

- Activity Set 2.1: bough, lap, sort

- Activity Set 2.2: out of sight, jig, full of glee, to no avail

- Activity Set 2.3: fetch, crown

- Activity Set 2.4: bough, crumb, spy

Print Awareness

Students will experience the left-to-right progression of word reading in the Rhyming Card Sort Game, the Rhyming Pictures Game, and the Bugs in Mugs Game found in Activity Sets 2.1–2.4. Also embedded in these Activity Sets is the awareness that the names of the rhymes are included directly under the pictures in several sets of game cards. Although this concept of print is presented at an awareness level only and is not intended as explicit instruction in teaching students to read printed words, it is intended to support their understanding that rhyming words can be translated into print. This is one of the core foundational understandings in learning to read.

General Tips for Implementing Activity Sets 2.1–2.4

- In Activity Set 2.1, you will introduce two words that do not rhyme. As you say the nonrhyming words, use your face as a way of guiding the students to know that the words do not rhyme—maintain an expression of looking puzzled or trying to decide if the words really do rhyme.

- When singing the words "Do they rhyme?" in the "Rhyming Exercise Song," show thumbs down and vigorously shake your head when you exclaim, "No, they don't rhyme." You are modeling the correct response for your students while cuing it for them at the same time.

- Introduce the **Rhyming Card Sort Game,** which you will continue to play in Activity Set 2.2. We found that it was a much-loved way to reinforce rhyme discrimination with our students. Because we used the rhyming cards many times, we invested in 50 pairs of good quality picture cards, although all 50 pairs would not be used in any given game. Commercial picture cards are used by speech-language pathologists (SLPs) for articulation practice. The kits contain several decks of brightly colored, motivational pictures printed on heavy, laminated stock. From these decks, we chose 50 pairs and built our own deck and scripted our own words to target rhyme discrimination for our students who were struggling. The cards have the picture name printed at the bottom so everyone working with or helping out in the classroom uses the same rhyming words. This is extremely important because the words associated with the pictures must be consistent in order for them to rhyme and the students to learn the concept of rhyming. Check with the SLP in your school to share his or her materials or use the Rhyming Card Sort Game word list from Appendix D: Games on the accompanying CD-ROM.

  In the target lessons, you will find a four-step approach to using the Rhyming Card Sort Game, and it is important to speak slowly, speak clearly, and exaggerate the rhymes. As you play, you will be using a simple, continual pattern of two rhyming pairs plus one card from the subsequent pair. For the following example, use *rake, wake,* and *ball* from the Rhyming Card Sort Game word List (see Appendix D: Games on the accompanying CD-ROM).

Lay out three cards face up in a triangle formation, saying the word on each card, one by one.

The first card at the top is rake.

The second card, either wake *or* ball, *is under the first card.*

The third card (the remaining word that was not used as the second card) *is next to the second card.*

Ask, Does rake (touch it) rhyme with wake (touch it)?

Or, does rake (touch it) rhyme with ball (touch it)?

Rake, wake? *Touch them as you say their names.*

Or, rake, ball? *Touch them as you say their names.*

Say, rake (touch it) rhymes with _____? Who can touch the rhyming word? *Call on a student to touch the rhyming card and say the word.*

▶ Child's response: Wake.

Instructional Tips for Playing the Rhyming Card Sort Game

- Mix up the rhyming pair—sometimes place the rhyming card on the left and other times place it on the right; otherwise, the students rely on the placement of the card rather than identifying the rhyme.

- Whenever you begin a new lesson that includes the Rhyming Card Sort Game, mix in some new rhyming pairs with the old ones. Eventually, you will rotate the whole deck and the students will become familiar with many new rhymes.

- Once your students learn to play this game, we recommend that you make a student game (using rhymes they know) and keep it in a center or workstation for independent play.

Game Management Tips

It is best to make a chart of the rhyming words and keep your deck in this order to minimize your time finding new rhymes for the students (see the Rhyming Card Sort Game word list from Appendix D: Games on the accompanying CD-ROM for more information). As you play, use a continual pattern of two rhyming pairs plus one card from the subsequent pair. Here are some tips on how to work with your rhyming deck of cards.

- Keep your deck face up and in the same order as the related Rhyming Card Sort Game word list from Appendix D: Games on the accompanying CD-ROM.

- Complete the three-card sort with the first student. Pick up the rhyming pair and turn them over in a discard pile so that students won't be distracted by past cards.

- Leave the unrhymed card on the table for the next round, and take the next two cards from your deck.

- At the end of the game, pick up your discard pile, turn it over, and put it at the bottom of your deck.

- At the start of the next lesson, take a few of the cards already used from the bottom and put them in the front of the deck. The students find success quickly with the previous rhymes and then move to new ones.

- **Rhyming Pictures Game:** In Activity Set 2.3, the students who have completed Activity Sets 2.1 and 2.2 are growing developmentally, and rhyme discrimination is probably beginning to emerge. All children develop differently, and we allow them to tell their rhymes at their own pace. In Activity Set 2.3, introduce the Rhyming Pictures Game in which the students are shown one card with three pictures—two rhyming and one nonrhyming—and ask which two pictures rhyme. We used commercially available rhyming cards with the names of the pictures on the back; however, we scripted our own words designed to target rhyme discrimination for our struggling students. We also used these cards for DROPP 10, as it contains several levels of phonological awareness cards—but again, we scripted our own words. You could also make your own cards for the Rhyming Pictures Game using the related Rhyming Pictures Game word list from Appendix D: Games on the accompanying CD-ROM.

Standard Teacher Talk for the Rhyming Pictures Game

In the intervention lessons, you will note how each student is progressing and developing his or her rhyme discrimination skill at his or her own comfortable pace. We scripted an easy approach that allows for student differences and gives them several opportunities for success. This is scaffolded instruction. While reviewing the following Teacher Talk, it is important to observe that some students can answer at *A* with only one prompt, some answer at *C* with two prompts, others may need three prompts to answer at *E*, and some may not be rhyming as yet and will actually be given the rhyming word at *F*. It is important to speak slowly, clearly, and exaggerate the rhymes. (As always, be positive and encouraging at all times.) For the following example, use bat, ball, and cat from the related Rhyming Pictures Game word list from Appendix D: Games on the accompanying CD-ROM.

Hold up the first card to the first student, say the words on all three pictures, and point to each one.

Top picture: bat (touch it)

Middle picture: ball (touch it)

Bottom picture: cat (touch it)

Touch bat *again and slowly and carefully say, Bat* rhymes with _____.

Give the student a chance to process the cards and answer.

A ▶ Child's response: Cat.

Yes, you get a point. *(Give a chip and move to the next student.)*

B ▶ **Child responds incorrectly or does not respond.**

Listen again. Does *bat (touch it)* rhyme with *ball (touch it)*?

Or, does *bat (touch it again)* rhyme with *cat (touch it)*?

C ▶ Child's response: Cat.

Yes, you get a point. *(Give a chip and move to the next student.)*

D ▶ **Child responds incorrectly or does not respond.**

Keep listening.

Bat, ball. *(Touch the pictures as you say them.)*

Bat, cat. *(Touch the pictures as you say them.)*

Bat rhymes with _____? *(Touch bat.)*

E ▶ Child's response: Cat.

Yes, you get a point. *(Give a chip and move to the next student.)*

F ▶ **Child responds incorrectly or does not respond.**

Bat rhymes with *cat. (Touch the pictures.)*

Instructional Tips for Playing the Rhyming Pictures Game

- Mix in some new cards with the old ones when you begin a new lesson that includes the Rhyming Pictures Game. Eventually, you will rotate the deck, and the students will become familiar with many new rhymes.

- Once your students learn to play this game, we recommend that you make a student game (using rhymes they know) and keep it in a center or workstation for independent play.

- **Bugs in Mugs Game:** In Activity Set 2.4, the students who have completed all of the prior Activity Sets for DROPP 2 should be close to having rhyme discrimination emerge as a phonological skill. In Activity Set 2.4, introduce the Bugs in Mugs Game, in which the students find a rhyming card and match it to a spot on a game board. We scripted words designed to target rhyme discrimination for our students who struggled. You can make your own game board and cards for this game by using the Rhyming Game Board in Appendix D: Games on the accompanying CD-ROM. An important element of this game is that it must be set up before the children arrive for group time, as set-up time takes a few minutes. (See using the Rhyming Game Board in Appendix D: Games on the accompanying CD-ROM for detailed game directions and set up.)

Standard Teacher Talk for Playing the Bugs in Mugs Game

Because each student is progressing and developing his or her rhyme discrimination skill at his or her own pace, continue to scaffold learning to give them several opportunities for success. This game's format for intervention is similar to the Rhyming Pictures Game. While reviewing the following Teacher Talk, it is important to observe that some students can answer at *A* with only one prompt, some answer at *C* with two prompts and limiting the choice of picture matches down to two pictures so the student can better target the rhymes, others may need three prompts combined with limited choices to answer at *E*, and some may not be rhyming as yet and will actually be given the rhyming word at *F*. It is important to speak slowly, clearly, and exaggerate the rhymes. (As always, be positive and encouraging at all times.) For the following example, use matching pairs from the Rhyming Game Board from Appendix D: Games on the accompanying CD-ROM and always review the picture names with the students at the beginning of the game and continue to prompt them throughout, if needed.

Let's start our game. *(Point to the first student.)* Pick a card from the cards lined up under the board and turn it over.

▶ Child responds by turning over a card with a picture of a bed.

Say the picture.

▶ Child's response: Bed. *(Child holds onto the card.)*

Yes, *bed*. Find a picture that rhymes with *bed*. Look over at this side of the game board. *Gesture to the side of the game board with the correct picture rhyme. Bed* rhymes with _____? Listen as I say the pictures on the board again. *(Touch them as you say them.)* Red. Pear. Frog. Mouse. *Bed* rhymes with _____?

A ▶ Child's response: Red.

Yes, *bed* rhymes with *red*. Place *bed* next to *red*. Let's say the rhyme. *Bed, red.*

▶ Child's response: Bed, red. *(Student places* bed *next to* red.*)*

Nice job. You get a point. *(Give a chip and move to the next student.)*

B ▶ Child responds incorrectly or does not respond.

Listen again. Does *bed* *(take bed and hold it next to red)* rhyme with *red*?

Or does *bed* *(hold bed next to pear)* rhyme with *pear*?

C   ▶ Child's response: Red.

Place *bed* next to *red*. Let's say the rhyme. *Bed, red.*

▶ Child's response: Bed, red. *(Student places* bed *next to* red *on the board.)*

Nice job. You get a point. *(Give a chip and move to the next student.)*

D   ▶ Child responds incorrectly or does not respond.

Keep listening. Does *bed* rhyme with *red*? *(Move* bed *back to* red.*)*

Or, does *bed* rhyme with *pear*? *(Move* bed *back to* pear.*)*

Bed, red? *(Move* bed *back to* red.*)*

Bed, pear? *(Move* bed *back to* pear.*)*

E   ▶ Child's response: Red.

Place *bed* next to *red*. Let's say the rhyme. *Bed, red.*

▶ Child's response: Bed, red. *(Student places* bed *next to* red *on the board.)*

Nice job. You get a point. *(Give a chip and move to the next student.)*

F   ▶ Child cannot respond correctly.

Bed rhymes with *red*. Say it with me.

▶ Child's response: *Bed* rhymes with *red*.

Okay. You will get another turn to rhyme. Put your card back here and keep your eye on it.

That will be your card next time so keep listening for rhymes.

Instructional Tips for Playing the Bugs in Mugs Game

- Mix in some new rhyming cards with the old ones when you begin a new lesson that includes the Bugs in Mugs Game. Eventually, you will use all of the cards and the students will become familiar with many new rhymes.

- Once your students learn to play this game, we recommend that you make a student game (using rhymes the students know) and keep it in a center or workstation for independent play.

Literature Link

There are four rhyming books used in DROPP 2 in order for students to hear rhyme in the context of stories. They are all presented at Lesson 3.

- Activity Set 2.1: *I Wish That I Had Duck Feet* (LeSieg, 1965)

- Activity Set 2.2: *Tumble Bumble* (Bond, 1996)

- Activity Set 2.3: *I Can't Said the Ant* (Cameron, 1965)

- Activity Set 2.4: *512 Ants on Sullivan Street* (Losi, 2006)

While reading books to students in Activity Sets 2.1–2.4, encourage them to anticipate and predict the rhyming words at the end of the sentences. The rhyming words should be read in an overemphasized voice for easy identification by the students. Read the rhyming lines slowly for the children to hear the rhymes and process the sound-alike qualities of the rhyming words.

Pause and Punch Technique

As you read, pause slightly just before the first rhyming word and then punch it with your voice to make an impact. Continue reading to its rhyming match, and pause again when you come to it to cue the students to supply (predict) the rhyming word. An example follows.

> A tiny bug went for a walk *(emphasize the last word in the line).*
> He met a cat and stopped to . . . talk! *Pause for the students to say the rhyming word and as they supply the rhyme, nod vigorously, and emphasize the word* talk.

It is best to choose easier and familiar rhyming words at first (e.g., *bear* and *chair*, *mouse* and *house*, *cat* and *hat*) so the students can make accurate choices when predicting or supplying the rhyme. Some students are strong at predicting rhyming words, whereas others are not. Observing this skill in students provides important insight into their continued rhyme development.

TEACHING TIP: **Expert Read-Alouds**

Always preview a book privately before reading aloud to the students to become familiar with the story and the rhyming words. Once you are comfortable with the storyline and the rhymes, you will be able to read the book "from the side" and hold it open for the children to see the pictures. Using this approach will keep the students actively engaged in the story.

Review

On the 10th day of each Activity Set, students get the opportunity to review the rhyme discrimination skills by practicing several of the games, songs, read-aloud books, and so forth from the prior 9 days before their skill assessment checkout. The review is taken from Lessons 1–3.

Skill Assessment Checkouts

After your review lesson is completed, set aside a few minutes during that same day to give each child an individual rhyme discrimination checkout. These take about 2 minutes per child to administer and provide useful information to guide your future small-group placements. Based on the checkout and collaborative conversations with all teachers, you will determine which students should continue on in Tier 2 small-group intervention and which students can successfully return to Tier 1 whole-class instruction.

Assessment Outcome: The student can discriminate between words that rhyme and words that do not rhyme.

ACTIVITY SET 2.1

Lesson Descriptions

Lessons	Sequence of daily activities	◇ Vocabulary
Lesson 1: Did You Ever See a Bear in a Chair?	Song for "Rock-a-Bye Baby" Target: Rhyming song—"Did You Ever See a Bear in a Chair?" Song for "Rock-a-Bye Baby"	Bough Lap
Lesson 2: Rhyming Card Sort Game	Fingerplay for "Grandmother's Cap" Target: Rhyming Card Sort Game Fingerplay for "Grandmother's Cap"	Sort
Lesson 3: I Wish that I Had Duck Feet	Song for "Rock-A-Bye Baby" Target: Rhyming book—*I Wish that I Had Duck Feet* (LeSieg, 1965) Fingerplay for "Grandmother's Cap"	
Lesson 4: Rhyme Discrimination Review	Fingerplay for "Grandmother's Cap" Target: Rhyming Card Sort Game; rhyming book—*I Wish that I Had Duck Feet* (LeSieg, 1965)	

Materials Needed

☑ Picture of a tree bough

☑ Any cards or objects that can be sorted (e.g., colors, animals, fruits)

☑ Book: *I Wish that I Had Duck Feet* (LeSieg, 1965)

☑ Tokens for behavior/participation

> ☑ DROPP 2 Skill Assessment Checkout (see Appendix B on the CD-ROM)   CD-ROM
>
> **Rhyming Card Sort Game**
>
> ☑ Game cards (see Appendix D on the CD-ROM)
>
> ☑ Word list (see Appendix D on the CD-ROM)
>
> ☑ Three colored chips per child

ACTIVITY SET

2.1 # 10-Day Planner

Day 1	**Lesson 1:** Did You Ever See a Bear in a Chair?
Day 2	**Lesson 1:** Did You Ever See a Bear in a Chair?
Day 3	**Lesson 2:** Rhyming Card Sort Game
Day 4	**Lesson 2:** Rhyming Card Sort Game
Day 5	**Lesson 3:** I Wish that I Had Duck Feet
Day 6	**Lesson 3:** I Wish that I Had Duck Feet
Day 7	**Lesson 1:** Did You Ever See a Bear in a Chair?
Day 8	**Lesson 2:** Rhyming Card Sort Game
Day 9	**Lesson 3:** I Wish that I Had Duck Feet
Day 10	**Lesson 4:** Rhyme Discrimination Review

LESSON 1: Did You Ever See a Bear in a Chair?

OBJECTIVES

Student will

- Know how to listen for rhyming words and be able to discriminate between rhyming and nonrhyming words in fingerplays and songs

Teacher will

- Emphasize the sounds of words that rhyme so students can clearly hear that the endings of rhyming words are the same
- Closely observe each student for focus and full participation
- Smile and ensure success for all children

RHYMES, SONGS, AND FINGERPLAYS

"Rock-a-Bye Baby"

"Did You Ever See a Bear in a Chair?"

MATERIALS

Picture of a tree bough

Tokens for behavior/participation

 TASK 1 Transition song to begin the lesson (approximately 3 minutes)

INTRODUCE the big idea.

Say the following to the group after calling the students together at a table. We are going to listen for words that rhyme. Don't forget that words that rhyme are words that sound the same. What do we call words that sound the same?

▶ Children's response: Rhyming words.

Yes, rhyming words. Like *tree* and *me.* Do it with me. *As you say* tree, *put your right palm out and tilt your head to the right. Do the same on the left side as you say* me.

▶ (Children respond by doing it with you.)

Nice job rhyming *tree* and *me.*

BEGIN the transition.

You are going to learn a rhyming song. It's called "Rock-a-Bye Baby." What's the name of our rhyming song?

▶ Children's response: "Rock-a-Bye Baby."

My turn to sing "Rock-a-Bye Baby." Watch what I do with my hands. *While saying the words, use your hands to imitate a cradle rocking on a tree bough.*

Rock-a-bye baby in the treetop.
When the wind blows the cradle will rock.
When the bough breaks the cradle will fall.
And down will come baby, cradle and all.
But we'll catch you!

Let's do "Rock-a-Bye Baby" together. Get ready.

 Multisensory Reinforcement

Use instructional moments to improve vocabulary and oral language. Explain vocabulary in a simple way.

Sing it with them and do the movements. Sing the song four times: first time in a normal voice, second time in a somewhat lower voice, third time in a whisper, fourth time in a normal voice. This helps them to modulate their tones and, later listen for changes in sounds, which helps them understand phonemes. Repeat the entire song with them and do the movements.

Good job using your voices and your rhymes singing "Rock-a-Bye Baby."

What is a bough? Touch your chin if you know.

▶ (If children cannot respond. . .)

 Vocabulary

BOUGH

Have the students repeat back the word or phrase. Follow a two-step approach. Step 1: Ask children to describe the vocabulary word.

A bough is a large tree branch. *Show a picture of a tree bough.* This holds the baby's cradle. What is a bough?

▶ **Children's response: A bough is a large tree branch.**

Show me how a cradle would rock on a bough of a tree. *Model a rocking motion with your arms.*

▶ **(Children should demonstrate a rocking motion.)**

Step 2: Give students the description and have them supply the word.

Yes, that's how a cradle would rock on a bough of a tree. A bough is a large tree branch. What's another way of saying a large tree branch?

▶ **Children's response: Bough.**

Yes, bough. John climbed up to the bough of the tree. *Use the word in a simple sentence.*

Guide students to use a complete sentence. Can someone say a sentence and use the word *bough*? *Take one or two correct student responses.*

 **TASK 2** | **Sing a rhyming song using different pairs of rhymes** (approximately 12–14 minutes)

INTRODUCE the lesson with the rhyming song.	You are going to learn a rhyming song called "Did You Ever See a Bear in a Chair?" What's the name of the song?
	▶ **Children's response: "Did You Ever See a Bear in a Chair?"**
	I think you may know this one. It's one of my favorite songs. You are going to think about rhyming words when we sing.
TEACH the rhyming song.	Sing with me. It's easy to learn. *Clearly emphasize the rhyming words.*
	Did you ever see a bear in a chair? *(Snap two times.)* Did you ever see a bear in a chair? *(Snap two times.)* No I never, no I never, no I never, no I never, no I never saw a bear in a chair. *(Shake head vigorously, then snap two times.)*
	▶ **(Children sing with you.)**
 **Multisensory Reinforcement**	*Sing the song as many times as time permits. When singing the repetitive parts, leave off the rhyming word at the end so students can predict the rhyme. Make movements to correspond with the words—for example, hold up your hands to show mittens, pretend to drive the truck. Always smile and nod with affirmation as they get it right and continue singing.*
	Did you ever see. . . *Continue the song using the following rhyming pairs:* kittens wearing mittens, a bug in a rug, a duck drive a truck, an ape eat a grape, a goat sail a boat, a cat wear a hat, a mouse build a house.
SING the "Rhyming Exercise Song."	Time to do rhyming words. Does *kittens* rhyme with *mittens?* What do you think?
	▶ **Children's response: Yes.**
Multisensory Reinforcement	Let's do our "Rhyming Exercise Song" to check for rhymes. *Do the movements with the children: Pause and flex your wrists with your palms up.*
	Put your hands in the sky. *On the word* hands, *stretch one arm up to the sky and then the other arm.* Do the rhyming exercise. *As you sing, switch and stretch arms one by one.*

Kittens *(Stretch one arm up.)*
Mittens *(Stretch the other arm up.)*
Kittens *(Switch arms.)*
Mittens *(Switch arms.)*
Kittens *(Switch arms.)*

Do they rhyme? *Pause here and allow them to show thumbs up or down before you respond. Look around at each student and make eye contact.* Yes. *Nod vigorously.* They rhyme. *Give two thumbs up.*

PRACTICE the "Rhyming Exercise Song" again, this time with two nonrhyming words.

Let's do another one. Does *bug* rhyme with *truck?* What do you think?

▶ **Children's response: No.**

Let's do our "Rhyming Exercise Song" to check for rhymes. *Do the movements with the children: Pause and flex your wrists with your palms up.*

Put your hands in the sky. *On the word* hands*, stretch one arm up to the sky and then the other arm.* Do the rhyming exercise. *As you sing, switch and stretch arms one by one.*

Bug *(Stretch one arm up.)*
Truck *(Stretch the other arm up. Show a puzzled expression on your face because the words do not rhyme.)*
Bug *(Switch arms.)*
Truck *(Switch arms. Show a puzzled expression on your face because the words do not rhyme.)*
Bug *(Switch arms.)*
Truck *(Switch arms. Show a puzzled expression on your face because the words do not rhyme.)*

Do they rhyme? *Pause here and allow them to show thumbs up or down. Look around at each student and make eye contact.* No. *Shake your head vigorously.* They don't rhyme. *Show thumbs down.*

PRACTICE the "Rhyming Exercise Song" one last time with two more rhyming words.

Let's do another one. Does *duck* rhyme with *truck?* What do you think?

▶ **Children's response: Yes.**

Sing the song again as you would with two rhyming words.

END the song.

Nice job everyone. Let's get out our cameras. *(Make a camera with your hands and click with your tongue as you take some pictures of students. They do the same.)*
Click. Click. Click. Looking good. *(Thumbs up. Big smile. Nod.)*

 TASK 3   Transition song to end the lesson *(approximately 3 minutes)*

MAKE THE TRANSITION to end the lesson.

You are going to practice the rhyming fingerplay you learned earlier. Can you remember the name? Sit up tall and proud if you remember. *Call on one student.*

▶ **Child's response: "Rock-a-Bye Baby."**

Yes, it's called "Rock-a-Bye Baby." *If the child responds incorrectly, then provide the name of the song.* The name of our rhyming song is "Rock-a-Bye Baby."

SING the song and include the rocking movements with your hands.

Let's get our cradles ready. *Repeat the entire song with the children four times and do the movements with them.*

Rock-a-bye baby in the treetop.
When the wind blows the cradle will rock.
When the bough breaks the cradle will fall.
And down will come baby, cradle and all.

Terrific job singing about the treetop. You are working hard learning your rhymes. Let's give ourselves a pat on the back.

END Lesson 1.

Everyone now gets their winnings for knowing words that rhyme and words that do not rhyme and for working hard. *Give out token rewards to each child.*

LESSON 2: Rhyming Card Sort Game

OBJECTIVES

Student will

• Know how to listen for rhyming words and be able to discriminate between rhyming and nonrhyming words in a card sorting game

Teacher will

• Emphasize the sounds of words that rhyme so students can clearly hear that the endings of rhyming words are the same
• Hold the cards so that each child can see every card sort
• Closely observe each student for focus and full participation
• Ensure that all children win the game

RHYMES, SONGS, AND FINGERPLAYS

"Grandmother's Cap"

MATERIALS

Any cards or objects you have that can be sorted (e.g., colors, animals, fruits)

> **Rhyming Card Sort Game**   CD-ROM
> ☑ Three colored chips per child
> ☑ Game cards (see Appendix D on the CD-ROM)
> ☑ Word List (see Appendix D on the CD-ROM)

 TASK 1   Transition fingerplay to begin the lesson *(approximately 3 minutes)*

INTRODUCE the big idea.

We are going to listen for words that rhyme.

Kiss your brain and remember to think big. *Kiss your palm and place it on your head.* Don't forget that words that rhyme are words that sound the same. What do we call words that sound the same?

▶ **Children's response: Words that rhyme.**

Yes, words that rhyme or rhyming words. Like *cap* and *lap. As you say* cap, *put your right palm out and tilt your head to the right. Do the same on the left side as you say* lap. *Do it with me.*

▶ **(Children respond by doing it with you.)**

Nice job rhyming *cap* and *lap.*

You are going to learn another rhyme. It's called "Grandmother's Cap." What's the name of the rhyme? *Coach the students for the correct response.*

BEGIN the transition.

▶ **Children's response: "Grandmother's Cap."**

My turn. *Say the fingerplay and make up motions that go with the words. This helps the students remember the words. Use exaggerated voice intonation and hand movements.*

These are Grandmother's glasses,
This is Grandmother's cap.
This is the way she folds her hands,
And lays them in her lap.

Your turn. *Repeat the fingerplay and do it with them.*

Nice job saying "Grandmother's Cap." You are learning rhyming words.

When we put something in our lap, where do we put it? Sit up tall and proud if you know. *Call on one or two children; confirm if the answer is correct.*

Follow a two-step approach.

 Vocabulary

LAP

Use instructional moments to improve vocabulary and oral language. Explain vocabulary in a simple way, and have the students repeat back the new word.

We have a lap when we sit down. It is right on top of our legs—like this. *Show them your lap.*

Step 1: Ask children to describe (or act out) the vocabulary word.

Where is your lap?

▶ **(Children respond by showing you their laps.)**

TEACHING TIP: Use the new word with a student's name. This will get students' attention.

Yes, that is your lap.

Step 2: Give students the description and have them supply the word.

Another way of saying I held Mekhi's sister on top of my legs is I held Mekhi's sister on my _____?

▶ **Children's response: Lap.**

Yes, lap. Everyone, I want you all to say, "I held Mekhi's sister on my lap." Get ready.

▶ **Children's response: I held Mekhi's sister on my lap.**

Where did you hold Mekhi's sister?

▶ **Children's respond: On my lap.**

Yes, on your lap.

 TASK 2   **Playing the Rhyming Card Sort Game** (approximately 12–14 minutes)

 Vocabulary

SORT

Explain vocabulary in a simple way.

Before we play our Rhyming Card Sort Game, let's talk about the word *sort*. *Sort* means putting things together that should be together.

Use any cards that can be sorted. We used color cards. Step 1: Allow children to sort cards.

Let's sort the colors. Look at these cards. Put all of the yellow cards in this pile, and put all of the blue cards in this pile. You are sorting the cards into two colors. What are the colors we are sorting?

▶ **Children's response: Yellow and blue.**

Yes, we are sorting yellow and blue. Another way of saying that we will put all of the yellow colors together and all of the blue colors together is saying we will sort the colors.

I want you all to say, "We will sort the colors." Get ready.

▶ **Children's response: We will sort the colors.**

Yes, we will sort the colors.

Step 2: Give students the description and have them supply the words.

What's another way of saying that we will put all of the yellow colors together and all of the blue colors together?

▶ **Children's response: We will sort the colors.**

Yes, we will sort the colors. Nice job learning about the word *sort*.

 PLAY the game.

 CD-ROM See Appendix D on the CD-ROM for the Rhyming Card Sort Game cards, instructions, and word list.

🪐 **TASK 3** Transition fingerplay to end the lesson *(approximately 3 minutes)*

MAKE THE TRANSITION to end the lesson.

You are going to practice the rhyming song you learned earlier. Can you remember the name of the song? Raise your hand if you remember. *Call on a child.*

▶ **Child's response: "Grandmother's Cap."**

Yes, it's called "Grandmother's Cap." Your turn. Everyone, what's the name of the song?

▶ **Children's response: "Grandmother's Cap."**

Eyes on me. Let's sing together. *Repeat fingerplay from beginning of lesson and sing one stanza. Children do the motions with you.*

END Lesson 2.

Everyone now gets their winnings for knowing words that rhyme and words that don't rhyme and for working hard. *Give out token rewards to each child.*

LESSON 3: I Wish that I Had Duck Feet

OBJECTIVES

Student will

*   Know how to listen for rhyming words and be able to discriminate between rhyming and nonrhyming words in an interactive rhyming book by accurately predicting the rhyming word in the story

Teacher will

*   Emphasize the sounds of words that rhyme so students can clearly hear that the endings of rhyming words are the same
*   Hold the book so that each child can see the pictures
*   Closely observe each student for focus and full participation
*   Lead children to participate in the interactive rhyming book by coaching them to accurately predict the rhyming word in the story

RHYMES, SONGS, AND FINGERPLAYS

"Rock-a-Bye Baby"
"Grandmother's Cap"

MATERIALS

Book: *I Wish that I Had Duck Feet* (LeSieg, 1965)
Tokens for behavior/participation

 **TASK 1**   **Transition song to begin the lesson** (approximately 3 minutes)

INTRODUCE the big idea.

We are going to listen for words that rhyme. Words that rhyme are words that sound the same. What do we call words that sound the same?

▶ **Children's response: Words that rhyme.**

Yes, words that rhyme or rhyming words. Like *why* and *dry.* Do it with me. *As you say* why, *put your right palm out and tilt your head to the right. Do the same on the left side as you say* dry.

▶ **(Children respond by doing it with you.)**

Nice job rhyming *why* and *dry.*

BEGIN the transition.

You are going to sing a rhyming song that you already know. It's called "Rock-a-Bye Baby." What's the name of our rhyming song?

▶ **Children's response: "Rock-a-Bye Baby."**

Let's sing "Rock-a-Bye Baby" together. Get ready. *Make rocking motions with your hands.*

 Multisensory Reinforcement

Sing the song four times: first time in a normal voice, second time in a lower voice, third time in a whisper, fourth time in a normal voice. This helps students modulate their tones and listen for changes in sounds, which helps them understand phonemes.

Rock-a-bye baby in the treetop.
When the wind blows the cradle will rock.
When the bough breaks the cradle will fall.
And down will come baby, cradle and all.
But we'll catch you!

Your turn to sing our rhyme. *Repeat the entire rhyme with them and do the movements.*

We will now read a story with rhyming words.

 **TASK 2**   **Listening to a rhyming book** (approximately 12–14 minutes)

INTRODUCE the lesson.

You are going to read a rhyming story with me and listen for some rhyming words. What about *brown* and *town?* Do they rhyme? Do they sound the same?

▶ **Children's response: Yes.**

Yes, *brown* and *town* sound the same. They rhyme. *Give a thumbs up.*

What about *brown* and *play?* Do they rhyme? Do they sound the same? Let's do our "Rhyming Exercise Song" and check it.

SING the "Rhyming Exercise Song."

Put your hands in the sky. *On the word* hands, *stretch one arm up to the sky and then the other arm. As you sing, switch and stretch arms one by one.* Do the rhyming exercise.

 Multisensory Reinforcement

Brown *(Stretch one arm up.)*
Play *(Stretch the other arm up. Show a puzzled expression on your face because the words do not rhyme.)*
Brown *(Switch arms.)*
Play *(Switch arms. Show a puzzled expression on your face because the words do not rhyme.)*

Brown *(Switch arms.)*

Play *(Switch arms. Show a puzzled expression on your face because the words do not rhyme.)*

Do they rhyme? *Pause here and allow them to show thumbs up or down. Look around at each student and make eye contact.* No. *Shake your head vigorously.* They don't rhyme. *Show thumbs down.*

What about *way* and *play?* Do they rhyme? Do they sound the same? Let's do the "Rhyming Exercise Song" and check it. *Do the movements—pause and flex your wrists with your palms up.*

Put your hands in the sky. *On the word hands, stretch one arm up to the sky and then the other arm. As you sing, switch and stretch arms one by one.* Do the rhyming exercise.

Way *(Stretch one arm up.)*
Play *(Stretch the other arm up.)*
Way *(Switch arms.)*
Play *(Switch arms.)*
Way *(Switch arms.)*
Play *(Switch arms.)*

Do they rhyme? *Pause here and allow them to show thumbs up or down. Look around at each student and make eye contact.* Yes. *Nod vigorously.* They rhyme. *Show two thumbs up.*

Pat yourselves on the back for fine rhyming work. *Students pat themselves on the back over the opposite shoulder.*

HOLD up the book and point to the title as you read.

This book has many rhyming words. The title of the book is *I Wish that I Had Duck Feet.* What do you think the story is about?

▶ **Children's response: A boy who wants duck feet.**

Yes. Why do you think the boy wants duck feet? *Call on one or two children for their response.*

Let's read to find out. *Read the book aloud and revisit the predictions.*

TEACHING TIP: Overemphasize the rhymes as you read.

SING the "Rhyming Exercise Song."

 Multisensory Reinforcement

Now let's see if we learned some rhyming words. Let's sing the "Rhyming Exercise Song" to check it out. Get ready. *Do the movements: Pause and flex your wrists with your palms up.*

Put your hands in the sky. *On the word hands, stretch one arm up to the sky and then the other arm. As you sing, switch and stretch arms one by one.* Do the rhyming exercise.

Floor *(Stretch one arm up.)*
Door *(Stretch the other arm up.)*
Floor *(Switch arms.)*
Door *(Switch arms.)*
Floor *(Switch arms.)*

Door *(Switch arms.)*

Do they rhyme? *Pause here and allow them to show thumbs up or down. Look around at each student and make eye contact.* **Yes.** *Nod vigorously.* **They rhyme.** *Show two thumbs up.*

SING the song several times and use the same format.

Use the following word pairs and do as many as time permits: don't/won't, fun/head, fun/one, strings/things, heat/school, heat/feet. Remember, some pairs will rhyme and some will not. Look puzzled and give a thumbs down at the end of the song when the pair does not rhyme. Remember to revisit the prediction.

 TEACHING TIP: Always end with a rhyming word to keep rhyming words in memory and further saturate the students in rhyme.

END the song.

You are working very hard. You are the rhyming kings and queens of _____ school. *Insert name of school.*

🌑 **TASK 3**   Transition fingerplay to end the lesson *(approximately 3 minutes)*

MAKE THE TRANSITION to end the lesson.

You are going to practice the rhyming fingerplay you learned before. The name of the fingerplay is "Grandmother's Cap."

What is the name of our fingerplay?

▶ **Children's response: "Grandmother's Cap."**

Yes, it's called "Grandmother's Cap." Eyes on me. Let's sing together. *Repeat the fingerplay.*

These are Grandmother's glasses,
This is Grandmother's cap.
This is the way she folds her hands,
And lays them in her lap.

END Lesson 3.

Everyone now gets their winnings for knowing words that rhyme and words that don't rhyme and for working hard. *Give out token rewards to each child.*

LESSON 4: Rhyme Discrimination Review

OBJECTIVES

Student will

- Know how to listen for rhyming words and be able to discriminate between rhyming and nonrhyming words in a card game
- Know how to listen for rhyming words and be able to discriminate between rhyming and nonrhyming words in an interactive rhyming book by accurately predicting the rhyming word in the story

Teacher will

- Emphasize the sounds of words that rhyme so that students can clearly hear that the endings of rhyming words are the same
- Hold the cards so that each child can see every card sort
- Ensure that all children win the game
- Hold the book so that each child can see the pictures
- Lead children to participate in the interactive rhyming book by coaching them to accurately predict the rhyming word in the story
- Closely observe each student for focus and full participation

RHYMES, SONGS, AND FINGERPLAYS

"Grandmother's Cap"

MATERIALS

Book: *I Wish that I Had Duck Feet* (LeSieg, 1965)

☑ DROPP 2 Skill Assessment Checkout (see Appendix B on the CD-ROM)

Rhyming Card Sort Game

☑ Game cards (see Appendix D on the CD-ROM)

☑ Three colored chips per child

☑ Word List (see Appendix D on the CD-ROM)

 TASK 1 | **Transition fingerplay to begin the lesson** (approximately 2 minutes)

INTRODUCE the big idea.	You are going to practice rhymes you learned before.
BEGIN the transition.	Let's sing together. The name of the fingerplay is "Grandmother's Cap." *Repeat the fingerplay.*

What is the name of our fingerplay?

▶ Children's response: "Grandmother's Cap."

Yes, it's called "Grandmother's Cap." Eyes on me. Let's sing together.

These are Grandmother's glasses,
This is Grandmother's cap.
This is the way she folds her hands,
And lays them in her lap.

Nice job singing "Grandmother's Cap." Pat yourselves on the back.

 **TASK 2A** | Reviewing the Rhyming Card Sort Game (approximately 8 minutes)

 PLAY the game. | **CD-ROM** See Appendix D on the CD-ROM for the Rhyming Card Sort Game cards, instructions, and word list.

🌍 **TASK 2B** | Reviewing a rhyming book (approximately 8–9 minutes)

INTRODUCE the lesson.

We're going to read a rhyming story and listen for some rhyming words. What can you tell me about rhyming words? *Give them a hint by tugging on your ear. Pause and allow them to respond.*

▶ **Children's response: They sound the same.**

Yes, rhyming words sound the same.

What about *right* and *night*? Do they rhyme? Do they sound the same?

▶ **Children's response: Yes.**

Yes, *right* and *night* sound the same. They rhyme. *Give a thumbs up.*

What about *did* and *kid*? Do they rhyme? Do they sound the same?

▶ **Children's response: Yes.**

Yes, *did* and *kid* sound the same. They rhyme. *Give a thumbs up.*

What about *hose* and *nose*? Do they rhyme? Do they sound the same?

▶ **Children's response: Yes.**

Yes, *hose* and *nose* sound the same. They rhyme. *Give a thumbs up.*

The title of the book is *I Wish that I Had Duck Feet. Hold up the book and point to the title as you read.* Let's say the title of the book together.

▶ **Children's response: I Wish that I Had Duck Feet.**

Raise your hand if you wish that you had duck feet.

▶ **(Children respond by raising their hands.)**

Describe what you would do with duck feet. *Call on one or two children to respond.*

Good job talking about duck feet. Now I'm ready to read. *Read the book aloud. Read slowly and emphasize rhyming words.*

Touch your ears if you still wish that you had duck feet.

▶ **(Children respond by touching their ears.)**

Tell me how you would use your duck feet. *Call on one or two students to answer the question.*

We will do a sit down cheer for everyone's terrific work today. *Sing to the tune of "Kiss Him Goodbye." Substitute the words "good job." Repeat the cheer.*

END Lesson 4.

Everyone now gets their winnings for knowing words that rhyme and words that don't rhyme and for working hard. *Give out token rewards to each child.*

CD-ROM | The DROPP 2 Skill Assessment Checkout will be completed for each student following this lesson.

ACTIVITY SET 2.2

Lesson Descriptions

Lessons	Sequence of daily activities	◇ Vocabulary
Lesson 1: Rhyming Card Sort Game	Fingerplay for "Five Little Pumpkins" Target: Rhyming Card Sort Game Fingerplay for "Five Little Pumpkins"	Out of sight
Lesson 2: Rhyming Card Sort Game	Song for "This Old Man" Target: Rhyming Card Sort Game Fingerplay for "This Old Man"	
Lesson 3: Tumble Bumble	Song for "Finger Family" Target: Rhyming book—*Tumble Bumble* (Bond, 1996) Song for "Grandmother's Cap"	Jig Full of glee To no avail
Lesson 4: Rhyme Discrimination Review	Fingerplay for "Grandmother's Cap" Target: Rhyming Card Sort Game; rhyming book—*Tumble Bumble* (Bond, 1996)	

Materials Needed

☑ Book: *Tumble Bumble* (Bond, 1996)

☑ Colored chips

☑ Tokens for behavior/participation

☑ DROPP 2 Skill Assessment Checkout (see Appendix B on the CD-ROM)

 CD-ROM

Rhyming Card Sort Game

☑ Game cards (see Appendix D on the CD-ROM)

☑ Word list (see Appendix D on the CD-ROM)

☑ Three colored chips per child

ACTIVITY SET

2.2 10-Day Planner

Day 1	**Lesson 1:** Rhyming Card Sort Game
Day 2	**Lesson 1:** Rhyming Card Sort Game
Day 3	**Lesson 2:** Rhyming Card Sort Game
Day 4	**Lesson 2:** Rhyming Card Sort Game
Day 5	**Lesson 3:** Tumble Bumble
Day 6	**Lesson 3:** Tumble Bumble
Day 7	**Lesson 1:** Rhyme Discrimination Review
Day 8	**Lesson 2:** Rhyming Card Sort Game
Day 9	**Lesson 3:** Tumble Bumble
Day 10	**Lesson 4:** Rhyme Discrimination Review

LESSON 1: Rhyming Card Sort Game

OBJECTIVES

Student will

- Know how to listen for rhyming words and be able to discriminate between rhyming and nonrhyming words in a fingerplay
- Know how to listen for rhyming words and be able to discriminate between rhyming and nonrhyming words in a card sorting game

Teacher will

- Emphasize the sounds of words that rhyme so students can clearly hear that the endings of rhyming words are the same
- Hold the cards so that each child can see every card sort
- Closely observe each student for focus and full participation
- Smile and ensure success for all children
- Ensure that all children win the game

RHYMES, SONGS, AND FINGERPLAYS

"Five Little Pumpkins"

MATERIALS

Tokens for behavior/participation

Rhyming Card Sort Game
- ☑ Game cards (see Appendix D on the CD-ROM)
- ☑ Word list (see Appendix D on the CD-ROM)

 TASK 1   Transition fingerplay to begin the lesson (approximately 3 minutes)

INTRODUCE the big idea.

Say the following to the group after calling the students together at a table. We are going to listen for words that rhyme. Don't forget, words that rhyme are words that sound the same. What do we call words that sound the same?

▶ Children's response: Words that rhyme.

Yes, words that rhyme or rhyming words. Like *gate* and *late*. *As you say* gate, *put out your right palm and tilt your head to the right. Do the same on the left side as you say* late. Do it with me.

▶ (Children respond by doing it with you.)

Nice job rhyming *gate* and *late*.

BEGIN the transition.

You are going to learn a rhyming fingerplay called "Five Little Pumpkins." What's the name of our rhyming song?

▶ Children's response: "Five Little Pumpkins."

Yes, "Five Little Pumpkins." My turn to say "Five Little Pumpkins." Watch what I do with my hands. *Put out your hand palm down and place your other hand upright on top with fingers extended.*

TEACHING TIP: Use drama to increase memory. Be very animated.

 **Model the Activity**

Five little pumpkins sitting on a gate. *(Wiggle fingers.)*
The first one says, my it's getting late. *(One finger talks.)*
The second one says, there are witches in the air. *(Look around and be scared.)*
The third one says, we don't care. *(Move shoulders and sound sassy.)*
The fourth one says, let's run, let's run. *(Hopeful voice.)*
The fifth one says, isn't Halloween fun? *(Smile and nod.)*
Ooooo, went the wind. *(Cup your mouth with both hands.)*

Out went the light. *(Clap.)*

Those five little pumpkins rolled quickly out of sight. *(Make rolling motions with your fists and hide hands behind back.)*

Everyone, let's do "Five Little Pumpkins" together. Get ready.

▶ **Children's response:**

Five little pumpkins sitting on a gate. *(Wiggle fingers.)*

The first one says, my it's getting late. *(One finger talks.)*

The second one says, there are witches in the air. *(Look around and be scared.)*

The third one says, we don't care. *(Move shoulders and sound sassy.)*

The fourth one says, let's run, let's run. *(Hopeful voice.)*

The fifth one says, isn't Halloween fun? *(Smile and nod.)*

Ooooo, went the wind. *(Cup your mouth.)*

Out went the light. *(Clap.)*

Those five little pumpkins rolled quickly out of sight. *(Make rolling motions with your fists and hide hands behind back.)*

Your turn to say our rhyme. *Repeat the entire song with them and do the movements.*

▶ **(Children respond.)**

Very good job using our voices and our rhymes singing "Five Little Pumpkins."

Follow a two-step approach.

We said our pumpkins rolled out of sight. When they rolled out of our sight, that means we couldn't see them anymore. Touch the place that gives us sight, or helps us see.

▶ **(Children touch their eyes.)**

Yes, we see with our eyes. We call this our eyesight. Say, we see with our eyes.

▶ **Children's response: We see with our eyes.**

Yes, we see with our eyes. This is called our eyesight.

Step 1: Ask children to describe the vocabulary word. Describe *eyesight. Call on one or two students.* Yes, your eyesight is when you see with your eyes.

When our pumpkins rolled out of sight, they went and hid. *Make rolling motions with your fists and hide hands behind back.* They rolled somewhere so no one could find them or see them. They went out of our eyesight or out of sight. *Touch your eyes.* Let's everyone show how our pumpkins rolled out of sight.

▶ **(Children respond with the rolling hand motion.)**

I am going to go out of sight right now. *Hide nearby so the students cannot see you.* Can you see me?

▶ **Children's response: No, we can't see you.**

Pop up. That's because I was out of sight. Where was I?

▶ **Children's response: You were out of sight.**

Step 2: Give students the description and have them supply the word.

✧ **Vocabulary**

OUT OF SIGHT

Use instructional moments to improve vocabulary and oral language. Always explain vocabulary in a simple way, and have the students repeat back the word or phrase.

99

TEACHING TIP: Use the new word in a sentence using your students' names. This always gets their attention.

Yes, I was out of sight. Just like those little pumpkins. Jabel, will you go out of sight? *Ask student to hide.* Everyone, where is Jabel?

▶ **Children's response: Jabel is out of sight.**

Yes, Jabel is out of sight. *Repeat the model with another student.*

Good job going out of sight. We will get ready for a fun rhyme. Now it's time to put your hand in your pocket and take out your magic wand. *(Reach across your body in an exaggerated manner, put your hand in your pocket, and pull out your imaginary wand.)*

Hocus, pocus. *(Wave your wand back and forth in the air.)*

Time to focus. *(Take the index fingers and thumbs of both hands and make eye-glasses on your face.)*

 TASK 2   **Rhyming Card Sort Game** (approximately 12–14 minutes)

◇ **Vocabulary**

SORT

Who remembers what sort out the rhyming cards means? Touch your right shoulder if you remember. *Call on one student.*

▶ **Child's response: To put the rhymes together.**

Explain vocabulary in a simple way and have the students repeat back the new word.

Yes, sort out the rhyming cards means to put the rhymes together. You will sort out the rhymes and put them together. Everyone, tell me another way of saying you will put the rhyming cards together?

▶ **Children's response: We will sort out the rhyming cards.**

TEACHING TIP: Use the new word with a student's name. This will get students' attention.

Yes, you will sort out the rhyming cards. Aallayah can sort out the rhyming cards. Let's all say that together.

▶ **Children's response: Aallayah can sort out the rhyming cards.**

Yes, Aallayah can sort out the rhyming cards. Can someone think of another sentence using the word *sort?* Touch your left shoulder if you know. *Call on one student.*

▶ **(Child responds with a sentence.)**

Great job using the word *sort.* Let's play the Rhyming Card Sort Game.

♣ **PLAY** the game.

CD-ROM   See Appendix D on the CD-ROM for the Rhyming Card Sort Game cards, instructions, and word list.

Your rhyming work was so good today. We are going to sing the "Give Me a Snap" song. *Sing to the tune of* The Addams Family *theme song.*

Give me a snap. *(Snap twice.)*

Give me a snap. *(Snap twice.)*

Give me a snap, give me a snap, give me a snap. *(Snap twice.)*

Repeat the tune but say, "Give me a cheer." Say "Hooray!" once instead of snapping twice.

Give me a cheer. Hooray!

 TASK 3   Transition fingerplay to end the lesson *(approximately 3 minutes)*

MAKE THE TRANSITION to end the lesson.	You are going to practice the rhyming fingerplay you learned earlier. What's the name of our fingerplay?
	▶ **Children's response: "Five Little Pumpkins."**
	Yes, it's called "Five Little Pumpkins."
SAY the rhyme and include the movements.	Let's get our pumpkins ready on our gate. *Repeat the entire rhyme with them and do the movements.*
	Five little pumpkins sitting on a gate. *(Wiggle fingers.)*
	The first one says, my it's getting late. *(One finger talks.)*
	The second one says, there are witches in the air. *(Look around and be scared.)*
	The third one says, we don't care. *(Move shoulders and sound sassy.)*
	The fourth one says, let's run, let's run. *(Hopeful voice.)*
	The fifth one says, isn't Halloween fun? *(Smile and nod.)*
	Ooooo, went the wind. *(Cup your mouth with both hands.)*
	Out went the light. *(Clap.)*
	Those five little pumpkins rolled quickly out of sight. *(Make rolling motions with your fists and hide hands behind back.)*
END Lesson 1.	Everyone now gets their winnings for knowing words that rhyme and words that don't rhyme and for working hard. *Give out token rewards to each child.*

LESSON 2: Rhyming Card Sort Game

OBJECTIVES

Student will

- Know how to listen for rhyming words and be able to discriminate between rhyming and nonrhyming words in a song with movement
- Know how to listen for rhyming words and be able to discriminate between rhyming and nonrhyming words in a card sorting game

Teacher will

- Emphasize the sounds of words that rhyme so students can clearly hear that the endings of rhyming words are the same
- Hold the cards so that each child can see every card sort
- Closely observe each student for focus and full participation
- Ensure that all children win the game

RHYMES, SONGS, AND FINGERPLAYS

"This Old Man"

MATERIALS

Tokens for behavior/participation

> **Rhyming Card Sort Game**
> ☑ Game cards (see Appendix D on the CD-ROM)
> ☑ Word list (see Appendix D on the CD-ROM)
>
> CD-ROM

TASK 1   Transition song to begin the lesson (approximately 3 minutes)

INTRODUCE the big idea.

We are going to listen for words that rhyme. Kiss your brain and remember to think big. *Kiss your palm and place it on your head.* Don't forget, words that rhyme are words that sound the same. What do we call words that sound the same?

▶ Children's response: Words that rhyme.

Yes, words that rhyme or rhyming words. Like *one* and *fun.* Do it with me. *As you say* one, *put your right palm out and tilt your head to the right. Do the same on the left side as you say* fun.

▶ (Children respond by doing it with you.)

Nice job rhyming *one* and *fun.* Let's try *two* and *shoe.* Do it with me. *As you say* two, *put your right palm out and tilt your head to the right. Do the same on the left side as you say* shoe.

▶ (Children respond by doing it with you.)

Nice job rhyming *two* and *shoe.*

You are going to learn another rhyming song. It's called "This Old Man." What's the name of the song?

▶ Children's response: "This Old Man."

BEGIN the transition.

Sing the song and make up motions that go with the words. This helps the students remember the words. Use exaggerated voice intonation and movements.

 Turn On Your Ears

 Model the Activity

My turn. Get ready to listen. It's a funny song.
This old man, he plays one,
He plays knick-knack just for fun.
With a knick-knack, paddy-whack, give your dog a bone.
This old man uses his cell phone.
This old man, he plays two,
He plays knick-knack on his shoe.
With a knick-knack, paddy-whack, give your dog a bone.
This old man uses his cell phone.
This old man, he plays three,
He plays knick-knack on his knee.
With a knick-knack, paddy-whack, give your dog a bone.
This old man uses his cell phone.
This old man, he plays four,
He plays knick-knack on the floor.
With a knick-knack, paddy-whack, give your dog a bone.
This old man uses his cell phone.

Your turn. Everyone stand up and sing with me. *Repeat the rhyme and do it with them.*

▶ Children's response:
This old man, he plays one,
He plays knick-knack just for fun.
With a knick-knack, paddy-whack, give your dog a bone.
This old man uses his cell phone.
This old man, he plays two,
He plays knick-knack on his shoe.
With a knick-knack, paddy-whack, give your dog a bone.
This old man uses his cell phone.
This old man, he plays three,
He plays knick-knack on his knee.

With a knick-knack, paddy-whack, give your dog a bone.
This old man uses his cell phone.
This old man, he plays four,
He plays knick-knack on the floor.
With a knick-knack, paddy-whack, give your dog a bone.
This old man uses his cell phone.

Nice job singing and moving to "This Old Man." You are learning rhyming words. Everyone go back to your seats.

 TASK 2 **Playing the Rhyming Card Sort Game** (approximately 12–14 minutes)

 PLAY the game.

> **CD-ROM** See Appendix D on the CD-ROM for the Rhyming Card Sort Game cards, instructions, and word list.

Excellent singing. Let's give ourselves a snap, crackle, pop. Do it with me.
Snap! *(Snap fingers once.)*
Crackle! *(Rub hands together quickly.)*
Pop! *(Clap hands once hard and quickly. Jet out hands with palms forward and fingers splayed.)*

 TASK 3 **Transition fingerplay to end the lesson** (approximately 3 minutes)

MAKE THE TRANSITION
to end the lesson.

You are going to practice the rhyming song you learned earlier. Everyone, what was the name of our rhyming song? *Prompt for correct response.*

▶ **Children's response: "This Old Man."**

Yes, "This Old Man." Let's stand and do it together. *Repeat song and movements from beginning of lesson.*

This old man, he plays one,
He plays knick-knack just for fun.
With a knick-knack, paddy-whack, give your dog a bone.
This old man uses his cell phone.
This old man, he plays two,
He plays knick-knack on his shoe.
With a knick-knack, paddy-whack, give your dog a bone.
This old man uses his cell phone.
This old man, he plays three,
He plays knick-knack on his knee.
With a knick-knack, paddy-whack, give your dog a bone.
This old man uses his cell phone.
This old man, he plays four,
He plays knick-knack on the floor.
With a knick-knack, paddy-whack, give your dog a bone.
This old man uses his cell phone.

 Turn On Your Ears

My turn. Listen to our "Have a Seat Song" as you go back to your seat. *Sing to the tune of "Shortnin' Bread."*

Everybody have a seat, have a seat, have a seat.

Everybody have a seat on your chair.

Not on the ceiling.

Not in the air.

Everybody have a seat on your chair.

▶ **(Children respond by going back to their seats.)**

Your turn to sing with me. *Sing with them as students are in their seats.*

▶ **Children's response:**

Everybody have a seat, have a seat, have a seat.

Everybody have a seat on your chair.

Not on the ceiling.

Not in the air.

Everybody have a seat on your chair.

| **END** Lesson 2. | Everyone now gets their winnings for knowing words that rhyme and words that don't rhyme and for working hard. *Give out token rewards to each child.* |

LESSON 3: Tumble Bumble

OBJECTIVES

Student will

- Know how to listen for rhyming words and be able to discriminate between rhyming and nonrhyming words in a fingerplay
- Know how to listen for rhyming words and be able to discriminate between rhyming and nonrhyming words in an interactive rhyming book by accurately predicting the rhyming word in the story

Teacher will

- Emphasize the sounds of words that rhyme so students can clearly hear that the endings of rhyming words are the same
- Hold the book so that each child can see the pictures
- Closely observe each student for focus and full participation
- Lead children to participate in the interactive rhyming book by coaching them to accurately predict the rhyming word in the story

RHYMES, SONGS, AND FINGERPLAYS

"Finger Family"

"Grandmother's Cap"

MATERIALS

Book: *Tumble Bumble* (Bond, 1996)

Tokens for behavior/participation

 TASK 1   Transition fingerplay to begin the lesson *(approximately 3 minutes)*

| **INTRODUCE** the big idea. | We are going to listen for words that rhyme. Don't forget, words that rhyme are words that sound the same. What do we call words that sound the same?

▶ **Children's response: Words that rhyme.**

Yes, words that rhyme or rhyming words. Like *all* and *small*. Do it with me. *As you say* all, *put out your right palm and tilt your head to the right. Do the same on the left side as you say* small.

▶ **(Children respond by doing it with you.)** |

BEGIN the transition.

Nice job rhyming *all* and *small.*

You are going to practice a rhyming fingerplay you all know and love. The name of our fingerplay is "Finger Family." Tell me the name of our fingerplay. *Guide for the correct response.*

▶ **Children's response: "Finger Family."**

Multisensory Reinforcement

Say the rhyme with them and do the finger movements. Use your fingers and voices for family members. Yes, it's called "Finger Family." Eyes on me. Let's sing together.

This is the Mama, kind and gentle,
Loving all the children dear.
This is the Papa, strong and faithful,
His bright smile is full of cheer.
This is the brother, full of mischief,
Growing up so straight and tall.
This is the sister, always happy,
Playing with her favorite doll.
This wee finger is the baby,
Dearest, sweetest, best of all.
Here you see the happy family,
All its members great and small.

Nice job saying "Finger Family." You are working very hard learning your rhymes.

Let's do our good job dance. *Sing to the tune of "Stayin' Alive," and substitute the words "we did a good job, we did a good job." Extend your right index finger in the air to the right of your body. Put your left hand on your hip. Move your right finger from the air to your other side as you sing.*

We will now read a story with rhyming words.

TASK 2　　**Listening to a rhyming book** (approximately 12–14 minutes)

INTRODUCE the lesson.

You are going to read a rhyming story with me and listen for some rhyming words. What about *glee* and *bee?* Do they rhyme? Do they sound the same?

▶ **Children's response: Yes.**

Yes, *glee* and *bee* sound the same. They rhyme. *Give a thumbs up.*

What about *jig* and *pig?* Do they rhyme? Do they sound the same?

▶ **Children's response: Yes.**

Yes, *jig* and *pig* sound the same. They rhyme. *Give a thumbs up.*

This book has many rhyming words. The title of the book is *Tumble Bumble. Hold up the book and point to the title as you read.* What do you think the story is about? Take a look at the picture on the cover. What kinds of animals can you see from the window?

▶ **(Children respond by naming the different animals.)**

Tell me about what the boy is thinking. *Call on one or two children for responses.*

Let's read to find out. *Read the book aloud.*

2.2

LESSON 3

TEACHING TIP: Overemphasize the rhymes as you read.

 Vocabulary

JIG

Explain vocabulary in a simple way, and have the students repeat back the new word.

Follow a two-step approach. Stand up and dance a silly little happy dance like the story. I am dancing a silly little dance because I'm happy. This silly little happy dance is called a jig. Everyone, when we do a silly little happy dance, what do we call it?

▶ **Children's response: It is called a jig.**

Step 1: Ask children to describe (or act out) the new word. Stand up and dance a jig.

▶ **(Children respond by standing and dancing for about 10 seconds.)**

Step 2: Give students the description and have them supply the word. We are dancing a jig just like the pig in *Tumble Bumble.* He was a happy pig. What's another way of saying Taleaha's sister was dancing a silly little dance?

TEACHING TIP: Use the new word with a student's name. This will get their attention.

Vocabulary

TO NO AVAIL

▶ **Children's response: Taleaha's sister was dancing a jig.**

Yes, Taleaha's sister was dancing a jig. Everyone, good job dancing a jig. Please be seated. You all danced a great jig—just like the pig.

Follow the same two-step approach as used with previous vocabulary word. Show students the picture on the page described below where the pig is crying.

In the book, the crocodile, cat, ant, and bee all stepped on the pig's tail while they were dancing a jig. They all said, "sorry," or apologized, but the pig kept on crying. Why did the pig keep crying? *Prompt for this response.*

▶ **Children's response: Because it hurt.**

So, even though all of the friends said, "sorry," or apologized, the pig's tail still hurt. Do you think they meant to step on his tail? *Prompt for this response.*

▶ **Children's response: No.**

Describe how you know that. *Call on one or two students.*

Yes, they were dancing a happy jig, so they really did not mean to step on his tail. So even though they did not mean to do it and they said, "sorry," or apologized, the pig kept on crying because his tail still hurt. That's what *to no avail* means. It means nothing helped because the poor pig's tail still really hurt. *Read from the book.* "Oink," he squealed. "That was my tail. They apologized to no avail." How did they apologize?

▶ **Children's response: To no avail.**

Yes, to no avail. *Prompt for this response.*

Yes, I apologized to no avail. Terrific job learning to say to no avail.

Follow the same two-step approach as used with previous two vocabulary words. Smile wide with glee and have the students mimic you.

<table>
<tr><td>

✧ **Vocabulary**

FULL OF GLEE

</td><td>

When we grin or smile with glee, it means we are full of happy or full of happiness. *Glee* means happy. Everyone, smile with glee. When are you full of glee? Sit up tall and proud if you can describe a time when you were full of glee.

Call on one or two students and use the same format for each. I was full of glee when . . . *You start the sentence. He or she repeats what you say and finishes it. Prompt with a broad smile.*

▶ **Child's response: I was full of glee when _____ (appropriate response).**

Yes, _____ *(student's name)* was full of glee when *(say whatever he or she says).*

Show me you are full of glee now. *Students all smile broadly.* What's another way of saying you are all full of being happy or full of happiness?

▶ **Children's response: We are full of glee.**

</td></tr>
</table>

SING the "Rhyming Exercise Song."

 Multisensory Reinforcement

Yes, we are all full of glee. Great job learning how to be full of glee. Now let's see if we learned some rhyming words. Let's sing the "Rhyming Exercise Song" to check it out. Follow me. Put your hands in the sky. *Stretch one arm up to the sky, then the other arm, on the word hands.* Do the rhyming exercise.

Bed *(Stretch one arm up as you say the word.)*
Head *(Stretch the other arm up.)*
Bed *(Switch arms.)*
Head *(Switch arms.)*
Bed *(Switch arms.)*
Head *(Switch arms.)*

Do they rhyme? *(Pause here and allow them to show thumbs up or down before you respond. Look around at each student and make eye contact.)* **Yes.** *(Nod vigorously.)* **They rhyme.** *(Give two thumbs up.)*

Sing the song several times and use the same format. Remember, some pairs will rhyme and some will not. Look puzzled and give a thumbs down at the end of the song when the pair does not rhyme. Use these words and do as many as time permits: tumble/jumble, song/mouse, song/along, friends/ends, big/well, well/bell.

TEACHING TIP: Always end with a rhyming word to keep rhyming words in memory and further saturate the students in rhyme.

END the song.

You are working very hard. You are the rhyming stars of _____ school. *(Insert name of school.)*

🪐 **TASK 3** Transition fingerplay to end the lesson *(approximately 3 minutes)*

MAKE THE TRANSITION to end the lesson.

You are going to practice the rhyming fingerplay you learned before. The name of the fingerplay is "Grandmother's Cap." What is the name of our fingerplay?

▶ **Children's response: "Grandmother's Cap."**

Yes, it's called "Grandmother's Cap." Eyes on me. Let's sing together. *Repeat the fingerplay.*

These are Grandmother's glasses,

This is Grandmother's cap.
This is the way she folds her hands,
And lays them in her lap.

We will do a sit down cheer for everyone's terrific work today. *Sing to the tune of "Kiss Him Goodbye." Substitute the words "good job." Repeat the cheer.*

END Lesson 3.

Everyone now gets their winnings for knowing words that rhyme and words that don't rhyme and for working hard. *Give out token rewards to each child.*

LESSON 4: Rhyme Discrimination Review

OBJECTIVES

Student will

- Know how to listen for rhyming words and be able to discriminate between rhyming and nonrhyming words in a fingerplay
- Know how to listen for rhyming words and be able to discriminate between rhyming and nonrhyming words in a card sorting game
- Know how to listen for rhyming words and be able to discriminate between rhyming and nonrhyming words in a song with movement
- Know how to listen for rhyming words and be able to discriminate between rhyming and nonrhyming words in an interactive rhyming book by accurately predicting the rhyming word in the story

Teacher will

- Emphasize the sounds of words that rhyme so students can clearly hear that the endings of rhyming words are the same
- Hold the cards so that each child can see every card sort
- Ensure that all children win the game
- Hold the book so that each child can see the pictures
- Lead children to participate in the interactive rhyming book by coaching them to accurately predict the rhyming word in the story
- Closely observe each student for focus and full participation

RHYMES, SONGS, AND FINGERPLAYS

"Grandmother's Cap"

MATERIALS

Book: *Tumble Bumble* (Bond, 1996)
Colored chips
Tokens for behavior/participation

☑ DROPP 2 Skill Assessment Checkout (see Appendix B on the CD-ROM) **CD-ROM**

Rhyming Card Sort Game

☑ Game cards (see Appendix D on the CD-ROM)

☑ Three colored chips per child

☑ Word list

 TASK 1   Transition fingerplay to begin the lesson *(approximately 2 minutes)*

INTRODUCE the big idea.

BEGIN the transition.

You are going to practice rhymes you learned before.

Let's sing together. The name of the fingerplay is "Grandmother's Cap." What is the name of our fingerplay?

▶ Children's response: "Grandmother's Cap."

Yes, it's called "Grandmother's Cap." Eyes on me. Let's sing together. *Repeat the fingerplay.*

These are Grandmother's glasses,
This is Grandmother's cap.
This is the way she folds her hands,

And lays them in her lap.

Nice job singing "Grandmother's Cap." Pat yourselves on the back.

 **TASK 2A**   Reviewing the Rhyming Card Sort Game (approximately 9 minutes)

 PLAY the game.

 CD-ROM   See Appendix D on the CD-ROM for the Rhyming Card Sort Game cards, instructions, and word list.

 **TASK 2B**   Reviewing a rhyming book (approximately 5 minutes)

INTRODUCE the lesson.

You are going to read a rhyming story with me and listen for some rhyming words. What about *glee* and *bee?* Do they rhyme? Do they sound the same?

▶ **Children's response: Yes.**

Yes, *glee* and *bee* sound the same. They rhyme. *Give a thumbs up.*

What about *jig* and *pig?* Do they rhyme? Do they sound the same?

▶ **Children's response: Yes.**

Yes, *jig* and *pig* sound the same. They rhyme. *Give a thumbs up.*

This book has many rhyming words. The title of the book is *Tumble Bumble.* *Hold up the book and point to the title as you read.* Who can describe what the story is about? *Call on one or two children for responses.* Let's read to see if you are right. *Read the book aloud.*

TEACHING TIP: Overemphasize the rhymes as you read.

 **TASK 2C**   A rhyming book game (approximately 3 minutes)

INTRODUCE the game.

That was fun. Can anyone remember any of the rhymes from *Tumble Bumble?* You can earn one point if you remember a rhyme. You only need one point to win. Touch your eyebrow if you remember any rhymes. *Call on individual students.*

▶ **(Children respond with a remembered rhyme.)**

Prompt their memory. Yes, _____ rhymes with _____. Point. *Give a chip.* Winner.

If necessary, turn to a rhyming page in the book, show the picture, read the passage, and leave off the last rhyming word.

▶ **(Child responds with the rhyming words.)**

Yes, _____ rhymes with ____. Point. *Give a chip.* Winner.

*****Correction procedure:* If students cannot remember or predict a rhyme, then give them a rhyming pair from the story.*

2.2

LESSON 4

Prompt for the rhyme. What about _____ and _____? Do they rhyme? Give me a thumbs up if they rhyme.

▶ **(Child responds with a thumbs up.)**

If students say two words that do not rhyme, then give a thumbs down.

Tell me a word that rhymes with *tumble*.

▶ **Child's response: Bumble.**

Yes, *tumble* rhymes with *bumble*. Let's try another. *Give them two new rhyming words.* What about *pig* and *jig?* Do they rhyme? Do they sound the same? Give me a thumbs up if they rhyme.

▶ **(Child responds with a thumbs up.)**

Repeat until everyone wins. Prompt for the rhyme, if needed. *
That was fun. Blow the whistle if you liked hearing and saying the rhyming words.

▶ **(Children respond with a "Whoo! Whoo!" as they pull an imaginary train whistle.)**

END Lesson 4.

Everyone now gets their winnings for knowing words that rhyme and words that don't rhyme and for working hard. *Give out token rewards to each child.*

The DROPP 2 Skill Assessment Checkout will be completed for each student following this lesson.

ACTIVITY SET 2.3

Lesson Descriptions

Lessons	Sequence of daily activities	◇ Vocabulary
Lesson 1: Rhyming Pictures Game	Song for "Pat-a-cake" Target: Rhyming Pictures Game Song for "Pat-a-cake"	
Lesson 2: Rhyming Pictures Game	Song for "Jack and Jill" Target: Rhyming Pictures Game Song for "Jack and Jill"	Fetch Crown
Lesson 3: I Can't Said the Ant	Song for "One, Two, Buckle My Shoe" Target: Rhyming book—*I Can't Said the Ant* (Cameron, 1965) Song for "This Old Man"	
Lesson 4: Rhyme Discrimination Review	Song for "This Old Man" Target: Rhyming Pictures Game; rhyming book—*I Can't Said the Ant* (Cameron, 1965)	

Materials Needed

☑ Book containing "One, Two, Buckle My Shoe" with pictures (e.g., Baker, 1994)

☑ Book: *I Can't Said the Ant* (Cameron, 1965)

☑ Tokens for behavior/participation

> ☑ DROPP 2 Skill Assessment Checkout (see Appendix B on the CD-ROM) **CD-ROM**
>
> **Rhyming Pictures Game**
>
> ☑ Game cards (see Appendix D on the CD-ROM)
>
> ☑ Word list (see Appendix D on the CD-ROM)
>
> ☑ Three colored chips per child

ACTIVITY SET

2.3 10-Day Planner

Day 1	**Lesson 1:** Rhyming Pictures Game
Day 2	**Lesson 1:** Rhyming Pictures Game
Day 3	**Lesson 2:** Rhyming Pictures Game
Day 4	**Lesson 2:** Rhyming Pictures Game
Day 5	**Lesson 3:** I Can't Said the Ant
Day 6	**Lesson 3:** I Can't Said the Ant
Day 7	**Lesson 1:** Rhyming Pictures Game
Day 8	**Lesson 2:** Rhyming Pictures Game
Day 9	**Lesson 3:** I Can't Said the Ant
Day 10	**Lesson 4:** Rhyme Discrimination Review

LESSON 1: Rhyming Pictures Game

OBJECTIVES

Student will

- Know how to listen for rhyming words and be able to discriminate between rhyming and nonrhyming words in a song with movements
- Know how to listen for rhyming words and be able to discriminate between rhyming and nonrhyming words in a rhyming picture game

Teacher will

- Emphasize the sounds of words that rhyme so students can clearly hear that the endings of rhyming words are the same
- Hold the cards so that each child can see every rhyming picture card
- Closely observe each student for focus and full participation
- Smile and ensure success for all children
- Ensure that all children win the game

RHYMES, SONGS, AND FINGERPLAYS

"Pat-a-cake"

MATERIALS

Tokens for behavior/participation

Rhyming Pictures Game

- ☑ Game cards (see Appendix D on the CD-ROM)
- ☑ Word list (see Appendix D on the CD-ROM)
- ☑ Three colored chips per child

🪐 **TASK 1** Transition song to begin the lesson (approximately 3 minutes)

INTRODUCE the big idea.

Say the following to the group after calling the students together at a table. We are going to listen for words that rhyme. Let's remember to think big today. Kiss your brain before we start. *Kiss your palm and place it on your head.* Don't forget, words that rhyme are words that sound the same. What do we call words that sound the same?

▶ Children's response: Words that rhyme.

Yes, words that rhyme or rhyming words. Like *man* and *can*. *As you say* man, *put out your right palm and tilt your head to the right. Do the same on the left side as you say* can. Do it with me.

▶ (Children respond by doing it with you.)

Nice job rhyming *man* and *can*.

You are going to learn a rhyming song that you will like very much. It's called "Pat-a-cake." What's the name of our rhyming song?

BEGIN the transition.

▶ Children's response: "Pat-a-cake."

✳ **Model the Activity**

Yes, "Pat-a-cake." My turn to say "Pat-a-cake." Watch what I do with my hands. *Pick one student to demonstrate with you the classic movements to this rhyme.*

✋ **Multisensory Reinforcement**

Pat-a-cake, Pat-a-cake, baker's man.
Bake me a cake as fast as you can.
Pat it, roll it, and mark it with a "B."
And put it in the oven for baby and me.

TEACHING TIP: Use drama to increase memory. Be very animated.

Put the students in pairs, practice the movements slowly, and check each pair.

Let's practice first. Hit, clap. Hit, clap. Hit, clap. Hit, clap. Hit, clap. Hit, clap. Hit, clap. *You may have to do the rhyme with each child separately because the criss-cross hand motions are usually difficult for young 4-year-olds.*

Now let's say the words and do "Pat-a-cake" together. Start with hit, clap. Get ready to say our rhyme. *Say the rhyme and do it together.*

▶ Children's response:
Pat-a-cake, Pat-a-cake, baker's man.
Bake me a cake as fast as you can.
Pat it, roll it, and mark it with a "B."
And put it in the oven for baby and me.

Good job using your hands, voices, and rhymes saying "Pat-a-cake."

 TASK 2

Rhyming Pictures Game (approximately 12–14 minutes)

 PLAY the game.

 CD-ROM See Appendix D on the CD-ROM for the Rhyming Pictures Game cards, instructions, and word list.

Your rhyming work was so good today. We are going to sing the "Give Me a Snap" song. *Sing to the tune of* The Addams Family *theme song. Snap twice after the words.*

Give me a snap. *(Snap twice.)*
Give me a snap. *(Snap twice.)*
Give me a snap, give me a snap, give me a snap. *(Snap twice.)*

Give me a cheer. Hooray! *Repeat the tune but say, "Give me a cheer." Say "Hooray!" once instead of snapping twice.*

 TASK 3

Transition song to end the lesson (approximately 3 minutes)

MAKE THE TRANSITION to end the lesson.

You are going to practice the rhyming song you learned earlier. Everyone, what's the name of our rhyme?

▶ Children respond: "Pat-a-cake."

Yes, it's called "Pat-a-cake."

You are going to practice "Pat-a-cake." How do we get ready? Get with your partner and get ready.

Start with hit, clap, hit, clap, hit, clap, hit, clap, hit, clap. Let's start now. *Say the rhyme and include the classic movements.*

▶ Children respond: Pat-a-cake, Pat-a-cake, baker's man.
Bake me a cake as fast as you can.
Pat it, roll it, and mark it with a "B."
And put it in the oven for baby and me.

Let's do "Pat-a-cake" again. *Repeat the entire rhyme and do the movements. Continue to work separately with those children who have trouble with the crisscross hand motions.*

TASK 3 *(continued)*

✱ **Model the Activity**	Your rhyming work was so good today. You deserve fireworks. Watch me first. *(Hold palms together in front as if praying.)* Sssssss. *(Wiggle your palms up in the air in front of you like a firecracker going off.)* AHHHHHHH! *(Clap them above your head. Wiggle your fingers around and down like the sparkles coming from a firecracker.)* Let's give ourselves fireworks together. Do it with me. *(Repeat.)*
END Lesson 1.	Everyone now gets their winnings for knowing words that rhyme and words that don't rhyme and for working hard. *Give out token rewards to each child.*

LESSON 2: Rhyming Pictures Game

OBJECTIVES

Student will

- Know how to listen for rhyming words and be able to discriminate between rhyming and nonrhyming words in a nursery rhyme
- Know how to listen for rhyming words and be able to discriminate between rhyming and nonrhyming words in a rhyming picture game

Teacher will

- Emphasize the sounds of words that rhyme so students can clearly hear that the endings of rhyming words are the same
- Hold the cards so that each child can see every rhyming picture card
- Closely observe each student for focus and full participation
- Ensure that all children win the game

RHYMES, SONGS, AND FINGERPLAYS

"Jack and Jill"

MATERIALS

Tokens for behavior/participation

> **Rhyming Pictures Game**
> ☑ Game cards (see Appendix D on the CD-ROM)
> ☑ Word list (see Appendix D on the CD-ROM)
> ☑ Three colored chips per child

🪐 **TASK 1** Transition song to begin the lesson *(approximately 3 minutes)*

INTRODUCE the big idea.	We are going to listen for words that rhyme. Let's put on our special magic glasses *(make circles with your fingers)* so we can see our rhyming pictures and listen for our rhyming words. What do we call words that sound the same? ▶ **Children's response: Words that rhyme.** Yes, words that rhyme or rhyming words. Like *Jill* and *hill*. *As you say* Jill, *put your right palm out and tilt your head to the right. Do the same on the left side as you say* hill. *Do it with me.* ▶ **(Children respond by doing it with you.)** Nice job rhyming *Jill* and *hill*.
BEGIN the transition.	You are going to learn another nursery rhyme. It's called "Jack and Jill." What's the name of the nursery rhyme? ▶ **Children's response: "Jack and Jill."**
◇ **Vocabulary** **NURSERY**	Who remembers what *nursery* means? *Prompt for the word.* What is a nursery? Touch your pointer finger if you know. *Call on one or two children.*

▶ Child's response: A nursery is a place where a baby sleeps.

What is a nursery? Everyone?

▶ Children's response: A nursery is a place where a baby sleeps.

Yes, a nursery is a place where a baby sleeps. Everyone, what's another way of saying a place where a baby sleeps?

▶ Children's response: A nursery is a place where a baby sleeps.

TEACHING TIP: Use the new word with a student's name. This will get students' attention.

Yes, a nursery is a place where a baby sleeps. We call this a nursery rhyme because some parents and grandparents sing these rhymes to their babies as they fall asleep. Everyone, what kinds of rhymes did Monet's mommy sing to her so she could fall asleep?

**Turn On
Your Ears**

▶ Children's response: Monet's mommy sang her nursery rhymes.

Great job knowing nursery rhymes. Listen to this nursery rhyme.

**Model
the Activity**

Sing the song. Use exaggerated voice intonation.
My turn.
Jack and Jill
went up the hill
to fetch a pail of water.
Jack fell down
and broke his crown
and Jill came tumbling after.

Your turn.

▶ Children respond by repeating "Jack and Jill."

TEACHING TIP: Personalizing the rhyme keeps students engaged and happy.

My turn again. Listen. *Use the students' names instead of the name Jack.*
Gabram and Jill
went up the hill
to fetch a pail of water.
Gabram fell down
and broke his crown
and Jill came tumbling after.

Your turn. Let's use Jabez's name.

▶ Children's response:
Jabez and Jill
went up the hill
to fetch a pail of water.
Jabez fell down
and broke his crown
and Jill came tumbling after.

Repeat the rhyme until all children's names are used.

Nice job saying "Jack and Jill." You are the rhyming superstars.

LESSON 2

◇ **Vocabulary**

FETCH

Explain vocabulary in a simple way, and have the students repeat back the new word.

Follow a two-step approach. Step 1: Ask children to describe (or act out) the new word. Jack and Jill fetched a pail of water. _____ *(call on a student),* will you fetch me a book from my desk?

▶ **(Child responds by bringing you a book from your desk.)**

Step 2: Give students the description and have them supply the word. Yes, _____ *(repeat student's name)* fetched me the book. Fetch means to get something. What's another way of saying get me my papers?

▶ **Children's response: Fetch me my papers.**

TEACHING TIP: Act it out. Use movement with the students.

Yes, fetch me my papers. Can somebody ask me to fetch something? Touch your head if you can ask me to fetch something. *Call on a student.*

▶ **(Child responds with a request to fetch.)**

Nice job saying *fetch. You respond by fetching it.*

Can somebody else ask me to fetch something? Make a muscle in your arm if you can ask me to fetch something. *Call on a student.*

▶ **(Child responds with a request to fetch.)**

Nice job saying *fetch. You respond by fetching it.* Everyone, good job fetching.

Follow the same two-step approach as used with the previous vocabulary word.

◇ **Vocabulary**

CROWN

In our nursery rhyme, Jack fell down the hill and broke his crown. Show me what he broke. Touch the place you think he broke.

▶ **(Children respond by not touching their heads.)**

I'll give you a clue. Where does a king or queen wear a crown?

▶ **Children's response: On their heads.**

Yes, so when Jack broke his crown, he really hurt his head. What's another way of saying that Jack hurt his head when he fell down the hill?

▶ **Children's response: Jack broke his crown.**

Yes, Jack broke his crown. Everybody touch the crown of your head.

▶ **(Children respond by touching their heads.)**

Everyone, what are you touching?

▶ **Children's response: The crown of our heads.**

Yes, you are touching the crown of your heads. Good job learning that another word for head is . . . *Pause for students to respond.*

▶ **Children's response: Crown.**

Yes, another word for head is crown. Everyone, say that with me.

▶ **Children's response: Another word for head is crown.**

TASK 2   Playing the Rhyming Pictures Game (approximately 12–14 minutes)

♣ **PLAY** the game.

CD-ROM   See Appendix D on the CD-ROM for the Rhyming Pictures Game cards, instructions, and word list.

TASK 3   Transition song to end the lesson (approximately 3 minutes)

MAKE THE TRANSITION to end the lesson.

You are going to practice the nursery rhyme you learned earlier. Everyone, what was the name of our rhyming song? *Prompt for correct response.*

▶ **Children's response: "Jack and Jill."**

Yes, "Jack and Jill." Let's sing together. *Repeat song from beginning of lesson.*

Jack and Jill
went up the hill
to fetch a pail of water.
Jack fell down
and broke his crown
and Jill came tumbling after.

Let's use Ebony's name. *Use the students' names instead of the name Jack. Repeat the rhyme until all children's names are used.*
Ebony and Jill
went up the hill
to fetch a pail of water.
Ebony fell down
and broke her crown
and Jill came tumbling after.

Nice job saying "Jack and Jill." You are learning lots of rhyming words.

Your rhyming work was so good today. Let's give ourselves the trucker cheer. Do it with me.

Grab your steering wheel. *(Put your hands on the "wheel" and "steer" it.)*
Rrrrrr. *(Make the sound of a truck.)*
Honk, honk. *(Put your fist in the air and pull the horn.)*
Grab your CB radio and say, "Good job, good buddy." *(Talk into your fist.)*

END Lesson 2.

Everyone now gets their winnings for knowing words that rhyme and words that don't rhyme and for working hard. *Give out token rewards to each child.*

LESSON 3: I Can't Said the Ant

OBJECTIVES

Student will

- Know how to listen for rhyming words and be able to discriminate between rhyming and nonrhyming words in an interactive rhyming book by accurately predicting the rhyming word in the story

Teacher will

- Emphasize the sounds of words that rhyme so students can clearly hear that the endings of rhyming words are the same
- Hold the book so that each child can see the pictures
- Closely observe each student for focus and full participation
- Lead children to participate in the interactive rhyming book by coaching them to accurately predict the rhyming word in the story

RHYMES, SONGS, AND FINGERPLAYS

"One, Two, Buckle My Shoe"

"This Old Man"

MATERIALS

A book containing "One, Two, Buckle My Shoe" with pictures (e.g., Baker, 1994)

Book: *I Can't Said the Ant* (Cameron, 1965)

Tokens for behavior/participation

 TASK 1   **Transition song to begin the lesson** (approximately 3 minutes)

INTRODUCE the big idea.

We are going to listen for words that rhyme. Don't forget, words that rhyme are words that sound the same. What do we call words that sound the same?

▶ **Children's response: Words that rhyme.**

Yes, words that rhyme or rhyming words. Like *clatter* and *matter*. *As you say* clatter, *put out your right palm and tilt your head to the right. Do the same on the left side as you say* matter. Do it with me.

▶ **(Children respond by doing it with you.)**

Nice job rhyming *clatter* and *matter*. We will read a story with rhyming words. Let's do another rhyme. *Kerplop* and *mop*. *As you say* kerplop *put out your right palm and tilt your head to the right. Do the same on the left side as you say* mop. Do it with me.

▶ **(Children respond by doing it with you.)**

Nice job rhyming *kerplop* and *mop*. Let's do one more. *Break* and *steak*. *As you say* break *put out your right palm and tilt your head to the right. Do the same on the left side as you say* steak. Do it with me.

▶ **(Children respond by doing it with you.)**

Nice job rhyming *break* and *steak*.

BEGIN the transition.

You are going to practice a rhyme you learned before. It's called "One, Two, Buckle My Shoe." What's the name of the rhyme? *Guide for the correct response.*

▶ **Children's response: "One, Two, Buckle My Shoe."**

Multisensory Reinforcement

Yes, it's called "One, Two, Buckle My Shoe." Let's say our rhyme together. *Say the rhyme and show each picture as you say that part of the rhyme.*

One, two,

Buckle my shoe;

Three, four,

Shut the door;

Five, six,

Pick up sticks;

Seven, eight,

Lay them straight;

Nine, ten,

A big fat hen.

Let's say our rhyme again, and this time try to guess the rhyme. I think you can do it. *Say the rhyme with them. Show each picture and pause for a few moments so they can look at the picture and say the rhyme.*

My turn to say the rhyme.

One, two,

Buckle my . . .

▶ **Children's response: Shoe.**

Three, four,

Shut the . . .

▶ **Children's response: Door.**

Five, six,

Pick up . . .

▶ **Children's response: Sticks.**

Seven, eight,

Lay them . . .

▶ **Children's response: Straight.**

Nine, ten,

A big fat . . .

▶ **Children's response: Hen.**

Nice job saying "One, Two, Buckle My Shoe." You are working hard learning your rhymes.

 TASK 2　　**Listening to a rhyming book** (approximately 12–14 minutes)

INTRODUCE the lesson.

You are going to read a rhyming story with me and listen for some rhyming words. This book has many rhyming words. The title of the book is *I Can't Said the Ant. Hold up the book and point to the title as you read.* What do you think the story is about? Take a look at the picture on the cover. What do you see on the cover? Pointer finger up if you know. *Call on one child.*

▶ **(Child responds by stating what he or she sees on the cover.)**

Everyone, who is talking in the title of the story? "I Can't Said the _____." *Prompt for response.*

▶ **Children's response: Ant.**

Let's read to find out what the ant thinks he can't do. This is one of my most favorite books. *Read the book aloud.*

TEACHING TIP: Overemphasize the rhymes as you read. There are many rhymes in this story that the students will learn quickly.

2.3

SING the "Rhyming Exercise Song."

 Multisensory Reinforcement

Now let's see if we learned some rhyming words. Let's sing the "Rhyming Exercise Song" to check them out. Get ready. *Do the movements: Pause and flex your wrists with your palms up.* Follow me.

Put your hands in the sky. *On the word hands, stretch one arm up to the sky and then the other arm.* Do the "Rhyming Exercise Song." *As you sing, switch and stretch arms one by one.*

Up *(Stretch one arm up.)*
Cup *(Stretch the other arm up.)*
Up *(Switch arms.)*
Cup *(Switch arms.)*
Up *(Switch arms.)*
Cup *(Switch arms.)*

Do they rhyme? *Pause here and allow them to show thumbs up or down before you respond. Look around at each student and make eye contact.* Yes. *Nod vigorously.* They rhyme. *Give two thumbs up. Dance a hip-hop two-step.* Let's sing more rhymes. My turn. Come on up, said the _____. *Pause for student response. Prompt for the first sound of the rhyming word (/c/).*

▶ Children's response: Cup.

Let's sing together. Come on up, said the cup (Ah-huh). Come on up, said the cup (Oh yeah). Come on up, said the cup (All right).

Sing the song several times and add the extra rhyme and dance. Prompt with the first sound of the word. Let's sing more rhymes. My turn. There's dust, said the _____.

Use the following word pairs and do as many as time permits:
   dust, crust

▶ Children's response: Crust.

Let's sing together. There's dust, said the crust (Ah-huh). There's dust, said the crust (Oh yeah). There's dust, said the crust (All right).

   bye-bye, pie

Let's sing our rhyme. My turn. Wave bye-bye, said the _____.

▶ Children's response: Pie.

Let's sing together. Wave bye-bye, said the pie (Ah-huh). Wave bye-bye, said the pie (Oh yeah). Wave bye-bye, said the pie (All right).

   today, tray

Let's sing our rhyme. My turn. It's today, said the _____.

▶ Children's response: Tray.

Let's sing together. It's today, said the tray (Ah-huh). It's today, said the tray (Oh yeah). It's today, said the tray (All right).

   shock, clock

Let's sing our rhyme. My turn. It's a shock, said the _____.

▶ Children's response: Clock.

Let's sing together. It's a shock, said the clock (Ah-huh). It's a shock, said the clock (Oh yeah). It's a shock, said the clock (All right).

   should, wood

Let's sing our rhyme. My turn. You should, said the _____.

▶ Children's response: Wood.

Let's sing together. You should, said the wood (Ah-huh). You should, said the wood (Oh yeah). You should, said the wood (All right).

   blink, sink

Let's sing our rhyme. My turn. Don't blink, said the _____.

▶ Children's response: Sink.

deal, peel

Let's sing together. Don't blink, said the sink (Ah-huh). Don't blink, said the sink (Oh yeah). Don't blink, said the sink (All right).

Let's sing our rhyme. My turn. It's a deal, said the _____.

▶ **Children's response: Peel.**

Let's sing together. It's a deal, said the peel (Ah-huh). It's a deal, said the peel (Oh yeah.). It's a deal, said the peel (All right).

END the song.

You are working hard learning how to rhyme.

🪐 **TASK 3**   Transition song to end the lesson *(approximately 3 minutes)*

MAKE THE TRANSITION to end the lesson.

You are going to practice a rhyming song you learned before. The name of our rhyming song is "This Old Man." What is the name of our rhyming song?

▶ **Children's response: "This Old Man."**

Yes, "This Old Man." Let's stand and do it together.

Sing the song and make up motions that go with the words. This helps the students remember the words. Use exaggerated voice intonation and movements.

This old man, he plays one,
He plays knick-knack just for fun.
With a knick-knack, paddy-whack, give your dog a bone.
This old man uses his cell phone.
This old man, he plays two,
He plays knick-knack on his shoe.
With a knick-knack, paddy-whack, give your dog a bone.
This old man uses his cell phone.
This old man, he plays three,
He plays knick-knack on his knee.
With a knick-knack, paddy-whack, give your dog a bone.
This old man uses his cell phone.
This old man, he plays four,
He plays knick-knack on the floor.
With a knick-knack, paddy-whack, give your dog a bone.
This old man uses his cell phone.

 Multisensory Reinforcement

👂 **Turn On Your Ears**

My turn. Listen to our "Have a Seat Song" as you go back to your seat. *Sing to the tune of "Shortnin' Bread."*

Everybody have a seat, have a seat, have a seat.
Everybody have a seat on your chair.
Not on the ceiling.
Not in the air.
Everybody have a seat on your chair.

▶ **(Children respond by going back to their seats.)**

Your turn to sing with me. *Sing with them as students are in their seats.*

▶ **Children's response:**
Everybody have a seat, have a seat, have a seat.
Everybody have a seat on your chair.
Not on the ceiling.
Not in the air.

Everybody have a seat on your chair.

END Lesson 3.

Everyone now gets their winnings for knowing words that rhyme and words that don't rhyme and for working hard. *Give out token rewards to each child.*

LESSON 4: Rhyme Discrimination Review

OBJECTIVES

Student will

- Know how to listen for rhyming words and be able to discriminate between rhyming and nonrhyming words in a nursery rhyme
- Know how to listen for rhyming words and be able to discriminate between rhyming and nonrhyming words in a rhyming picture game
- Know how to listen for rhyming words and be able to discriminate between rhyming and nonrhyming words in an interactive rhyming book by accurately predicting the rhyming word in the story

Teacher will

- Emphasize the sounds of words that rhyme so students can clearly hear that the endings of rhyming words are the same
- Hold the cards so that each child can see every card sort
- Ensure that all children win the game
- Hold the book so that each child can see the pictures
- Lead children to participate in the interactive rhyming book by coaching them to accurately predict the rhyming word in the story
- Closely observe each student for focus and full participation

RHYMES, SONGS, AND FINGERPLAYS

"This Old Man"

MATERIALS

Book: *I Can't Said the Ant* (Cameron, 1965)

☑ DROPP 2 Skill Assessment Checkout

☑ Tokens for behavior/participation

Rhyming Pictures Game

☑ Game cards (see Appendix D on the CD-ROM)

☑ Word list (see Appendix D on the CD-ROM)

☑ Three colored chips per child

 TASK 1   Transition song to begin the lesson (approximately 2 minutes)

INTRODUCE the big idea.

MAKE THE TRANSITION to begin the lesson.

Sing the song and make up motions that go with the words. This helps the students remember the words. Use exaggerated voice intonation and movements.

You are going to practice rhymes you learned before.

You are going to practice a rhyming song you learned before. The name of our rhyming song is "This Old Man." What is the name of our rhyming song?

▶ **Children's response: "This Old Man."**

Yes, "This Old Man." Let's stand and do it together.

This old man, he plays one,
He plays knick-knack just for fun.
With a knick-knack, paddy-whack, give your dog a bone.
This old man uses his cell phone.
This old man, he plays two,
He plays knick-knack on his shoe.
With a knick-knack, paddy-whack, give your dog a bone.
This old man uses his cell phone.
This old man, he plays three,

He plays knick-knack on his knee.
With a knick-knack, paddy-whack, give your dog a bone.
This old man uses his cell phone.
This old man, he plays four,
He plays knick-knack on the floor.
With a knick-knack, paddy-whack, give your dog a bone.
This old man uses his cell phone.

Let's all sing our "Have a Seat Song" as you go back to your seat. *Sing to the tune of "Shortnin' Bread." Sing with them as students are in their seats.*

▶ **(Children respond by going back to their seats and singing.)**
Everybody have a seat, have a seat, have a seat.
Everybody have a seat on your chair.
Not on the ceiling.
Not in the air.
Everybody have a seat on your chair.

 **TASK 2A**   Reviewing the Rhyming Pictures Game *(approximately 9 minutes)*

 PLAY the game.

 CD-ROM   See Appendix D on the CD-ROM for the Rhyming Pictures Game cards, instructions, and word list.

 TASK 2B   Reviewing a rhyming book *(approximately 5 minutes)*

INTRODUCE the lesson.

You are going to read a rhyming story with me and listen for some rhyming words. This book has many rhyming words. The title of the book is *I Can't Said the Ant. Hold up the book and point to the title as you read.* Describe what the ant can't do. Pointer finger up if you know. *Call on one child.*

▶ **(Child responds by stating what the ant can't do.)**

Let's listen as I read. *Read the book aloud.*

TEACHING TIP: Overemphasize the rhymes as you read. There are many rhymes in this story that the students will learn quickly.

SING the "Rhyming Exercise Song."

Now let's see if we learned some rhyming words. Let's sing the "Rhyming Exercise Song" to check them out. Get ready. *Do the movements: Pause and flex your wrists with your palms up.* Follow me.

🖐 **Multisensory Reinforcement**

Put your hands in the sky. *On the word hands, stretch one arm up to the sky and then the other arm.* Do the rhyming exercise. *As you sing, switch and stretch arms one by one.*

Up *(Stretch one arm up.)*
Cup *(Stretch the other arm up.)*
Up *(Switch arms.)*
Cup *(Switch arms.)*
Up *(Switch arms.)*
Cup *(Switch arms.)*

Do they rhyme? *Pause here and allow them to show thumbs up or down before you respond. Look around at each student and make eye contact.* Yes. *Nod vigorously.* They rhyme. *Give two thumbs up. Dance a hip-hop two-step.* Let's sing more rhymes. My turn. Come on up, said the _____. *Pause for student response. Prompt with the first sound of the rhyming word (/c/).*

▶ **Children's response: Cup.**

Let's sing together. Come on up, said the cup (Ah-huh). Come on up, said the cup (Oh yeah). Come on up, said the cup (All right).

Sing the song several times and add the extra rhyme and dance. Let's sing more rhymes. My turn. There's dust, said the _____.

▶ **Children's response: Crust.**

Let's sing together. There's dust, said the crust (Ah-huh). There's dust, said the crust (Oh yeah). There's dust, said the crust (All right).

Use the following word pairs and do as many as time permits:
   dust, crust

   bye-bye, pie

Let's sing our rhyme. My turn. Wave bye-bye, said the _____.

▶ **Children's response: Pie.**

Let's sing together. Wave bye-bye, said the pie (Ah-huh). Wave bye-bye, said the pie (Oh yeah). Wave bye-bye, said the pie (All right).

   today, tray

Let's sing our rhyme. My turn. It's today, said the _____.

▶ **Children's response: Tray.**

Let's sing together. It's today, said the tray (Ah-huh). It's today, said the tray (Oh yeah). It's today, said the tray (All right).

   shock, clock

Let's sing our rhyme. My turn. It's a shock, said the _____.

▶ **Children's response: Clock.**

Let's sing together. It's a shock, said the clock (Ah-huh). It's a shock, said the clock (Oh yeah). It's a shock, said the clock (All right).

   should, wood

Let's sing our rhyme. My turn. You should, said the _____.

▶ **Children's response: Wood.**

Let's sing together. You should, said the wood (Ah-huh). You should, said the wood (Oh yeah). You should, said the wood (All right).

   blink, sink

Let's sing our rhyme. My turn. Don't blink, said the _____.

▶ **Children's response: Sink.**

Let's sing together. Don't blink, said the sink (Ah-huh). Don't blink, said the sink (Oh yeah). Don't blink, said the sink (All right).

   deal, peel

Let's sing our rhyme. My turn. It's a deal, said the _____.

▶ **Children's response: Peel.**

Let's sing together. It's a deal, said the peel (Ah-huh). It's a deal, said the peel (Oh yeah.). It's a deal, said the peel (All right).

END the song.

You are working hard learning how to rhyme.

Great job singing and dancing your rhyming words. You are a gold star class. You know what that means.

Take out your star box.
Get your star.
Cup one hand. Pretend to get a star on the pointer finger of the other hand, lick it, and put it on your forehead. You are all gold star kids.

END Lesson 4.

Everyone now gets their winnings for knowing words that rhyme and words that don't rhyme and for working hard. *Give out token rewards to each child.*

 CD-ROM   The DROPP 2 Skill Assessment Checkout will be completed for each student following this lesson.

ACTIVITY SET 2.4

Lesson Descriptions

Lessons	Sequence of daily activities	◇ Vocabulary
Lesson 1: Bugs in Mugs	Song for "Rock-a-Bye Baby" Target: Bugs in Mugs Game Song for "Rock-a-Bye Baby"	Bough
Lesson 2: Bugs in Mugs	Fingerplay for "Five Little Ducks" Target: Bugs in Mugs Game Fingerplay for "Five Little Ducks"	
Lesson 3: 512 Ants on Sullivan Street	Song for "One, Two, Buckle My Shoe" Target: Rhyming book—*512 Ants on Sullivan Street* (Losi, 2006) Song for "The Itsy-Bitsy Spider"	Crumb Spy
Lesson 4: Rhyme Discrimination Review	Song for "One, Two, Buckle My Shoe" Target: Bugs in Mugs Game; rhyming book— *512 Ants on Sullivan Street* (Losi, 2006)	

Materials Needed

☑ Book containing "One, Two, Buckle My Shoe" with pictures (e.g., Baker, 1994)

☑ Book: *512 Ants on Sullivan Street* (Losi, 2006)

☑ Tokens for behavior/participation

> ☑ DROPP 2 Skill Assessment Checkout   **CD-ROM**
>
> **Bugs in Mugs Game**
>
> ☑ Game board (see Appendix D on the CD-ROM)
>
> ☑ Game cards (see Appendix D on the CD-ROM)
>
> ☑ Word list (see Appendix D on the CD-ROM)
>
> ☑ Two colored chips per child

ACTIVITY SET

2.4 **10-Day Planner**

Day 1	**Lesson 1:** Bugs in Mugs
Day 2	**Lesson 1:** Bugs in Mugs
Day 3	**Lesson 2:** Bugs in Mugs
Day 4	**Lesson 2:** Bugs in Mugs
Day 5	**Lesson 3:** 512 Ants on Sullivan Street
Day 6	**Lesson 3:** 512 Ants on Sullivan Street
Day 7	**Lesson 1:** Bugs in Mugs
Day 8	**Lesson 2:** Bugs in Mugs
Day 9	**Lesson 3:** 512 Ants on Sullivan Street
Day 10	**Lesson 4:** Rhyme Discrimination Review

LESSON 1: Bugs in Mugs

OBJECTIVES

Student will

- Know how to listen for rhyming words and be able to discriminate between rhyming and nonrhyming words in a song with movements
- Know how to listen for rhyming words and be able to discriminate between rhyming and nonrhyming words in a rhyming picture game

Teacher will

- Emphasize the sounds of words that rhyme so students can clearly hear that the endings of rhyming words are the same
- Hold the cards so that each child can see every rhyming picture card
- Closely observe each student for focus and full participation
- Smile and ensure success for all children
- Ensure that all children win the game

RHYMES, SONGS, AND FINGERPLAYS

"Rock-a-Bye Baby"

MATERIALS

Tokens for behavior/participation

> **Bugs in Mugs Game**
> CD-ROM
> ☑ Game board (see Appendix D on the CD-ROM)
> ☑ Game cards (see Appendix D on the CD-ROM)
> ☑ Word list (see Appendix D on the CD-ROM)
> ☑ Two colored chips per child

TASK 1   **Transition song to begin the lesson** (approximately 3 minutes)

INTRODUCE the big idea.

Say the following to the group after calling the children together at a table.

We are going to listen for words that rhyme. Let's remember to think big today. Kiss your brain before we start. *Kiss your palm and place it on your head.*

Don't forget, words that rhyme are words that sound the same. What do we call words that sound the same?

▶ **Children's response: Words that rhyme.**

Yes, words that rhyme or rhyming words. Like *bug* and *mug*. *As you say* bug, *put out your right palm and tilt your head to the right. Do the same on the left side as you say* mug.

Do it with me.

▶ **(Children respond by doing it with you.)**

Nice job rhyming *bug* and *mug*.

BEGIN the transition.

You are going to practice the rhyming song you already know. The name of our rhyme is "Rock-a-Bye Baby."

What is the name of our rhyming song?

▶ **Children's response: "Rock-a-Bye Baby."**

Yes, it's called "Rock-a-Bye Baby." Let's get our cradles ready.

 **Multisensory Reinforcement**

Do the entire song with them and do the movements. Sing the song four times: the first time in a normal voice, the second time in a somewhat lower voice, the third time in a whisper, the fourth time in a normal voice. This helps them to modulate their tones and listen for changes in sounds, which helps them understand phonemes.

Rock-a-bye baby in the treetop.
When the wind blows the cradle will rock.

When the bough breaks the cradle will fall.
And down will come baby, cradle and all.
But we'll catch you!

Terrific job singing about our tree. You are working hard learning your rhymes. Let's give ourselves a pat on the back.

 Vocabulary

BOUGH

Who remembers what a bough is? Put your hands on your head if you know. *Call on one student.*

▶ (Child responds.)

Yes, a bough is a large tree branch. Everyone, what is a bough? *Prompt the students.*

▶ Children's response: A bough is a large tree branch.

Show me how a cradle would rock on a bough of a tree.

TEACHING TIP: Act it out. Use exaggerated movements with the students.

▶ (Students show the cradle rocking with their hands.)

Bryan's cradle is rocking in the bough of a tree.

Can someone say a sentence and use the word bough? Put your hands on your head if you know. *Take one or two student responses.*

Great job using the word *bough.*

 TASK 2   **Bugs in Mugs Game** *(approximately 12–14 minutes)*

 PLAY the game.

CD-ROM See Appendix D on the CD-ROM for the Bugs in Mugs Game cards, board, instructions, and word list.

TASK 3   Transition song to end the lesson *(approximately 3 minutes)*

MAKE THE TRANSITION to end the lesson.

You are going to practice the rhyming song we did earlier. The name of our rhyme is "Rock-a-Bye Baby." Everyone, what is the name of our rhyming song?

▶ Children's response: "Rock-a-Bye Baby."

Yes, it's called "Rock-a-Bye Baby." Let's get our cradles ready.

Do the entire song with them and do the movements. Sing the song four times: the first time in a normal voice, the second time in a somewhat lower voice, the third time in a whisper, the fourth time in a normal voice.

Multisensory Reinforcement

Rock-a-bye baby in the treetop.
When the wind blows the cradle will rock.
When the bough breaks the cradle will fall.
And down will come baby, cradle and all.
But we will catch you!

Nice job everyone. Let's get out our cameras. *(Make a camera with your hands and click with your tongue as you take some pictures of students. They do the same.)*

Click. Click. Click. Lookin' good. *(Thumbs up. Big smile. Nod.)*

END Lesson 1.

Everyone now gets their winnings for distinguishing between rhyming and non-rhyming words and for working hard. *Give out token rewards to each child.*

LESSON 2: Bugs in Mugs

OBJECTIVES

Student will

- Know how to listen for rhyming words and be able to discriminate between rhyming and nonrhyming words in a rhyming fingerplay
- Know how to listen for rhyming words and be able to discriminate between rhyming and nonrhyming words in a rhyming picture game

Teacher will

- Emphasize the sounds of words that rhyme so students can clearly hear that the endings of rhyming words are the same
- Hold the cards so that each child can see every rhyming picture card
- Closely observe each student for focus and full participation
- Ensure that all children win the game

RHYMES, SONGS, AND FINGERPLAYS

"Five Little Ducks"

MATERIALS

Tokens for behavior/participation

Bugs in Mugs Game
- ☑ Game board (see Appendix D on the CD-ROM)
- ☑ Game cards (see Appendix D on the CD-ROM)
- ☑ Word list (see Appendix D on the CD-ROM)
- ☑ Two colored chips per child

 TASK 1   Transition fingerplay to begin the lesson *(approximately 3 minutes)*

INTRODUCE the big idea.

We are going to listen for words that rhyme. Let's put on our special magic glasses *(make circles with your fingers)* so we can see our rhyming pictures. Listen so that you can hear our rhyming words. What do we call words that sound the same?

▶ Children's response: Words that rhyme.

Yes, words that rhyme or rhyming words. Like *Jill* and *hill*. Do it with me. *As you say* Jill, *put your right palm out and tilt your head to the right. Do the same on the left side as you say* hill.

▶ (Children respond by doing it with you.)

Nice job rhyming *Jill* and *hill*.

BEGIN the transition.

You are going to learn to sing a rhyming song. You may know this one. It's called "Five Little Ducks." What's the name of the song? *Coach the students for the correct response.*

▶ Children's response: "Five Little Ducks."

My turn. *Sing the first two lines of the fingerplay until you have sung two rhyming words. Use exaggerated, easy, consistent, and space-conscious finger and hand movements that mimic the song.*

Five little ducks went out one day,
over the hill and far away.

Your turn to sing. *Sing with them and do the finger movements. Sing the next two lines until you have sung two more rhyming words.*

▶ **Children's response:**
**Five little ducks went out one day,
over the hill and far away.**

Mother duck said "Quack, quack, quack,"
But only four little ducks came back.

Your turn to sing. *Sing with them and do the finger movements.*

▶ **Children's response:**
**Mother duck said "Quack, quack, quack,"
But only four little ducks came back.**

Let's start from the beginning and sing our rhyming song together. *Repeat the fingerplay, do it with them, and count down to one little duck.*

TEACHING TIP: For the last verse, use drama to increase memory. Look sad for the mother duck, but get happy quickly as the ducks come back.

Let's sing the last verse.

Sad mother duck went out one day,
Over the hill and far away.
The sad mother duck said "Quack, quack, quack,"
And all of the five little ducks came back.

Nice job singing "Five Little Ducks." You are working hard. Let's give ourselves a round of applause. *Clap hands in a circle for a round of applause.*

 TASK 2　Play Bugs in Mugs Game *(approximately 12–14 minutes)*

♣ **PLAY** the game.

 See Appendix D on the CD-ROM for the Bugs in Mugs Game cards, board, instructions, and word list.

 TASK 3　Transition fingerplay to end the lesson *(approximately 3 minutes)*

BEGIN the transition.

You are going to practice the rhyming fingerplay you sang earlier. Everyone, can you remember the name of the song? Touch your knee if you remember. *Guide for the correct response.*

▶ **Children's response: "Five Little Ducks."**

Yes, it's called "Five Little Ducks." Eyes on me. Let's sing together. *Repeat the earlier transition. Sing the entire song and do the finger movements.*

Your rhyming work was so good today. Let's give ourselves the old cowboy and cowgirl cheer. Do it with me. Ye-haw. *Put one finger in the air. Circle it like a lasso.*

| **END** Lesson 2. | Everyone now gets their winnings for knowing words that rhyme and words that do not rhyme and for working hard. *Give out token rewards to each child.* |

LESSON 3: 512 Ants on Sullivan Street

OBJECTIVES

Student will

- Know how to listen for rhyming words and be able to discriminate between rhyming and nonrhyming words in an interactive rhyming book by accurately predicting the rhyming word in the story

Teacher will

- Emphasize the sounds of words that rhyme so students can clearly hear that the endings of rhyming words are the same
- Hold the book so that each child can see the pictures
- Closely observe each student for focus and full participation
- Lead children to participate in the interactive rhyming book by coaching them to accurately predict the rhyming word in the story

RHYMES, SONGS, AND FINGERPLAYS

"One, Two, Buckle My Shoe"
"The Itsy-Bitsy Spider"

MATERIALS

Book containing "One, Two, Buckle My Shoe" with pictures (e.g., Baker, 1994)
Book: *512 Ants on Sullivan Street* (Losi, 2006)
Tokens for behavior/participation

🪐 **TASK 1**   **Transition song to begin the lesson** (approximately 3 minutes)

| **INTRODUCE** the big idea. | We are going to listen for words that rhyme. Words that rhyme are words that sound the same. What do we call words that sound the same? |

▶ **Children's response: Words that rhyme.**

Yes, words that rhyme or rhyming words. Like *clatter* and *matter*. Do it with me. *As you say clatter, put out your right palm and tilt your head to the right. Do the same on the left side as you say matter.*

▶ **(Children respond by doing it with you.)**

Nice job rhyming *clatter* and *matter*. We will read a story with rhyming words.

Let's do another rhyme. *Kerplop* and *mop*. Do it with me. *Repeat movements when rhyming other pairs.*

▶ **(Children respond by doing it with you.)**

Nice job rhyming *kerplop* and *mop*. Let's do one more. *Break* and *steak*. Do it with me.

▶ **(Children respond by doing it with you.)**

Nice job rhyming *break* and *steak*.

| **BEGIN** the transition. | You are going to practice a rhyme you learned before. It's called "One, Two, Buckle My Shoe." What's the name of the rhyme? *Guide for the correct response.* |

▶ **Children's response: "One, Two, Buckle My Shoe."**

Yes, it's called "One, Two, Buckle My Shoe." Let's say our rhyme together. *Show children the book, pointing to the pictures as you go along.*

One, two,

Buckle my shoe;

Three, four,

Shut the door;

Five, six,

Pick up sticks;

Seven, eight,

Lay them straight;

Nine, ten,

A big fat hen.

Let's say our rhyme again, and this time try to guess the rhyme. I think you can do it. *Say the rhyme with them, show each picture, and pause for a few moments so they can look at the picture and say the rhyme.* My turn to say the rhyme.

One, two,

Buckle my . . .

▶ **Children's response: Shoe.**

Three, four,

Shut the . . .

▶ **Children's response: Door.**

Five, six,

Pick up . . .

▶ **Children's response: Sticks.**

Seven, eight,

Lay them . . .

▶ **Children's response: Straight.**

Nine, ten,

A big fat . . .

▶ **Children's response: Hen.**

Nice job saying "One, Two, Buckle My Shoe." You are working hard learning your rhymes.

 TASK 2   **Listening to a rhyming book** (approximately 12–14 minutes)

INTRODUCE the lesson.

You are going to read a rhyming story with me and listen for some rhyming words. This book has many rhyming words. The title of the book is *512 Ants on Sullivan Street. Hold up the book and point to the title as you read.* Take a look at the picture on the cover. Where do you think the story is happening? I'll give you clues. It takes place outside, usually in the spring or summer; sometimes your whole family gets together, you eat food, maybe play games. Two thumbs up if you know. *Call on one child. Prompt for the response.*

▶ **(Child responds with appropriate response.)**

Yes, it is a picnic. How do you know this is a picnic? Two thumbs up if you know. *Call on one child.*

▶ **(Child responds with appropriate response.)**

Describe what the ants are doing. Look at the picture. Two thumbs up if you know. *Call on one child.*

▶ (Child responds with appropriate response.)

Do you think 512 ants are a lot of ants? Two thumbs up if you know. *Call on one child.*

▶ (Child responds with appropriate response.)

How do you know? Look at the picture. Two thumbs up if you know. *Call on one child.*

▶ (Child responds with appropriate response.)

Let's read to find out what 512 ants do at the picnic. *Read the book aloud.*

TEACHING TIP: Overemphasize the rhymes as you read. There are many rhymes in this story that the students will learn quickly.

✦ Vocabulary

CRUMB

Explain vocabulary in a simple way, and have the students repeat back the new word.

The ant carried a crumb. What did he carry?

▶ Children's response: He carried a crumb.

Yes, the ant carried a crumb. This is a crumb. *Show the picture from the book.* A crumb is a little, tiny piece of food that breaks off from the bigger piece. Everyone, what's a crumb?

Follow a two-step approach. Step 1: Ask children to describe (or act out) the new word.

▶ Children's response: A crumb is a little, tiny piece of food that breaks off from the bigger piece.

Step 2: Give students the description and have them supply the word.

Yes, a crumb is a little, tiny piece of food that breaks off from the bigger piece. What happens if you have lots of little, tiny pieces of food that break off from the bigger piece? Everyone, you will have lots of _____?

▶ Children's response: Crumbs.

What happens when you have lots of crumbs and they get all over the house? Touch your right shoulder if you know. *Prompt for the following types of responses: they are tiny, they make a mess, and you could get ants.*

TEACHING TIP: Use the new word with a student's name. This will get students' attention.

Yes, we have to be careful with our crumbs because ants love crumbs. After we have our snack today, Maleika will check for crumbs on our table. What will she be checking for?

▶ Children's response: Maleika will check for crumbs.

Yes, Maleika will check for crumbs. Nice job learning about crumbs.

✦ Vocabulary

SPY

Follow the same two-step approach as used with previous vocabulary word. In our story, the ants spied some take-out Chinese food. What does it mean to spy something? Sit up tall and proud if you know. *Call on one child.*

▶ (Child responds with appropriate response.)

The ants spied some Chinese food. That means they found some food they didn't know was there. *Spy* means to find out something you didn't know about. What's another way of saying the ants found some food they didn't know was there?

133

▶ **Children's response: The ants spied some Chinese food.**

Yes, the ants spied some Chinese food. *Spy* means to find out something you didn't know about. I spy something green and blue on my desk. Who can tell me what I spy? Touch the bridge of your nose if you know. *Show them the bridge of their nose. Call on one child.*

▶ **(Child responds with appropriate response.)**

TEACHING TIP: Use a game format to practice words. Students love anything in a game format.

Let's play a quick game. It's called "I Spy." I'm going to spy a color on one of you—maybe something you are wearing, your eye color, or your hair color. Then you show all of us what I found or spied on you. It's so much fun. Listen. I spy. . . . *Make glasses with your fingers.* Now you say, "What do you spy?" *Prompt the students for the whole game.*

▶ **Children's response: What do you spy? (Students make glasses with their fingers.)**

A color. Now you say, "What color?"

▶ **Children's response: What color?**

Look at a color that one of the students has on. Yellow. Now you say, "On who?"

▶ **Children's response: On who?**

Y-o-u. *Point to a student and spell out the word.* Find your yellow and show us.

▶ **(Child responds by touching yellow and showing the others.)**

Y-o-u spells _____? *Look expectantly at the students.* It spells *you. Point to a student.* Everyone, y-o-u spells _____.

▶ **Children's response: You.**

Yes, y-o-u spells *you. Point to an individual.* Let's try our game again. It's called "I Spy."

Now let's see if we learned some rhyming words. Let's sing the "Rhyming Exercise Song" to check them out. Get ready. Follow me. Put your hands in the sky. *Do the movements: Pause and flex your wrists with your palms up. Stretch one arm up to the sky, then the other arm, on the word hands.* Do the rhyming exercise.

SING the "Rhyming Exercise Song."

 **Multisensory Reinforcement**

Who *(Stretch one arm up as you say the word.)*
You *(Stretch the other arm up.)*
Who *(Switch arms.)*
You *(Switch arms.)*
Who *(Switch arms.)*
You *(Switch arms.)*

Do they rhyme? *(Pause here and allow them to show thumbs up or down before you respond. Look around at each student and make eye contact.)* Yes. *(Nod vigorously.)* They rhyme. *(Give two thumbs up.)*

Sing the song several times and use the same format. Remember, some pairs will rhyme and some will not. Look puzzled and give a thumbs down at the end of the song when the pair does not rhyme. Use the following words and do as many as time permits: dine/line, fudge/head, fudge/budge, chore/more, hurray/school, hurray/tray.

TEACHING TIP: Always end with a rhyming word to keep rhyming words in memory and further saturate the students in rhyme.

| **END** the song. | You are working hard exercising your rhyming muscles. You are the strongest rhymers I know. |

 TASK 3   **Transition fingerplay to end the lesson** (approximately 3 minutes)

| **MAKE THE TRANSITION** to end the lesson. | You are going to practice the rhyming fingerplay you learned before. The name of our song is "The Itsy-Bitsy Spider." Everyone, what's the name of our rhyming fingerplay? |

▶ **Children's response: "The Itsy-Bitsy Spider."**

Yes, it's called "The Itsy-Bitsy Spider." Let's get our spiders ready. *Sing the entire song with them and do the movements.*

The itsy-bitsy spider went up the water spout.
Down came the rain and washed the spider out.
Out came the sun and dried up all the rain.
So the itsy-bitsy spider came up the spout again.

Great job singing rhymes about your spiders.

Your rhyming work was so good today. We are going to sing the "Give Me a Snap" song. *Sing to the tune of* The Addams Family *theme song.*

Give me a snap. *(Snap twice.)*
Give me a snap. *(Snap twice.)*
Give me a snap, give me a snap, give me a snap. *(Snap twice.)*

Repeat the tune but say, "Give me a cheer." Say "Hooray!" once instead of snapping twice.

Give me a cheer. Hooray!

| **END** Lesson 3. | Everyone now gets their winnings for knowing words that rhyme and words that don't rhyme and for working hard. *Give out token rewards to each child.* |

LESSON 4: Rhyme Discrimination Review

OBJECTIVES

Student will

- Know how to listen for rhyming words and be able to discriminate between rhyming and nonrhyming words in a rhyming song and fingerplay
- Know how to listen for rhyming words and be able to discriminate between rhyming and nonrhyming words in a rhyming picture game
- Know how to listen for rhyming words and be able to discriminate between rhyming and nonrhyming words in an interactive rhyming book by accurately predicting the rhyming word in the story

Teacher will

- Emphasize the sounds of words that rhyme so students can clearly hear that the endings of rhyming words are the same
- Hold the cards so that each child can see every card sort
- Ensure that all children win the game
- Hold the book so that each child can see the pictures
- Lead children to participate in the interactive rhyming book by coaching them to accurately predict the rhyming word in the story
- Closely observe each student for focus and full participation

RHYMES, SONGS, AND FINGERPLAYS

"One, Two, Buckle My Shoe"

MATERIALS

Book: *512 Ants on Sullivan Street* (Losi, 2006)

Tokens for behavior/participation

- ☑ DROPP 2 Skill Assessment Checkout (see Appendix B on the CD-ROM)

Bugs in Mugs Game

- ☑ Game board (see Appendix D on the CD-ROM)
- ☑ Game cards (see Appendix D on the CD-ROM)
- ☑ Word list (see Appendix D on the CD-ROM)
- ☑ **Two colored chips per child**

 TASK 1 | Transition song to begin the lesson (approximately 2 minutes)

INTRODUCE the big idea.	You are going to practice rhymes you learned before. It's called "One, Two, Buckle My Shoe." What's the name of the rhyme? *Guide for the correct response.*
BEGIN the transition.	

▶ **Children's response:** "One, Two, Buckle My Shoe."

Yes, it's called "One, Two, Buckle My Shoe." Let's say our rhyme together. *Say the rhyme and point to each picture in the book as you say that part of the rhyme.*

One, two,

Buckle my shoe;

Three, four,

Shut the door;

Five, six,

Pick up sticks;

Seven, eight,

Lay them straight;

Nine, ten,

A big fat hen.

Let's say our rhyme again, and this time try to guess the rhyme. I think you can do it. *Say the rhyme with them. Show each picture and pause for a few moments so they can look at the picture and say the rhyme.* My turn to say the rhyme.

One, two,

Buckle my . . .

▶ **Children's response:** Shoe.

Three, four,
Shut the . . .

▶ **Children's response: Door.**

Five, six,
Pick up . . .

▶ **Children's response: Sticks.**

Seven, eight,
Lay them . . .

▶ **Children's response: Straight.**

Nine, ten,
A big fat . . .

▶ **Children's response: Hen.**

Nice job saying "One, Two, Buckle My Shoe." You are working hard learning your rhymes.

 **TASK 2A**   Reviewing the Bugs in Mugs Game *(approximately 9 minutes)*

 PLAY the game.

CD-ROM See Appendix D on the CD-ROM for the Bugs in Mugs Game cards, board, instructions, and word list.

 TASK 2B   Reviewing a rhyming book *(approximately 5 minutes)*

INTRODUCE the big idea.

We are going to listen for words that rhyme. Everyone, what can you tell me about rhyming words? *Give them a hint by tugging on your ear.* They . . . *Pause to allow them to respond.*

▶ **Children's response: They sound the same.**

Yes, words that rhyme or rhyming words sound the same. Like *lunch* and *munch*. Do it with me. *As you say* lunch, *put your right palm out and tilt your head to the right. Do the same on the left side as you say* munch.

▶ **(Children respond by doing it with you.)**

Do they rhyme? Do they sound the same?

▶ **Children's response: Yes, they rhyme.**

Yes, *lunch* and *munch* sound the same. They rhyme. *Give a thumbs up.*

▶ **(Children respond with a thumbs up.)**

What about *plum* and *crumb?* Do it with me. *Repeat the movements.*

▶ **(Children respond by doing it with you.)**

Do they rhyme? Do they sound the same?

▶ **Children's response: Yes, they rhyme.**

Yes, *plum* and *crumb* sound the same. They rhyme. *Give a thumbs up.*

▶ (Children respond with a thumbs up.)

Nice job rhyming *lunch* and *munch* and *plum* and *crumb.*

You are going to read a rhyming story with me and listen for more rhyming words. The title of the book is *512 Ants on Sullivan Street. Hold up the book and point to the title as you read.* Take a look at the picture on the cover. Everyone, where does the story take place?

▶ **Children's response: At a picnic.**

Yes, at a picnic. How do you know this is a picnic? Touch your nose if you know. *Call on one child.*

▶ (Child responds with appropriate response.)

Everyone, who is talking in the title of the story? *Prompt for the response.*

▶ **Children's response: 512 Ants on Sullivan Street.**

INTRODUCE the lesson.

Yes, 512 Ants on Sullivan Street. Let's read to find out what the ants did at the picnic on Sullivan Street. *Read the book aloud.*

TEACHING TIP: Overemphasize the rhymes as you read.

 ◇ **Vocabulary**

SPY

In our story, the ants spied some take-out Chinese food. Everyone, what does it mean to spy something?

▶ **Children's response: It means to find out something you didn't know about.**

Yes, spy means to find out something you didn't know about.

TEACHING TIP: Use a game format to practice the word. Students love anything in a game format.

Let's play "I Spy." Do you remember how? I'm going to spy a color on one of you—maybe something you are wearing, your eye color, or your hair color. Then you show all of us what I found or spied on you. Get ready. I spy____. *Make glasses with your fingers. Prompt the students for the whole game.*

▶ **Children's response: What do you spy? (Students make glasses with their fingers.)**

A color.

▶ **Children's response: What color?**

Look at a color that one of the students has on. Pink.

▶ **Children's response: On who?**

Y-o-u. *Point to a student and spell out the word.* Find your pink.

▶ (Child responds by touching pink.)

Let's play again. *Play one or two more times, if time permits.*

Let's do our good job dance. *Sing to the tune of "Stayin' Alive," and substitute the words "we did a good job, we did a good job." Extend your right index finger in the air to the left of your body. With your left hand on your hip, move your right finger from the air to your side as you sing.*

| **END** Lesson 4. | Everyone now gets their winnings for knowing words that rhyme and words that don't rhyme and for working hard. *Give out token rewards to each child.* |

CD-ROM   **The DROPP 2 Skill Assessment Checkout will be completed for each student following this lesson.**

Sentence Segmentation

Overview

WHY SENTENCE SEGMENTATION IS IMPORTANT

Sentence segmentation is important because when children understand that spoken sentences are composed of separate words, this helps them to eventually understand word boundaries in print. Clapping once for each word in a sentence demonstrates the critical developmental step of understanding that a word is a unit of language. This word awareness is strongly linked to the ability to read and write.

HOW DROPP 3 IS STRUCTURED

DROPP 3 has two Activity Sets: 3.1 and 3.2. Each Activity Set consists of four scripted lessons (Teacher Talk) that are used on 10 sequential learning days (the four lessons are repeated over the 10-day span). DROPP 3 has 20 days of intervention lessons designed to develop and practice students' word awareness and sentence segmentation skills. During the first 9 days of each set, students practice hearing and identifying individual words in nursery rhymes, songs, and short sentences. On the 10th day, students review the skills to prepare for a short skill assessment checkout. (See the CD-ROM for the DROPP 3 Skill Assessment Checkout.)

Length of Activity Sets and Lessons

Each Activity Set is designed to be delivered across 10 sequential learning days. Each day's intervention lesson, including the transition activities, takes about 20 minutes to complete.

Goal and Emphasis of the Sentence Segmentation Lessons

The goal of Activity Sets 3.1 and 3.2 is to strengthen your students' awareness of individual words in short sentences. The emphasis is completely on spoken words and sentences at this stage. There are a number of action songs and nursery rhymes in these Activity Sets that extend children's love of learning through movement and song. Students learn the first steps of segmenting sentences into words when they repeat the sentences, act out individual words, or supply a word in the action songs.

Student Objectives

Students will be able to segment sentences into words by doing the following activities:

- Clapping once for each word in a short sentence

- Standing and saying one word as part of a "human sentence"

- Moving a chip for each word that is heard in a short sentence

- Building and reading a picture sentence and clapping once for each word

Teacher Objectives

- Develop students' awareness of word boundaries in speech through scaffolded, multisensory activities.

- Define and demonstrate the meaning of the terms *word* and *sentence*.

- Model how to hear individual words in familiar nursery rhymes, and help students repeat words and short sentences from those rhymes.

- Use movement and music to help students link individual words with actions in songs.

- Teach children to clap out words in short and long sentences.

- Guide children in using manipulatives (pictures and colored chips) to represent individual words in sentence segmentation games.

How the Sentence Segmentation Activity Sets Develop Early Literacy

Multisensory Techniques

There are action songs, stand-up sentences, word clapping, and manipulative chips and pictures in Activity Sets 3.1 and 3.2 that provide multisensory learning opportunities for the children. These activities will deepen your students' emerging phonological awareness of sounds and words. Children make an important leap from hearing spoken language as a stream of speech to hearing words as individual units of speech as they use their whole bodies to represent words in stand-up sentences, their hands for clapping out words, and their eyes and ears for matching pictures and words.

Making Meaning and Building Vocabulary

As your students learn to listen to words in sentences, they will begin to understand that words are spoken in a particular order to convey meaning. This is an important developmental step that is linked to later reading comprehension. To further develop students' thinking skills, the nursery rhymes and action songs in Activity Sets 3.1 and 3.2 are developed around a common theme—the sun, moon, and stars. This builds students' oral vocabulary as they develop their knowledge of the world around them. New vocabulary is listed at the beginning of each Activity Set. We recommend that you use the new words throughout the day to reinforce student vocabulary growth.

Print Awareness

Students will experience the left-to-right progression of word reading in the Stand-Up Sentences and Move the Chip activities of Activity Sets 3.1 and 3.2. Also embedded in these Activity Sets is the printed word awareness that comes from the teacher saying and pointing to words in the nursery rhymes. Although these concepts about print are presented at an awareness level and not intended for explicit instruction, they will support your students' understanding that the sounds of speech can be mapped onto print, which is the foundation for reading.

GENERAL TIPS FOR IMPLEMENTING ACTIVITY SETS 3.1 AND 3.2

- Substitute the Child's Name in Nursery Rhyme Sentences: Both Activity Sets follow the format of introducing word awareness in short sentences from familiar nursery rhymes. In the Teacher Talk, you will see the suggestion to occasionally substitute your students' names for the name in the nursery rhyme. This is a fun way to develop the children's ability to hear differences between what they expect to hear and what you say instead.

- Rhyme Review: In Set 3.1, the words *diddle* and *fiddle* are chosen for rhyming practice. Be alert for other chances throughout your day to reinforce the skill of rhyming using the "Rhyming Exercise Song."

TEACHING TIP: **Helpful Technology for Success**

If you have forgotten the tunes to the nursery rhymes, go to http://www.gardenofsong.com, where you can hear hundreds of traditional children's songs played on the piano. If you like, you can download them to accompany your lesson.

- Creative Word Usage: In the song "Aiken Drum," introduced in Activity Set 3.1, the children will be encouraged to make up creative phrases that describe Aiken Drum's apparel. This will work best if you familiarize yourself with the rhyme ahead of time and think of some suggestions to get the children started. This is an entertaining way to teach the children to play with language.

- From Songs to Speech: Throughout these sets, you will convert lines from the lesson's songs into spoken sentences. Whenever you do this, first say the line slowly just after singing it, and then repeat it in a conversational tone. This will help the children focus on the meaning of the sentence, which is often lost when the words are sung. Think aloud about the fact that the words make a sentence that tells something.

- Stand-Up Sentence Clapping: The students who are part of a Stand-Up Sentence do *not* clap when you and the remaining students clap out the words. Because these young children are working hard to grasp a new concept, it is best to simplify the task of the students who are standing by giving them only one step to follow—saying their individual word when you point to them.

TEACHING TIP: **Check for Success**

Maintain eye contact with the students, and ensure they are responding correctly and on cue. By doing this, you are conducting a mini assessment for each child to see who may need additional help.

- Shorter or Longer Sentences: By watching closely, you will see if children are successfully demonstrating word awareness in the lesson activities. *Shorter:* If a child shows any confusion during the group response, then give him or her a short two- or three-word sentence for individual response. Pause between each word and make a cupping gesture with your hands around each word to assist the child and ensure his or her success. *Longer:* Children who grasp the concept of separate words by clapping successfully can be given increasingly longer sentences, up to seven words, on the exit tasks.

- Checking for Success on Move the Chip: First, see that every child says the word when moving a chip down to the line. Second, when checking the whole sentence, be sure that the children say each word and touch the chip as they repeat each sentence.

- Difference Between Activity Set 3.1 and Activity Set 3.2: Activity Set 3.2 has shorter sentences in its exercises. The students in Activity Set 3.2 are being given another 10 days to develop their sentence segmentation skills because they did not fully grasp the concept in Activity Set 3.1. Therefore, the practice sentences are intentionally shorter to assure basic recognition of individual words in sentences.

TEACHING TIP: **Celebrate Success**

Always give students a specific compliment at the end of every task. Praise them and tell them what they did. For example, say, "You did a great job hearing and clapping the words in our nursery rhyme sentence. Pat yourself on the back."

Skill Assessment Checkouts

The assessment outcome for DROPP 3 is that students will segment sounds in spoken sentences by clapping words in a sentence. This is aligned with most states' curriculum guidelines for general reading processes and phonemic awareness. After your review lesson is completed on the 10th day, set aside a few minutes during that day to give each child an individual sentence segmentation checkout. These take about 2 minutes per child to administer and provide useful information to guide your small-group placements. Based on the checkout and collaborative conversations with all teachers, you will determine which students should continue in Tier 2 small-group intervention and which students can successfully return to Tier 1 whole-class instruction.

Assessment Outcome: The student can segment short spoken sentences into individual words.

ACTIVITY SET 3.1

Lesson Descriptions

Lessons	Sequence of daily activities	✧ Vocabulary
Lesson 1: Stand-Up Sentences	Movement song: "Bend and Stretch" Target: Clap and stand to segment sentences into words Movement song: "Bend and Stretch"	Nursery Twinkle
Lesson 2: Move the Chip	Nursery rhyme: "Hey Diddle, Diddle" Target: Move the Chip to segment sentences into words Silly song: "Aiken Drum"	Fiddle
Lesson 3: What Do You Like?	Silly song: "Aiken Drum" Target: Form picture sentences, segment sentences into words Nursery rhymes: "Twinkle, Twinkle, Little Star" and "Star Light, Star Bright"	Ladle
Lesson 4: Sentence Segmentation Review	Movement song: "Bend and Stretch" Review: Stand-Up Sentences Review: Move the Chip Nursery rhyme: "Star Light, Star Bright"	Sentence

Materials Needed

☑ Large nursery rhyme book(s) with "Twinkle, Twinkle, Little Star," "Hey Diddle Diddle," "Aiken Drum," and "Star Light, Star Bright"
☑ Up to eight large colored circles
☑ Up to eight colored chips for each child
☑ Ladle or a picture of a ladle
☑ Three small buckets
☑ Optional: Toy star or picture of star
☑ Optional: Toy moon or a picture of the moon
☑ Tokens for behavior/participation

> ☑ DROPP 3 Skill Assessment Checkout (see Appendix B on the CD-ROM) **CD-ROM**
> **Move the Chip Game**
> ☑ Display board (see Appendix D on the CD-ROM)
> ☑ Game pieces (see Appendix D on the CD-ROM)
> **What Do You Like? Game**
> ☑ Three buckets
> ☑ Heart, teacher, subject, and object cards (see Appendix D on the CD-ROM)
> ☑ Word list (see Appendix D on the CD-ROM)

ACTIVITY SET 3.1 10-Day Planner

Day 1	**Lesson 1:** Stand-Up Sentences
Day 2	**Lesson 1:** Stand-Up Sentences
Day 3	**Lesson 2:** Move the Chip
Day 4	**Lesson 2:** Move the Chip
Day 5	**Lesson 3:** What Do You Like?
Day 6	**Lesson 3:** What Do You Like?
Day 7	**Lesson 1:** Stand-Up Sentences
Day 8	**Lesson 2:** Move the Chip
Day 9	**Lesson 3:** What Do You Like?
Day 10	**Lesson 4:** Sentence Segmentation Review

LESSON 1: Stand-Up Sentences

OBJECTIVES

Student will

- Learn how to separate (segment) words in short sentences by clapping out each word
- Stand up as one word in a human sentence

Teacher will

- Review word awareness in a familiar rhyme
- Model how to clap out words in sentences
- Guide students to stand and say each word in a sentence

RHYMES, SONGS, AND FINGERPLAYS

"Bend and Stretch"

"Twinkle, Twinkle, Little Star"

MATERIALS

Large nursery rhyme book with "Twinkle, Twinkle, Little Star"

Six large colored circles

Optional: Toy star or picture of star

Tokens for behavior/participation

TECHNOLOGY LINK

View the following video clip to learn the song "Bend and Stretch" and movements:
http://www.youtube.com/watch?v=alRu8-5Nyek.

 TASK 1 | **Movement song to begin the lesson** (approximately 3 minutes)

INTRODUCE the big idea: sentences.

Settle the children at a table and say the following. We are going to learn about sentences. Sentences are made of words that we can say. It is fun saying and listening for the words that make a sentence.

BEGIN the transition activity.

You are going to learn an action song called "Bend and Stretch." An action song is a song we can sing while we learn an action, or a thing to do, with our bodies. Who can think of an action that we might do with a song called "Bend and Stretch?" Raise your hand.

▶ **Children's response: Bend down, stretch our bodies.**

 Turn On Your Ears

Yes. The song will tell us when to bend and stretch and do other things. Listen to this song and do what I do.

 TEACHING TIP: Use exaggerated movements.

SING the song.

 Multisensory Reinforcement

(Sing.) Bend and stretch. *(Touch toes.)*
Reach for the stars. *(Raise fingertips toward ceiling.)*
There goes Jupiter. *(Sway body back and forth.)*
Here comes Mars. *(Continue to sway.)*
Bend and stretch. *(Touch toes.)*
Reach for the sky. *(Raise fingertips toward ceiling.)*
Standing on tippy-toes. *(Rise up onto tiptoes.)*
Oh, so high. *(Big smile as you bring hands back to your sides.)*

 **TASK 2A** | **Stand-Up Sentences** (approximately 10 minutes)

INTRODUCE the skill through song.

That was fun reaching all the way up to the stars. Now you are going to learn a nursery rhyme about stars.

Who remembers what a nursery is? Raise your hand. *Accept several responses.*

▶ **Children's response: A place where a baby sleeps.**

Vocabulary

NURSERY

That's right. A nursery is a place where a baby sleeps, and a nursery rhyme is something that some parents sing to their babies as they fall asleep. Some of you may know this one. It's called "Twinkle, Twinkle, Little Star."

My turn to sing "Twinkle, Twinkle, Little Star." *Use a large nursery rhyme picture book. Point to each word while singing the entire song.*

SING the song.

Twinkle, twinkle, little star, how I wonder what you are.
Up above the world so high, like a diamond in the sky.
Twinkle, twinkle, little star, how I wonder what you are.

SING the song with the children.

Good job listening to "Twinkle, Twinkle, Little Star." Now I want you to sing the first part with me.

TEACHING TIP: Sing just the first two lines with the children. Do not use the nursery rhyme book any longer. Look at each child's face and smile while singing to encourage all to participate.

▶ **Children sing: Twinkle, twinkle, little star, how I wonder what you are.**

Great job singing with me. *If any child seems uncertain, then repeat once or twice.*

◇ **Vocabulary**

TWINKLE

That sounded wonderful. You sang the words in the first part. One of the words we sang was *twinkle*. What does *twinkle* mean? Raise your hand if you know. *Accept one or two reasonable responses.*

Twinkle means to shine or give out light. So we want the little star to twinkle or shine. Everyone, what does *twinkle* mean?

▶ **Children's response: Shine.**

Yes. *Twinkle* means shine. *Twinkle* is one of the **words** in the first part of our song. The words go together to make a **sentence**. Everyone, what do the words go together to make?

▶ **Children's response: A sentence.**

✶ **Model the Activity**

Watch me say a sentence slowly, while I clap my hands for each word in the sentence.

Say slowly, clapping softly with each word.
Twinkle *(clap)* twinkle *(clap)* little *(clap)* star *(clap)*.

Do that with me. Let's clap our hands once for each word.
Twinkle *(clap)* twinkle *(clap)* little *(clap)* star *(clap)*.

*Correction procedure: Demonstrate correctly and repeat until firm. If a child claps twice for a two-syllable word, such as twinkle, *then say the following: Wait.* Twinkle *is just one word, even though you heard two parts in it. So only clap your hands once for* twinkle *because* twinkle *is one word.**

LINK to Stand-Up Sentences.

We clapped for each word in the first sentence of our rhyme. Now it's time to make a Stand-Up Sentence. *Choose four students to stand up in a row, shoulder to shoulder. Continue the following until each child says his or her one word.*

Each of you will stand for one word from our first sentence. _____ , you are *twinkle*. Say your word.

▶ **Child 1's response: Twinkle.**

Assign the remaining words to the other three students. Okay, each of you stands for a word. Now, when you each say your word, your words will go together to make our whole sentence. When I point to you, say your word. Get ready.

Point at a moderate pace at first. Gradually quicken the pace so that the words flow together like a sentence.

▶ Children say, in turn: Twinkle, twinkle, little star.

Listen, everyone. We have a Stand-Up Sentence. Say it again.

▶ Children say, in turn: Twinkle, twinkle, little star.

Wow! You each said one word and together they made a sentence from our nursery rhyme. You made a sentence that tells our little star to twinkle and shine.

Say that sentence one more time, and this time I will clap once for each word.

▶ Standing children's response: Twinkle, twinkle, little star.

Students who are not standing may clap with the teacher. Children who are standing do not clap. (Simplify the standing students' action by giving them only one task.)

Good job clapping and saying the words that make our first sentence.

Follow previous format, rotating children's turns.
Now, let's make a different Stand-Up Sentence.
Here is our next sentence.
Reach - for - the - sky. *Choose four children.*
When I point to you, say your word. Get ready.

▶ Children's response: Reach - for - the - sky.

Everyone, say that sentence again.

▶ Children's response: Reach for the sky.

Say it again, a little faster. *Point at a faster pace.*

▶ Children's response: Reach for the sky.

Emphasize that the words make a sentence that tells us something. Comment on what the sentences tell the children to do. You made a sentence that tells us to reach for the sky, like we did in "Bend and Stretch."

Repeat each Stand-Up Sentence several times. Then clap out the words several more times. Here is a new sentence to try. I like hamburgers.

▶ Children's response: I - like - hamburgers.

Everyone, say that sentence again.

▶ Children's response: I like hamburgers.

Say it again, a little faster.

▶ Children's response: I like hamburgers.

Wow. *Hamburgers* is a big word. It's a long word, but it's still just one word, so I only will clap for it one time.

Repeat. Additional sentence options include "I have a new bike," "I see stars," and "I ride my bike."

Tell students the skill that they have mastered. I like the way you took turns being the words in our Stand-Up Sentences. Each student stood for one word.

Turn On Your Ears

Multisensory Reinforcement

Teacher claps four times.

PRACTICE Stand-Up Sentences.

LINK meaning to sentences.

 **TASK 2B**   **Preview of upcoming lesson** (approximately 3 minutes)

PREPARE the display board ahead of time.	*Place six large different-colored circles at the top of chart paper with a blank line beneath.*
INTRODUCE the upcoming activity.	Now I will show you something else I like to do when I hear words in sentences.

I am a teacher. *Repeat more slowly.* I - am - a - teacher.

Watch this. *Move a circle down to the line for each word while slowly saying the word.*

I - am - a - teacher. Look. I moved down one chip for each word I said in my sentence. I am a teacher. Say it with me. *Touch each circle while repeating the sentence with students.*

▶ **Children's response: I am a teacher.**

Good job saying the words in my sentence. *Move circles back to top.*

PRACTICE with students.

Here's another sentence.

I - love - this - class. *Repeat more slowly.*

 Multisensory Reinforcement

I - love - this - class. *Touch each circle while repeating the sentence with students.* I love this class. Say it with me.

▶ **Children's response: I love this class.**

Now I will choose a student to touch the circles for our words. *Choose a student.* Touch one circle for each word we say.

▶ **Children's response: I love this class. (One student touches each circle.)**

Let's practice some more sentences.

If students' responses are correct with four-word sentences, increase sentence length. Follow same procedure with the following sentences: "I love this whole class" and "I love this whole wonderful class."

Compliment the students' performance. You did a great job hearing the words in the sentences.

 **TASK 3**   **Transition song to end the lesson** (approximately 3 minutes)

SING a transition song.

You worked hard today hearing the words in sentences. You are my shining stars! I think I can see you twinkling and giving off light.

Let's stand up and reach up to the sky where the stars live. Do you remember the action song we learned earlier? Let's sing "Bend and Stretch" again.

Everybody, stand up. Watch me and do what I do. Sing along if you remember any of the words. *Sing the song.*

Bend and stretch. *(Touch toes.)*
Reach for the stars. *(Raise fingertips toward ceiling.)*
There goes Jupiter. *(Sway body back and forth.)*
Here comes Mars. *(Continue to sway.)*
Bend and stretch. *(Touch toes.)*
Reach for the sky. *(Raise fingertips toward ceiling.)*
Standing on tippy-toes. *(Rise up onto tiptoes.)*
Oh, so high. *(Big smile as you bring hands back to your sides.)*

Excellent singing. Now, line up to show me if you can clap for each word in the sentence I will give you.

Use an exit task to assess skill mastery. Let each child have one turn. Use these sentences, giving shorter sentences to students who are not yet proficient at hearing and clapping out the words. Help them to complete the task successfully, if necessary.

_____, *(choose a child)* your turn. Twinkle means shine. Say it and clap it.

▶ **Child's response: Twinkle *(clap)* means *(clap)* shine *(clap).***

(Additional exit sentences include "Reach for the stars" [four claps], "I have a new bike" [five claps], and "I did my best today" [five claps].)

END Lesson 1.

Everyone now gets their winnings for hearing the words in sentences and for working hard. *Give out token rewards to each child.*

LESSON 2: Move the Chip

OBJECTIVES

Student will

- Learn how to segment words in sentences by moving chips to show how many words are heard

Teacher will

- Model how to segment three- to six-word sentences

- Guide students to hear the individual words in short sentences

RHYMES, SONGS, AND FINGERPLAYS

"Hey Diddle, Diddle"

"Aiken Drum"

MATERIALS

Large nursery rhyme book with "Hey Diddle, Diddle" and "Aiken Drum"

Optional: Toy moon or a picture of the moon

Move the Chip Game

☑ Display board

☑ Game pieces

 CD-ROM

 TASK 1   **Nursery rhyme to begin the lesson** (approximately 3 minutes)

INTRODUCE the lesson.

Say the following to the group after settling the students together at a table. We are going to practice hearing words in sentences, and we'll do some new Stand-Up Sentences. Then we'll play a game called Move the Chip.

Introduce the nursery rhyme. We already learned a nursery rhyme about something that twinkles in the sky at night. Who can tell me what twinkles at night?

▶ **Children's response: Stars.**

That's right. We learned "Twinkle, Twinkle, Little Star." Today we'll learn a nursery rhyme and a song about something else that can shine up in the sky at night. What else can you see shining in the night sky besides a star?

▶ **Children's response: The moon.**

That's right. The moon can shine up in the night sky. *Optional: Show a picture or toy moon and hold it up high like in the sky.*

Turn On Your Ears

Listen to this funny nursery rhyme. It's called "Hey Diddle, Diddle." Some of you may already know it. If you know it, say it softly with me. *Use a large nursery rhyme picture book. Point to each word while saying the rhyme.*

Hey diddle, diddle,
The cat and the fiddle,
The cow jumped over the moon.
The little dog laughed to see such sport,
And the dish ran away with the spoon.

Repeat the rhyme before moving on if it seems new to most of the children.

Good job listening to "Hey Diddle, Diddle." Now say the first part with me. *Build auditory awareness and listening awareness. Stop using the nursery rhyme book. Look at each child's face and smile while reciting to encourage all to participate.*

▶ **Children's response:**
Hey diddle, diddle,
The cat and the fiddle,
The cow jumped over the moon.

Great job saying that with me. *If any child seems uncertain, then repeat once or twice.*

Isn't that funny? That nursery rhyme has words that sound funny. Let's say some of them. *Diddle* and *fiddle.* Say it with me. *Place your hands in front of you, palms forward; move each hand forward slightly as you say each rhyming word.*

▶ **Children's response: Diddle, fiddle, diddle, fiddle.**

Do those words rhyme? *Look around at each student.*

▶ **Children's response: Yes.**

SING the "Rhyming Exercise Song."

Yes. They rhyme. Let's sing our "Rhyming Exercise Song". Get your rhyme muscles nice and firm so our rhymes are in great shape. Follow me.

 Multisensory Reinforcement

Do the movements: Pause and flex your wrists with your palms up. Put your hands in the sky. *On the word hands, stretch one arm up to the sky and then the other arm.* Do the rhyming exercise.

Diddle *(Stretch one arm up as you say the word.)*
Fiddle *(Stretch the other arm up.)*
Diddle *(Switch arms.)*
Fiddle *(Switch arms.)*
Diddle *(Switch arms.)*
Fiddle *(Switch arms.)*

Do they rhyme? *Pause here and allow them to show thumbs up or thumbs down before you respond. Look around at each student and make eye contact.* Yes. *Nod vigorously.* They rhyme. *Give two thumbs up.*

 **TASK 2**   Move the Chip (approximately 12–14 minutes)

LINK the transition song to the big idea.

I like that nursery rhyme and the way that you said the words in the sentences.

Diddle is a silly word that doesn't mean anything, but *fiddle* is a real word. Who knows what a fiddle is? *Accept one or two responses.*

◇ **Vocabulary**

A fiddle is a musical instrument that you play on your shoulder with a long stick called a bow—you saw one in the nursery rhyme book. See the fiddle? *Show a picture of a fiddle from a book.*

Let's all play the fiddle. *Pretend to have a fiddle on your shoulder and a bow in the other hand; move the bow and pretend to play. Have the children do the same.*

What are we playing?

▶ **Children's response: The fiddle.**

Yes, the fiddle. A fiddle is also called a violin. What is another name for a fiddle?

▶ **Children's response: Violin.**

Yes, violin. Good job. *Practice hearing and clapping words in sentences.*

Listen to this part of the nursery rhyme: The little dog laughed. The words go together to make a sentence. What do the words go together to make?

▶ **Children's response: A sentence.**

Watch me say the sentence slowly while I clap my hands for each word in the sentence. *Say the words slowly, clapping once with each word.* The *(clap)* little *(clap)* dog *(clap)* laughed *(clap).*

Say that with me. Let's clap our hands once for each word.

▶ **Children's response: The *(clap)* little *(clap)* dog *(clap)* laughed *(clap).***

Great. We clapped for each word in the first sentence. Now it's time to make a Stand-Up Sentence.

Each of you will stand for one word from our sentence. *Choose four students to stand shoulder to shoulder for the words* the, little, dog, *and* laughed.

Okay. Now, when you each say your word, your words will go together to make our whole sentence. When I point to you, say your word. *Point at a moderate pace.*

▶ **Children say, in turn: The - little - dog - laughed.**

Listen, everyone. We have a Stand-Up Sentence. Say it again. *Point at a faster pace.*

▶ **Children say, in turn: The - little - dog - laughed.**

Wow! You each said one word and together they made a sentence from our nursery rhyme. The little dog laughed. You made a sentence that tells what the dog did when he saw the cat playing a fiddle.

Teacher demonstrates clapping out sentences. Say that sentence one more time, and this time I will clap once for each word.

▶ **Children's response: The little dog laughed.**

If there are other children, they will also clap. Standing students do not clap. Simplify the task of the standing students by giving them only one step.

Now, let's make a different Stand-Up Sentence. *Continue in the same format, giving all students a turn to stand. Practice two more sentences.*

Mary had a little lamb. *(Choose students.)*

▶ **Children's response: Mary had a little lamb.**

You made a sentence from a different nursery rhyme. Let's try a new sentence: Mary ate four cheeseburgers.

▶ **Children's response: Mary ate four cheeseburgers.**

REVIEW the big idea: practice hearing and clapping words in sentences.

 Turn On Your Ears

PRACTICE Stand-Up Sentences.

 Turn On Your Ears

ENGAGE in group practice.

Teacher claps four times.

Teacher and remaining students clap five times.

3.1

Wow. *Cheeseburgers* is a big word, but it's still just one word, so I only will clap for it one time.

Tell students the skill they have mastered. I like the way you took turns being the words in our Stand-Up Sentences. Each student stood for one word, and your words went together to make a sentence that tells us something.

♣ **PLAY** the game.

 CD-ROM   See Appendix D on the CD-ROM for the Move the Chip Game instructions, display board, and game pieces.

 TASK 3   **Transition song to end the lesson** (approximately 3 minutes)

SING a transition song.

Your good work makes me very proud. Look at my smile. I am like the big moon shining at you *(show children a picture of the moon or a toy moon)*; you are my shining stars. I think I can see you twinkling and giving off light.

Now I am going to sing you a song about a man who lives in the moon. Wouldn't that be funny to live way up in the sky in the moon?

Play music from http://www.gardenofsong.com, if desired.
There was a man who lived in the moon, in the moon, in the moon.
There was a man who lived in the moon, and his name was Aiken Drum.
And he played upon a ladle, a ladle, a ladle.
And he played upon a ladle, and his name was Aiken Drum.

Repeat.

DO the exit task to assess skill mastery.

Good job listening to the first part of the song about a man named Aiken Drum who lives in the moon. Later you will hear some more funny parts of that song. Now show me if you can clap for each word in the sentence I give you.

Say one sentence for each child. Have the child repeat the sentence and clap it out, helping if necessary. Use the following exit sentences (match sentence length to child's skill at hearing words): "There was a man" (four claps), "He lived in the moon" (five claps), "His name was _____ (substitute child's first name) Drum" (five claps), "The cow jumped over the moon" (six claps), and "A man lived in the moon" (six claps).

END Lesson 2.

Everyone now gets their winnings for hearing the words in sentences and for working hard. *Give out token rewards to each child.*

LESSON 3: What Do You Like?

OBJECTIVES

Student will

- Learn how to build short oral sentences using pictures
- Clap to segment the sentences into words

Teacher will

- Model how to hear the individual words in short sentences by building oral sentences from given pictures

RHYMES, SONGS, AND FINGERPLAYS

"Aiken Drum"

"Twinkle, Twinkle, Little Star"

"Star Light, Star Bright"

MATERIALS

Large nursery rhyme book(s) with "Aiken Drum" and "Star Light, Star Bright"

Ladle or a picture of a ladle

Tokens for behavior/participation

What Do You Like? Game

☑ Three buckets

☑ Heart, teacher, subject, and object cards (see Appendix D on the CD-ROM)

☑ Word list (see Appendix D on the CD-ROM)

CD-ROM

 TASK 1   **Song to begin the lesson** (approximately 3 minutes)

INTRODUCE the lesson.	*Settle the group at a table and say the following.* We are going to practice hearing words in sentences in a funny nursery song. Then we'll clap out words in sentences and play a game called What Do You Like?
INTRODUCE the song.	Yesterday you heard a nursery song called "Aiken Drum" about a funny man who lives up in the moon. *Show children the picture of the moon or the toy moon.* I like that song because it's fun to add more words to it to make it sound silly. Let's sing the first part together.

Play music from http://www.gardenofsong.com, if desired.

There was a man who lived in the moon, in the moon, in the moon.

There was a man who lived in the moon, and his name was Aiken Drum.

And he played upon a ladle, a ladle, a ladle.

And he played upon a ladle, and his name was Aiken Drum.

 **Vocabulary**	Nice job singing with me. In the second part, we said that Aiken Drum plays upon a ladle. *Show a ladle or picture of a ladle.*
LADLE	Did any of you ever see a ladle? *Accept several responses.*
	Where did you see a ladle? You may have seen a ladle in a kitchen because a ladle is a kind of spoon. What is a ladle?

▶ **Children's response: A kind of spoon.**

Yes, a ladle is a big spoon for serving food that is liquid or drippy. Who can think of something you eat that could be served with a ladle?

▶ **Children's response: Soup, beans, punch.**

 **Multisensory Reinforcement**	*Pretend to pour soup. Get children to join in.* Let's all take our ladles and serve up some soup. What are we using to serve up our soup? Yes, our ladles.

So, isn't it funny that Aiken Drum played upon a ladle? That is so funny. He must have thought it was a musical instrument. Maybe he thought it was a fiddle or a guitar. Maybe he took the ladle and played it like this. *Pretend to strum.*

DEVELOP creative word usage.

Encourage children to make up their own descriptions of Aiken Drum.

I can think of some new, funny words for this song to tell what I think Aiken Drum looked like.

Sing two or three funny verses.
There was a man who lived in the moon, in the moon, in the moon.
There was a man who lived in the moon, and his name was Aiken Drum.
And his hat was made of cream cheese, of cream cheese, of cream cheese.
And his hat was made of cream cheese, and his name was Aiken Drum.

Can you think of some words that tell something about what Aiken Drum looked like? Let's describe him in interesting ways with food. *Examples might include the following: "His eyes were made of peaches." "His coat was made of pork chops." "His mouth was a carrot."*

 TASK 2

What Do You Like? (approximately 12 minutes)

LINK the transition song to hearing words in sentences.

You did a nice job making up sentences to sing about a funny man who lived in the moon. We have been having fun this week listening to words in sentences and clapping them out. Let's practice some sentences together, clapping once for each word in a sentence.

The stars can twinkle. Say that sentence again with me, and clap one time for each word. *Clap four times while repeating the sentence.*

▶ **Children's response: The *(clap)* stars *(clap)* can *(clap)* twinkle *(clap)*.**

Good job clapping out the words in a sentence. Let's do some more together. *Complete four or five sentences following the same format.*

I like fried chicken. *(four claps)*
Mother sang a nursery rhyme. *(five claps)*
Sally likes to sing. *(four claps)*
The man has a fiddle. *(five claps)*
We see stars at night. *(five claps)*
I pour soup with a ladle. *(six claps)*

 PLAY the game.

 CD-ROM   See Appendix D on the CD-ROM for the What Do You Like? Game instructions, cards, and word list.

 TASK 3

Transition rhymes to end the lesson (approximately 3 minutes)

END Lesson 3 with transition nursery rhymes.

Let's sing our nursery rhyme about stars that twinkle up in the sky.

▶ **Children's response: Twinkle, twinkle, little star, how I wonder what you are.**
Up above the world so high, like a diamond in the sky.
Twinkle, twinkle, little star, how I wonder what you are.

Isn't that a nice nursery rhyme? There are many babies who fall right asleep when they hear that song in their nurseries. Children like to look up at the stars in the sky at night. Did you know that when you see a star, you can make a wish? Here is another nursery rhyme about making a wish on a star. *Option:*

Show pictures from a large read-aloud book as you read "Star Light, Star Bright."

Star light, star bright,
First star I see tonight.
I wish I may, I wish I might,
Have this wish I wish tonight.

Say it with me. *Repeat the nursery rhyme several times with the children.*

▶ **Children's response:**
Star light, star bright,
First star I see tonight.
I wish I may, I wish I might,
Have this wish I wish tonight.

DO the exit task to demonstrate skill mastery.

Good job saying some rhymes about the stars. Here's my wish: I wish there were more hard-working students like you! Now, show me if you can clap for each word in the sentence I give you.

Say one sentence for each child. Have the child repeat the sentence and clap it out, helping if necessary. Use the following exit sentences (match sentence length to child's skill at hearing words): "I see a star" (four claps), "I see a twinkly star" (five claps), "I wished on a star" (five claps), "_____ (substitute child's name) wished on a star" (five claps), "A cow jumped over the moon" (six claps), and "A man lived in the moon" (six claps).

END Lesson 3.

You all did a good job building sentences and clapping out the words in them. Everyone gets their winnings for hearing the words in sentences and for working hard. *Give out token rewards to each child.*

LESSON 4: Sentence Segmentation Review

OBJECTIVES

Student will

- Demonstrate the ability to listen carefully to the separate words in sentences, clap them out in multisensory practice, and move chips to show the number of words

Teacher will

- Review and reinforce the segmenting of brief oral sentences
- Guide students to demonstrate the skill independently in two activities

RHYMES, SONGS, AND FINGERPLAYS

"Bend and Stretch"

"Star Light, Star Bright"

MATERIALS

Eight colored chips for each child

Tokens for behavior/participation

☑ DROPP 3 Skill Assessment
  Checkout

Move the Chip Game

☑ Display board   ☑ Game pieces

CD-ROM

TASK 1 | Song to begin the lesson (approximately 3 minutes)

INTRODUCE the lesson.	*Settle the group at a table and say the following.* You have been learning how to listen to the words in sentences. Today we are going to practice all the ways we know to hear words in sentences. *View the following video clip for a demonstration of music and song motions: http://www.youtube.com/watch?v=aIRu8-5Nyek.*
INTRODUCE the song with motions.	Let's begin with an action song you learned before. Remember, an action is something we do. Everyone, what is an action?

► **Children's response: Something we do.**

Our action song is called "Bend and Stretch." Let's get our bodies ready. *Shake your arms and legs.* Eyes on me. Let's sing it together.

SING the song.

(Sing.) Bend and stretch. *(Touch toes.)*
Reach for the stars. *(Raise fingertips toward ceiling.)*
There goes Jupiter. *(Sway body back and forth.)*
Here comes Mars. *(Continue to sway.)*
Bend and stretch. *(Touch toes.)*
Reach for the sky. *(Raise fingertips toward ceiling.)*
Standing on tippy-toes. *(Rise up onto tiptoes.)*
Oh, so high. *(Big smile as you bring hands back to your sides.)*

TASK 2A | Reviewing sentence segmentation (approximately 6 minutes)

 Vocabulary

SENTENCE

 Turn On Your Ears

 Multisensory Reinforcement

BEGIN Stand-Up Sentences.

Nice job singing "Bend and Stretch." Now you are ready to show what you know about words in sentences.

Listen to this sentence: We all like apples. The words go together to make a sentence. What do the words go together to make?

► **Children's response: A sentence.**

Yes, a sentence. Watch me say that sentence slowly while I clap my hands for each word in the sentence. *Say the sentence slowly, clapping softly once with each word.*

We *(clap)* all *(clap)* like *(clap)* apples *(clap)*.

Do that with me. Let's clap our hands once for each word.

► **Children's response: We *(clap)* all *(clap)* like *(clap)* apples *(clap)*.**

Great. We clapped for each word in the first sentence. Now it's time to make a Stand-Up Sentence. *Choose four students to stand up shoulder to shoulder.*

Each of you will get to be one word from our sentence. *Continue until each child says his or her one word.*

► **Children say, in turn: We - all - like - apples.**

Okay. Now when you each say your word, your words will go together to make our whole sentence. When I point to you, say your word. Get ready. *Point at a moderate pace at first. Gradually, point at a faster pace so that the words flow together like a sentence.*

► **Children say, in turn: We - all - like - apples.**

Listen, everyone, we have a Stand-Up Sentence. Say it again.

► **Children's response: We all like apples.**

Wow. You each said one word and together they made a sentence.

Add clapping to the Stand-Up Sentence. Say that sentence one more time, and this time I will clap once for each word.

▶ **Standing children's response: We** *(clap)* **all** *(clap)* **like** *(clap)* **apples** *(clap)*.

Teacher claps four times.

Students who are not standing may clap with teacher. Children who are standing do not clap. I clapped one time for each word in our Stand-Up Sentence. Good job saying the words that make our first sentence.

PRACTICE the task.

Now, let's make a different Stand-Up Sentence. *Choose five children. Follow previous format, rotating children's turns.*

Mary - had - a - little - lamb.

Everyone, say that sentence again.

▶ **Children's response: Mary had a little lamb.**

Say it a little faster, so it sounds just the way we talk.

▶ **Children's response: Mary had a little lamb.**

Emphasize that the words make a sentence that tells us something. Comment on what the sentences tell the children to do. You made a sentence that tells us about the lamb in a nursery rhyme we know.

Here's another sentence.

Mother ate two cheeseburgers.

Everyone, say that sentence again.

▶ **Children's response: Mother ate two cheeseburgers.**

Say it the way we talk.

▶ **Children's response: Mother ate two cheeseburgers.**

Comment on what the sentences tell the children to do. Wow! *Cheeseburgers* is a big word, but it's still just one word, so I only will clap for it one time.

Repeat each Stand-Up Sentence several times. Then clap out the words several more times. Additional sentence options include "The cat had a fiddle" (five claps), "The cow jumped over the moon" (six claps), and "I ride my bike" (four claps).

Tell students the skill they have mastered. I like the way you took turns being the words in our Stand-Up Sentences. Each student stood for one word.

 TASK 2B   Move the Chip *(approximately 8 minutes)*

 PLAY the game.

 See Appendix D on the CD-ROM for the Move the Chip Game instructions, display board, and game pieces.

TASK 3 Transition nursery rhyme to end the lesson (approximately 3 minutes)

END Lesson 4 with a transition nursery rhyme.	Do you remember that you can make a wish when you see a star? Let's finish our lesson by saying our nursery rhyme about making a wish on a star. Say it with me. ▶ Children recite: Star light, star bright, First star I see tonight. I wish I may, I wish I might, Have this wish I wish tonight. *Repeat the nursery rhyme several times with the children.*
DO the exit task to demonstrate skill mastery.	Here's my wish. I wish there were more hard-working students like you around! Now stand up to show me if you can clap for each word in the sentence I give you. *Let each child step forward and say one of the sentences. Scaffold the exit task to ensure success for every student. Give the shorter sentences to students who are not yet skilled at hearing and clapping out the words. Help them to complete the task successfully, if necessary. Exit sentences include the following: "I like school" (three claps), "I worked hard today" (four claps), "I have fun in school" (five claps), "We eat pizza at lunch" (five claps), and "Now we go back to class" (six claps).*
END Lesson 4.	You all did a good job today building sentences and clapping out the words in them. Everyone now gets their winnings for hearing the words in sentences and for working hard. *Give out token rewards to each child.*

CD-ROM The DROPP 3 Skill Assessment Checkout will be completed for each student following this lesson.

ACTIVITY SET 3.2

Lesson Descriptions

Lessons	Sequence of daily activities	✧ Vocabulary
Lesson 1: Stand-Up Sentences	Movement song: "Amy Finds a Friend" Target: Clap and stand in a row to segment sentences into words Movement song: "Ring Around the Rosie"	Action Posies
Lesson 2: Move the Chip	Nursery rhyme: "Down by the Station" Target: Move the Chip to segment sentences into words Movement song: "Amy Finds a Friend"	Pufferbellies Station
Lesson 3: What Do You Like?	Movement song: "Sally Go Round the Sun" Target: Form picture sentences, segment into words Nursery rhymes: "Humpty Dumpty"	Chimney
Lesson 4: Sentence Segmentation Review	Movement song: "Sally Go Round the Sun" Review: Stand-Up Sentences Review: Move the Chip Nursery rhyme: "Star Light, Star Bright"	Sentence

Materials Needed

☑ Large nursery rhyme book(s) with "Ring Around the Rosie," "Down by the Station," "Sally Go Round the Sun," and "Humpty Dumpty"

☑ Up to eight large colored circles

☑ Up to eight colored chips for each child

☑ Picture of a chimney

☑ Three small buckets

☑ Optional: Toy train car

☑ Tokens for behavior/participation

☑ DROPP 3 Skill Assessment Checkout (see Appendix B on the CD-ROM)

 CD-ROM

Move the Chip Game

☑ Display board (see Appendix D on the CD-ROM)

☑ Game pieces (see Appendix D on the CD-ROM)

What Do You Like? Game

☑ Three buckets

☑ Heart, teacher, subject, and object cards (see Appendix D on the CD-ROM)

☑ Word list (see Appendix D on the CD-ROM)

ACTIVITY SET

3.2 **10-Day Planner**

Day 1	**Lesson 1:** Stand-Up Sentences
Day 2	**Lesson 1:** Stand-Up Sentences
Day 3	**Lesson 2:** Move the Chip
Day 4	**Lesson 2:** Move the Chip
Day 5	**Lesson 3:** What Do You Like?
Day 6	**Lesson 3:** What Do You Like?
Day 7	**Lesson 1:** Stand-Up Sentences
Day 8	**Lesson 2:** Move the Chip
Day 9	**Lesson 3:** What Do You Like?
Day 10	**Lesson 4:** Sentence Segmentation Review

LESSON 1: Stand-Up Sentences

OBJECTIVES

Student will

- Learn how to separate (segment) words in short sentences by clapping out each word
- Stand up as one word in a human sentence

Teacher will

- Review word awareness in a familiar rhyme, model how to clap out words in sentences, and guide students to stand and say each word in a sentence

RHYMES, SONGS, AND FINGERPLAYS

"Amy Finds a Friend"

"Ring Around the Rosie"

MATERIALS

Large nursery rhyme book with "Ring Around the Rosie"

Six large colored circles

Tokens for behavior/participation

TECHNOLOGY LINK

View the following video clip to learn the song and movements: http://www.youtube.com/watch?v=yWWOpGnYVXkto learn song and movements

---

 TASK 1 Movement song to begin the lesson (approximately 3 minutes)

INTRODUCE the big idea: sentences.	*Settle the students in their seats and say the following.* We are going to learn about sentences. Sentences are made of words that we can say. It is fun saying and listening for the words that make a sentence.
BEGIN the transition activity.	First, you are going to learn an action song called "Amy Finds a Friend." We learned that an action song is a song we can sing while doing something with our bodies.
Vocabulary **ACTION**	Everybody, what is an action? ▶ **Children's response: Something we can do.** *Arrange the children in a circle.* Yes. An action is something we can do. In this song, the action is to skip around our circle, then choose a friend. I'll go first to show you how it works.
SING the song.	*Sing to the tune of "Farmer in the Dell." Walk or skip around the circle; then choose someone to join you. Sing it again, and let that child choose a friend.*
Multisensory Reinforcement	_____ *(insert your own name)* finds a friend; _____ finds a friend; hi, ho, away we go, _____finds a friend. _____ *(insert a child's name)* finds a friend; _____ finds a friend; hi, ho, away we go, _____finds a friend. *Continue until all are children's names have been used.*

 TASK 2A Stand-Up Sentences (approximately 10 minutes)

INTRODUCE the skill through song.	That was fun singing and skipping and finding all our friends. Now we're going to learn another nursery rhyme about a circle game that we can play with friends. It's called "Ring Around the Rosie." My turn to sing "Ring Around the Rosie." *Use a large nursery rhyme picture book.*

Point to each word while singing the entire song.

Ring around the rosie,
A pocket full of posies,
Ashes! ashes!
We all fall down!

Good job listening to "Ring Around the Rosie." Now I want you to sing it with me. *Build listening awareness by closing the nursery rhyme book. Look at each child's face and smile while singing to encourage all to participate.*

▶ Children's response:
Ring around the rosie,
A pocket full of posies,
Ashes! Ashes!
We all fall down!

Great job singing with me. *Repeat once or twice.*

That sounded wonderful. You sang the words in the nursery rhyme. One of the words we sang was *rosie. Rosie* is a funny way of saying roses. In the song, *rosie* rhymes with *posies.* What are posies? Raise your hand if you know.

Posies are flowers. What is another word for posies? *Call on one or two children.*

▶ Children's response: Flowers.

Yes, flowers. Let's smell our bouquet of posies. *Pretend to smell a bouquet of flowers.* In a little while, when we play the circle came "Ring Around the Rosie," we will pretend to stand in a circle around some pretty flowers, or posies.

Demonstrate clapping out sentences. Posies is one of the words in our song. The words go together to make a sentence. Everyone, what do the words go together to make?

▶ Children's response: A sentence.

Yes, words go together to make a sentence. Watch me say a sentence slowly, while I clap my hands for each word in the sentence. *Say the sentence slowly, clapping softly with each word.*

Ring *(clap)* around *(clap)* the *(clap)* rosie *(clap).*

Do that with me. Let's clap our hands once for each word.

▶ Children's response: Ring *(clap)* around *(clap)* the *(clap)* rosie *(clap).*

Correction procedure: Demonstrate correctly and repeat until firm. If a child claps twice for a two-syllable word, such as rosie, say the following: Wait. Rosie is just one word, even though you heard two parts in it. So only clap your hands once because rosie is one word.

Great. We clapped for each word in the first sentence of our rhyme. Now it's time to make a Stand-Up Sentence. *Choose four students to stand up in a row, shoulder to shoulder.* Each of you will stand for one word from our first sentence. *To Child 1:* You're first. Your word is *ring. (Child 1 says the word.) Assign words to the four students. Continue until each child says his or her one word.*

Okay, each of you stands for a word. Now, when you each say your word, your words will go together to make our whole sentence. When I point to you, say your word. *Point at a moderate pace at first. Gradually, point at a faster pace so that the words flow together like a sentence.*

▶ Child 1: Ring; Child 2: around; Child 3: the; Child 4: rosie.

 Vocabulary

POSIES

 Model the Activity

LINK clapping out words to Stand-Up Sentences.

161

Listen, everyone. We have a Stand-Up Sentence. Say it again.

▶ **Children say, in turn: Ring - around - the - rosie.**

Wow! You each said one word and together they made a sentence from our nursery rhyme. You made a sentence that tells us to make a ring, or circle, around some pretty flowers.

Add clapping to the Stand-Up Sentence. Say that sentence one more time, and this time I will clap once for each word.

▶ **Standing children's response: Ring around the rosie.**

Teacher claps after each word.

Students who are not standing can clap with the teacher. Children who are standing do not clap. Simplify the standing students' action by giving them only one task. Good job clapping and saying the words that make our first sentence.

Now, let's make a different Stand-Up Sentence. Here is our next sentence.

PRACTICE the task, linking meaning to sentences.

Amy - finds - a - friend. *Choose four children.*

When I point to you, say your word. *Follow previous format, rotating children's turns.*

▶ **Children's response: Amy - finds - a - friend.**

Everyone, say that sentence again.

▶ **Children's response: Amy finds a friend.**

Say it again, a little faster. *Point at a faster pace.*

▶ **Children's response: Amy finds a friend.**

Emphasize that the words make a sentence that tells us something. Comment on what the sentences tell the children to do. You made a sentence about our first action song. Here's our next sentence. I like pufferbellies. *Choose three children.*

▶ **Children's response: I - like - pufferbellies.**

Everyone, say that sentence again.

▶ **Children's response: I like pufferbellies.**

Say it again, a little faster.

▶ **Children's response: I like pufferbellies.**

Wow. *Pufferbellies* is a big word. It's a long word, but it's still just one word, so I only will clap for it one time.

Repeat each Stand-Up Sentence several times; then clap out the words several more times. Additional sentence options include: "I have a new friend." "Posies are flowers." and "I ride the bus."

Tell students the skill they have mastered. I like the way you took turns being the words in our Stand-Up Sentences. Each student stood for one word.

 **TASK 2B**   **Preview of upcoming lesson** *(approximately 3 minutes)*

INTRODUCE the upcoming activity.

 Turn On Your Ears

Prepare the display board ahead of time. Place seven large different-colored circles at the top of chart paper, with a blank line beneath. Now I will show you something else I like to do when I hear words in sentences. Listen.

Repeat more slowly.

Away we go.

Watch this. *Move one colored circle down to the line for each word while saying the words slowly.*

Away - we - go. *Point to and touch each of the three circles while repeating the sentence.* Look. I moved down one chip for each word I said in my sentence.

Away we go. *Point to each circle.* Say it with me.

▶ Children's response: **Away we go.**

Good job saying the words in my sentence. *Move circles back to top.*

PRACTICE with the students.

Here's another sentence: I rode my bike. *Move circles down, repeating the sentence word by word.*

Repeat more slowly.

I - rode - my - bike. *Touch each circle while repeating the sentence.*

Say it with me.

▶ Children's response: **I rode my bike.**

Now I will choose a student to touch the circles for our words. *Choose a student.* Touch one circle for each word we say.

▶ Children's response: **I rode my bike.** *(Student touches the circles.)*

Let's practice some more sentences. *If students' responses are correct with four-word sentences, increase sentence length. Follow the same procedure with "I rode my bike today" and "I rode my bike with Diamond today."*

Compliment the students' performance. You did a great job hearing the words in sentences.

 **TASK 3**   Transition song to end the lesson *(approximately 3 minutes)*

SING a transition song.

You worked hard today hearing the words in sentences. I would like to give you some pretend posies for all your hard work. Here, each of you can have some pretty posies. *Pretend to pick some flowers and hand them to the children. Then, pretend to smell a bouquet of flowers.* These posies smell sweet!

 Multisensory Reinforcement

Now let's stand up and make a circle, or a ring, around our posies. *Put imaginary flowers in the middle of the carpet; then, hold hands with the children to form a circle.*

Who remembers the name of the nursery rhyme we sang earlier?

▶ Children's response: **"Ring Around the Rosie."**

That's right, "Ring Around the Rosie." Let's sing it, and this time we will walk in a circle. At the end, we will pretend to fall down.

Watch me and do what I do. Sing along if you remember the words. *Walk around in a circle, holding hands.*

▶ Children's response:

**Ring around the rosie,
A pocket full of posies,
Ashes! Ashes!
We all fall down!** *(Stoop down at the end.)*

DO the exit task to demonstrate skill mastery.

Good job. Now line up to show me if you can clap for each word in a sentence.

_____ , *(choose a child)* your turn. Listen: Away we go. Say it and clap it.

▶ Child's response: Away *(clap)* we *(clap)* go *(clap)*.

Let each child have one turn. Use additional sentences, giving shorter sentences to students who are not yet skilled at hearing and clapping out the words. Help them to complete the task successfully, if necessary. Additional exit sentences include the following: "Posy means flower" *(three claps),* "_____ (insert child's name) finds a friend" *(four claps),* "I have a pufferbelly" *(four claps),* "I have a new friend" *(five claps),"* and *"I did my best today" (five claps).*

END Lesson 1.

Everyone now gets their winnings for hearing the words in sentences and for working hard. *Give out token rewards to each child.*

LESSON 2: Move the Chip

OBJECTIVES

Student will

- Learn how to segment words in sentences by moving chips to show how many words are heard

Teacher will

- Model how to segment three- to six-word sentences
- Guide students to hear the individual words in short sentences

RHYMES, SONGS, AND FINGERPLAYS

"Down by the Station"

"Amy Finds a Friend"

MATERIALS

Large nursery rhyme book with "Down by the Station"

Optional: Toy train car

Six to eight large colored circles

Five to eight colored chips for each child

Move the Chip Game

☑ Display board

☑ Game pieces

 TASK 1   Nursery rhyme to begin the lesson *(approximately 3 minutes)*

INTRODUCE the lesson.

Say the following to the group after settling the students together at a table. We are going to practice hearing words in sentences, and we'll do some new Stand-Up Sentences. Then we'll play our game called Move the Chip.

INTRODUCE the nursery rhyme.

We already learned a nursery rhyme about having our pockets full of posies. Who can tell me what posies are?

▶ Children's response: Flowers.

That's right. Posies are flowers. We got in a circle and sang "Ring Around the Rosie." Today we'll learn a song about getting in a straight line, not a circle. Our new nursery rhyme song is called "Down by the Station." It is about trains. Have you ever seen train cars lined up all in a row? *Accept several answers.*

In the front car, a person called the station master pulls a handle down to make the train go down the track. Then it can pull the whole row of train cars.

 Vocabulary

PUFFERBELLIES

In this nursery rhyme, the train cars are called pufferbellies. They have that funny name because when the train starts to go, it puffs out smoke. Pufferbelly is an old-fashioned name for a train car. Everybody, what is an old-fashioned name for train cars?

▶ Children's response: Pufferbellies.

Yes, a pufferbelly is a train car. Everybody, what is a pufferbelly?

▶ Children's response: A train car.

SAY the rhyme.

Yes, a train car. Now I will sing a nursery rhyme about pufferbellies called "Down by the Station." Some of you may already know it. If you know it, sing it with me. *Use a large nursery rhyme picture book. Point to each word while singing.*

Down by the station, early in the morning.
See the little pufferbellies, all in a row.
See the station master turn the little handle.
Puff, puff, toot, toot, off we go.

Repeat the song one or two times.

 **Vocabulary**

STATION

Didn't that sound nice? We sang about what it is like to see the trains going out of the train station. Who knows what a station is?

▶ **Children may answer "A place you go," "I went to the bus station," and so forth.**

A station is a special building or place. Everybody, what can you call a special building or place?

▶ Children's response: A station.

That's right, a station. The train station is a special building for trains. What can we call a special building for trains?

▶ Children's response: A train station.

Yes, a train station. It has tracks, special oil for the train wheels, and special places for people to buy train tickets and wait for the train. Has anyone ever been in a train or bus station? What did you see/do there? *Accept all answers.*

🪐 **TASK 2**   **Move the Chip** (approximately 12–14 minutes)

LINK the transition song to the big idea: sentences.

I like that nursery rhyme about the trains. It had sentences that told us about the train station. *Teach children the last section of the rhyme song.*

Now I want you to sing the last part with me. *Sing with the children. Do not use nursery rhyme book any longer. Look at each child's face and smile while reciting to encourage all to participate.*

See the station master turn the little handle,
Puff, puff, toot, toot, off we go.

Let's sing that last part again. Great job singing with me.

INTRODUCE a new idea.

Change a song to spoken sentences. I like the way you sang part of that song. Let's listen to the words we sang. Listen to me as I say them like we talk. See the station master. *Slowly say the words in a conversational tone.* Say that with me.

▶ Children's response: See the station master.

Again.

▶ Children's response: See the station master.

Good job.

3.2

REVIEW the big idea.

Review hearing and clapping words in sentences. I like the way you said that just like you were talking. Those words go together to make a sentence. What do the words go together to make?

▶ **Children's response: A sentence.**

Watch me say those words slowly while I clap my hands for each word. *Say slowly, clapping once with each word.*

See *(clap)* the *(clap)* station *(clap)* master *(clap)*.

Do that with me. Let's clap our hands once for each word.

▶ **Children's response: See *(clap)* the *(clap)* station *(clap)* master *(clap)*.**

Great. We clapped for each word in the first sentence.

PRACTICE Stand-Up Sentences.

Review stand-up sentences. Now it's time to make a Stand-Up Sentence. Each of you will stand for one word from our sentence. *Choose four students to stand shoulder to shoulder for* see, the, station, *and* master. Okay. When you each say your word, they will go together to make our whole sentence. When I point to you, say your word. *Point at a moderate pace at first and then get faster.*

▶ **Individual children: See - the - station - master.**

Listen, everyone. We have a Stand-Up Sentence. Say it again.

Turn On Your Ears

▶ **Individual children: See the station master.**

Wow! You each said one word and together they made a sentence from our nursery rhyme. You made a sentence that tells us to look at the master person in charge of the train station.

ENGAGE in group practice.

Practice saying and clapping out sentences. Let's make another Stand-Up Sentence.

Off they go. That is a short sentence. It tells us that the train is going off on a trip. Say that sentence one more time, and this time I will clap once for each word.

Teacher claps three times.

▶ **Children's response: Off they go.**

Continue in the same format, giving all students a turn. Practice several more sentences, including the following: "Go to the station" (four claps), "Stand in a row" (four claps), and "Twinkle, twinkle, little star" (four claps).

Give specific praise to tell the students the skill they have mastered. I like the way you took turns being the words in our Stand-Up Sentences. Each student stood for one word, and your words went together to make a sentence that tells us something.

♣ **PLAY** the game.

CD-ROM See Appendix D on the CD-ROM for the Move the Chip Game instructions, display board, and game pieces.

 TASK 3 **Transition song to end the lesson** (approximately 3 minutes)

SING a new transition song.

You worked hard today. You are a group of hard-working friends! So let's practice the action song we learned called "Amy Finds a Friend." The action you will each do is skip around our circle, choose a friend, and then get in line.

Arrange the children in a circle. Sing to the tune of "Farmer in the Dell." Child 1 skips around the circle and chooses a child. Sing it again while Child 2 chooses a friend.

Continue until all children have had a turn, using this format: _____ (say first child's name) finds a friend; _____ finds a friend; hi, ho, away we go, _____ finds a friend.

USE an exit task to assess skill mastery.	Now show me that you can clap for each word in the sentence I give you.

Let each child have one turn. Have the child repeat the sentence and clap it out, helping if necessary. Give short sentences to children who are not yet proficient. Exit sentences include the following (match sentence length to child's skill at hearing words.): "_____ (child's name) works hard" (three claps), "_____ (child's name) found a friend" (four claps), "_____ (child's name) rode a train" (four claps), "I went to the station" (five claps), "That train went so fast" (five claps), and "I like to ride a train" (six claps).

END Lesson 2.	Everyone now gets their winnings for hearing the words in sentences and for working hard. *Give out token rewards to each child.*

LESSON 3: What Do You Like?

OBJECTIVES

Student will

- Learn how to build short oral sentences using pictures
- Clap to segment the sentences into words

Teacher will

- Model how to hear the individual words in short sentences by building oral sentences from given pictures

RHYMES, SONGS, AND FINGERPLAYS

"Sally Go Round the Sun"

"Humpty Dumpty"

MATERIALS

Large nursery rhyme book(s) with "Sally Go Round the Sun" and "Humpty Dumpty"

Picture of a chimney

Tokens for behavior/participation

What Do You Like? Game

☑ Three buckets

☑ Heart, teacher, subject, and object cards (see Appendix D on the CD-ROM)

☑ Word list (see Appendix D on the CD-ROM)

CD-ROM

 TASK 1 — Action song to begin the lesson (approximately 3 minutes)

INTRODUCE the lesson.	*Settle the group at a table and say the following.* We are going to practice hearing and clapping words in sentences in a new action song. Then we'll play a game you know called "What Do You Like?"

You are going to learn an action song called "Sally Go Round the Sun." An action is a thing to do. Everybody, what is an action?

▶ **Children's response: A thing to do.**

Yes. An action is a thing we can do. In this song, the action is to skip around our circle in one direction. When we say "boom-boom" we will skip in the other direction. *Show children pictures from the song in the nursery rhyme book.*

Let's try it. *Form a circle holding hands. Walk or skip in one direction, singing to the tune of "Here We Go Loop-de-Loo."*

3.2

INTRODUCE the song.

Sally go round the sun,
Sally go round the moon,
Sally go round the chimney top
Every afternoon (boom-boom).

Now, sing it with me. *Change the direction of your circle and go the other way. Sing the song three times.*

▶ Children's response:
Sally go round the sun,
Sally go round the moon,
Sally go round the chimney top
Every afternoon (boom-boom).

TEACHING TIP: In later lessons, when the song is well known by all children, you can introduce or reinforce directional vocabulary by calling out "turn left" or "turn right" when you change directions.

 Vocabulary

CHIMNEY

You did a nice job singing a new action song. In one part, we said that Sally goes around a chimney top. Did any of you ever see a chimney on top of a house? *Children may mention that Santa Claus comes down the chimney.*

The chimney is on top of the house where it lets smoke come out of the heaters in the winter time. A chimney is up on the roof. *Show a picture of a chimney—ideally, one that shows smoke coming out.* Everyone, where is a chimney?

▶ Children's response: Up on the roof.

Yes, a chimney is up on the roof.

TASK 2   **What Do You Like?** *(approximately 12 minutes)*

LINK the transition song to hearing words in sentences.

We have been listening to words in sentences. It's fun to clap out the words in the sentences. Let's practice together, clapping once for each word in a sentence.

Sally go round the sun. Say that sentence again with me and clap one time for each word. *Clap five times while repeating sentence.*

▶ Children's response: Sally *(clap)* go *(clap)* round *(clap)* the *(clap)* sun *(clap)*.

Good job clapping out the words in a sentence. Let's do some more together from all of the nursery rhymes you've been learning.

Complete four to five sentences following the same format.
Ring around the rosie. (four claps)
Down by the station. (four claps)
Twinkle, twinkle, little star. (four claps)
Mary had a little lamb. (five claps)
A man lived in the moon. (six claps)

 PLAY the game.

CD-ROM See Appendix D on the CD-ROM for the What Do You Like? Game instructions, cards, and word list.

 **TASK 3** | Transition rhymes to end the lesson and exit task *(approximately 3 minutes)*

END Lesson 3 with a transition nursery rhyme.

Now we will say another nursery rhyme that some of you may know. It's called "Humpty Dumpty." My turn to say "Humpty Dumpty." *Read the nursery rhyme and show children pictures from a large read-aloud book. Point to each word while reciting.*

Humpty Dumpty sat on a wall.
Humpty Dumpty had a great fall.
All the king's horses and all the king's men
Couldn't put Humpty together again.

Good job listening to "Humpty Dumpty." Now say it with me. *Repeat the nursery rhyme several times with the children.*

▶ Children recite:
Humpty Dumpty sat on a wall.
Humpty Dumpty had a great fall.
All the king's horses and all the king's men
Couldn't put Humpty together again.

DO the exit task to demonstrate skill mastery.

Gee, there is a lot of falling down in these nursery rhymes. First, in "Ring Around the Rosie," we all fell down. Now poor Humpty Dumpty fell off the wall.

So be careful and don't fall down when you stand up to show me that you can clap for each word in the line I give you.

Say one line for each child. Have the child repeat the line and clap it out, helping if necessary. Use these exit lines: "Humpty Dumpty sat on a wall" (six claps), "Humpty Dumpty had a great fall" (six claps), "All the king's horses" (four claps), "All the king's men" (four claps), and "Couldn't put Humpty together again" (five claps).

END Lesson 3.

You all did a good job today building sentences and clapping out the words in them. Everyone now gets their winnings for hearing the words in sentences and for working hard. *Give out token rewards to each child.*

LESSON 4: Sentence Segmentation Review

OBJECTIVES

Student will

- Demonstrate the ability to listen carefully to the separate words in sentences, clap them out in multisensory practice, and move chips to show the number of words

Teacher will

- Review and reinforce the segmenting of brief oral sentences

- Guide students to demonstrate the skill independently in two activities

RHYMES, SONGS, AND FINGERPLAYS

"Sally Go Round the Sun"

"Star Light, Star Bright"

MATERIALS

Eight colored chips for each child

Tokens for behavior/participation

☑ DROPP 3 Skill Assessment Checkout (see Appendix B on the CD-ROM)

Move the Chip Game

☑ Display board

☑ Game pieces

 **TASK 1** Action song to begin the lesson (approximately 3 minutes)

INTRODUCE the lesson.	*Settle the group at a table and say the following.* You have been learning how to listen to the words in sentences. Today we are going to practice all the ways we know to hear words in sentences.
INTRODUCE the song with motions.	Let's begin with an action song you learned before. Remember, an action is something we do. Everyone, what is an action?

▶ Children's response: Something we do.

In this song, the action is to walk around our circle in one direction. When we say "boom-boom" we will walk in the other direction. *Form a circle holding hands. Walk in one direction; then change the direction of your circle and go the other way. Sing the song three times.*

Sally go round the sun,
Sally go round the moon,
Sally go round the chimney top
Every afternoon (boom-boom).

 TASK 2A Stand-Up Sentences (approximately 6 minutes)

 Vocabulary

SENTENCE

 Turn On Your Ears

Nice job singing "Sally Go Round the Sun." Now you are ready to show what you know about words in sentences.

Listen to this sentence: We all like pizza.

The words go together to make a sentence. What do the words go together to make?

▶ Children's response: A sentence.

Yes, a sentence. Watch me say that sentence slowly while I clap my hands for each word in the sentence. *Clap slowly and softly with each word.* We all like pizza.

Do that with me. Let's clap our hands once for each word.

▶ Children's response: We *(clap)* all *(clap)* like *(clap)* pizza *(clap)*.

BEGIN Stand-Up Sentences.

Great! We clapped for each word in the first sentence. Now it's time to make a Stand-Up Sentence. *Choose four students to stand up shoulder to shoulder.* Each of you will get to be one word from our sentence.

Okay. Now, when you each say your word, they will go together to make our whole sentence. When I point to you, say your word. Get ready. _____ , you're first. Your word is *we*. *Continue until each child says his or her one word. Point at a moderate pace at first. Gradually, point at a faster pace so that the words flow together like a sentence.*

▶ Children say, in turn: We - all - like - pizza.

Listen, we have a Stand-Up Sentence. Say it again.

▶ Children's response: We all like pizza.

Wow! You each said one word and together they made a sentence.

Add clapping to the Stand-Up Sentence. Say that sentence one more time, and this time I will clap once for each word.

▶ Children's response: We all like pizza.

PRACTICE the task, linking meaning to sentences.

Students who are not standing clap with the teacher. Children who are standing do not clap. I clapped one time for each word in our Stand-Up Sentence. Standers, good job saying the words that make our first sentence.

Now, let's make a different Stand-Up Sentence. *Choose three children. Follow previous format, rotating children's turns. Point to each child.*

▶ Children's response: Dad - likes - hamburgers.

Everyone, say that sentence again.

▶ Children's response: Dad likes hamburgers.

Say it a little faster, so it sounds just the way we talk.

▶ Children's response: Dad likes hamburgers.

Emphasize that the words make a sentence that tells us something. You made a sentence that tells us what Dad likes to eat. Here is a new sentence. *Choose four new children.*

Mother likes fried chicken.

Everyone, say that sentence. *Point to each child standing.*

▶ Children's response: Mother - likes - fried - chicken.

Everyone, say that sentence again. *Point to each, at a quicker pace.*

▶ Children's response: Mother likes fried chicken.

Say it the way we talk.

▶ Children's response: Mother likes fried chicken.

Repeat each Stand-Up Sentence several times, then clap out the words several more times. Additional options include the following: "Sister likes pork chops" (four claps), "Brother likes cookies" (three claps), and "I ride my bike" (four claps).

Give specific praise to tell the students the skill they have mastered. I like the way you took turns being the words in our Stand-Up Sentences. Each student stood for one word.

 TASK 2B | Move the Chip *(approximately 8 minutes)*

 PLAY the game.

 CD-ROM See Appendix D on the CD-ROM for the Move the Chip Game instructions, board, and game pieces.

 TASK 3 | Transition nursery rhyme to end the lesson *(approximately 3 minutes)*

END Lesson 4 with a transition nursery rhyme.

Do you remember that you can make a wish when you see a star? Let's finish our lesson by saying our nursery rhyme about making a wish on a star. Say it with me.

▶ Children recite:
Star light, star bright,
First star I see tonight.
I wish I may, I wish I might,
Have this wish I wish tonight.

3.2

LESSON 4

DO the exit task to demonstrate skill mastery.	*Repeat the nursery rhyme several times with the children.* Here's my wish: I wish there were more hard-working students like you around! Now stand up to show me if you can clap for each word in the sentence I give you. *Let each child step forward, then say one of the sentences. Give the shorter sentences to students who are not yet skilled at hearing and clapping out the words. Help them to complete the task successfully, if necessary. Use these additional exit sentences: "I like school" (three claps), "I worked hard today" (four claps), "I have fun in school" (five claps), "We eat pizza at lunch" (five claps), and "Now we go back to class" (six claps).*
END Lesson 4.	You all did a good job today building sentences and clapping out the words in them. Everyone now gets their winnings for hearing the words in sentences and for working hard. *Give out token rewards to each child.*

 CD-ROM   The DROPP 3 Skill Assessment Checkout will be completed for each student following this lesson.

Compound Word Blending

Overview

WHY COMPOUND WORD BLENDING IS IMPORTANT

As young children play with the sounds in words, they develop the awareness that words are made up of parts, or segments. In compound words, each segment has meaning, which makes it easier for the child to understand that a spoken word can have several parts. Children who can hear and blend together the two segments of compound words are mastering an important step toward more advanced phonological awareness of syllables and then phonemes. This awareness is strongly linked to the ability to decode and spell words.

HOW DROPP 4 IS STRUCTURED

DROPP 4 has one Activity Set that consists of four scripted lessons (Teacher Talk) that are used on 10 sequential learning days (the four lessons are repeated over the 10-day span). DROPP 4 has 10 days of intervention lessons designed to develop and practice students' compound word awareness and compound blending skills. During the first 9 days of the Activity Set, students are given guidance and practice in hearing and blending together the two small words in compound words from songs, nursery rhymes, fingerplays, and picture cards. On the 10th day, they review the skills to prepare for a short skill assessment checkout. (See the CD-ROM for the DROPP 4 Skill Assessment Checkout.)

Length of Activity Set and Lessons

Activity Set 4.1 is designed to be delivered across 10 sequential learning days. Each day's intervention lesson, including the transition activities, takes about 20 minutes to complete.

Goal and Emphasis of the Compound Word Blending Lessons

The goal of Activity Set 4.1 is to develop your students' awareness of the two small words in compound words and their ability to hear the separate segments and blend them into one spoken word. This Activity Set emphasizes using the meaningful segments of compound words to support students' ability to hear and blend word parts. Word meaning is also emphasized in the compound word lists, which are grouped by themes—the outdoors, types of food, and places. This gives students a meaning-filled foundation from which to select and say the correct answers. These themed lessons incorporate action songs, puzzles, and blending games to increase the likelihood that students will be able to blend spoken compound words successfully.

Student Objective

- Develop an awareness of word segments by hearing two small words and blending them together to say a compound word.

Teacher Objectives

- Develop students' awareness of word segments through scaffolded, multisensory activities.

- Define and demonstrate the meaning of the terms *compound word* and *blend*.

- Model how to hear the two small words that make a compound word in familiar songs, nursery rhymes, and fingerplays.

- Use movement and music to help students understand that words are made up of segments of sound.

How the Compound Blending Activity Set Develops Early Literacy

Multisensory Techniques

In Activity Set 4.1, children learn to hear and say compound words and move their hands wider apart or closer together to demonstrate their awareness of word length, word segments, and word blending. There are manipulative picture puzzles, fingerplays, and a dramatic song that provide multisensory learning opportunities for the children. These activities were chosen because they contain short compound words. Playing with these words in songs and actions makes learning fun while deepening your students' emerging phonological awareness of words and word segments. As they use their fingers to make a *bee - hive*; their bodies to make a *tea - pot*; and their eyes, ears, and hands to match compound word pictures, the children make an important leap from hearing multisyllabic words as one large unit to hearing and blending the smaller segments within larger words.

Making Meaning and Building Vocabulary

Students' understanding of word meanings is greatly enhanced when they work with compound words because they discover that words are composed of units of sound and units of meaning. Linking two smaller words (e.g., *dog* and *house*) with the longer and more descriptive word (*doghouse*) lays the foundation for later ability to comprehend unfamiliar words by analyzing word parts.

As your students listen to and repeat themed sets of compound words, they will begin to understand that the objects named are grouped together because they have similarities. For example, in Lesson 1, they will repeat *classroom*, *bedroom*, and other place names as they are asked to tell where they might see a *teapot*. They will enjoy this as a funny guessing game, whereas you realize that the activity has the additional benefits of building the children's thinking skills, awareness of categories, and oral vocabulary while extending their understanding of the world around them.

New vocabulary is found at the beginning of the Activity Set and is presented in a two-step approach described in Chapter 2. We recommend that you use the new words throughout the day to reinforce students' vocabulary growth. The vocabulary words in Activity Set 4.1 are *spout*, *beehive*, *hive*, *meadow*, and *haystack*.

Print Awareness

In the compound blending procedure of Activity Set 4.1, students will experience the left-to-right progression of word reading as they see and feel the first small word on their left hands, then progress to the right hand. Also embedded in this Activity Set is the printed word awareness that comes from the teacher saying and pointing to words in the nursery rhyme, "Little Boy Blue." Although these concepts about print are presented at an awareness level and not intended for explicit instruction, they will support your students' understanding that the sounds of the compound words they hear can be mapped onto print and that some words are longer than others. This links their emerging phonological awareness of word sounds with the reading of print, which is the foundation for reading.

GENERAL TIPS FOR IMPLEMENTING ACTIVITY SET 4.1

Using hand gestures gives the children multisensory supports for compound word awareness and blending. You will use your hands in two different ways to help the children grasp the concept that compound words are made of two smaller words.

1. Awareness: Facing the children, hold up both hands, palms forward, 1 foot apart. As you say a compound word, slowly emphasize each word part by widening your fingers and slightly moving your hands toward the children. Begin with your right hand, then do the same with your left for the second word part (which they will see as a left-to-right progression). Do not bring hands together at this point. Your goal is for the children to be aware and see that there are two small words in the compound word. Practice this step until all children show they are firm with it by saying the two small words in several compound words.

2. Blending: After students understand that compound words have two small words, you can progress to the more advanced steps of hearing and blending the two parts into a compound word. Now, move your hands together to visually reinforce the auditory blending of the two small words while saying the word parts with the children. Repeat several times, more quickly, until children can hear and say the compound word.

Start small! Begin by choosing two-syllable compound words in Lessons 1 and 2. Select puzzle pieces and picture cards of compound words that are made up of two one-syllable words (e.g., *teapot*, *goldfish*). Lists of longer compound words are provided in Lesson 3. Incorporate these words into the compound blending activities and games after the children are secure in their understanding of basic word blending.

In Activity Set 4.1, the words *spout* and *stout* are chosen for rhyming practice. Be alert for other chances throughout your day to reinforce the skill of rhyming using the "Rhyming Exercise Song."

Teaching for Success with Longer Compound Words

As longer words are introduced, the children must comprehend that some of the compound word parts are longer than others but are still a single word with meaning. Do not emphasize the three separate syllables in words such as *ham-bur-ger*; instead, emphasize the two units of meaning: *ham-burger* (say both small words quickly). Do not discuss the concept of syllables at this point. Just tell the children that some words are longer, such as *burger*, but they are still one word.

TEACHING TIP: **Check for Success**

During every activity, maintain eye contact with the students, and ensure they are responding correctly and on cue. In this way, you are doing a mini assessment for each child to see who may need additional help at every step of the way.

Compound Word Puzzles

- Use a commercial compound word puzzle or download 12 simple compound word pictures from http://www.carlscorner.us.com/Compounds.htm. On the first day of the game, choose only pictures of compound words that are made of one-syllable segments, such as *blue - bird* and *dog - house*. Use a mixture of shorter and longer compound words on Days 2, 7, and 10 because children's compound word awareness skills will grow.

- For the first round, control the students' cards by giving only two puzzle parts that match. This round is a demonstration/practice round, and your goal is to assure the students' successful understanding of how to

  ▲ Pull the picture pieces together

▲ Say each picture name in the correct order

▲ Blend the two names together to say the entire compound word

- Scaffold support for struggling students by continuing to give only two matching puzzle pieces at a time. Children who show a good understanding of the skill may be given four or six puzzle pieces at once.

TEACHING TIP: **Celebrate Success**

Always give the class a specific compliment at the end of every task or game. Praise students and tell them what they did. For example, say, "You did a great job saying the compound word picture names and blending their two word parts to say one longer word. Let's give ourselves a cheer."

Coco Compound's Blend-It Game

- Preparing the game materials: Use a generic game board that has a "start" and "finish" square and 12–16 squares in between. Visuals, short cuts, and special squares may certainly be incorporated.

- Game piece (for team game): Because the students play as one team, you need just one game piece (see the game board on the CD-ROM), which you will name Coco. When a student blends a compound word correctly, he or she gets to move Coco ahead one space.

- Compound word picture cards: Assemble or purchase a deck of cards with pictures of compound words. For each game, select 12–16 cards, beginning with only single-syllable word parts. In later games, mix longer and shorter word parts as the children's blending skills grow.

- Procedure: The teacher holds the deck during the game, preventing the children from seeing the pictures. For each turn, the teacher says the two word parts slowly, and when the child correctly blends and says the compound word, shows the picture while repeating the compound several times with the child. This will reinforce the correctness and meaning of the word for all of the children.

Scaffold Your Instruction for Greater Success

Using hand gestures and picture cards helps students by providing visual and movement cues for learning and remembering the compound blending skill. Be alert and remove these extra supports when you see evidence that students are grasping the skill and can practice it using only auditory cues. This will enhance their phonological development.

Review

On the 10th day of the Activity Set, students get the opportunity to review compound word awareness and blending skills by practicing the Compound Word Puzzle, Coco Compound's Blend-It Game, and the "Beehive" fingerplay from the prior 9 days before their skill assessment checkout.

Skill Assessment Checkouts

After your review lesson is completed, set aside a few minutes to give each child an individual compound-blending checkout. These take about 2 minutes per child to administer and provide useful information to guide your small-group placements. Based on the checkout and collaborative conversations with all teachers, you will determine which students should continue in Tier 2 small-group intervention and which students can successfully return to Tier 1 whole-class instruction.

Assessment Outcome: The student can blend two short spoken words into a compound word.

ACTIVITY SET 4.1

Lesson Descriptions

Lessons	Sequence of daily activities	◇ Vocabulary
Lesson 1: Compound Word Puzzles	Song: "I'm a Little Teapot" Target: Blend Compound Word Puzzles Fingerplay: "Here Is the Beehive"	Spout Beehive Hive
Lesson 2: Coco Compound's Blend-It Game (Short Words)	Fingerplay: "Here Is the Beehive" Target: Blend short words into compounds Nursery rhyme: "Little Boy Blue"	Meadow
Lesson 3: Coco Compound's Blend-It Game (Longer Words)	Song: "I'm a Little Teapot" Target: Blend longer words into compounds Nursery Rhyme: "Little Boy Blue"	Spout Spout off Haystack
Lesson 4: Compound Word Blending Review	Fingerplay: "Here Is the Beehive" Review: Compound Word Puzzles Review: Coco Compound's Blend-It Game (Longer Words) Nursery Rhyme: "Wee Willie Winkie"	

Materials Needed

☑ Nursery rhyme picture book with "Little Boy Blue"

☑ Teapot or picture of a teapot

☑ Optional: Large Nursery Rhyme book with "Wee Willie Winkie"

☑ Optional: Pictures of a bedroom, a classroom, and a doghouse

☑ Tokens for behavior/participation

☑ DROPP 4 Skill Assessment Checkout (see Appendix B on the CD-ROM) **CD-ROM**

Compound Word Puzzles

☑ Compound Word Puzzles cards

☑ Colored chips (at least two per child)

Coco Compound's Blend-It Game

☑ Game board (see Appendix D on the CD-ROM)

☑ Game cards (see Appendix D on the CD-ROM)

☑ Game piece (see Appendix D on the CD-ROM)

☑ Word list (see Appendix D on the CD-ROM)

ACTIVITY SET

4.1 # 10-Day Planner

Day 1	**Lesson 1:** Compound Word Puzzles
Day 2	**Lesson 1:** Compound Word Puzzles
Day 3	**Lesson 2:** Coco Compound's Blend-It Game (Short Words)
Day 4	**Lesson 2:** Coco Compound's Blend-It Game (Short Words)
Day 5	**Lesson 3:** Coco Compound's Blend-It Game (Longer Words)
Day 6	**Lesson 3:** Coco Compound's Blend-It Game (Longer Words)
Day 7	**Lesson 1:** Compound Word Puzzles
Day 8	**Lesson 2:** Coco Compound's Blend-It Game (Short Words)
Day 9	**Lesson 3:** Coco Compound's Blend-It Game (Longer Words)
Day 10	**Lesson 4:** Compound Word Blending Review

LESSON 1: Compound Word Puzzles

OBJECTIVES

Student will

- Learn how to listen to the separate parts of compound words
- Blend word parts together to say a compound word

Teacher will

- Model blending of single-syllable word parts into compound words
- Guide students to hear and blend separate compound word parts in a puzzle
- Watch each student's success and provide multisensory supports as needed

RHYMES, SONGS, AND FINGERPLAYS

"I'm a Little Teapot"

"Here Is the Beehive"

MATERIALS

Teapot or picture of a teapot

Optional: Pictures of a bedroom, a classroom, and a doghouse

Tokens for behavior/participation

Compound Word Puzzles Game

Compound Word Puzzles cards

Colored chips (at least two per child)

 TASK 1 | **Song to begin the lesson** (approximately 3 minutes)

INTRODUCE the big idea: compound words.

Say the following to the group after settling the students together at a table. You know how to listen to words in sentences. Some words are short, but some are long and have two parts in them. They are called compound words. Starting today, you are going to learn how to listen to two small words and blend them into compound words.

BEGIN the transition activity.

We will start with a fun song and dance called "I'm a Little Teapot."

This is an action song because when we sing it, we have some actions that we can do with our bodies to act like a teapot that is pouring out some nice hot tea. *Show a picture of a teapot.*

When you listen to the song, do what I do and see if you can learn the actions in "I'm a Little Teapot." What's the name of the song and dance we will learn today?

▶ Children's response: "I'm a Little Teapot."

✳ Model the Activity

Yes, "I'm a Little Teapot." My turn to sing. Watch me dance. *Model the song and dance movements. Use exaggerated, easy, consistent, and space-conscious movements that mimic the song.*

I'm a little teapot, short and stout. *Place both hands on hips.*
Here is my handle, here is my spout. *Extend one arm in the shape of a spout.*
When I get all steamed up, then I shout.
Just tip me over and pour me out. *Tip to one side.*

Your turn to sing and dance with me. Everyone stand up. *Each child should have his or her own space. Sing with them and lead them in their dance movements.*

Multisensory Reinforcement

▶ Children's response:

I'm a little teapot, short and stout.

Here is my handle, here is my spout.

When I get all steamed up, then I shout.

Just tip me over and pour me out.

Let's everyone sing and dance one more time. *Repeat the song and dance.* Now go back to your seats. Nice job being teapots.

Vocabulary

SPOUT

Let's sit back down and talk about the word *spout. Point to the spout on the teapot or picture of a teapot.* The spout of the teapot is the part where the tea pours out. *Point to spout on picture.* What do we call the part where the tea pours out?

▶ **Children's response: Spout.**

Yes, the spout is the part where the tea pours out. When we tip over in the teapot dance, we are pretending that one of our hands is the spout pouring out tea.

Show me where the spout is with your hand. *Students place hands at the same position as in the song—mirroring yours to bend one down and pour.*

Your turn to sing and dance again with me. Everyone stand up. *Repeat the song and dance.*

 TASK 2   **Compound Word Puzzles** (approximately 12–14 minutes)

LINK the transition song to the skill of compound word blending.

Introduce hand gestures for compound word awareness.

Multisensory Reinforcement

Turn On Your Ears

Introduce hand gestures for compound word blending

Turn On Your Ears

PRACTICE and extend the skill.

That was fun being little teapots! Now I am going to say *teapot* slowly in two parts. Listen. *Say the word slowly, without stopping.*

Tea-pot. *Repeat.* Tea --- pot.

Hold up your hands, palms toward the children, 1 foot apart. When you say the first small word, emphasize your right hand by spreading your fingers and moving your hand slightly toward the children. Do the same with the second small word and the left hand.

Tea-pot.

Who can hear the whole word I am saying? Everyone, give me a thumbs up if you hear the whole word. *Look around to gauge who understands.*

Listen. Tea-pot. Everyone, what word did I say?

▶ **Children's response: Teapot.**

Yes, teapot. I said the two small words, *tea* and *pot*, and you heard the whole compound word, *teapot*.

Look at my hands. Let's say the two small words in teapot together. Get ready.

▶ **Children say in conjunction with hand gestures: Tea-pot.**

Modify the compound word awareness gestures for each example by holding hands up with palms forward. After showing two word parts on your hands, demonstrate blending by moving your hands together.

Now, turn on your ears! It is fun to hear the two small words in compound words. Sit up and listen for some more two-part compound words while you answer my questions about a teapot. *Warm up awareness of hearing parts of compound words by saying short, familiar ones very slowly, with a 2-second pause.*

Would you be likely to see a teapot in a . . . bed --- room? What word did I just say?

▶ **Children's response: Bedroom.**

Yes, bedroom. *Continue to use the hand gestures described. If desired, show pictures of a bedroom, a classroom, and a doghouse.*

Do you think a teapot would be in the bedroom?

▶ **Children's response: No.**

No, we do not usually pour tea in our bedrooms.

4.1

 Turn On Your Ears

Listen again. Would we usually have a teapot in the . . . class --- room? Everyone, what word did I just say?

▶ **Children's response: Classroom.**

Yes, classroom. Good job hearing the two small words in *classroom.* Do we pour tea in the classroom?

▶ **Children's response: No.**

Listen again. Would we usually have a teapot in a . . . dog --- house? What word did I just say?

▶ **Children's response: Doghouse.**

Yes, doghouse. Do we pour tea in a doghouse?

▶ **Children's response: No.**

Who knows where we might really see a teapot or have a cup of tea? *(Accept two or three answers.)*

Good thinking. Some good places for a teapot are in the kitchen or the dining room or maybe in a cafeteria.

♣ **PLAY** the game.

CD-ROM See Appendix D of the CD-ROM for the Compound Word Puzzles Game instructions.

 TASK 3   Fingerplay and exit task *(approximately 3 minutes)*

 Vocabulary

HIVE, BEEHIVE

You worked hard today hearing the two small words in compound words. You were just like a hive of busy bees. Does anyone know what a beehive is? Raise your hand if you do. *Accept one or two answers.*

A beehive is a home for bees. Everyone, what is a beehive?

▶ **Children's response: A home for bees.**

Yes. A beehive is a home for bees. It is shaped like this. *Put both hands together to make a hive shape.*

Now we will learn a fingerplay about bees and their home, or beehive. Watch me and do what I do. We will practice a few times so you can all learn the finger movements that make this a fun fingerplay.

 Model the Activity

Here is the beehive. *Close one hand on top of the other.*
But where are the bees? *Act puzzled; look back and forth.*
Hidden inside where nobody sees. *Look in the hole made by your finger and thumb.*
Watch them closely come out of the hive. *Look at children's faces with excitement.*
1, 2, 3, 4, 5, Bzzzz. *Pop one finger up for each number until your hand shows five fingers, palm forward. Make buzzing sound.*

Repeat fingerplay.

DO the exit task to demonstrate skill mastery.

Good job! Now show me if each of you can hear and blend two words together to make one bigger, compound word. Let's all practice one together.

Use the compound blending procedure: Hold up hands, palms toward children. Emphasize your right hand when saying door *and left hand when saying* knob.

Door --- knob. Everybody, what compound word did I say?

▶ **Children's response: Doorknob.**

Yes, doorknob. We open doors by turning the doorknob.

Let each child have one turn. Say the following words, using the previous format. After the child blends the two-syllable word successfully, repeat it in the suggested sentence or in a meaningful short sentence of your choice.

REINFORCE word meanings.

Rain --- coat (Yes, raincoat. Put on your raincoat when it rains.)

Wash --- cloth (Yes, washcloth. Wash your face with a washcloth.)

Foot --- ball (Yes, football. Kick the football and run fast.)

Note --- book (Yes, notebook. We can write in a notebook.)

Doll --- house (Yes, dollhouse. Little kids play with a dollhouse.)

Everyone now gets their winnings for blending compound words and for working hard. *Give out token rewards to each child.*

END Lesson 1.

LESSON 2: Coco Compound's Blend-It Game (Short Words)

OBJECTIVES

Student will

- Learn how to listen carefully to the separate parts of compound words
- Blend word parts together to say a compound word

Teacher will

- Model blending of single-syllable word parts into compound words
- Guide students to hear and blend separate word parts
- Watch each student's success and provide multisensory supports as needed

RHYMES, SONGS, AND FINGERPLAYS

"Here Is the Beehive"

"Little Boy Blue"

MATERIALS

Nursery rhyme picture book with "Little Boy Blue"

Tokens for behavior/participation

Coco Compound's Blend-It Game

☑ Game board and piece (see Appendix D on the CD-ROM)

☑ Game cards (see Appendix D on the CD-ROM)

☑ Word list (see Appendix D on the CD-ROM)

 TASK 1   **Fingerplay to begin the lesson** (approximately 3 minutes)

INTRODUCE the lesson.

Say the following to the group after settling the children together at a table. We are going to listen to compound words and hear their two small words. Then we'll play a game called Coco Compound's Blend-It Game.

PERFORM the fingerplay with the children.

We learned a fingerplay about bees and their home, called a beehive. Everyone, what is the bee's home called?

▶ **Children's response: A beehive.**

Multisensory Reinforcement

Yes, a beehive. Let's practice the fingerplay and use the finger movements to make it fun. Get ready.

Here is the beehive. *Close one hand on top of the other.*
But where are the bees? *Act puzzled; look back and forth.*
Hidden inside where nobody sees. *Look in the hole made by your finger and thumb.*
Watch them closely come out of the hive. *Look at children's faces with excitement.*
1, 2, 3, 4, 5. Bzzzz. *Pop one finger up for each number until your hand shows five fingers, palm forward. Make buzzing sound.*

Repeat one time.

 **TASK 2**   Coco Compound's Blend-It Game *(approximately 12 minutes)*

LINK the fingerplay to the big idea.

Listen to the word that we said in our fingerplay. *Use the compound blending procedure: Hold up hands, palms toward children. Emphasize your right hand when saying bee and left hand when saying hive.*

Bee --- hive.

REVIEW compound blending.

Who can hear the whole word I am saying? Listen! Give me a thumbs up if you hear the whole word. *Look around to gauge who remembers and understands.*

 Turn On Your Ears

Listen. *Pause, then use the compound blending procedure by holding hands up, palms forward.* Bee --- hive. Everyone, what word did I say?

▶ Children's response: Beehive.

Yes, beehive. I said the two small words, *bee* and *hive*, and you heard the compound word *beehive*.

 Multisensory Reinforcement

Now sit up and listen for some more two-part compound words while you answer my questions about a beehive.

Okay, listen for a two-part compound word. Do you think we might see a beehive…

Out --- side? Everybody, what word did I just say?

▶ Children's response: Outside.

Yes, outside. Do you think a beehive would be outside?

▶ Children's response: Yes.

Yes. We hope the bees will build their beehives outside.

Listen again. If a beehive is outside, do you think the bees would like to come out and fly in the . . .

Sun --- shine? Everybody, what word did I just say?

▶ Children's response: Sunshine.

Yes, sunshine. Do you think bees would like to fly in the sunshine?

▶ Children's response: Yes.

Yes, bees do like to fly in the sunshine and visit the pretty flowers.

Listen again. Do you think the bees would like to come out and fly around when there is a . . .

Snow --- storm? Everybody, what word did I just say?

▶ **Children's response: Snowstorm.**

Yes, snowstorm. Do you think bees would like to fly around in a snowstorm?

▶ **Children's response: No.**

You are right. Bees would not like to fly in a snowstorm because they would get all wet. When it snows, bees like to stay in their hive.

Here is another compound word that goes with beehive.

Farm --- house. *Repeat.* Everyone, what word did I say?

▶ **Children's response: Farmhouse.**

Yes, farmhouse. We might see a beehive out in the country at a farmhouse.

 PLAY the game.

CD-ROM See Appendix D on the CD-ROM for the Coco's Compound Blend-It Game instructions, board, piece, cards, and word list. *(Use word list for one-syllable segments.)*

 TASK 3   **Nursery rhyme to end the lesson** *(approximately 3 minutes)*

PRACTICE using the outdoor theme vocabulary, pausing between word parts to build students' ability to hear and blend parts.

You worked hard today hearing the two small words in compound words. We talked about bee - hives. *Use a 2-second pause between parts.* Everyone, what word?

▶ **Children's response: Beehives.**

Yes, beehives. And sun - shine. Everyone, what word?

▶ **Children's response: Sunshine.**

Yes, sunshine. And snow - storm. Everyone, what word?

▶ **Children's response: Snowstorm.**

END with the nursery rhyme.

Now I am going to sing a nursery rhyme about a little boy who spends all day out - side. Everybody, what word?

▶ **Children's response: Outside.**

He lives out in the country at a farm - house. Everyone, what word?

▶ **Children's response: Farmhouse.**

 **Vocabulary**

MEADOW

Yes, a farmhouse. He takes care of a cow and a sheep. His name is Little Boy Blue. *Show the children a picture of Little Boy Blue from nursery rhyme book.* His job is to keep the cow and sheep from running away into the meadow. What could a meadow be? Can anyone guess? *Allow children to guess.*

A meadow is a big grassy field. Everyone, what can we call a big grassy field?

▶ **Children's response: A meadow.**

Yes, a meadow is a big grassy field on a farm.

This story tells what happened one day when Little Boy Blue was doing his job. Listen. *Point to each word and the pictures as you read the nursery rhyme.*

 Turn On Your Ears

Little Boy Blue, come blow your horn.
The sheep's in the meadow, the cow's in the corn.
Where is the boy who looks after the sheep?

TASK 3 (continued)

He's under the haystack, fast asleep.

Oh, my! Look at Little Boy Blue sleeping on the haystack. Do you think he knows where the cow and the sheep are? *Discuss the nursery rhyme for a few minutes.*

DO the exit task to demonstrate skill mastery.

Repeat the nursery rhyme. I hope you enjoyed listening to that nice nursery rhyme. Now, get ready to show me who can hear word parts and guess the compound word all by yourself.

Say the following word pairs slowly, using hand gestures if necessary for success. Let each child blend one of these exit compound words: hay-stack, bee-hive, out-side, snow-storm, sun-shine.

END Lesson 2.

Everyone now gets their winnings for blending word parts to say compound words and for working hard. *Give out token rewards to each child.*

LESSON 3: Coco Compound's Blend-It Game (Longer Words)

OBJECTIVES

Student will

- Learn how to listen carefully to the separate parts of compound words
- Blend word parts together to say a compound word

Teacher will

- Model blending of multisyllabic word parts into compound words
- Guide students to hear and blend separate word parts
- Watch each student's success and provide multisensory supports as needed

RHYMES, SONGS, AND FINGERPLAYS

"I'm a Little Teapot"
"Little Boy Blue"

MATERIALS

Nursery rhyme picture book with "Little Boy Blue"

Teapot or picture of a teapot

Tokens for behavior/participation

Coco Compound's Blend-It Game CD-ROM

- ☑ Game board and piece (see Appendix D on the CD-ROM)
- ☑ Game cards (see Appendix D on the CD-ROM)
- ☑ Word list (see Appendix D on the CD-ROM)

 TASK 1   **Fingerplay to begin the lesson** (approximately 3 minutes)

INTRODUCE the lesson, reviewing the big idea.

Settle the group at a table and say the following. You have been learning how to listen to the two small words in longer compound words and blend them together to say the whole compound word. Today we are going to listen to some new compound words and hear their two small words. Then we'll play Coco Compound's Blend-It Game with some longer words.

Let's begin with our fun song and dance called "I'm a Little Teapot" because it has a compound word we know: tea --- pot. Everyone, say it fast.

▶ Children's response: Teapot.

Yes, teapot.

INTRODUCE the song.	Sing and dance with me. Everyone stand up. *Make sure each child has his or her own space. Sing with the children and lead them in their dance movements.*

 Multisensory Reinforcement

▶ Children sing and dance.
I'm a little teapot, short and stout.
Here is my handle, here is my spout.
When I get all steamed up, then I shout.
Just tip me over and pour me out.

Good job singing and dancing! Let's do it one more time. *Repeat the song and movements.*

 Vocabulary

SPOUT

Who remembers where the spout is on a teapot? *Show the teapot or picture and let several children point to the spout.*

Great. The spout is like the mouth of the teapot. That's why it can be called "spouting off" when people talk a lot. Having lots of words pour out of your mouth is like having lots of tea pour out of the teapot. If one of you kept talking and talking, I might say, "What are you spouting off about?" Isn't that a funny thing to say?

Turn On Your Ears

Listen. Spouting off means talking a lot. Everybody, what does spouting off mean?

▶ Children's response: Talking a lot.

Vocabulary

TO SPOUT OFF

Yes, spouting off means talking a lot. What is another way to say talking a lot?

▶ Children's response: Spouting off.

Listen. The man was talking and talking about his new outfit. He was spouting off about it. Everybody, what was the man doing?

▶ Children's response: Spouting off.

Everybody, let's ask the man what he's spouting off about. My turn.

What are you spouting off about? Say it with me.

▶ Children's response: What are you spouting off about?

Isn't that funny?

Multisensory Reinforcement

"I'm a Little Teapot" has some words that go together. Listen. *Put hands with palms facing toward the children.* Spout, stout. Spout, stout. Hey, do they rhyme? *Look around at each student.*

Yes. They rhyme. Let's sing our rhyming song.

SING the "Rhyming Exercise Song."

Get your rhyme muscles nice and firm so our rhymes are in great shape. Follow me. Put your hands in the sky. *On the word hands, stretch one arm up to the sky and then the other arm.* Do the "Rhyming Exercise Song." *As you sing, switch and stretch arms one by one.*

Spout *(Stretch one arm up.)*
Stout *(Stretch the other arm up.)*
Spout *(Switch arms.)*
Stout *(Switch arms.)*
Spout *(Switch arms.)*
Stout *(Switch arms.)*

Do they rhyme? *Pause here and allow them to show thumbs up or down before you respond. Look around at each student and make eye contact.* Yes. *Nod vigorously.* They rhyme. *Give two thumbs up.*

 TASK 2 Coco Compound's Blend-It Game (approximately 12 minutes)

LINK the transition song to compound blending.

 Multisensory Reinforcement

REVIEW compound blending.

Turn On Your Ears

INTRODUCE compound blending of longer words.

 Multisensory Reinforcement

PRACTICE blending longer compound words.

Listen to this word that we said in our action song. *Use the compound blending procedure: Hold up your hands, palms toward children. Emphasize your right hand when saying tea and your left hand when saying* pot.

Tea --- pot. I bet you can hear the whole word I am saying.

Listen. Tea - pot. *Look around to gauge who remembers and understands.* Everyone, what word did I say?

▶ Children's response: Teapot.

Yes, teapot. I said the two small words, *tea* and *pot*, and you heard the compound word *teapot*.

Now sit up and listen for some more two-part compound words while you answer my questions about a teapot. Listen for a two-part compound word. Here's a clue—the words will tell you about things you can eat and drink. Are you ready?

Do you like to drink a . . . *Pause, then use the blending procedure by holding your hands up, palms forward.*

milk --- shake? Everybody, what word did I just say?

▶ Children's response: Milkshake.

Yes, milkshake. Do you like to drink a milkshake?

▶ Children's response: Yes.

Yes, a milkshake is tasty.

Listen again. Could you eat a . . . *Use compound blending procedure by holding your hands up, palms forward.*

ham --- burger? Everybody, what word did I just say?

▶ Children's response: Hamburger.

Yes, hamburger. Could you eat a hamburger?

▶ Children's response: Yes.

Yes, a hamburger is good to eat.

Listen. Hamburger is a longer word. Watch my hands. *Use exaggerated movements to show ham on your right hand; then say burger quickly while emphasizing your left hand with a single movement (not two movements for the two syllables).*

TEACHING TIP: As longer words are introduced, the children need to realize that some words are longer than others. Do not emphasize the three separate syllables in words such as *hamburger*; instead, emphasize the two units of meaning: *ham-burger* (say both small words quickly).

Ham --- burger. Say those two words with me.

▶ Children's response: Ham-burger.

Yes, ham --- burger. Good job hearing the two small words in a longer compound word.

Listen again. Could you eat a . . .
straw --- berry? Everybody, what word did I just say?

▶ Children's response: Strawberry.

186

Yes, strawberry. Could you eat a strawberry?

 Turn On Your Ears

▶ **Children's response: Yes.**

Yes, a strawberry is a delicious fruit that you can eat.

Listen again. Could you eat a . . .

water --- melon? Everybody, what word did I just say?

▶ **Children's response: Watermelon.**

Yes, watermelon. Could you eat a watermelon?

▶ **Children's response: Yes.**

Yes, you can eat watermelon. It is so cool and tasty.

Listen again. Could you put this on your bread?

Butter --- fly. Everybody, what word did I just say?

▶ **Children's response: Butterfly.**

Yes, butterfly. Could you put butterfly on your bread?

▶ **Children's response: No.**

No. We can put butter on our bread. If we put a butterfly on our bread, it would probably fly away.

 ♣ **PLAY** the game.

CD-ROM See Appendix D on the CD-ROM for the Coco's Compound Blend-It Game instructions, board, piece, cards, and word list. *(Use word list for multisyllable segments.)*

 TASK 3   Nursery rhyme to end the lesson *(approximately 3 minutes)*

REVIEW today's big idea.

You worked hard today hearing the two small words in compound words. We talked about straw --- berries. Everybody, what word?

▶ **Children's response: Strawberries.**

Yes, strawberries.

And ham --- burgers. Everybody, what word?

▶ **Children's response: Hamburgers.**

Yes, hamburgers.

And water --- melon. Everybody, what word?

▶ **Children's response: Watermelon.**

Yes, watermelon.

 Turn On Your Ears

Now get ready to listen again to the nursery rhyme about Little Boy Blue. *(Show children a picture from the nursery rhyme.)* Do you remember that he got so sleepy that he fell asleep under a hay --- stack? Everybody, what word?

▶ **Children's response: Haystack.**

 ✧ **Vocabulary**

HAYSTACK

What could a haystack be? Can anyone guess?

(Allow children to guess.)

A haystack is a big pile, or stack, of hay. Hay is a nice sweet grass that horses and cows like to eat. So the farmers stack it up and save it in a big soft pile. No won-

END with the nursery rhyme.

der Little Boy Blue fell asleep on the hay --- stack. Everybody, what is that word I just said?

▶ **Children's response: Haystack.**

Yes, haystack. Little Boy Blue fell asleep on a nice soft haystack. *Point to each word and the pictures as you read the nursery rhyme.*

Little Boy Blue, come blow your horn.
The sheep's in the meadow, the cow's in the corn.
Where is the boy who looks after the sheep?
He's under the haystack, fast asleep.

Turn On Your Ears

Listen again. If you know any parts of this nursery rhyme, you can say them with me. *(Repeat the nursery rhyme. Don't be surprised if students cannot recite most of the rhyme. See if students can fill in the rhyming word in every other line.)*

Little Boy Blue, come blow your horn.
The sheep's in the meadow, the cow's in the _____ (corn).
Where is the boy who looks after the sheep?
He's under the haystack, fast a _____ (sleep).

DO the exit task to demonstrate skill mastery.

Aren't you smart to learn a new nursery rhyme? Now, get ready to show me who can hear word parts and say compound words all by yourself. These are some things Little Boy Blue might see in the meadow.

Let each child have a turn. Say one of the following word pairs slowly, without using hand gestures; ask the child to say the compound word. Use these compound words for the exit task: sun-flower, butter-fly, lady-bug, river-bank, dragon-fly.

END Lesson 3.

Everyone now gets their winnings for blending word parts to say compound words and for working hard. *Give out token rewards to each child.*

LESSON 4: Compound Word Blending Review

OBJECTIVES

Student will

- Demonstrate the ability to blend two shorter and two longer spoken words into compound words

Teacher will

- Review blending of compound words
- Guide students to demonstrate the skill independently in two game formats
- Support students' success with careful item selection and multisensory supports

RHYMES, SONGS, AND FINGERPLAYS

"Here is the Beehive"
"Wee Willie Winkie"

MATERIALS

Optional: Large nursery rhyme book with "Wee Willie Winkie"

Tokens for behavior/participation

Compound Word Puzzles

Compound word puzzle cards

Colored chips (at least two per child)

☑ DROPP 4 Skill Assessment Checkout (see Appendix B on the CD-ROM)   **CD-ROM**

Coco Compound's Blend-It Game

☑ Game board and piece (see Appendix D on the CD-ROM)

☑ Game cards (see Appendix D on the CD-ROM)

☑ Word list (see Appendix D on the CD-ROM)

TEACHING TIP: As you deliver this lesson, note where students' individual comfort zones occur to help you assess their varying degrees of skill mastery.

 TASK 1   **Fingerplay to begin the lesson** (approximately 3 minutes)

INTRODUCE the lesson.	*Settle the group at a table and say the following.* Today we are going to practice all the ways we know to blend two small words together to make compound words.
INTRODUCE the fingerplay.	We learned a fingerplay about bees and their home, which is called a beehive. Everyone, what is the bee's home called?

▶ **Children's response: A beehive.**

Yes, beehive. Let's practice that fingerplay and use the finger movements to make it fun.

 **Multisensory Reinforcement**

DO the fingerplay with the children.

Everyone, do this with me. *Children say and mirror your actions.*

Here is the beehive. *(Close one hand on top of the other.)*
But where are the bees? *(Act puzzled; look back and forth.)*
Hidden inside where nobody sees. *(Look in the hole made by your finger and thumb.)*
Watch them closely come out of the hive. *(Look at children's faces with excitement.)*
1, 2, 3, 4, 5. Bzzzz. *(Pop one finger up for each number until your hand shows five fingers, palm forward. Make buzzing sound.)*

Repeat fingerplay.

 **TASK 2A**   **Compound word practice** (approximately 7 minutes)

REVIEW the big idea: compound word blending.

You have learned how to listen hard and blend two small words together into a longer word, called a compound word. Now we will practice our puzzles to blend some more compound words.

For students who are struggling, scaffold support by only giving two matching pieces at a time. Children who show good understanding may be given up to six matching pieces.

 PLAY the game.

 See Appendix D of the CD-ROM for the Compound Word Puzzles Game instructions.

 **TASK 2B**   **Coco Compound's Blend-It Game** (approximately 8 minutes)

 PLAY the game.

 See Appendix D on the CD-ROM for the Coco's Compound Blend-It Game instructions, board, piece, cards, and word list. *(Choose a mix of words from both the one-syllable and multisyllable segment word lists.)*

TASK 3 **Transition nursery rhyme** (approximately 3 minutes)

DO the exit activity, which uses the compound words *sunshine, nightgown, upstairs,* and *downstairs.*

Turn On Your Ears

You worked hard today hearing the two small words in compound words. Some of them were shorter words and some were longer. You did a wonderful job and I am proud of you.

Listen to these two small words: *sun --- shine.* Everyone, get ready to blend those two small words and say them the fast way. Sun --- shine. Everybody, what word?

▶ **Children's response: Sunshine.**

Yes, sunshine. Your good work makes me smile like the sun! (*Give a great big smile.*)

Now think about this: When the sun goes down, people put on their sleeping clothes and go to bed. They can put on their pajamas, or they might put on a . . . night --- gown. Listen: night - gown. What word did I just say?

▶ **Children's response: Nightgown.**

Yes, nightgown! Now, I have a nursery rhyme about a tiny little boy who runs around in his . . . night --- gown!

Turn On Your Ears

Listen to this nursery rhyme, and then you can say some of the words in it with me. (*Optional: Show the rhyme and pictures in a large nursery rhyme book as you say it.*)

Wee Willie Winkie runs through the town
Upstairs and downstairs, in his nightgown.
Rapping at the window, crying through the lock,
Are the children in their beds, for now it's eight o'clock?

Repeat one or two times. When the children seem familiar with it, drop the final rhyming words, as follows:

Wee Willie Winkie, runs through the . . . (*emphasize*) town
Upstairs and downstairs, in his night . . .

▶ **Children: Gown.**

Rapping at the window, crying through the…(*emphasize*) lock
Are the children in their beds, for now it's eight o' . . .

▶ **Children: Clock.**

END Lesson 4.

Everyone now gets their winnings for hearing and blending the two small words in compound words and for working hard. *Give out token rewards to each child.*

 CD-ROM The DROPP 4 Skill Assessment Checkout will be completed for each student following this lesson.

Compound Word Segmentation

Overview

WHY COMPOUND WORD SEGMENTATION IS IMPORTANT

When children can separate a compound word into its smaller words, they are acquiring a vital skill that carries them beyond the earlier tasks of segmenting sentences and hearing rhymes toward the ability to hear the individual phonemes in words. Clapping, hopping, and moving chips to represent the segments of compound words are enjoyable ways for children to see that they can break spoken words into parts. This prepares them for the eventual understanding that those word parts correspond to letter symbols, which they will learn to read.

HOW DROPP 5 IS STRUCTURED

DROPP 5 has two Activity Sets—5.1 and 5.2. Each Activity Set consists of four scripted lessons (Teacher Talk) that are used on 10 sequential learning days (the four lessons are repeated over the 10-day span). DROPP 5 has 20 days of intervention lessons designed to develop and practice students' compound word awareness and segmentation skills. During the first 9 days of each set, students are given guidance and practice in hearing and segmenting compound words in songs and games. On the 10th day, they review the skills to prepare for a short skill assessment checkout. (See the CD-ROM for the DROPP 5 Skill Assessment Checkout.)

Length of Activity Sets and Lessons

Each Activity Set is designed to be delivered across 10 sequential learning days. Each day's intervention lesson, including the transition activities, takes about 20 minutes to complete.

Goal and Emphasis of the Compound Word Segmentation Lessons

In Activity Sets 5.1 and 5.2, the goal is to develop your students' ability to segment compound words into their two small word parts. These Activity Sets emphasize the meaning of the small words in compound words to support students' phonological awareness of word segments. Throughout Activity Sets 5.1 and 5.2, the themes of school, the weather, and food and drink are evident in the choices of compound words and transition songs. This categorizing of words helps to develop students' vocabulary and comprehension as aids to compound word segmentation. This makes it easier for children to concentrate on the segmenting tasks because it removes the "cognitive load" of wondering about words' meanings.

Student Objectives

Students will be able to segment compound words by doing the following activities:

- Clapping once for each small word in a compound word

- Hopping on squares to demonstrate the whole and parts of a compound word

- Moving a chip for each small word in a compound word

Teacher Objectives

- Develop students' awareness of compound word segments through scaffolded, multisensory activities.

- Use movement and music to help students understand that words are made up of segments of sound.

- Model and practice how to segment compound words by clapping and hopping for the two small words.

- Teach children how to move colored chips to represent the separate word parts in compound words.

How the Compound Word Segmentation Activity Sets Develop Early Literacy

Multisensory Techniques

In Activity Sets 5.1 and 5.2, your students' auditory and phonological skills are enhanced through visual, kinesthetic, and tactile channels in every activity. The learning activities in these sets incorporate both large and small motor movements in entertaining, noncompetitive games that will deepen students' understanding and memory of the skills being addressed. In Lesson 1, there are action songs containing compound words, followed by Clap-Out Compounds in which the children see the compound word picture, say the whole compound word, and stand and clap the word parts. In Lesson 2, students use their whole bodies in Happy Hopscotch to hop out a whole compound word and its separate word parts. In Lesson 3, the Gumdrop Game uses colorful charts and chips to prompt the students to see, say, hear, and feel the parts of compound words. As students practice these activities over multiple days, they will solidify their ability to hear parts of words, which is a requirement for learning letter–sound correspondences in order to become good readers and writers.

Making Meaning and Building Vocabulary

Students' understanding of word meanings is greatly enhanced when they work with compound words because they discover that words are composed of units of sound and units of meaning. Linking two smaller words (e.g., *dog* and *house*) with the longer and more descriptive word (e.g., *doghouse*) lays the foundation for comprehending unfamiliar words by analyzing word parts.

New vocabulary words are found at the beginning of the Activity Set and are presented in the two-step approach described in Chapter 2. We recommend that you use the new words throughout the day to reinforce students' vocabulary growth. The vocabulary words in Activity Sets 5.1 and 5.2 are *gumdrop, compound, beam, sunbeam, action, verse,* and *grapefruit.*

Print Awareness

In Lesson 3 of both Activity Sets 5.1 and 5.2, students play the Gumdrop Game in which they segment compound words by moving a colored chip for each small word. After the children pull the two chips down on their individual boards, they check their work by putting their index finger under the left chip, then the right chip, while saying each word part. This gives them the experience of left-to-right progression, which is an important part of print awareness.

GENERAL TIPS FOR IMPLEMENTING ACTIVITY SETS 5.1 AND 5.2

- Whole body learning helps to catch the meaning. Activity Sets 5.1 and 5.2 begin with songs that prompt the children to use their whole bodies to experience the ideas and words of the songs. Whether children are recalling the meaning of *spout* as they mimic a teapot or singing while creating a visual image of candy raining down on them, you can be assured that they are catching, remembering, and understanding the vocabulary or concept much more than if they had only heard about it.

- Hand gestures for manipulating compound words: Give them a hand! In Lesson 1 of each Activity Set, you will continue to use the hand gestures for compound word awareness introduced in Activity Set 4.1 in this way: Face the children, holding up both hands, palms forward, 1 foot apart. As you say a compound word slowly, emphasize each word part by widening your fingers and moving that hand slightly toward children. Begin with your right hand, then do the same with your left for the second word part (which they will see as a left-to-right progression). Do not bring hands together at this point. Your goal is for the children to be aware and see that there are two small words in the compound word. Practice this step until all children show that they are firm with it by saying the two small words in several compound words.

TEACHING TIP: **Act It Out for Long-Term Success**

Incorporate movement in your students' response options whenever you can. Hand gestures and other little motions that demonstrate a new word can fit right into your lessons. Building in the use of additional learning channels does not take a long time, but it will make a long-term difference in your students' understanding and retention of the important words and ideas you are teaching.

Begin with Two-Syllable Compound Words

In Lesson 1 of Activity Sets 5.1 and 5.2, select picture cards of compound words that are made up of two one-syllable small words (e.g., *raindrop, sunshine*). Lists of longer compound words are provided in Lesson 2 so that you can introduce two-syllable small words after the children understand compound words.

Teach Compound Words Before Syllables and Phonemes

Do not worry if some of your students have trouble hearing the separate parts of words at first. This is common among younger preschoolers who typically need a lot of practice with bigger, more holistic (and hence, more meaningful) units of speech, such as compound words. Use the extra word lists that accompany all of the DROPP 5 games to give additional practice to any students who need it. This will assure that your students will be better prepared to tackle syllables, onset-rimes, and phonemes in the future.

Teach Longer Compound Words without Introducing Syllables

As longer words are introduced, the children must comprehend that some of the compound word parts are longer than others but are still a single word with meaning. Do not emphasize the three separate syllables in words such as *straw-ber-ry*; instead, emphasize the two units of meaning: *strawberry* (say both small words quickly). Do not discuss the concept of syllables at this point. Just tell the children that some words are longer, such as *strawberry*, but they are still one word.

Make the Most of Transition Activities

- You will see that all of the transition songs and fingerplays were chosen to reinforce compound word segmentation because they provide additional musical and tactile opportunities for students to repeat compound words.

- An added bonus to DROPP 5 is that every transition activity contains rhyming words. Whenever you have an extra few minutes, repeat any of the songs as a vehicle for rhyming reinforcement. Use the "Rhyming Exercise Song" or just Pause and Punch the rhyming pairs to reinforce the skill of rhyming.

- Reinforce directional vocabulary. Activity Set 5.1 uses the action song "Sally Go Round the Sun." As the children skip in a circle, they will change direction whenever you sing "boom-boom." If the song appears to be well known by all the children, then introduce and reinforce directional vocabulary by calling out "turn left" or "turn right" when they change directions.

- Fingerplays such as "This Little Boy" and "This Little Girl" give children a chance to tell what steps they take to get ready for school. Guide them to think of two to four activities they do each morning before leaving for school. This will build their sequential thinking skills.

TEACHING TIP: **Check for Success**

During every activity, maintain eye contact with the students to ensure they are responding correctly and on cue. In this way, you are doing a mini assessment for each child to see who may need additional help at every step of the way.

Clap-Out Compounds

- Prepare picture cards before beginning the lesson. Use a commercial deck of compound word pictures or download 12–16 simple compound word pictures from http://www.carlscorner.us.com/Compounds.htm. On the first day of the game, choose only pictures of compound words that are made of one-syllable segments, such as *rain-drop* and *sun-shine*. In later games, as children's compound word awareness skills grow, you can use a mixture of shorter and longer compound words.

- First round: Show the children the first short compound word card and say the whole word smoothly. If the chosen student is unable to clap out the two small words correctly, then use the compound word awareness hand gestures (from Activity Set 4.1) to help him or her clap out the answer correctly (e.g., *rain-drop*).

- Subsequent rounds: Do not use pictures in additional rounds in order to emphasize auditory recognition of separate small words.

When the skill is being introduced, the visual support provided by picture cards is helpful. Once your children are able to repeat compound words consistently and accurately, however, stop using the picture cards in order to de-emphasize the visual supports. This will promote the development of better listening skills, which leads to deeper phonological awareness.

Happy Hopscotch

- Prepare the game materials before the lesson. Place tape on the floor or cut a yoga mat in half and draw a four-square hopscotch board (see the CD-ROM for a diagram). Select 10–12 words from the suggested list, beginning with shorter words.

- Have the whole group repeat your chosen words before preparing to hop. This will improve their segmentation ability by familiarizing them with the words. Model how to clap out, then hop, stamp, or jump out a short compound word.

  - Jump with both feet in first single box, saying *schoolgirl* as one smooth word.

  - Hop with one foot into left box, saying *school*.

  - Hop with one foot into right box, saying *girl*.

- Jump with both feet in final box, repeating *schoolgirl* as one smooth word.

- After landing on both feet, raise your hands overhead triumphantly (like a winning athlete).

TEACHING TIP: **Celebrate Success**

Always give students a specific compliment at the end of the game. Praise them and tell them what they did. For example, "You did a great job hopping to show the two small words in a compound word."

Gumdrop Game

- Prepare the materials before the lesson. Select 12–16 words from suggested lists in the lesson. Assemble "gumdrops" with two large different-colored circles for demonstration and sets of two small colored circles per child. Prepare a large demonstration copy and individual copies of the frame (see Appendix D on the accompanying CD-ROM).

- Directions for playing the game are as follows.

  - Demonstrate how to say the entire compound word while pointing to the top circles on the demonstration frame.

  - Pull down a large colored circle for each small word in the compound while saying that word part slowly.

  - Check your answer by touching the circles at the bottom while saying the individual word parts, from left to right.

  - Sweep your pointer finger from left to right a second time while repeating the entire compound word.

TEACHING TIP: **Scaffold Your Instruction for Greater Success**

If the children cannot move the chips to segment the compound word correctly, then guide them in clapping out the word first. Then, help them touch and say the word segments in the top box before touching, saying, and moving the chips down. Practice until they meet with success, then have them repeat the process independently with the same word.

Review

On the 10th day of each Activity Set, students get the opportunity to review compound word awareness and blending skills by practicing the Clap-Out Compounds, Happy Hopscotch, and Gumdrop Game from the prior 9 days before their skill assessment checkout.

Skill Assessment Checkouts

After your review lesson is completed on the 10th day, set aside a few minutes to give each child an individual compound word segmentation checkout. Students will clap once for each of the two small words in a whole compound word. This is aligned with most states' curriculum guidelines for general reading processes and phonemic awareness. These take about 2 minutes per child to administer and provide useful information to guide your small-group placements. Based on the checkout and collaborative conversations with all teachers, you will determine which students should continue in Tier 2 small-group intervention and which students can successfully return to Tier 1 whole-class instruction.

Assessment Outcome: The student can segment short spoken sentences into individual words.

ACTIVITY SET 5.1

Lesson Descriptions

Lessons	Sequence of daily activities	◇ Vocabulary
Lesson 1: Clap-Out Compounds	Silly song: "Oh, What a Rain" (Verse 1) Target: Segment short compound words by clapping Nursery Rhyme: "Two Blackbirds"	Gumdrop Compound
Lesson 2: Happy Hopscotch	Silly song: "Oh, What a Sun" (Verse 2) Target: Segment compound words in multisensory game Action song: "Sally Go Round the Sun"	Beam Sunbeam Action
Lesson 3: Gumdrop Game	Silly song: "Oh, What a Snow" (Verse 3) Target: Segmenting compound words by moving chips Nursery Rhyme: "Wee Willie Winkie"	
Lesson 4: Compound Word Segmentation Review	Silly song: "Oh, What a Rain" (All verses) Target: Review all activities Silly song: "Oh, What a Rain"	Verse

Materials Needed

☑ Picture or a sample of a gumdrop

☑ Picture of a sunbeam or flashlight beam

☑ Five to six pictures/objects of short compound words or a compound words card deck

☑ Optional: Large nursery rhyme book with "Wee Willie Winkie"

> ☑ DROPP 5 Skill Assessment Checkout (see Appendix B on the CD-ROM)
> ☑ Tokens for behavior/participation
>
> **CD-ROM**
>
> **Happy Hopscotch**
> ☑ Happy Hopscotch board diagram (see Appendix D on the CD-ROM)
> ☑ Happy Hopscotch word list (see Appendix D on the CD-ROM)
>
> **Gumdrop Game**
> ☑ Gumdrop Game game board (see Appendix D on the CD-ROM)
> ☑ Two large different-colored chips for the teacher and two smaller different-colored chips for each student

ACTIVITY SET

5.1 **10-Day Planner**

Day 1	**Lesson 1:** Clap-Out Compounds
Day 2	**Lesson 1:** Clap-Out Compounds
Day 3	**Lesson 2:** Happy Hopscotch
Day 4	**Lesson 2:** Happy Hopscotch
Day 5	**Lesson 3:** Gumdrop Game
Day 6	**Lesson 3:** Gumdrop Game
Day 7	**Lesson 1:** Clap-Out Compounds
Day 8	**Lesson 2:** Happy Hopscotch
Day 9	**Lesson 3:** Gumdrop Game
Day 10	**Lesson 4:** Compound Word Segmentation Review

LESSON 1: Clap-Out Compounds

OBJECTIVES

Student will

- Learn how to separate (segment) compound words into their two small words by clapping once for each small word

Teacher will

- Review compound word awareness in a song
- Model and guide students to clap out the two small words in compound words

RHYMES, SONGS, AND FINGERPLAYS

"Oh, What a Rain"

"Two Blackbirds"

MATERIALS

Picture or a sample of a gumdrop

Five to six pictures/objects of short compound words or a compound words card deck

Tokens for behavior/participation

TECHNOLOGY LINK

Visit the following site to hear the music for "Oh, What a Rain": http://kids.niehs.nih.gov/lyrics/raindrops.htm

---

 TASK 1   **Song to begin the lesson** (approximately 3 minutes)

INTRODUCE the big idea: compound word segmentation.

Settle the group in their seats and say the following. You know how to listen to two small words and blend them together to make one long word called a compound word. Starting today, you are going to learn how to listen to some new compound words and hear their two small words.

BEGIN the song.

 Multisensory Reinforcement

I am going to sing a song about something funny that could happen when it rains. You may know this song, and if you do, you can sing along with me. Listen; here we go. *Stand up and look up at the ceiling with a happy face, with hands open and facing upward at your sides. Sway in rhythm as you sing.*

If all of the raindrops were lemonade and gumdrops,
Oh, what a rain it would be.
Standing outside with my mouth open wide. *(Put head back.)*
Ah, ah, ah, ah, ah, ah, ah, ah, ah, ah. *(Open mouth wide.)*
If all of the raindrops were lemonade and gumdrops,
Oh, what a rain it would be.

Repeat the song.

Your turn to sing with me. Everyone stand up. *Make sure each child has space. Repeat the song, leading them in the song and movements.*

▶ Children sing and copy the movements.

Good job singing our funny song. Let's do it one more time.

▶ Children repeat first verse with movements.

 TASK 2   **Clap-Out Compounds** (approximately 12–14 minutes)

LINK the big idea to the song.

That was fun pretending to catch treats that come down with the rain. Some of the words in the song are two-part words, like *gum-drops.*

Show a picture of a gumdrop or an actual gumdrop. Who knows what this is? Raise your hand.

197

5.1

 Vocabulary

GUMDROP

▶ Children's response: Candy.

This candy is called a gumdrop. What is this candy called?

▶ Children's response: A gumdrop.

Yes, a gumdrop. What is a gumdrop?

▶ Children's response: Candy.

Yes, candy.

REVIEW compound word awareness.

We sang a song about some yummy things coming down out of the sky, like gumdrops. Listen. *Gumdrop* has two small words. It is a compound word. Let's listen for both small words.

 Multisensory Reinforcement

Gum-drop.

Repeat, using your hands to demonstrate as follows. Hold up both hands about a foot apart, palms toward children. When you say the first syllable, emphasize your right hand by spreading your fingers and moving your hand slightly away from the other and toward the children. Do the same with the second syllable and the left hand. Repeat the target word.

INTRODUCE clapping out compounds.

Now let's learn a way to show that our ears can hear both small words in a compound word. Ears ready? Listen. My turn. *Say the whole word, quickly; then repeat it, pausing between the two parts and clapping once for each part.*

Turn On Your Ears

Gumdrop. Gum *(clap)* drop *(clap)*. Gumdrop.

Now let's do it together. Get ready to say it and clap it.

▶ Children's response: Gum *(clap)* drop *(clap)*. Gumdrop.

Good job saying and clapping the two word parts in *gumdrop*.

TEACHING TIP: Link the skill with previous learning to build understanding.

Let's think about the smart thing you are doing. When you learned about words in sentences, you listened very well and then you clapped to show that you could hear the words, like this. *Say the sentence, clapping six times, once with each word:*

Mother bought gumdrops at the supermarket. Everyone, say and clap out the words in that sentence with me.

▶ Children's response: Mother bought gumdrops at the supermarket *(clap six times)*.

 Turn On Your Ears

Be sure the children are firm in this task. Repeat the same sentence, with clapping support if necessary. That's wonderful. Now, get your ears ready to hear the two small words in the compound words in that same sentence.

Model the Activity

Listen: Mother bought . . .

▶ Children's response: Gumdrops.

Yes, gumdrops.

Think aloud about compound words. Does *gumdrops* have two small words? Let's see. My turn to say it and clap it.

Gum *(clap)* drops *(clap)*. Gumdrops.

Yes! I clapped two times because I heard the two small words in a compound word. Okay, listen again. Mother bought gumdrops at the supermarket.

Okay, listen again. Mother bought gumdrops at the . . .

▶ Children's response: Supermarket.

Yes, supermarket. Does *supermarket* have two small words? Let's see. Watch me say it and clap it. Super *(clap)* market *(clap)*. Supermarket.

Yes, I did it again! I clapped out the two small words in the compound word *supermarket*.

PRACTICE clapping out compound words.

Engage in group practice: Assemble pictures or objects representing five to six short compound words. If you have a compound words card deck, then choose only the two-syllable words. Let's clap out some more compound words together. Listen.

Raindrop. *Show first picture [e.g., raindrop].* This is a rain-drop. What word?

▶ Children's response: Raindrop.

Yes, raindrop. Let's clap out the two small words in *raindrop.* Say it and clap it.

▶ Children's response: Rain *(clap)* drop *(clap)*. Raindrop.

Good job clapping out the two small words in the compound word *raindrop.*

**Correction procedure: If a child repeats or claps the word incorrectly, then say the following.* Do it with me. Rain-drop. Say it.

▶ Child's response: Raindrop. *Say with child.*

Yes, raindrop. Let's clap it out.

▶ Child's response: Rain *(clap)* drop *(clap)*. Raindrop. *Do all steps with child.*

Good. One more time clapping it out.

▶ Child's response: Rain *(clap)* drop *(clap)*. Raindrop.

Good job.*****

Let's try some more. *Follow the initial format for four or five compound words. Show the picture and use this wording each time.*

This is a _____. What word?

▶ Children's response: _____.

Yes, _____. Let's clap out the two small words in _____. Say it and clap it.

▶ Children's response: _____ *(clap)* _____ *(clap)*. _____. **(Say whole word.)**

Good job clapping out the two small words in the compound word _____.

INTRODUCE individual practice.

Here are some sample words for individual clapping out of short compound words: sunshine, airplane, haystack, outside, teapot, bedroom, *and* doghouse.

Now you will clap out your own compound word.

Follow the previous format and wording. Give each child a turn to answer individually. First round: If you have a compound word deck, then show each child a new compound picture card from the deck. Otherwise, reuse the group pictures for individual practice.

Ready? Sun-shine. Say it fast.

▶ Child's response: Sunshine.

Yes, sunshine. Say it and clap it.

▶ Child's response: Sun *(clap)* shine *(clap)*. Sunshine.

5.1

Use these additional short compound words for clapping out practice: dollhouse, farmhouse, football, flashlight, cowboy, baseball, beehive, snowman, goldfish, *and* milkshake.

 Turn On Your Ears

Yes, sunshine. Good job clapping two times for the two small words in *sunshine.*

Ready? _____. Say it fast.

▶ **Child's response:** _____.

Yes, _____. Say it and clap it.

▶ **Child's response:** ___ *(clap)* _____ *(clap)*. _____. **(Say whole word.)**

Yes, _____.

Good job clapping two times for the two small words in _____.

This time around we will not look at the pictures. But you will each get more turns to clap out your own compound word. Listen carefully.

Subsequent rounds: Do not show pictures for two to three additional rounds in order to shift the emphasis to auditory recognition of separate small words. Follow the same format for each child, using short compound words. Continue for several more rounds and use the above wording each time.

🪐 **TASK 3**   **Transition nursery rhyme and exit task** (approximately 3 minutes)

END the lesson with the transition song and exit task.

You worked hard today clapping out the two small words in compound words. You did a wonderful job and I am proud of you. Your good work makes me smile like the sun.

Even though we were singing about the rain earlier, now let's listen to a nursery rhyme about two birds who like to fly around out in the . . . sun - shine. Say it fast.

▶ **Children's response: Sunshine.**

Yes, sunshine.

These two birds are called . . . black - birds. What kind of birds? Say it fast.

▶ **Children's response: Blackbirds.**

Yes, blackbirds.

READ the nursery rhyme.

There were two blackbirds,
Sitting on a hill,
The one named Jack,
The other named Jill,
Fly away, Jack! Fly away, Jill!
Come again, Jack! Come again, Jill!

DO the exit task.

Now show me if you can clap out one last compound word all by yourself. *Let each child have one turn to clap out one of the following words, using today's lesson format and words. Clap out these exit compound words:* blackbird, sunshine, teapot, goldfish, raindrop, *and* haystack.

END Lesson 1.

Everyone now gets their winnings for hearing and blending the two small words in compound words and for working hard. *Give out token rewards to each child.*

LESSON 2: Happy Hopscotch

OBJECTIVES

Student will

- Learn how to separate (segment) short compound words into their two small words by hopping or clapping once for each small word

Teacher will

- Review compound word awareness in a song
- Model and guide students to hop once for each of the two small words in compound words

RHYMES, SONGS, AND FINGERPLAYS

"Oh, What a Sun"

"Sally Go Round the Sun"

MATERIALS

Picture of a sunbeam or flashlight beam

Tokens for behavior/participation

Happy Hopscotch   **CD-ROM**

☑ Happy Hopscotch board diagram (see Appendix D on the CD-ROM)

☑ Happy Hopscotch word list

 TASK 1   **Transition song to begin** (approximately 3 minutes)

INTRODUCE the lesson.	We are going to listen to compound words and hear their two small words. Then we'll use the words in a fun game called Happy Hopscotch.
BEGIN the transition activity.	You learned the first part of a song about something funny that could happen when it rains. Now I'm going to sing the second part of that song about something great that could happen when the sun shines. Listen so that you'll be able to sing it with me.
	Stand up and look up at the ceiling with a happy face, with hands open and facing upward at your sides. Sway in rhythm as you sing.
SING the song.	If all of the sunbeams were bubble gum and ice cream
	Oh, what a sun it would be.
	Standing outside with my mouth open wide. *(Put head back.)*
	Ah, ah, ah, ah, ah, ah, ah, ah, ah, ah. *(Open mouth wide.)*
	If all of the sunbeams were bubble gum and ice cream
	Oh, what a sun it would be.
Multisensory Reinforcement	Your turn to sing with me. Everyone stand up. *Make sure each child has space. Lead them in the song and movements.*
	▶ Children sing and copy the movements.
	Good job singing our funny song. Let's do it one more time. *Repeat the song and movements.*

 TASK 2   **Happy Hopscotch** (approximately 12–14 minutes)

Vocabulary **BEAM/SUNBEAM**	*Show a picture of a sunbeam or flashlight beam.* Who knows what this is? Raise your hand. *Accept several answers.*
	This is a beam of light. When you can see a line of light shining on something we call it a beam of light. What kind of light do we call it?
	▶ Children's response: A beam.

Yes, a beam.

We sang about sunbeams in our song. Sunbeams are lines or rays of light that shine down from the sun. What do we call lines of light that shine down from the sun?

▶ **Children's response: Sunbeams.**

Yes, sunbeams.

REVIEW and practice compound word awareness by clapping out compounds.

Turn On Your Ears

We sang about some yummy things coming down out of the sky with the sunbeams. Listen. *Sunbeam* is a compound word. It is made up of two small words. Let's listen for both small words. Turn on your ears! Get ready. Sun-beam.

Repeat while clapping with each word part. Sun *(clap)* beam *(clap)*. Sunbeam. Can you hear both parts of the compound word *sunbeam*?

Let's clap out some new compound words to show that our ears can hear both parts of a compound word. Everybody, ears ready?

Listen. Class-room. Say it fast.

▶ **Children's response: Classroom.**

Yes, classroom. Say it and clap it out.

▶ **Children's response: Class *(clap)* room *(clap)*. Classroom.**

Yes, classroom. Good job clapping two times for the two small words in *classroom*.

Listen. Wash-cloth. Say it fast.

▶ **Children's response: Washcloth.**

Yes, washcloth. Clap it out.

▶ **Children's response: Wash *(clap)* cloth *(clap)*. Washcloth.**

Yes, washcloth. Good job.

Repeat this format, clapping out four to five additional words, such as snowflake, bluebird, haystack, doorknob, fireman, *and* backpack.

♣ **PLAY** the game.

CD-ROM See Appendix D on the CD-ROM for the Happy Hopscotch board diagram and the Happy Hopscotch word list.

🪐 **TASK 3**   Transition action song and exit task *(approximately 3 minutes)*

INTRODUCE the action song.

✧ **Vocabulary**

ACTION

SING the song.

Some of you know our action song called "Sally Go Round the Sun." Remember, an action is a thing to do. Everybody, what is an action?

▶ **Children's response: A thing to do.**

Yes. An action is a thing we can do. In this song, the action is to skip around our circle in one direction, then when we say "boom-boom" we will skip in the other direction.

Form a circle holding hands. Walk in one direction, singing to the tune of "Here We Go Loop-de-Loo."

Sally, go round the sun,
Sally, go round the moon,

Sally, go round the chimney top
Every afternoon (boom-boom).

Change the direction of your circle and go the other way. Sing the song three times.

> TEACHING TIP: If the song appears to be well known by all children, then you can introduce or reinforce directional vocabulary by calling out "turn left" or "turn right" when you change directions.

CONDUCT the exit task to demonstrate skill mastery.

Now get ready to show me if you can clap out one last compound word all by yourself. *Use this format with each child.*

> TEACHING TIP: Scaffold your teaching by giving short, basic words to any child who seems to struggle with clapping at the right times. Guide responses to ensure success. Give longer words to students who clapped correctly.

Listen. Dog-house. Say it fast.

▶ **Children's response: Doghouse.**

Yes, doghouse. Clap it out.

▶ **Children's response: Dog *(clap)* house *(clap)*. Doghouse.**

Yes, doghouse. Good job clapping two times for the two word parts in *doghouse*.

Word options for exit task:

Basic	Three syllables	Four syllables
teapot	superstar	pufferbelly
raindrop	butterfly	butterfinger
sunshine	grandfather	coffeemaker
haystack	cheeseburger	watermelon
goldfish	sunflower	

END Lesson 2.

Everyone now gets their winnings for hearing and blending the two small words in compound words and for working hard. *Give out token rewards to each child.*

LESSON 3: Gumdrop Game

OBJECTIVES

Student will

- Learn how to separate (segment) short compound words into their two small words by moving a chip for each small word

Teacher will

- Review how to segment compound words by clapping out the two small words
- Model how to move colored chips to represent the separate word parts in compound words

RHYMES, SONGS, AND FINGERPLAYS

"Oh, What a Snow"
"Wee Willie Winkie"

MATERIALS

Optional: Large nursery rhyme book with "Wee Willie Winkie"

Tokens for behavior/participation

Gumdrop Game

☑ Gumdrop Game game boards (see Appendix D on the CD-ROM)

☑ Two large different-colored chips for the teacher and two smaller different-colored chips for each student

TASK 1 | Transition song to begin (approximately 3 minutes)

INTRODUCE the lesson.

We are going to listen to some new compound words and hear their two small words. Then we'll play a new game called the Gumdrop Game with some longer words.

BEGIN the transition activity.

We sang two parts of a song about yummy treats that could fall out of the sky when it rains or when the sun shines. Today we're going to sing another part of that song. This part is about something that could happen when it snows. Listen so that you'll be able to sing it with me.

Stand up and look up at the ceiling with a happy face, with hands open and facing upward at your sides. Sway in rhythm as you sing.

SING the song.

If all of the snowflakes were candy bars and milkshakes,
Oh, what a snow it would be.
Standing outside with my mouth open wide. *(Put head back.)*
Ah, ah, ah, ah, ah, ah, ah, ah, ah, ah. *(Open mouth wide.)*
If all of the snowflakes were candy bars and milkshakes,
Oh, what a snow it would be.

Your turn to sing with me. Everyone stand up. *Make sure each child has space.*

▶ **Children sing and copy the movements.**

Good job singing our funny song. Let's do it one more time. *Repeat the song and movements.*

TASK 2 | Gumdrop Game (approximately 12–14 minutes)

REVIEW compound word awareness by clapping out compounds.

We sang about some yummy food coming down like snowflakes. Listen. *Snowflakes* is a compound word. It is made up of two small words. Let's listen for both small words. *Repeat while clapping with each word part.* Snow-flakes.

Snow *(clap)* flakes *(clap)*. Snowflakes. Can you hear both parts of the compound word *snowflakes?*

 Turn On Your Ears

Today we will clap out some longer compound words to show that our ears can hear the small words in a compound word. Everybody, ears ready?

Listen. Lady-bug. Say it.

▶ **Children's response: Ladybug.**

Yes, ladybug. Everybody, get ready to clap it out. Remember, even though it is a longer word, we will still clap just two times, once for each small word. Get ready. Lady-bug. Say it fast.

▶ **Children's response: Ladybug.**

Yes, ladybug. Clap it out.

▶ **Children's response: Lady *(clap)* bug *(clap)*. Ladybug.**

Yes, ladybug. Good job clapping two times for the two small words in *ladybug.*

TEACHING TIP: Teach longer compounds without introducing syllables. Emphasize the two units of meaning (straw-berry) instead of the three syllables (straw-ber-ry).

Listen. Straw-berry. Say it fast.

▶ **Children's response: Strawberry.**

Yes, strawberry. Clap it out.

▶ Children's response: Straw *(clap)* berry *(clap)*. Strawberry.

Yes, strawberry. Good job.

Repeat format, clapping out four to five additional words. Clap out additional words, such as grasshopper, hamburger, peppermint, afternoon, *and* pineapple.

 PLAY the game.

> **CD-ROM** See Appendix D on the CD-ROM for the Gumdrop Game instructions and game boards.

 TASK 3   Transition nursery rhyme and exit task *(approximately 3 minutes)*

END the lesson with a transition nursery rhyme.

You worked hard today. You showed me that you can say the two small words in compound words by moving down your colored gumdrops, I mean chips, in the Gumdrop Game. I am proud of you.

PAUSE AND PUNCH.

Now, let's say our nursery rhyme about Wee Willie Winkie, the tiny little boy who runs around in his . . . night - gown! Say it fast!

▶ Children's response: Nightgown.

Yes, nightgown. Say it and clap it.

▶ Children's response: Night *(clap)* gown *(clap)*. Nightgown.

Yes, nightgown!

Optional: Show the rhyme and pictures in a large nursery rhyme book as you say it.

First, listen to the nursery rhyme, and then you can say some of the words in it with me.

Wee Willie Winkie runs through the town
Upstairs and downstairs, in his nightgown.
Rapping at the window, crying through the lock,
Are the children in their beds, for now it's eight o'clock?

Repeat the nursery rhyme one or two times. When the children seem familiar with it, drop the final rhyming words, as follows:

PAUSE AND PUNCH.

Wee Willie Winkie, runs through the . . . town *(emphasize)*
Upstairs and downstairs, in his night . . .

▶ Children: Gown.

Rapping at the window, crying through the . . . lock *(emphasize)*
Are the children in their beds, for now it's eight o' . . .

▶ Children: Clock.

CONDUCT the exit task to demonstrate skill mastery.

Get ready to show me if you can clap out one last compound word all by your-self. *Use this format with each child. Match word difficulty to each child's ability.*

Listen. Dog-house. Say it fast.

▶ Child's response: Doghouse.

Yes, doghouse. Clap it out.

▶ Child's response: Dog *(clap)* house *(clap)*. Doghouse.

Yes, doghouse. Good job clapping two times for the two small words in dog-house.

Clap out these exit compound words:

Basic	Three syllables	Four syllables
upstairs	dragonfly	watermelon
downstairs	grandmother	butterfinger
eyelid	cheeseburger	coffeemaker
earthworm	butternut	pufferbelly
sunfish		
sweetheart		
headache		

END Lesson 3.

Everyone now gets their winnings for hearing and blending the two small words in compound words and for working hard. *Give out token rewards to each child.*

LESSON 4: Compound Word Segmentation Review

OBJECTIVES

Student will

- Demonstrate the ability to separate (segment) shorter, then longer, compound words into their two small words by clapping, hopping, or moving a chip for each small word

Teacher will

- Review compound word awareness and segmentation

- Guide students to demonstrate the skill independently in three game formats

- Support students' success with careful item selection and multisensory supports

RHYMES, SONGS, AND FINGERPLAYS

"Oh, What a Rain" (all verses)

MATERIALS

DROPP 5 Skill Assessment Checkout (see Appendix B on the CD-ROM)

Tokens for behavior/participation

> **Happy Hopscotch**
> - ☑ Happy Hopscotch board diagram (see Appendix D on the CD-ROM)
> - ☑ Happy Hopscotch word list
>
> **Gumdrop Game**
> - ☑ Gumdrop Game game board
> - ☑ Two large different-colored chips for the teacher and two smaller different-colored chips for each student

---

 TASK 1   Transition song to begin *(approximately 5 minutes)*

INTRODUCE the lesson.	Today we will practice all the ways we know of hearing the two small words in compound words.
REVIEW the song.	First we will get to sing all three verses, or parts, of our song about yummy treats coming down out of the sky.
✧ **Vocabulary** **VERSE**	When we sing a song that has more than one part, each part is called a verse. Say that word. ▶ **Children's response: Verse.** Yes, verse. A verse is a part of a song. What is a verse?

► Children's response: A part of a song.

Yes. A verse is part of a song. The first verse of our song was about raindrops, lemonade, and gumdrops. Let's practice the first verse. *Stand in a circle and sway in rhythm as you sing.*

If all of the raindrops were lemonade and gumdrops,
Oh, what a rain it would be.
Standing outside with my mouth open wide. *(Put head back.)*
Ah, ah, ah, ah, ah, ah, ah, ah, ah, ah. *(Open mouth wide.)*
If all of the raindrops were lemonade and gumdrops,
Oh, what a rain it would be.

Good job singing the first part, or the first verse. What did I call the first part?

► Children's response: The first verse.

Yes, we just sang the first verse. The second verse of our song was about sunbeams, bubble gum, and ice cream. Let's practice the second verse.

If all of the sunbeams were bubble gum and ice cream,
Oh, what a sun it would be.
Standing outside with my mouth open wide. *(Put head back.)*
Ah, ah, ah, ah, ah, ah, ah, ah, ah, ah. *(Open mouth wide.)*
If all of the sunbeams were bubble gum and ice cream,
Oh, what a sun it would be.

Wow. You are my superstar singers. Or shall I call you the Sunbeam Singers? You just sang the second part, or the second verse, of our song. What did I call the second part?

► Children's response: The second verse.

Yes, we sang the second verse. The third verse of our song was about snowflakes, candy bars, and milkshakes. Let's practice the third verse.

If all of the snowflakes were candy bars and milkshakes,
Oh, what a snow it would be.
Standing outside with my mouth open wide. *(Put head back.)*
Ah, ah, ah, ah, ah, ah, ah, ah, ah, ah. *(Open mouth wide.)*
If all of the snowflakes were candy bars and milkshakes,
Oh, what a snow it would be.

In that song the weather brings down some really sweet treats. It gives me a toothache just to think about it. You did a great job singing all three verses of that song. You remembered all three parts, or verses. What do we call the parts?

► Children's response: Verses.

Yes, verses. Good job remembering that new word. Later on, we'll sing all three verses again.

SING all three verses of the song.

 **Multisensory Reinforcement**

 **TASK 2A**　　Clap-Out Compounds *(approximately 3 minutes)*

REVIEW compound words: definition and blending.

A lot of the words in our song were compound words because they each have two small words. Listen and say these words after me.

Rain-drop. Say it fast.

► Children's response: Raindrop.

5.1

Yes, raindrop.

Gum-drop. Say it fast.

▶ **Children's response: Gumdrop.**

Yes, gumdrop.

Sun-beam. Say it fast.

▶ **Children's response: Sunbeam.**

Yes, sunbeam.

Snow-flake. Say it fast.

▶ **Children's response: Snowflake.**

Yes, snowflake.

Milk-shake. Say it fast.

▶ **Children's response: Milkshake.**

Yes, milkshake.

**Turn On
Your Ears**

PRACTICE clapping out
compound words.

Good job. Each of those compound words has two small words. Let's listen for the small words and clap them out. Everybody, turn on your ears. Ears ready?

Listen. Rain-drop. Say it and clap it.

▶ **Children's response: Rain** *(clap)* **drop** *(clap)***.**

What word?

▶ **Children's response: Raindrop.**

Yes, raindrop. Good job clapping two times for the two small words in *raindrop*. *Repeat the format, clapping out additional words.*

Listen. Gum-drop. Say it and clap it.

▶ **Children's response: Gum** *(clap)* **drop** *(clap)***.**

What word?

▶ **Children's response: Gumdrop.**

Yes, gumdrop. Good job. *Repeat with* sunbeam, snowflake, *and* milkshake.

 TASK 2B   **Gumdrop Game** (approximately 5 minutes)

 PLAY the game.

CD-ROM   See Appendix D on the CD-ROM for the Gumdrop Game instructions and game board.

 TASK 2C   **Happy Hopscotch** (approximately 5 minutes)

 PLAY the game.

CD-ROM   See Appendix D on the CD-ROM for the Happy Hopscotch board diagram and the Happy Hopscotch word list.

TASK 3 | Transition song (approximately 3 minutes)

END the lesson with a transition song.

You worked hard today and showed me that you can hear the two small words in compound words. Some of them were short words, and some of them were long words. You did a wonderful job and I am proud of you.

Let's pretend our winnings are floating out of the sky as we sing our song about "Oh, What a Rain." Do you remember all three verses?

SING the song.

Ready? First verse.

If all of the raindrops were lemonade and gumdrops,
Oh, what a rain it would be.
Standing outside with my mouth open wide. *(Put head back.)*
Ah, ah, ah, ah, ah, ah, ah, ah, ah, ah. *(Open mouth wide.)*
If all of the raindrops were lemonade and gumdrops,
Oh, what a rain it would be.

Continue singing the remaining verses.

END Lesson 4.

Everyone now gets their winnings for hearing and blending the two small words in compound words and for working hard. *Give out token rewards to each child.*

CD-ROM The DROPP 5 Skill Assessment Checkout will be completed for each student following this lesson.

ACTIVITY SET 5.2

Lesson Descriptions

Lessons	Sequence of daily activities	◇ Vocabulary
Lesson 1: Clap-Out Compounds	Song: "I'm a Little Teapot" Target: Segment short compound words by clapping Song: "Oh, What a Rain" (All verses)	Grapefruit Verse
Lesson 2: Happy Hopscotch	Song: "This Little Boy" Target: Segment short compound words in a multisensory game Song: "This Little Girl"	
Lesson 3: Gumdrop Game	Song: "Tiny Tim" Target: Segment compound words by moving chips Song: "Tiny Tim"	
Lesson 4: Compound Word Segmentation Review	Song: "I'm a Little Teapot" Target: Review all activities Song: "Oh, What a Rain"	

Materials Needed

☑ Pictures of or an actual teapot, teacup, and grapefruit

☑ Five to six pictures/objects of short compound words or a compound words card deck

☑ Plastic toy lizard

☑ Tokens for behavior/participation

☑ DROPP 5 Skill Assessment Checkout (see Appendix B on the CD-ROM)   **CD-ROM**

Happy Hopscotch

☑ Happy Hopscotch board diagram (see Appendix D on the CD-ROM)

☑ Happy Hopscotch word list (see Appendix D on the CD-ROM)

Gumdrop Game

☑ Gumdrop Game game board (see Appendix D on the CD-ROM)

☑ Two large different-colored chips for the teacher and two smaller different-colored chips for each student

ACTIVITY SET

5.2 10-Day Planner

Day 1	**Lesson 1:** Clap-Out Compounds
Day 2	**Lesson 1:** Clap-Out Compounds
Day 3	**Lesson 2:** Happy Hopscotch
Day 4	**Lesson 2:** Happy Hopscotch
Day 5	**Lesson 3:** Gumdrop Game
Day 6	**Lesson 3:** Gumdrop Game
Day 7	**Lesson 1:** Clap-Out Compounds
Day 8	**Lesson 2:** Happy Hopscotch
Day 9	**Lesson 3:** Gumdrop Game
Day 10	**Lesson 4:** Compound Word Segmentation Review

LESSON 1: Clap-Out Compounds

OBJECTIVES

Student will

- Learn how to separate (segment) compound words into their two small words by clapping once for each small word

Teacher will

- Review compound word awareness in a song
- Model and guide students to clap out the two small words in compound words

RHYMES, SONGS, AND FINGERPLAYS

"I'm a Little Teapot"

"Oh, What a Rain"

MATERIALS

Picture of or an actual grapefruit

Five to six pictures/objects of short compound words or a compound words card deck

Tokens for behavior/participation

TECHNOLOGY LINK

Visit the following site to hear the music for "Oh, What a Rain": http://kids.niehs.nih.gov/lyrics/raindrops.htm

---

 TASK 1   Transition song to begin (approximately 3 minutes)

REVIEW the big idea: compound word segmentation.	You know that a compound word is a longer word that is made up of two small words. You have been learning how to listen to compound words and clap out their two small words. Starting today, you will listen to some new compound words and have fun hearing their two small words.
BEGIN the song.	Today we'll learn some compound words that name things we eat and drink. I'm thinking of a song we can sing that tells about a pot that pours tea. Who knows which action song talks about something that pours tea?
	▶ Children's response: "I'm a Little Teapot."
Multisensory Reinforcement	That's right. "I'm a Little Teapot." Let's sing and dance to that song. *Have everyone stand up. Make sure each child has space. Sing and dance to the song, leading children in the song and movements.*
	I'm a little teapot, short and stout.
	Here is my handle, here is my spout.
	When I get all steamed up, then I shout.
	Just tip me over and pour me out.
REPEAT the song.	Good job singing our funny song. Let's do it one more time. *Repeat.*

 **TASK 2**   Clap-Out Compounds (approximately 12–14 minutes)

Vocabulary **GRAPEFRUIT**	*Show a picture or an actual grapefruit.* Who knows what this is? Raise your hand. *Accept several answers.* This is called a grapefruit. What is this fruit called?
	▶ Children's response: Grapefruit.
	Yes, a grapefruit. *Grapefruit* has the word *grape* in it, but it is not like a grape. A grapefruit is more like an orange, but the inside is pink or red. We can eat grapefruit for breakfast. What fruit is this?
	▶ Children's response: Grapefruit.

REVIEW compound word awareness.

Multisensory Reinforcement

Turn On Your Ears

PRACTICE clapping out compounds.

Yes, grapefruit.

We sang a song about a teapot. Listen. *Teapot* has two small words in it. It is a compound word. Let's listen for both small words.

Repeat, using your hands to demonstrate, as follows. Hold up both hands about a foot apart, palms toward children. When you say the first syllable, emphasize your right hand by spreading your fingers and moving your hand slightly away from the other. Do the same with the second syllable and the left hand. Repeat the target word.

Tea-pot. Can you hear both small words in the compound word *teapot?*

Now let's practice a way to show that our ears can hear both small words in a compound word. Everybody, turn on your ears. Ears ready? Listen. My turn. *Say the whole word quickly, then repeat it, pausing between the two small words and clapping once for each part. Repeat the whole word.*

Teapot.
Tea-pot. *Clap hands with each small word.*
Teapot.

Now let's do it together. Get ready to say it and clap it.

▶ **Children's response: Teapot. Tea** *(clap)* **pot** *(clap)*. **Teapot.**

Good job saying and clapping the two small words in *teapot.*

TEACHING TIP: Link the skill with previous learning to build students' understanding.

Let's think about the smart thing you are doing. When you learned about words in sentences, you listened very well, and then you clapped to show that you could hear the words, like this. *Say this sentence, clapping six times—once with each word:*

Grandfather put tea in the teapot. Everyone, say and clap out the words in that sentence with me. Get ready.

▶ **Children's response: Grandfather put tea in the teapot.** *(Clap six times.)*

Be sure the children are firm in this task. Repeat the same sentence, with clapping support, if necessary. That's wonderful. *Think aloud about compound words.* Now, get your ears ready to hear the two small words in the compound words in that same sentence.

Everyone, who put tea in the teapot?

▶ **Children's response: Grandfather.**

Yes, grandfather. *Review the activity of clapping out compound words with the children.* Say it and clap it.

▶ **Children's response: Grand** *(clap)* **father** *(clap)*. **Grandfather.**

Yes. We clapped out the two small words in a compound word. Okay, listen again. Grandfather put tea in the teapot.

Grandfather put tea in the . . .

▶ **Children's response: Teapot.**

Yes, teapot. Does *teapot* have two small words? Let's find out. Clap it out with me.

▶ **Children's response: Tea** *(clap)* **pot** *(clap)*. **Teapot.**

Turn On Your Ears

Yes, we did it again! We clapped out the two small words in the compound word *teapot.* Good job.

PRACTICE clapping out compound words.

Assemble pictures or objects representing five to six short compound words. If you have a compound words card deck, then choose only the two-syllable words. Let's clap out some more compound words together. Listen.

Toothpaste. *Show first picture [e.g., toothpaste].* This is toothpaste. What word?

▶ **Children's response: Toothpaste.**

Yes, toothpaste. Let's clap out the two small words in toothpaste. Say it and clap it.

▶ **Children's response: Tooth** *(clap)* **paste** *(clap).* **Toothpaste.**

Good job clapping out the two small words in the compound word *toothpaste.* Let's try some more. *Follow this format for four to five compound words. Show the picture and use this wording each time.* This is a _____. What word?

▶ **Children's response: _____.**

Yes, _____. Let's clap out the two small words in _____. Say it and clap it.

▶ **Children's response: ____** *(clap)* **____** *(clap).* **_____.** *(Say whole word.)*

Good job clapping out the two small words in the compound word _____.

INTRODUCE individual practice.

Use these related words for clapping: cheesecake, gumball, popcorn, *and* peanut.

Here are some sample words for individual clapping out of short compound words: daydream, railroad, eyeball, whitefish, schoolboy, friendship, blackboard, *and* firehouse.

Now you will clap out your own compound word. *Follow the previous format and wording. Give each child a turn to answer individually. First round: If you have a compound word deck, then show each child a new compound picture card from the deck. Otherwise, reuse the group pictures for individual practice.*

This time around we will not look at the pictures. But you will each get more turns to clap out your own compound word. Listen carefully. *Subsequent rounds: Do not show pictures for two to three additional rounds in order to shift the emphasis to auditory recognition of separate small words. Follow the same format for each child, using short compound words.* Ready? Day-dream. Say it fast.

▶ **Child's response: Daydream.**

Yes, daydream. Say it and clap it.

▶ **Child's response: Day** *(clap)* **dream** *(clap).* **Daydream.**

Yes, daydream. Good job clapping two times for the two small words in daydream! *Continue for several more rounds and use the above format each time.*

***Correction procedure:** If a child repeats or claps the word (e.g., rainbow) incorrectly, say,* Do it with me. Rain-bow. Say it.

▶ **Child's response: Rainbow.** *(Say with child.)*

Yes, rainbow. Let's clap it out.

Return to group practice: Use these additional short compound words for clapping out practice: dollhouse, farmhouse, football, flashlight, cowboy, baseball, beehive, snowman, goldfish, *and* milkshake.

▶ **Child's response: Rain** *(clap)* **bow** *(clap).* **Rainbow.** *(Do all steps with the child.)*

*Repeat until firm.**

TASK 3   **Transition song and exit task** (approximately 3 minutes)

END the lesson with a transition song and exit task.

SING the song.

You worked hard today clapping out the two small words in compound words. Your ears are really working well, helping you listen hard.

We heard the two small words in some compound words about food.

Now, let's sing our song that tells about a time when it was raining food. The song is "Oh, What a Rain." We learned all three verses of the song. Each part of the song is called a verse. Everyone, what is a part of a song called?

▶ **Children's response: A verse.**

Yes, a verse. *Sing as many verses as time allows.*

The first verse of our song was about raindrops, lemonade, and gumdrops. Let's sing the first verse.

If all of the raindrops were lemonade and gumdrops,
Oh, what a rain it would be.
Standing outside with my mouth open wide. *(Put head back.)*
Ah, ah, ah, ah, ah, ah, ah, ah, ah, ah. *(Open mouth wide.)*
If all of the raindrops were lemonade and gumdrops,
Oh, what a rain it would be.

The second verse of our song was about sunbeams, bubble gum, and ice cream. Let's sing the second verse.

If all of the sunbeams were bubble gum and ice cream
Oh, what a sun it would be.
Standing outside with my mouth open wide. *(Put head back.)*
Ah, ah, ah, ah, ah, ah, ah, ah, ah, ah. *(Open mouth wide.)*
If all of the sunbeams were bubble gum and ice cream,
Oh, what a sun it would be.

The third verse of our song was about snowflakes, candy bars, and milkshakes. Let's sing the third verse:

If all of the snowflakes were candy bars and milkshakes,
Oh, what a snow it would be.
Standing outside with my mouth open wide. *(Put head back.)*
Ah, ah, ah, ah, ah, ah, ah, ah, ah, ah. *(Open mouth wide.)*
If all of the snowflakes were candy bars and milkshakes,
Oh, what a snow it would be.

DO the exit task.

Now show me if you can clap out one last compound word all by yourself. *Clap out these exit compound words:* railroad, whitefish, schoolboy, friendship, *and* day-dream. *Let each child have a turn to clap out one of the words, using today's lesson format and words.*

END Lesson 1.

Everyone now gets their winnings for hearing and blending the two small words in compound words and for working hard. *Give out token rewards to each child.*

LESSON 2: Happy Hopscotch

OBJECTIVES

Student will

- Learn how to separate (segment) short compound words into their two small words by hopping or clapping once for each small word

Teacher will

- Review compound word awareness in a fingerplay
- Model and guide students to hop once for each of the two small words in compound words

RHYMES, SONGS, AND FINGERPLAYS

"This Little Boy" and "This Little Girl"

MATERIALS

Tokens for behavior/participation

> **Happy Hopscotch**
> ☑ Happy Hopscotch board diagram (see Appendix D on the CD-ROM)
> ☑ Happy Hopscotch word list

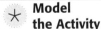 **TASK 1**   Transition song to begin (approximately 3 minutes)

INTRODUCE the lesson.	We are going to listen to compound words and hear their two small words. Then we'll use the words in a fun game called Happy Hopscotch.
BEGIN the transition activity.	Today we're going to say our fingerplay called "This Little Boy." Show me if you remember it by saying it with me and doing the finger movements.
RECITE the fingerplay with the children.	This little boy is going to bed. On the pillow, he lays his head. Covers himself up tight. And falls asleep for the rest of the night. In the morning, he opens his eyes; Throws back the covers with great surprise.
⁎ **Model the Activity**	He . . . *(Demonstrate motions for several actions the little boy might do, such as brush his teeth, eat his breakfast, and put on his backpack.)* Now he's ready and on his way To do his best at school all day.

 TASK 2   Happy Hopscotch (approximately 12–14 minutes)

REVIEW and practice compound word awareness by clapping out compounds.	Our fingerplay was about a little boy who gets ready to go to school. We can call him a schoolboy. Listen. *Schoolboy* is a compound word. It is made up of two small words. Let's listen for both small words.
	Repeat while clapping with each word part. School *(clap)* boy *(clap)*. Schoolboy. Can you hear both parts of the compound word *schoolboy*?
Turn On Your Ears	Let's clap out some new compound words to show that our ears can hear both parts of a compound word. Listen. Little boy went to his classroom. Class-room. Say it fast.

▶ Children's response: Classroom.

Yes, classroom. Say it and clap it out.

▶ Children's response: Class *(clap)* room *(clap)*. Classroom.

Yes, classroom. Good job clapping two times for the two small words in *classroom*. Listen: Little Boy wore his backpack. Back-pack. Say it fast.

▶ Children's response: Backpack.

Yes, backpack. Clap it out.

TASK 2 *(continued)*

Sample words include lunch-box, notebook, playground, sandbox, *and* bathroom.

 PLAY the game.

▶ Children's response: Back *(clap)* pack *(clap)*. Backpack.

Yes, backpack. Good job! *Repeat this format, clapping out four to five additional words.*

> **CD-ROM** See Appendix D on the CD-ROM for the Happy Hopscotch board diagram and the Happy Hopscotch word list.

 TASK 3   Transition song to close *(approximately 3 minutes)*

REVIEW the fingerplay.

RECITE the fingerplay.

⭐ **Model the Activity**

CONDUCT the exit task to demonstrate skill mastery.

Word options for exit tasks:

Basic: daytime, schoolboy, blackboard, lunchroom

Three syllables: teenager, butterscotch, thunderstorm, cheeseburger, cabdriver

Four syllables: babysitter, superhero, coffeemaker, watermelon

END Lesson 2.

Now we'll say our fingerplay, but this time it is about a little girl. Say it with me and do the finger movements.

This little girl is going to bed. On the pillow, she lays her head.
Wraps the covers around her tight. And falls asleep for the rest of the night.
In the morning, she opens her eyes;
Throws back the covers with great surprise.

She. . . *(Demonstrate motions for several actions the little girl might do, such as comb her hair, put on her jacket, and get her backpack.)*
Now she's ready and on her way
To do her best in school all day.

Now get ready to show me if you can clap out one last compound word all by yourself. *Scaffold your lesson. Use this format with each child. Match word difficulty to child's ability. Give longer words to students who correctly clap the lesson.*

Listen. Play-ground. Say it fast.

▶ Child's response: Playground.

Yes, playground. Clap it out.

▶ Child's response: Play *(clap)* ground *(clap)*. Playground.

Yes, playground. Good job clapping two times for the two word parts in *playground.*

Everyone now gets their winnings for hearing and blending the two small words in compound words and for working hard. *Give out token rewards to each child.*

LESSON 3: Gumdrop Game

OBJECTIVES

Student will

- Learn how to separate (segment) short compound words into their two small words by moving a chip for each small word

Teacher will

- Review how to segment compound words by clapping out the two small words
- Model how to move colored chips to represent the separate word parts in compound words

RHYMES, SONGS, AND FINGERPLAYS

"Tiny Tim"

MATERIALS

Plastic toy lizard

Tokens for behavior/participation

> **Gumdrop Game**
> ☑ Gumdrop Game game board
>   (see Appendix D on the CD-ROM)   **CD-ROM**
>
> ☑ Two large different-colored chips for the teacher and two smaller different-colored chips for each student

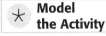 **TASK 1** | Transition song to begin (approximately 3 minutes)

INTRODUCE the lesson.

We are going to listen to some new compound words and hear their two small words. Then we'll play the Gumdrop Game with some longer words.

Today we'll begin with a song about a little lizard named Tiny Tim.

BEGIN the transition activity.

My turn to sing.

SING the song.

 Model the Activity

I had a little lizard, *(Put the lizard on your hand like a little pet.)*
I named him Tiny Tim.
I put him in the bathtub,
To see if he could swim. *(Move arms in a swimming motion.)*
He drank up all the water. *(Pretend to drink.)*
He ate up all the soap.
And now he's sick in bed,
With bubbles in his throat.
Brrrrr. *(Blow your lips together, making a "raspberry" sound.)*

Your turn to sing with me. *Repeat the song, leading children in the song and movements.*

▶ Children sing and copy the movements.

Good job singing our funny song. Let's do it one more time. *Repeat the song and movements.*

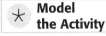 **TASK 2** | Gumdrop Game (approximately 12–14 minutes)

REVIEW compound word awareness by clapping out compounds.

We sang about Tiny Tim going for a swim in the bathtub. *Bathtub* is a compound word. It is made up of two small words. Let's listen for both small words.

Bath-tub. Bath *(clap)* tub *(clap)*. Bathtub. Can you hear both parts of the compound word *bathtub*?

 Turn On Your Ears

Today we will clap out some longer compound words to show that our ears can hear the small words in a compound word. Everybody, turn on your ears.

Instead of eating soap, Tiny Tim might have preferred a bug, like a dragon-fly. Say it.

▶ Children's response: Dragonfly.

Yes, dragonfly. Everybody, get ready to clap it out. Remember, even though it is a longer word, we will still clap just two times, once for each small word.

TEACHING TIP: Teach longer compound words without introducing syllables. Emphasize word units, not syllables.

Get ready. Dragon-fly. Say it fast.

▶ Children's response: Dragonfly.

Yes, dragonfly. Clap it out.

▶ Children's response: Dragon *(clap)* fly *(clap)*. Dragonfly.

Yes, dragonfly. Good job clapping two times for the two small words in *dragonfly*.

Listen: Do you think Tiny Tim would like to eat a grass-hopper? Say it fast.

▶ Children's response: Grasshopper.

Yes, grasshopper. Clap it out.

217

5.2

Clap out additional words, such as firecracker, blueberry, honeymoon, afternoon, and shoemaker.

♣ **PLAY** the game.

▶ **Children's response: Grass** *(clap)* **hopper** *(clap)***. Grasshopper.**

Yes, grasshopper. Good job!

Repeat format, clapping out four to five additional words..

 CD-ROM See Appendix D on the CD-ROM for the Gumdrop Game instructions and game board.

 TASK 3   Transition song and exit task *(approximately 3 minutes)*

END the lesson with a transition song.

SING the transition song.

Let's sing our song again about the little lizard named Tiny Tim. Sing it with me.

I had a little lizard, *(Put the lizard on your hand like a little pet.)*
I named him Tiny Tim.
I put him in the bathtub,
To see if he could swim. *(Move arms in a swimming motion.)*
He drank up all the water. *(Pretend to drink.)*
He ate up all the soap.
And now he's sick in bed,
With bubbles in his throat.
Brrrrr. *(Blow your lips together, making a "raspberry" sound.)*

Let's sing it again. *Repeat the song, leading children in the song and movements.*

Good job singing our funny song. Let's do it one more time. *Repeat the song and movements.*

CONDUCT the exit task to demonstrate skill mastery.

Clap out these exit compound words:

Basic: sunfish, headache, eyelid, earthworm, sweetheart

Three syllables: butternut, dragonfly, grandmother, cheeseburger

Four syllables: pufferbelly, butterfinger, coffeemaker, watermelon

END Lesson 3.

Now get ready to show me if you can clap out one last compound word all by yourself. *Use this format with each child. Match word difficulty to child's ability.* Listen. Cheese-cake. Say it fast.

▶ **Child's response: Cheesecake.**

Yes, cheesecake. Clap it out.

▶ **Child's response: Cheese** *(clap)* **cake** *(clap)***. Cheesecake.**

Yes, cheesecake. Good job clapping two times for the two small words in *cheesecake.*

Everyone now gets their winnings for hearing and blending the two small words in compound words and for working hard. *Give out token rewards to each child.*

LESSON 4: Compound Word Segmentation Review

OBJECTIVES

Student will

- Demonstrate the ability to separate (segment) shorter, then longer, compound words into their two small words by clapping, hopping, or moving a chip for each small word

Teacher will

- Review compound word awareness and segmentation
- Guide students to demonstrate the skill independently in three game formats
- Support students' success with careful item selection and multisensory supports

RHYMES, SONGS, AND FINGERPLAYS

"I'm a Little Teapot"

"Oh, What a Rain"

MATERIALS

☑ DROPP 5 Skill Assessment Checkout (see Appendix B on the CD-ROM)

 CD-ROM

☑ Tokens for behavior/participation

Happy Hopscotch

☑ Happy Hopscotch board diagram (see Appendix D on the CD-ROM)

☑ Happy Hopscotch word list

Gumdrop Game

☑ Gumdrop Game game board

☑ Two large different-colored chips for the teacher and two smaller different-colored chips for each student

---

 TASK 1   Transition song to begin (approximately 3 minutes)

INTRODUCE the lesson.	Today we will practice all the ways we know of hearing the two small words in compound words. Let's start with our action song that talks about pouring tea. Which of our songs is about pouring tea?
	▶ Children's response: "I'm a Little Teapot."
	That's right. "I'm a Little Teapot." Let's sing and dance to that song. *Repeat.*
SING the song.	Everyone stand up. *Make sure each child has space. Sing and dance to the song, leading children in the song and movements.*
	I'm a little teapot, short and stout. *(Place both hands on hips.)* Here is my handle, here is my spout. *(Extend one arm in the shape of a spout.)* When I get all steamed up, then I shout. Just tip me over and pour me out. *(Tip to one side.)*
	Good job singing our funny song. Let's do it one more time. *Repeat.*

TASK 2A | Clap-Out Compounds (approximately 3 minutes)

REVIEW compound words: definition and blending.

Some words are compound words because they each have two small words. Listen and say some of those words after me.

Tooth-paste. Say it fast.

▶ **Children's response: Toothpaste.**

Yes, toothpaste.

School-boy. Say it fast.

▶ **Children's response: Schoolboy.**

Yes, schoolboy.

Class-room. Say it fast.

▶ **Children's response: Classroom.**

Yes, classroom.

Back-pack. Say it fast.

▶ **Children's response: Backpack.**

Yes, backpack.

Friend-ship. Say it fast.

▶ **Children's response: Friendship.**

Yes, friendship.

Lunch-room. Say it fast.

▶ **Children's response: Lunchroom.**

Yes, lunchroom.

PRACTICE clapping out the compound words.

Good job. Each of those compound words has two small words. Let's listen for the small words and clap them out. Everybody, turn on your ears. Ears ready?

Listen: Lifeguard. Say it and clap it.

▶ **Children's response: Life** *(clap)* **guard** *(clap).*

What word?

▶ **Children's response: Lifeguard.**

Yes, lifeguard. Good job clapping two times for the two small words in *lifeguard.*
Repeat the format, clapping out additional words.

Listen: Rainbow. Say it and clap it.

▶ **Children's response: Rain** *(clap)* **bow** *(clap).*

What word?

▶ **Children's response: Rainbow.**

Yes, rainbow. Good job.

Repeat with sunbeam, beehive, fireworks, *and* airport.

🔊 **Turn On Your Ears**

 TASK 2B | Gumdrop Game (approximately 5 minutes)

♣ **PLAY** the game.

 CD-ROM See Appendix D on the CD-ROM for the Gumdrop Game instructions and game board.

TASK 2C   Happy Hopscotch *(approximately 5 minutes)*

 PLAY the game.

CD-ROM   See Appendix D on the CD-ROM for the Happy Hopscotch board diagram and the Happy Hopscotch word list.

 TASK 3   Transition song *(approximately 3 minutes)*

END the lesson with a transition song.

You worked hard today and showed me that you can hear the two small words in compound words. Some were short words and some were long. You did a wonderful job and I am proud of you! Let's pretend our winnings are floating out of the sky as we sing our song "Oh, What a Rain." Do you remember all three verses?

The first verse of our song was about raindrops, lemonade, and gumdrops. Let's sing the first verse.

SING the song.

If all of the raindrops were lemonade and gumdrops,
Oh, what a rain it would be.
Standing outside with my mouth open wide. *(Put head back.)*
Ah, ah, ah, ah, ah, ah, ah, ah, ah, ah. *(Open mouth wide.)*
If all of the raindrops were lemonade and gumdrops,
Oh, what a rain it would be.

The second verse of our song was about sunbeams, bubble gum, and ice cream. Let's sing the second verse.

If all of the sunbeams were bubble gum and ice cream,
Oh, what a sun it would be.
Standing outside with my mouth open wide. *(Put head back.)*
Ah, ah, ah, ah, ah, ah, ah, ah, ah, ah. *(Open mouth wide.)*
If all of the sunbeams were bubble gum and ice cream,
Oh, what a sun it would be.

The third verse of our song was about snowflakes, candy bars, and milkshakes. Let's sing the third verse:

If all of the snowflakes were candy bars and milkshakes,
Oh, what a snow it would be.
Standing outside with my mouth open wide. *(Put head back.)*
Ah, ah, ah, ah, ah, ah, ah, ah, ah, ah. *(Open mouth wide.)*
If all of the snowflakes were candy bars and milkshakes,
Oh, what a snow it would be.

END Lesson 4.

Everyone now gets their winnings for hearing and blending the two small words in compound words and for working hard. *Give out token rewards to each child.*

 CD-ROM   **The DROPP 5 Skill Assessment Checkout will be completed for each student following this lesson.**

Syllable Awareness

Overview

WHY SYLLABLE AWARENESS IS IMPORTANT

Students must become aware of the segments of spoken words in order to eventually understand that words are made up of individual sounds that correspond to letters. Through syllable play, young children learn to recognize the larger units of sounds in words, which is a necessary step toward being able to detect the individual sounds, or phonemes, in words. This phonemic awareness is strongly linked to the ability to read and write.

HOW DROPP 6 IS STRUCTURED

DROPP 6 has a single Activity Set that consists of four scripted lessons (Teacher Talk) that are used on 10 sequential learning days (the four lessons are repeated over the 10-day span). DROPP 6 has 10 days of intervention lessons designed to develop and practice students' word length awareness and syllable awareness skills. During the first 9 days of the Activity Set, students are given guidance and practice in hearing and comparing short and long words and detecting word parts, or syllables, using songs, picture cards, a nursery rhyme, and a fingerplay. On the 10th day, they review the skills to prepare for a short skill assessment checkout. (See the CD-ROM for the DROPP 6 Skill Assessment Checkout.)

Length of Activity Set and Lessons

Activity Set 6.1 is designed to be delivered across 10 sequential learning days. Each day's intervention lesson, including the transition activities, takes about 20 minutes to complete.

Goal and Emphasis of the Syllable Awareness Lessons

In Activity Set 6.1, the goal is to develop your students' awareness of word length and syllables and their ability to detect the separate syllables in spoken words. The emphasis at this stage of phonological instruction is helping children discern whether a word is composed of a single syllable or multiple syllables. The object is not for the children to specifically count the number of syllables, but to deepen their awareness of word segments through a range of enjoyable multisensory activities. When your students sort short and long picture names and tap out their syllables, they are progressing toward the more advanced skill of hearing individual phonemes.

Student Objectives

Students will be able to demonstrate syllable awareness by doing the following activities:

- Repeating multisyllabic words accurately

- Sorting picture cards to show which have one syllable and which have more than one syllable

- Telling which word is longer in a pair of spoken words

- Tapping once for each syllable in spoken words with up to four syllables

Teacher Objectives

- Teach children that words are made of segments called syllables.

- Use pictures and gestures to help students understand that words are made up of segments of sound and have varying lengths.

- Model and practice how to sort pairs of spoken words and picture cards into two sets composed of short words and longer words.

- Teach children how to tap a "syllable stick" one time for each syllable heard in spoken words.

How the Syllable Awareness Activity Set Develops Early Literacy

Multisensory Techniques

In Activity Set 6.1, children learn a procedure for measuring word length using hand gestures, and they are guided to use this procedure throughout all four lessons. This prompts them to see the length of a short word or long word between their cupped hands, to feel the progressive distance that comes with longer words, and to say and hear the elaborated syllables in words. In addition, students learn how to say and tap out the syllables in words in Lesson 3. The students use multiple learning channels in all of these activities to gain a thorough understanding of the segments of sounds in words.

Making Meaning and Building Vocabulary

The students repeat the names of many animals while pointing to their pictures in Lessons 1 and 2. You may use the suggested categories of animal names, chosen for their clearly distinguishable syllables, or select multisyllabic words from your content area teaching (such as science) to practice your students' oral vocabulary and extend their understanding of the natural world while reinforcing their awareness of syllables. New vocabulary words are found at the beginning of the Activity Set and are presented in the two-step approach described in Chapter 2. We recommend that you use the new words and phrases in a variety of ways (e.g., conversation, dramatic play, storytelling) throughout the day to reinforce student vocabulary and oral language growth.

Print Awareness

In the syllable awareness hand gestures activity, students see the left-to-right progression of word reading as your left hand sweeps to the left for each progressive syllable you say in words. Also embedded in this Activity Set is the printed word awareness that comes from the teacher saying and pointing to words in the nursery rhyme "Jack Be Nimble." Although these concepts about print occur at an awareness level and are not explicitly taught, they show students that syllables occur in a left-to-right progression even in verbal word pronunciation. In the nursery rhyme, students will see that some words are longer than others. Therefore, their emerging phonological awareness of word segments is linked with the reading of those syllables in print.

GENERAL TIPS FOR IMPLEMENTING ACTIVITY SET 6.1

- Have students repeat words of different lengths. Before you explain syllables to the students, you will give them the opportunity to feel the difference in the lengths of spoken words by repeating sets of words that are discernibly short or long. Be sure that every student responds as you begin with one-syllable words. Listen carefully to the students and practice any word that is difficult for them until all can say it completely and correctly. This is particularly important when longer words are presented.

- To make a big difference in students' word awareness skills, compare words that have different lengths to build word length and syllable awareness. As your children begin to hear the differences between short and long words, it is best to compare one-syllable words with four- to five-syllable words. If you choose to supplement the lesson activities with additional words of your own, then skip the two-syllable words and save the introduction of three-syllable words until students are firm in their syllable awareness.

TEACHING TIP: **Supplement for Success with Content Area Words**

Each lesson of Activity Set 6.1 provides words for repetition and sorting in syllable awareness tasks. Repeat the activities using words of your choice from any of your core curriculum lessons to provide further practice and extend your students' success. Saying new math, science, or general vocabulary words multiple times or comparing their length has the additional advantage of helping the students pronounce and familiarize themselves with the concepts you are teaching in other areas. Whether you practice the activities in small groups or with the whole class, your children will really benefit from this extra practice with new vocabulary while reinforcing their syllable awareness.

- Sharpen students' listening skills by switching words in familiar songs. Throughout Activity Set 6.1, you will use the transition activities to heighten students' enjoyment of language and syllable awareness by switching key words with unexpected replacements. In the familiar counting song "Five Little Ducks," you will replace the short word *duck* with the multisyllabic words *caterpillar* and *elephant*. In "Jack Be Nimble, with a Twist," you will make surprising swaps for the word *candlestick*. Children get a great kick out of the surprise of hearing something different from what they expect to hear in a familiar song or rhyme. This improves not only their general listening skills, but also their specific awareness of word length and syllables.

- Rhyme reinforcement: In Activity Set 6.1, the words *stick* and *quick* are chosen for rhyming practice. Be alert for other chances throughout your day to reinforce the skill of rhyming using the "Rhyming Exercise Song."

TEACHING TIP: **Check for Success**

During every activity, maintain eye contact with the students, and ensure that every child is responding correctly and on cue. It is important that they all engage their brains and their voices in every phonological practice activity. Furthermore, their responses provide a mini assessment for each task, telling who may need additional help at every step of the way.

- Multisensory supports for syllable awareness: As in DROPPS 4 and 5, you will use your hands as a teaching tool to help the children visualize and understand the big idea—the understanding that words can be short or long and are made of syllables. Here's how to do it:

  - Syllable awareness hand gestures for short words: Place your hands in front of you, palms facing each other about 6 inches apart. Say one-syllable words quickly while moving hands down a little as if to cup the word in a small space to measure its short length. Guide children to use their hands to "measure" the short words by seeing and feeling the short distance while saying the word quickly.

- Syllable awareness hand gestures for long words: Use your hands as before, palms facing each other as if measuring length. As you introduce and repeat the multisyllabic words, extend the distance between your hands by moving your left hand about 8 inches to the left with each new syllable until your hands are wide apart. When the children join you in this exercise, they can easily see the difference in word lengths by the short or wide distance between their hands.

Long or Short?

- Prepare the Long or Short? Sorting Chart ahead of time. Set up a display chart with two columns. Draw a short line at the top of the left column, and draw a long line at the top of the right column. Make six rows under each column for pictures.

- Assemble 12 animal pictures—six with one-syllable names and six with at least three-syllable names. On the first day, use words that are very different lengths, such as *cat* and *caterpillar*, to demonstrate how to hear and sort word pairs by length. On days 2, 7, and 10, you can scaffold your students' learning by introducing three-syllable words to fine-tune their listening skills.

- Procedure: Beginning with a picture of an animal with a short name, guide and model for children how to say the animal's name and measure it (by hearing and with hand gestures) to see if it is long or short. Elicit students' participation in finding that it is a short name. Show the children how the lines at the top of the columns represent "short" and "long." Tape the first picture under the short column. Continue with the remaining word pairs. As each word pair is sorted by you and the children, tape the short name picture in the left column and the longer name in the right column.

- Reinforce with word repetition: When all of the word pairs are sorted, give the students another opportunity to experience the differences between the short and long words by repeating each column's word list. As they say the words, gesture with your hands to show short or long distances.

- End the activity with a skill-based compliment. For example, you might say, "You have all done a fine job of listening hard to say and hear short words and long words."

Sorting Sticks

- Prepare the Long or Short? Sorting Chart before you begin Lesson 2. In this lesson, the chart will be used for group demonstration of sorting spoken words by word lengths prior to individual student practice. Assemble eight large animal pictures for demonstration and a deck of multisyllabic picture cards for individual practice. Any commercial picture cards or your own laminated pictures will do. Make sure that they do not include the printed names of the pictures.

- Provide two sorting sticks per child—one short and one long. We found that 7-inch craft sticks and 4-inch popsicle sticks are easy for children to handle and can lay flat on the work table. These sticks mirror the short and long lines at the top of the sorting chart. The children will place the sticks on their work tables with the short stick to the left and long stick to the right.

- Procedure: After reviewing the sorting chart with the eight large pictures, distribute a pair of small picture cards to each child and guide them to say the card names as many times as necessary for determining which word is short and which is long. Place the short word picture under the short stick and the long word picture under the long stick. Play the sorting game according to the directions on the CD-ROM (as directed in Lesson 2), distributing the cards in pairs for three to six rounds.

Tapping Syllable Sticks

- Sorting stick or syllable stick? When advancing from the syllable sorting task of Lesson 2 to the more specific syllable recognition task of Lesson 3, we used the 7-inch craft sticks for tapping out syllables. To avoid confusion, we told the children that the bigger sorting stick helps find the longer words and then it becomes a syllable tapping stick to help tap out the syllables in the words.

- Why not clap out syllables? We reserved the clapping out segmenting task for the more holistic whole words and compound words activities. Although the difference between compound word units and syllables will not be emphasized in pre-K, in order to prevent future confusion, we do not want the children to equate the two concepts.

- Why not tap with fingers instead of sticks? The sound of tapping out syllables with sticks provides an additional auditory cue that really helps the children learn to distinguish the syllables in words.

Review

On the 10th day of the Activity Set, students get the opportunity to revisit word length awareness in the nursery rhyme "Jack Be Nimble, with a Twist." They will then refresh their syllable awareness by sorting short and long picture names and tapping out words to show one or more than one word part before completing their skill assessment checkout.

Skill Assessment Checkouts

After your review lesson is completed, set aside a few minutes during that day to give each child an individual syllable awareness checkout. This will take about 2 minutes per child to administer and provides useful information to guide your small-group placements. Based on the checkout and collaborative conversations with all teachers, you will determine which students should continue in Tier 2 small-group intervention and which students can successfully return to Tier 1 whole-class instruction.

Assessment Outcome: The student can identify the longer word in a pair of words.

ACTIVITY SET 6.1

Lesson Descriptions

Lessons	Sequence of daily activities	✧ Vocabulary
Lesson 1: Long or Short?	Song: "Five Little Ducks" Target: Repeat and sort short and long words Song: "Five Little Caterpillars"	Caterpillar Butterfly
Lesson 2: Sorting Sticks	Fingerplay: "Sleepy Caterpillars" Target: Say and sort pictures of short and long words Song: "Five Little Elephants"	
Lesson 3: Tapping Syllable Sticks	Rhyme: "Jack Be Nimble" Target: Tap to show one or more than one word part Rhyme: "Jack Be Nimble"	Syllable Nimble
Lesson 4: Syllable Awareness Review	Rhyme: "Jack Be Nimble, with a Twist" Review Task 2A: Say and sort pictures Reveiw Task 2B: Tapping syllable sticks Fingerplay: "Sleepy Caterpillars"	Syllable

Materials Needed

☑ Pictures of a caterpillar, a butterfly, and an elephant

☑ Pictures of three-syllable words, including microwave, pineapple, and umbrella

☑ 12 large animal pictures: six with one-syllable names and six with three or more syllable names

☑ 10 pictures: Five with one-syllable names and five with at least three-syllable names.

☑ Long or Short? Sorting Chart (see Appendix D on the CD-ROM)

CD-ROM

☑ Nursery rhyme book with "Jack Be Nimble"

☑ One short and one long sorting stick for each student (e.g., 7-inch craft stick and 4-inch popsicle stick)

☑ One syllable stick (e.g., tongue depressor) for each student

☑ DROPP 6 Skill Assessment Checkout (see Appendix B on the CD-ROM)

☑ Tokens for behavior/participation

Sorting Sticks Game

☑ Long or Short? Sorting Chart (see Appendix D on the CD-ROM)

☑ "Joe" and "Desdemona" game pieces (see Appendix D on the CD-ROM)

☑ A list of the names of the children in the group sorted from shortest name to longest

☑ Eight large animal picture cards: four with one-syllable names and four with three or more syllable names

☑ Sorting sticks for each child: 7-inch craft stick and 4-inch popsicle stick (or equivalent)

☑ Tokens for behavior/participation

ACTIVITY SET

6.1 **10-Day Planner**

Day 1	**Lesson 1:** Long or Short?
Day 2	**Lesson 1:** Long or Short?
Day 3	**Lesson 2:** Sorting Sticks
Day 4	**Lesson 2:** Sorting Sticks
Day 5	**Lesson 3:** Tapping Syllable Sticks
Day 6	**Lesson 3:** Tapping Syllable Sticks
Day 7	**Lesson 1:** Long or Short?
Day 8	**Lesson 2:** Sorting Sticks
Day 9	**Lesson 3:** Tapping Syllable Sticks
Day 10	**Lesson 4:** Syllable Awareness Review

LESSON 1: Long or Short?

OBJECTIVES

Student will

- Learn how to listen carefully to and repeat short and long words

- Compare and sort spoken words with one or more than one syllable

Teacher will

- Provide multisensory activities and cues that emphasize varying word lengths

- Model how to hear and sort words by length

- Use a silly song to introduce and reinforce the sounds of multisyllabic words

RHYMES, SONGS, AND FINGERPLAYS

"Five Little Ducks"

"Five Little Caterpillars"

MATERIALS

Pictures of a caterpillar and a butterfly

12 large animal pictures: six with one-syllable names and six with three or more syllable names

Long or Short? Sorting Chart (prepared ahead of time; see directions in lesson)

Tokens for behavior/participation

TECHNOLOGY LINK

View the following video clip to hear the music for the song: http://www.youtube.com/watch?v= ixYagchvzIE.

 TASK 1 **Transition song to begin** (approximately 3 minutes)

INTRODUCE the big idea: word length awareness.

Settle the students in their seats and say the following. We are going to listen to words to see if they are short words or long words. Some words are short little words, such as *duck,* and some are longer, such as *caterpillar.* It is fun to listen and say short and long words.

BEGIN the song.

Today we will start with a rhyming song that some of you know. It's called "Five Little Ducks." If you know it, then you can sing along with me. Here we go.

Sing the song using the suggested gestures and finger movements. Emphasize the rhyming words.

Five little ducks went out one day,
Over the hill and far away. *Show the shape of a hill, gesturing up, then down.*
Mother duck said "quack, quack, quack,"
But only four little ducks came back. *Show four fingers.*

Continue with the song and movements, reducing the number of ducks each time. Make a sad face on fifth verse. Sing slowly.

But none of her little ducks came back.

Sing the last verse.

So, sad mother duck went out one day,
Over the hill and far away.
The sad mother duck said "quack, quack, quack,"
And all of the five little ducks came back. *Show all five fingers.*

Nice job singing "Five Little Ducks"!

TASK 2   Long or Short? (approximately 12–14 minutes)

INTRODUCE word length awareness with short words.

 Multisensory Reinforcement

We sang a song about some little ducks. Listen. *Duck* is a short word. It does not take long to say it. Everyone, say it with me.

▶ **Children's response: Duck.**

Yes, duck. *Duck* is a short little word. *While saying the word, emphasize its short length with hand motions. Place your hands in front of you, palms facing each other about 6 inches apart. Say words quickly while moving hands down a little as if to measure the short length.*

Let's say some more short, little words. Say each of these words after me. *Practice and repeat one-syllable words. Continue using your hands to measure the short words*

Bear. Say it.

▶ **Children's response: Bear.**

Yes, bear.

Boy. Say it.

▶ **Children's response: Boy.**

Yes, boy.

Use all of the following words: dog, girl, bird, chair, bug, moon, fly, *and* goat.

Turn On Your Ears

INTRODUCE and practice hearing long words with syllable awareness hand gestures.

 Multisensory Reinforcement

Good job saying small words. Now watch me and listen. Turn on your ears! I'm going to say some long words. Listen to my first long word: alligator. *Repeat slowly, emphasizing each syllable and extending hands. Use your hands as before, palms facing each other as if measuring length.*

Al-li-ga-tor. *Pause. Alligator* is a long word. *As you introduce and repeat the multi-syllabic words, extend the distance between your hands by moving your left hand about 8 inches to the left with each new syllable until your hands are wide apart. By moving your left hand, the children get the idea of left-to-right progression of word reading.* Here are some more long words. Listen.

Helicopter. Hel-i-cop-ter. *(Pause.)* Is helicopter a long word?

▶ **Children's response: Yes.**

Yes, helicopter is a long word.

Hippopotamus. Hip-po-pot-a-mus. *(Pause.)* Is that a long word?

▶ **Children's response: Yes.**

Yes, *hippopotamus* is a very long word.

One more. Thermometer. Ther-mom-et-er. *(Pause.)* Is thermometer a long word?

▶ **Children's response: Yes.**

Yes, *thermometer* is a long word.

ENGAGE in group practice for saying long words.

Follow the same format for the following words: macaroni, Thanksgiving, jack-o-lantern, rodeo, cauliflower, elephant, cafeteria, refrigerator, *and* caterpillar.

Good job listening to some long words. Now it's your turn to say some long words. Everyone, listen and say these long words after me. *Use hand gestures: Emphasize the different syllables while you measure out the word's length with your hands.*

Kangaroo. Say it.

▶ **Children's response: Kangaroo.**

Yes, kangaroo.

Wow! You said some very long words. Pat yourself on the back.

6.1

LESSON 1

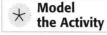 **Vocabulary**

CATERPILLAR
BUTTERFLY

Now let's look at the picture of something that has a long name.

Who knows what this is? *Show a picture of a caterpillar.* Raise your hand if you know. *Accept several answers.* This insect is called a caterpillar. Everybody, what is this insect called?

▶ **Children's response: A caterpillar.**

Yes, a caterpillar. A caterpillar is an insect that starts out like a worm and then turns into a butterfly. *Show a picture of a butterfly.* Everybody, what does a caterpillar turn into?

▶ **Children's response: A butterfly.**

Yes, a caterpillar turns into a butterfly. Have any of you ever seen a caterpillar *(show picture again)*? Raise your hands. What did you see?

▶ **Children's response: A caterpillar.**

Have you ever seen a butterfly *(show picture again)*? Raise your hands. What did you see?

▶ **Children's response: A butterfly.**

Good job learning about caterpillars and butterflies and saying their long names.

Assemble 12 animal pictures (six with one-syllable names and six with at least three-syllable names) and prepare a Long or Short? Sorting Chart ahead of time. Draw a short line at the top of the left column, draw a long line at the top of the right column, and make rows under each column for pictures.

 Model the Activity

Turn On Your Ears

Now I am going to say the names of some animals. Some of the names will be short and some will be long. I wonder if my ears can hear which words are short *(pause and show a short distance with your hands)* and which words are long *(spread your hands wide apart)*. I will turn on my ears and listen hard. The short names will be ones I can say fast. The long names will have more word parts.

Place pictures of a cat and caterpillar where all children can see them.

Watch me. Cat. *Point to the picture of the cat. Say the word and show a small distance with your hands, with your palms facing each other.* I said that name fast. It is a short name.

Caterpillar. *Point to the picture of the caterpillar. Say the word and move your hands further apart with each syllable. Repeat action and word slowly.* Cat-er-pill-ar. That is a longer name.

DEMONSTRATE task response.

Cat. Caterpillar. Cat. Caterpillar. *Look at both pictures. Repeat their names while pointing to each.* I can hear that the cat's name is short and the caterpillar's name is long. I am going to put the short names in one column and the longer names in the other column.

This is a short line. So I will put the cat here because *cat* is a short word. *Point to the short line at the top of the left column.* This is a long line. So I will put the caterpillar here because *caterpillar* is a long word with more word parts. *Point to the long line at the top of the right column.*

PRACTICE saying long and short words and comparing word lengths.

Let's say the names of some more animals together. Some of the names will be short and some will be long. Let's see if your ears can hear which words are short and which words are long. We will all turn on our ears and listen hard. Watch my hands to see if they show a short word *(demonstrate by indicating a short distance with your hands)* or a longer word *(demonstrate by indicating a wider distance with your hands)* with more word parts.

Turn On Your Ears

The short names will be ones we can say fast, like cat. *Point to the cat picture.* Say it.

▶ Children's response: Cat.

Yes, cat.

The long names will have more word parts, like caterpillar. *Point to the caterpillar picture.* Say it.

▶ Children's response: Caterpillar.

Yes, caterpillar.

Set two new pictures up with the short name first—for example, pictures of an ant and an alligator. Okay, here are some more animals. This is an ant. *Show short distance with hands.* Say it.

▶ Children's response: Ant.

Yes, ant.

This is an alligator. *Show wider distance with hands, moving left hand toward the left to emphasize left-to-right progression of word length.* Say it.

▶ Children's response: Alligator.

Yes, alligator.

Let's say both names and try to find the short name. Ant. Alligator. Everyone, say them with me.

▶ Children's response: Ant. Alligator.

Say them again.

▶ Children's response: Ant. Alligator.

Who can tell me which of these animals has the short name? Raise your hand.

▶ Children's response: Ant.

Yes, *ant* is a short name. We can say it fast. Ant. Good job hearing that *ant* is a short word! Now let's say both names and find the long name. Ant. Alligator. Everyone, say them with me.

▶ Children's response: Ant. Alligator.

Say them again.

▶ Children's response: Ant. Alligator.

Which of these animals has a *(pause and spread hands wide apart)* long name? Get ready.

▶ Children's response: Alligator.

Yes, *alligator* is a very long name. Good job hearing that *alligator* is a long word!

Let's put the short name in the short name column. Who can show us which column has a short line at the top? *Choose a child to point to the short line.* Yes, this is a short line. So, we will put the ant here because *ant* is a short word, like *cat.*

Let's put the long name in the long name column. Who can show us which column has a long line at the top? *Choose a child to point to the long line.* Yes, this is a long line. *Spread hands wide apart.* So, we will put the alligator here because *alligator* is a long word, like *caterpillar.*

ENGAGE in group practice.

 **Multisensory Reinforcement**

Practice two to three more word pairs. Place the long name first on the second practice set. Use these additional words for saying and sorting by length:

One syllable	Three syllables	Four Syllables	Five syllables
duck	kangaroo	armadillo	hippopotamus
bear	buffalo	rhinoceros	tyrannosaurus
pig	elephant		

**Correction procedure: Show the word's length with your hands, palms facing each other. Guide the child's hands to mirror your hand motions, feeling and seeing the difference between the short and long words. If a child selects the wrong word/ picture when asked to identify the short or long name, then say the following.*

Watch my hands. Pig. Say it with me.

▶ **Child's response: Pig.**

Yes, pig. Let's measure that name to see if it is short or long. *Practice several times until the child can say whether a word is long or short.******

SUMMARIZE the activity by checking and saying the sorted names.

Let's check our lists. First we will say all of the short names. Get ready. Cat. Say it.

▶ **Children's response: Cat.**

Yes, cat.

Ant. Say it.

▶ **Children's response: Ant.**

Yes, ant.

Continue reading all of the short picture names in the left column. Great job saying all of those *(hands a short distance apart)* short names! Now, let's say all of the long names. Get ready. *Say all of the long picture names in the right column.*

Caterpillar. Say it.

▶ **Children's response: Caterpillar.**

Yes, caterpillar.

Alligator. Say it.

▶ **Children's response: Alligator.**

GIVE specific praise to show students the skills they are mastering.

Yes, alligator. *Continue reading all of the long names.*

Great job saying all of those *(hands wide apart)* long names! You just said some very long names.

 TASK 3   Transition song and exit task *(approximately 3 minutes)*

END the lesson with a transition song and exit task.

You worked hard today saying words that were short *(hands a short distance apart)* and long *(hands wide apart)*. You did a wonderful job, and I am proud of you!

TEACHING TIP: Sharpen listening skills by switching words in familiar songs. Students will get a kick out of hearing a different phrase and will learn to listen carefully.

Now we will have fun by changing our rhyming song about the five little ducks to the same song about five little caterpillars. Listen how funny our song will be when we change the short word *duck* to the longer word *caterpillar.* Sing it with me.

Multisensory Reinforcement

Gesture with your hands and count down from 5 on your fingers to dramatize the song. Show the caterpillar picture and emphasize the length of the word caterpillar, looking surprised every time you say it.

Five little caterpillars went out one day,
Over the hill and far away.
Mother caterpillar said "quack, quack, quack,"
But only four little caterpillars came back.

Continue with the song and movements, reducing the number of caterpillars each time. Make a sad face on the fifth verse. Sing slowly.

None of her little caterpillars came back.

Sing the last verse.

So, sad mother caterpillar went out one day,
Over the hill and far away.
The sad mother caterpillar said "quack, quack, quack,"
And all of the five little caterpillars came back.

Isn't that funny singing about five little caterpillars? Do you think a caterpillar would really say "quack?"

▶ **Children's response: No.**

No. You are right. Caterpillars don't say much of anything. They are quiet.

DO the exit task.

Now get ready to show me that you can each say a long word all by yourself. *Let each child have a turn repeating one of the following words.*

Exit multisyllabic words to repeat:

alligator	kangaroo
armadillo	dinosaur
caterpillar	jellyfish
rhinoceros	elephant
hippopotamus	

If too difficult, try these:

END Lesson 1.

Everyone now gets their winnings for saying and sorting words that were short and long and for working hard. *Give out token rewards to each child.*

LESSON 2: Sorting Sticks

OBJECTIVES

Student will

- Learn how to listen carefully to and repeat short and long words

- Compare and sort spoken words into two columns to show one or more than one syllable

Teacher will

- Teach a new fingerplay that guides children to pronounce long words

- Provide pictures and hand gesture cues that emphasize varying word lengths

- Model how to hear and sort words by length

- Use a silly song to introduce and reinforce the sounds of multisyllabic words

RHYMES, SONGS, AND FINGERPLAYS

"Sleepy Caterpillars"

"Five Little Elephants"

MATERIALS

Pictures of a caterpillar, a butterfly, and an elephant

Tokens for behavior/participation

Sorting Sticks Game

☑ Long or Short? Sorting Chart (see Appendix D on the CD-ROM)

☑ "Joe" and "Desdemona" game pieces (see Appendix D on the CD-ROM)

☑ A list of the names of the children in the group sorted from shortest name to longest

☑ Eight large animal picture cards: four with one-syllable names and four with three or more syllable names

☑ Sorting sticks for each child: 7-inch craft stick and 4-inch popsicle stick (or equivalent)

 TASK 1　Transition fingerplay to begin (approximately 3 minutes)

INTRODUCE/REVIEW the big idea: word length awareness.	We are going to listen to and say short and long words to hear their word parts. Then we will say the names of pictures and sort them into two groups—short names and long names.
	Who remembers what this is? *Show the caterpillar picture.* Raise your hand.
	▶ Children's response: A caterpillar.
BEGIN the transition activity.	Yes, this insect is called a caterpillar. Everybody, what is this insect called?
	▶ Children's response: A caterpillar.
	Yes, a caterpillar. We learned that a caterpillar is a kind of insect that starts out like a worm and then turns into a butterfly. What does a caterpillar turn into?
	▶ Children's response: A butterfly.
	Yes, a caterpillar turns into a butterfly. *Show the butterfly picture.*
Model the Activity	It's my turn to show you a fingerplay about sleepy caterpillars. Watch my fingers and try to do what I do to tell a story about caterpillars turning into butterflies. Listen, watch, and move your fingers like me. *Recite the fingerplay.*
	Let's go to sleep, the caterpillars said, *(Wiggle pointer finger.)*
	As they tuck themselves into their beds. *(Close fist around that finger.)*

They will awaken by and by, *(Rock closed hand like a cradle.)*

And each one will be a lovely butterfly. *(Open hand, one finger at a time; make your hand "fly" away while flapping the thumb and little finger like wings.)*

 **Multisensory Reinforcement**

Your turn to say the fingerplay with me. *(Repeat each line of the fingerplay slowly, leading them in the words and movements. Make sure each child has space to let the butterfly "fly" away.)*

Good job learning a new fingerplay! Let's do it one more time. *(Repeat the fingerplay and movements.)*

TASK 2   Sorting Sticks: Say and sort pictures of short and long words *(approximately 12–14 minutes)*

REVIEW saying short words.

We have been hearing and saying short words and long words. Let's remember some of the short words we can say. Say these short words after me: Get ready.

 **Multisensory Reinforcement**

Duck. *Show short distance between your hands. Continue using your hands to "measure" the short words.* Say it.

▶ **Children's response: Duck.**

Yes, duck.

Bear. Say it.

▶ **Children's response: Bear.**

Yes, bear.

Girl. Say it.

▶ **Children's response: Girl.**

Yes, girl.

Additional short words for repeating include ham, web, bread, pig, cake, *and* nurse.

Continue in this format, using the suggested words or other one-syllable words from your content area teaching.

REVIEW saying long words.

Good job saying short words! Now let's say some long words. *Continue using your hands to "measure" the long words. Show an increasingly wider distance with your hands as you say each syllable. Follow the same format for all of the words.*

Our first long word is *macaroni. Repeat slowly, emphasizing each syllable and extending hands.*

Mac-a-ro-ni. *Macaroni* is a long word. Say it with me.

▶ **Children's response: Macaroni.**

Yes, macaroni.

Additional long words for repeating include armadillo, rhinoceros, stegosaurus, thermometer, porcupine, *and* jack-o-lantern.

Our next word is *television.* Say it.

▶ **Children's response: Television.**

Yes, television.

 PLAY the game.

> **CD-ROM**   See Appendix D on the CD-ROM for the Sorting Sticks Game instructions.

TASK 3   Transition song and exit task (approximately 3 minutes)

INTRODUCE/REVIEW
the transition song.

You worked hard today saying and sorting words that were short and long. I am proud of you! Now we will have fun by changing our rhyming song about the five little ducks to the same song about five little elephants. Listen how funny our song will be when we change the short word, *duck,* to a longer animal name, *elephant.* Sing it with me.

Multisensory Reinforcement

Sing to the tune of "Five Little Ducks" and do the finger counting movements. Show the elephant picture and emphasize the length of the word elephant, looking surprised every time you say it.

Five little elephants went out one day,
Over the hill and far away.
Mother elephant said "quack, quack, quack,"
But only four little elephants came back.

Continue with the song and movements, reducing the number of elephants each time. Make a sad face on the fifth verse. Sing slowly.

None of her little elephants came back.

Sing the last verse.

So, sad mother elephant went out one day,
Over the hill and far away.
The sad mother elephant said "quack, quack, quack,"
And all of the five little elephants came back.

Isn't that funny, singing "Five Little Elephants." Do you think an elephant would really say "quack?"

▶ **Children's response: No.**

No. You are right. Elephants don't usually make sounds unless they are in danger. Then they make a noise like a trumpet horn. But they don't quack.

Turn On Your Ears

Now get ready to show me if you can say two words, and tell me which one is a long word. Turn on your ears! *Let each child stand up and repeat a word pair. Use these word pairs: ant, alligator; armadillo, dog; caterpillar, cow; rat, rhinoceros; and* hen, hippopotamus.

DO the exit task to demonstrate skill mastery.

Which of your words is long—ant or alligator?

▶ **Child's response: Alligator.**

Yes. *Alligator* is long because it has more word parts.

Good job hearing and saying the word parts in a long word. *Continue until each child answers successfully.*

END Lesson 2.

Everyone now gets their winnings for saying and sorting words that were short and long and for working hard. *Give out token rewards to each child.*

LESSON 3: Tapping Syllable Sticks

OBJECTIVES

Student will

- Practice hearing and repeating short and long words using students' names
- Learn the meaning of the word *syllable*
- Tap out the syllables in spoken words to show one syllable or multiple syllables

Teacher will

- Teach a nursery rhyme that will guide children to hear names of varying lengths
- Model how to hear and tap out words by length

RHYMES, SONGS, AND FINGERPLAYS

"Jack Be Nimble"

MATERIALS

Nursery rhyme book with "Jack Be Nimble"
Syllable stick (e.g., tongue depressor) for each child
Tokens for behavior/participation

 TASK 1   Transition rhyme (approximately 3 minutes)

REVIEW the big idea: syllable awareness.

Today we will listen to and say short and long words to hear their word parts, which are also called syllables. Then we will tap out the word parts using sticks called syllable sticks.

BEGIN the transition activity.

I am going to read you a nursery rhyme about a boy who loves to jump. His name is Jack. *Show children a picture from the nursery rhyme.* Everyone, what is his name?

▶ **Children's response: Jack.**

Yes, Jack. Listen to this rhyme about funny Jack. *Recite the nursery rhyme using the book. Point to the words while reciting.*

Jack be nimble, Jack be quick,
Jack jump over the candlestick.

CONDUCT a rhyme review.

Good job listening to "Jack Be Nimble." Now I want you to listen hard and see if you can hear a rhyme in it. *Place your hands in front of you, palms forward; move each hand forward slightly as you say each rhyming word.*

Jack be nimble, Jack be quick,
Jack jump over the candle . . .

▶ **Children's response: Stick.**

Yes, stick. You filled in the word *stick.* I think your ears heard a rhyme. Listen. Quick, stick. Do they rhyme?

▶ **Children's response: Yes.**

Yes. They rhyme. Let's sing the "Rhyming Exercise Song."

SING the "Rhyming Exercise Song."

Get your rhyme muscles nice and firm so our rhymes are in great shape. Follow me. Put your hands in the sky. *Stretch one arm up to the sky, then the other arm, on the word hands.* Do the rhyming exercise.

Quick *(Stretch one arm up as you say the word.)*
Stick *(Stretch the other arm up.)*
Quick *(Switch arms.)*
Stick *(Switch arms.)*

Quick *(Switch arms.)*
Stick *(Switch arms.)*

Do they rhyme? *Pause here and allow them to show thumbs up or down before you respond. Look around at each student and make eye contact.* **Yes.** *Nod vigorously.* **They rhyme.** *Give two thumbs up.*

 **TASK 2** | **Tapping Syllable Sticks** *(approximately 12 minutes)*

REVIEW word length awareness.

Multisensory Reinforcement

Good job hearing a rhyme in the nursery rhyme about Jack. Listen while I say his name again. Jack. *Gesture a short distance with your hands.* Is Jack's name a short name or a long name?

▶ **Children's response: A short name.**

Yes. Jack is a short name *(gesture with hands)*. Say his name. Get ready.

▶ **Children's response: Jack.**

Yes, Jack. Now we will practice saying more short names. Say these short names after me. Get ready.

Joan. Say it.

▶ **Children's response: Joan.**

Yes, Joan.

Bob. Say it.

▶ **Children's response: Bob.**

Yes, Bob.

Use the names Jim, May, Tom, John, Ann, *and* Beth *or choose your own one-syllable names.*

Jill. Say it.

▶ **Children's response: Jill.**

Yes, Jill. *Continue in this format, "measuring" the short words with your hands.*

Good job saying short names. Now let's say some long names. Carolina. *Show a long distance between your hands.* Say it.

▶ **Children's response: Carolina.**

Yes, Carolina.

Antonio. Say it.

▶ **Children's response: Antonio.**

Yes, Antonio.

Use the names Christiana, Desdemona, Cornelius, Demetrius, Alexandra, *and* Henrietta *or use the long names of any of your students.*

Continue with this format, "measuring" the long names with your hands. Good job saying long names.

Listen. I said that a word part is called a syllable. Say that word.

▶ **Children's response: Syllable.**

Yes, syllable. *Repeat the word until everybody can say it.* A syllable is a word part. What is a syllable?

 Vocabulary

SYLLABLE

▶ **Children's response: A word part.**

Yes, a syllable is a word part. Short words such as *bat* have just one little syllable. *Snap your fingers once while saying bat.*

But long words, such as ballerina, can have a lot of syllables. Bal-le-ri-na. *Snap your fingers for each syllable.* Ballerina has a lot of syllables. What does ballerina have a lot of?

▶ **Children's response: Syllables.**

INTRODUCE syllable sticks.

Yes, *ballerina* is a long word that has a lot of syllables. This is my syllable stick. I use it to tap every time I hear a word part, or syllable, in a word. Watch.

Multisensory Reinforcement

Auditorium. Au-di-to-ri-um. *Tap loudly for each syllable.* Gee, I tapped a lot of times for that long word. *Auditorium* has a lot of word parts, or syllables.

Now I will tap out a short word. Gym. *Tap loudly one time.* Did I tap one time or more than once? Gym. *Repeat and tap once.* Who can tell me if I tapped once or more than once? Raise your hands.

▶ **Child's response: Once.**

New word: pie *(tap once).*

Did you hear one tap or more than one tap?

▶ **Children's response: One tap.**

Yes, you heard one tap for *pie* because *pie* only has one word part, or one syllable.

New word: refrigerator. Re-frig-er-a-tor *(tap five times).*

Did you hear one tap or more than one tap?

▶ **Children's response: More than one.**

Turn On Your Ears

Yes. You heard more than one tap because *refrigerator* has more than one syllable. Your ears are listening carefully to hear the syllables in words. Let's practice some more words. After I tap out each word, tell me if you heard one tap or more than one tap. Get ready to turn on your ears. Listen.

Next word: macaroni. Mac-a-ro-ni *(tap four times).* Did you hear one tap or more than one tap?

▶ **Children's response: More than one.**

Yes, more than one.

Additional words for tapping out syllables include ham, watermelon, motorcycle, hat, bulldozer, kite, *and* moon.

Next word: cake. Cake *(tap once).* Did you hear one tap or more than one tap?

▶ **Children's response: One tap.**

Yes, one tap. *Continue to practice, using the same format.*

TEACHING TIP: At this point, do not count the number of taps because that introduces another element of learning that can be confusing. The goal is to help the children hear the difference between a single-syllable word and a multisyllabic word. This is a broad, initial step to understand the qualities of words, which leads to later reading success.

PRACTICE syllable sticks.

Good job listening to hear the syllables in words. Now it's your turn to tap out the syllables. *Distribute syllable sticks.* I will say each word. Then you will say it with me, and we will tap for every word part we hear. We will tap out the syllables. Let's practice.

First word: boat. Say it and tap it.

Multisensory Reinforcement

▶ **Children's response: Boat (one tap).**

Did you make one tap or more than one tap?

Multisensory Reinforcement

▶ Children's response: One.

Yes. You made one tap because *boat* has one syllable. Let's tap out a longer word. Listen carefully. Magazine. Say it and tap it.

▶ Children's response: Mag-a-zine (three taps).

Did you make one tap or more than one tap?

▶ Children's response: More than one.

Yes. You made more than one tap because *magazine* is a longer word with more syllables.

New word: basketball. Say it and tap it.

▶ Children's response: Bas-ket-ball (three taps).

Did you make one tap or more than one tap?

▶ Children's response: More than one.

Yes. *Basketball* has more than one syllable. Good; your ears are hearing more syllables.

Next word: zoo. Say it and tap it.

▶ Children's response: Zoo (one tap).

Did you make one tap or more than one tap?

▶ Children's response: One tap.

Use words from your content area of teaching or these suggested words: coat, sun, telephone, cat, computer, marshmallow, book, *and* face.

Yes. *Zoo* has only one syllable. *Continue to practice, using the same format.*

Correction procedure: If any children have difficulty tapping at the right times, then slow down and practice only one-syllable words until they are completely successful. Then, go to three-syllable words and work slowly and clearly to help say, hear, and tap out the three word parts. Practice each word as many times as necessary until all children tap it out successfully.

 Vocabulary

SYLLABLE

Good job using your syllable sticks. Remember, a syllable is a word part. What is a syllable?

▶ Children's response: A word part.

Yes, a syllable is a word part. You are learning how to hear the syllables in words. That means you can hear how word parts go together to make words. Good learning.

🪐 **TASK 3**   Transition nursery rhyme and exit task *(approximately 5 minutes)*

✧ **Vocabulary**

NIMBLE

You worked hard today! You showed me that you can tap out the syllables in words. You are very nimble at hearing word parts. Say nimble.

▶ Children's response: Nimble.

Yes, nimble. What do you think *nimble* means? *Accept children's responses. Nimble* means to be quick and clever in how you do something. So if you are quick and clever at hopping in hopscotch, we can say you are a nimble player. What kind of player?

▶ Children's response: A nimble player.

Yes. A nimble player is quick and clever. If you are quick at thinking, what kind of thinker are you?

▶ Children's response: A nimble thinker.

Good. If you are quick at jumping rope, what kind of jumper are you?

▶ Children's response: A nimble jumper.

RECITE the transition rhyme.

Today we learned a nursery rhyme about a boy who is nimble at jumping. Let's say that rhyme again. It's called "Jack Be Nimble." Get ready to say it with me. *Show children the nursery rhyme and point to the words. Repeat the rhyme.*

Jack be nimble, Jack be quick,
Jack jump over the candlestick.
Let's say it again.

Jack is a nimble jumper. Is he a quick jumper?

▶ Children's response: Yes.

Is he a clever jumper?

▶ Children's response: Yes.

Yes, you are right. We know that Jack is quick and clever because *nimble* means quick and clever. Let's say our rhyme one last time.

Jack be nimble, Jack be quick,
Jack jump over the candlestick.

Nice job saying our new nursery rhyme. Now get ready to show me if you can tap out a long word all by yourself.

DO the exit task to demonstrate skill mastery.

Listen. Magazine. Say it and tap it.

▶ Children's response: Mag-a-zine (three taps).

Yes, mag-a-zine. Good job making more than one tap. You showed me that you heard more than one word part in magazine.

On the first day of this lesson, use only three-syllable words. On subsequent days, match word difficulty to child's ability, giving short words to students who aren't firm in their understanding of syllables. Use this format with each child.

Additional multisyllabic words to tap out:

Three syllables	*Four syllables*
basketball	alligator
telephone	helicopter
computer	caterpillar
marshmallow	rhinoceros
woodpecker	macaroni

END Lesson 3.

Everyone now gets their winnings for hearing and tapping out syllables and for working hard. *Give out token rewards to each child.*

LESSON 4: Syllable Awareness Review

OBJECTIVES

Student will

- Practice hearing, saying, and sorting short and long words
- Review the meaning of the word *syllable*
- Tap out the syllables in spoken words to show one or more than one syllable

Teacher will

- Provide pictures and hand gesture cues that emphasize varying word lengths
- Model how to hear, sort, and tap out words by length

RHYMES, SONGS, AND FINGERPLAYS

"Jack Be Nimble, with a Twist"
"Sleepy Caterpillars"

MATERIALS

Pictures of three-syllable words, including microwave, pineapple, and umbrella

10 pictures: Five with one-syllable names and five with at least three-syllable names

☑ Long or Short? Sorting Chart (see Appendix D on the CD-ROM)

☑ One short and one long sorting stick for each student

☑ One syllable stick for each student

☑ DROPP 6 Skill Assessment Checkout (see Appendix B on the CD-ROM)

☑ Tokens for behavior/participation

 TASK 1   Transition nursery rhyme (approximately 3 minutes)

INTRODUCE the lesson and review the big idea: syllable awareness.	Today we are going to practice all the ways we know of hearing the syllables in short and long words. *Prepare pictures of these or any three-syllable words:* microwave, pineapple, *and* umbrella.
	I want to say the nursery rhyme "Jack Be Nimble." But I am going to trick you. I am going to change the long word *candlestick* to something else. Let's see if your sharp ears can hear a different long word in our rhyme.
REVIEW the rhyme, with a twist.	My turn to say the rhyme. Listen.
	Jack be nimble, Jack be quick. Jack jump over the . . . microwave. *Show picture of a microwave.* Did I change the nursery rhyme?
Turn On Your Ears	▶ Children's response: Yes.
	Did I say Jack jumped over the candlestick?
	▶ Children's response: No.
	What did I say Jack jumped over? *Point to the picture.*
	▶ Children's response: The microwave.
	The microwave. Wouldn't that be funny if Jack came in your kitchen and jumped over your microwave? Good job using your ears carefully. Listen again.
	Jack be nimble, Jack be quick. Jack jump over the pineapple. *Show picture of a pineapple.* Did I change the nursery rhyme?
	▶ Children's response: Yes.
	What did I say Jack jumped over? *Point to the picture.*
	▶ Children's response: The pineapple.
Turn On Your Ears	The pineapple. Wouldn't that be funny if Jack jumped over a . . . pineapple? Listen again.

Jack be nimble, Jack be quick. Jack jump over the . . . umbrella. *Show a picture of an umbrella.* What did I say Jack jumped over?

▶ **Children's response: The umbrella.**

The umbrella. Jack had better not jump over an umbrella because it might poke him. Now let's say the rhyme one more time the right way. Get ready to say it with me.

Jack be nimble, Jack be quick. Jack jump over the candlestick.

Good job!

 **TASK 2A**   Say and sort pictures *(approximately 7 minutes)*

REVIEW short and long words.

Prepare the activity materials ahead of time. Assemble 10 pictures: five with one-syllable names and five with at least three syllables in their names. Use a Long or Short? Sorting Chart. (See the CD-ROM.)

 Multisensory Reinforcement

Prepare pictures for this activity in advance. Group short and long words together, putting the short word first. Do not show all of the pictures at once. Show each short and long word pair while saying the words, so that pointing can occur for the relevant words. Set up the pictures where all children can see them.

Set up two new pictures, short name first. Now I want you to listen to some picture names. Some will be short and some will be long.

Use your ears to hear which words are short and which words are long. Listen hard. The short names will be ones I can say fast. The long names will have more word parts, or syllables.

Cat, caterpillar. Watch me. Cat. *Pause and show a short distance with your hands.* Caterpillar. *Spread your hands wide apart.* Tell me which of these pictures has a short name? Get ready.

▶ **Children's response: Cat.**

Yes, *cat* is a short name. *Show a small distance with your hands.* It has only one syllable.

We will put the cat in the short name column. Who can show us which column has a short line at the top? *Choose a child to point to the short line in the sorting chart.* Yes, this is a short line. So we will put the cat here because *cat* is a short word.

Caterpillar. *Point to caterpillar. Show a wide gesture with your hands.* Say it.

▶ **Children's response: Caterpillar.**

Yes, caterpillar. Is *caterpillar* a short word?

▶ **Children's response: No.**

Is *caterpillar* a long word?

▶ **Children's response: Yes.**

Yes, *caterpillar* is a long word because it has more word parts. *Spread your hands wide apart.* We'll put the caterpillar in the long name column. Who can show us which column has a long line at the top? *Choose a child to point to the long line.* Yes, this is a long line. So we will put the caterpillar here because it is a long word.

Let's say the names of some more pictures. Some of the names will be short and some will be long. Let's see if your ears can hear which words are short and which words are long.

Repeat the activity—for example, with cake *and* motorcycle. Here are some more pictures. This is a cake. Say it.

▶ Children's response: Cake.

Yes, cake.

This is a motorcycle. Say it.

▶ Children's response: Motorcycle.

Yes, motorcycle.

Let's say both names and try to find the short name. Cake, motorcycle. Everyone, say them with me.

▶ Children's response: Cake, motorcycle.

Again.

▶ Children's response: Cake, motorcycle.

Tell me which picture has a short name. Get ready.

▶ Children's response: Cake.

Yes, *cake* is a short name. So we will put it in the short name column. What kind of name is *motorcycle?* Short or long?

▶ Children's response: Long.

Yes, *motorcycle* is a long name. So we will put it in the long name column.

ENGAGE in group practice.

Practice the three remaining word pairs you have chosen, following the previous format. Change the order so that long words are sometimes presented first. Let's check our lists. First we will say all of the short names.

Get ready. Cat. Say it.

▶ Children's response: Cat.

Continue, saying all words. Great job hearing, saying, and sorting short and long names.

ENGAGE in individual practice.

Now it's your turn to sort short and long picture names. *Give each child one long and one short stick.* Put your two sticks in order, small to large, like on the chart. *Help students place small sticks on the top left part of their workspaces and large sticks on the top right part of their workspaces.*

I will give you each two picture cards. We will say the names together, and then you can listen hard and figure out which picture has a short word name and which one has a long name.

Give each child a pair of picture cards containing a one-syllable name and a multisyllabic name. Have the whole group repeat the names of each picture pair. Let the children work independently to match the short name with their short stick and the long name with their long stick. Continue with three more word pairs. Check work by having all students repeat each student's columns of short and long names. Collect the picture cards and short sticks.

TASK 2B | Tapping Syllable Sticks (approximately 7 minutes)

REVIEW syllable sticks.

Watch me use my syllable stick to tap every time I hear a word part, or syllable, in a word. My turn. *Hold up one of the longer sticks.*

Tyrannosaurus. Ty-ran-no-saur-us. *Tap loudly for each syllable.* Everyone, did I tap one time or more than one time for that word?

▶ Children's response: More than one time.

Good. I tapped out a long word with more than one word part.

Next word: Plate. *Tap loudly one time.* Did you hear one tap or more than one tap?

▶ Children's response: One tap.

Good. You heard me tap one time because *plate* has just one syllable.

TEACHING TIP: Do not count the number of taps. The goal is to help the children hear the difference between a single-syllable word and a word with three or more syllables.

PRACTICE syllable sticks.

Continue to practice with words of your choice or the following suggested words: bug, ballerina, pajamas, moon, fly, photographer, banana, magician, goat, *and* ham.

Your turn to tap out the syllables. I will say each word. Then you will say it with me, and we will tap for every word part we hear. We will tap out the syllables. Let's practice.

First word: web. Say it and tap it.

▶ Children's response: Web (one tap).

Did you make one tap or more than one tap?

▶ Children's response: One tap.

Yes. You made one tap because *web* has one syllable.

New word: bulldozer. Say it and tap it.

▶ Children's response: Bulldozer (three taps).

Did you make one tap or more than one tap?

▶ Children's response: More than one.

Yes. *Bulldozer* has more than one syllable. Good ears hearing more syllables.

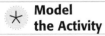 **TASK 3** | Transition fingerplay (approximately 3 minutes)

END the lesson with a transition fingerplay.

★ **Model the Activity**

You worked very hard today and showed me that you can hear, and say, and sort, and tap out syllables in short and long words. You did a beautiful job and I am proud of you!

Sometimes when I work hard, I get sleepy, like the sleepy caterpillars. Let's say the rhyme and do the fingerplay about the sleepy caterpillars. Do it with me. *Recite the fingerplay.*

Let's go to sleep, the caterpillars said, *(Wiggle pointer finger.)*
As they tuck themselves into their beds. *(Close fist around that finger.)*
They will awaken by and by, *(Rock closed hand like a cradle.)*
And each one will be a lovely butterfly. *(Open one finger at a time; make your hand "fly" away while flapping the thumb and little finger like wings.)*

6.1

END Lesson 4.

Everyone now gets their winnings for saying and sorting words that were short and long and for working hard. *Give out token rewards to each child.*

 The DROPP 6 Skill Assessment Checkout will be completed for each student following this lesson.

Syllable Blending

Overview

WHY SYLLABLE BLENDING IS IMPORTANT

Blending separate syllables into words prepares young children for the later skill of blending word parts in order to read. Practicing syllable blending helps children pronounce longer words by increasing the ability to hold sounds in memory. This is particularly important for learners who are at risk and who may not have experience saying and understanding multisyllabic words. As children learn to blend sets of syllables together into a word, they are manipulating sounds—an important step toward learning to read.

HOW DROPP 7 IS STRUCTURED

DROPP 7 has two Activity Sets—7.1 and 7.2. Each Activity Set consists of four scripted lessons (Teacher Talk) that are used on 10 sequential learning days (the four lessons are repeated over the 10-day span). DROPP 7 has 20 days of intervention lessons designed to develop and practice students' syllable awareness and blending skills. During the first 9 days of each set, students are given guidance and practice in hearing, saying, and blending syllables into words through manipulative games, songs, and a fingerplay. On the 10th day, they review the skills to prepare for a short skill assessment checkout. (See the CD-ROM for the DROPP 7 Skill Assessment Checkout.)

Length of Activity Sets and Lessons

Each Activity Set is designed to be delivered across 10 sequential learning days. Each day's intervention lesson, including the transition activities, takes about 20 minutes to complete.

Goal and Emphasis of the Syllable Blending Lessons

The goal of Activity Sets 7.1 and 7.2 is to heighten your students' awareness of syllables and their ability to blend spoken syllables into whole words by saying them "the fast way." These lessons emphasize syllable play through enjoyable games, songs, and fingerplays that will guide children to recognize and manipulate spoken words and syllables. As your students learn to hear and blend progressively longer words, they are making headway toward the more advanced skill of segmenting words into syllables. This will prepare them to become skilled readers who will better understand and decode multisyllabic words.

Student Objectives

Students will be able to demonstrate syllable blending by doing the following activities:

- Repeating multisyllabic words accurately

- Listening carefully to the separate sounds of multisyllabic words and blending those syllables to say the entire word smoothly

Teacher Objectives

- Develop students' syllable awareness and blending skills through scaffolded, multisensory activities.

- Use music to help hear the syllables in words.

- Assemble simple games that provide practice in blending spoken syllables into words.

How the Syllable Blending Activity Sets Develop Early Literacy

Multisensory Techniques

Activity Sets 7.1 and 7.2 incorporate the key multisensory support of hand gestures that reinforce both syllable awareness and syllable blending. Beginning in Lesson 1, students learn to move their hands in ways that visually and kinesthetically reinforce the concept of syllables as separate word parts that can be brought together. As students practice these gestures over multiple days, they learn to use multiple channels to solidify their understanding and memory of important reading processes.

Making Meaning and Building Vocabulary

Your students' understanding of longer words is reinforced in Lessons 1 and 2 of each Activity Set, in which you are given short sentences to say that demonstrate the meaning of the new words. In all of the lessons, showing pictures of the words attaches meaning to the words being blended. To further develop students' thinking skills, the songs, fingerplays, and word lists in Activity Sets 7.1 and 7.2 are developed around the common themes of animals and insects. Providing a known category of words, along with contextual clues, scaffolds students' success in blending words by narrowing the range of possible answers. New vocabulary words are found at the beginning of the Activity Set and are presented in the two-step approach described in Chapter 2. We recommend that you use the new words throughout the day to reinforce student vocabulary growth. The emphasized words in these sets are *syllable, minnow, nimble, nursery,* and *twinkle.*

Print Awareness

In the syllable awareness and syllable blending hand gestures of DROPP 7, students see the left-to-right progression of word reading as the syllables are spoken. Also embedded in these Activity Sets is the printed word awareness that comes from the teacher saying and pointing to words while reading three nursery rhymes. Here, students will see that some words look and sound longer than others. This supports their emerging awareness that sounds can be "mapped" onto printed symbols that make words.

GENERAL TIPS FOR IMPLEMENTING ACTIVITY SETS 7.1 AND 7.2

- The difference Between Activity Set 7.1 and Activity Set 7.2: Activity Set 7.2 has more multisensory supports and shorter words than Activity Set 7.1 in order to provide extra help to the children who require another 10 days to develop their syllable blending skills. In addition, we found it helpful to revisit some compound word blending at the beginning of Activity Set 7.2 because the word meaning of compound word segments provide extra support for students who struggle to hear separate word parts.

- Scaffolding for Success: There are a number of suggestions for adapting the activities of DROPP 7 to ensure students' mastery of progressively more challenging phonological skills.

  - Blend Two-Syllable Words at First: In the Blend-It Game, select only two-syllable names for blending from the themed word lists. Lists of longer words are provided in Lesson 2 so that you can introduce multisyllabic words after the children are secure in their understanding of basic syllable blending.

  - Multisensory Cues: As in the previous three DROPPS, you will use your hands as a teaching tool to help the children visualize and understand that syllables can be blended into whole words. The procedure, as described in Lesson 1, is as follows: Hold up both hands, about a foot apart, palms toward children. When you say the first syllable, emphasize your right hand by spreading fingers and moving that hand slightly away from the other and closer to the children. Do the same with the second syllable on the left hand. Then, bring your hands together while saying the whole word smoothly.

  - Two-Second Pause: When saying multisyllabic words in segments for children to hear and blend, it is important to pause for 2 seconds between each syllable. This ensures that the children are hearing and blending distinct word parts, not just repeating the word slowly without detecting separate syllable units. This critical skill also builds their auditory memory.

  - Use Pictures: As the children are learning to blend and pronounce longer words, such as *porcupine*, provide pictures to verify the correctness of their blending responses. This allows students to build background knowledge, and the phonological aspect of the task is made easier without the cognitive load of wondering about the word's meaning.

TEACHING TIP: **Withdrawing Extra Supports for Increased Skill Success**

As soon as a child is able to repeat and blend longer words consistently, try removing the scaffolded supports to allow him or her to respond more independently. By de-emphasizing the multisensory supports and contextual cues, you will promote the development of deeper phonological awareness.

- Rhyming Reinforcement: In Activity Set 7.1, the words *box* and *rocks* are chosen for rhyming practice with the "Rhyming Exercise Song." By reciting the songs in the lessons, you have another opportunity to reinforce rhymes by pausing to prompt students to fill in the missing rhyming word. If students cannot guess the missing word, then scaffold support by repeating the verse while providing the first sound of the rhyme. Be alert for other chances throughout your day to reinforce the skill of rhyming.

TEACHING TIP: **Check for Success**

During every activity, maintain eye contact with the students, and ensure they are responding correctly and on cue. In this way, you are doing a mini assessment for each child to see who may need additional help at every step of the way.

Blend-It Game

- Prepare picture cards or small objects before the lesson. Use a commercial deck of multisyllabic word pictures, or prepare your own cards or a collection of small toys. On the first day of each syllable blending Activity Set, choose only pictures of two-syllable words for both skill introduction and the Blend-It Game. You will need several specific pictures (e.g., a pizza, a candle) as well as enough pictures or toys to provide each student with at least three items to blend in the game. It is fine to use the same item with several students in different rounds of the game.

- Tell the children that you have pictures or toys (prompts) that you will name by saying their word parts. (Follow the detailed scripted directions provided in the lessons.) Keep the prompts out of sight while segmenting their names orally, and after a child blends the name successfully, show the prompt, and repeat its name as reinforcement of the correctly blended word. Give a colored chip or make a tally mark by each child's name for each successful response.

- Continue to administer items until every child in the group has blended an equal number of words correctly.

TEACHING TIP: **Smile**

Smile often and show the children how happy you are to be with them. All of these syllable blending games are clearly instructional, but the content is fun, and your delivery should be easy and happy.

Sammy Syllable's Blend-It Game

- Prepare materials before the lesson. Print the game cards and board from Appendix D on the CD-ROM. A game piece also appears on the right side of the game board. This game piece represents "Sammy" and is for the whole group.

- Tell the children that you have pictures or toys (prompts) that you will name by saying their word parts. (Follow the detailed scripted directions provided in the lessons.) For each word that a student blends correctly, the Sammy game piece is moved ahead one square. Show the card prompt after the student blends a word successfully. The whole team wins when Sammy reaches the finish line.

- Do not use visual or gestural prompts unless a child is unable to respond correctly. As students' skill levels increase on Sammy Syllable's Blend-It Game, increase the length of the words being blended, and gradually reduce the prompts in order to shift the learning emphasis to auditory recognition of syllables.

Skill Assessment Checkouts

After your review lesson is completed, set aside a few minutes during that day to give each child an individual sentence segmentation checkout. These take about 2 minutes per child to administer and provide useful information to guide your small-group placements. Based on the checkout and collaborative conversations with all teachers, you will determine which students should continue in Tier 2 small-group intervention and which students can successfully return to Tier 1 whole-class instruction.

Assessment Outcome: The student can orally blend two or three syllables into a whole word.

ACTIVITY SET 7.1

Lesson Descriptions

Lessons	Sequence of daily activities	◇ Vocabulary
Lesson 1: Two-Syllable Blend-It Game	Nursery rhyme: "Jack Be Nimble" Target: Game—blending two-syllable words Rhyme: "Down by the Station"	Syllable
Lesson 2: Sammy Syllable's Blend-It Game	Nursery rhyme: "Jack Be Nimble, with a Twist" Target: Game—blending two- and three-syllable words Nursery rhyme: "Jack Be Nimble"	Syllable
Lesson 3: More Syllables with Sammy	Fingerplay: "There Was a Little Turtle" Target: Game—blending two- and three-syllable words Fingerplay: "There Was a Little Turtle"	Minnow
Lesson 4: Syllable Blending Review	Rhyme: "I Say—You Say" Review Task 2A: Blending two- and three-syllable words Review Task 2B: Sammy Syllable's Blend-It Game with multisyllabic words	Syllable

Materials Needed

☑ Large nursery rhyme book(s) with "Jack Be Nimble" and "Down by the Station"

☑ 10–15 large picture cards depicting two-syllable objects, including a candle and a pizza

☑ 5–10 large picture cards depicting animals with three-syllable names

☑ Optional: Small toy turtle

☑ Optional: Insect pictures or objects—mosquito, dragonfly, bumblebee, grasshopper, ladybug, worm

☑ Syllable blending checklist

☑ DROPP 7 Skill Assessment Checkout (see Appendix B on the CD-ROM)

☑ Tokens for behavior/participation

Two-Syllable Blend-It Game

☑ Game cards (see Appendix D on the CD-ROM)

☑ Colored chips (up to three per child)

Sammy Syllable's Blend-It Game

☑ Game board (see Appendix D on the CD-ROM)

☑ Game cards (see Appendix D on the CD-ROM)

☑ One game piece (see Appendix D on the CD-ROM)

☑ Word list (see Appendix D on the CD-ROM)

ACTIVITY SET 7.1 — 10-Day Planner

Day 1	**Lesson 1:** Two-Syllable Blend-It Game
Day 2	**Lesson 1:** Two-Syllable Blend-It Game
Day 3	**Lesson 2:** Sammy Syllable's Blend-It Game
Day 4	**Lesson 2:** Sammy Syllable's Blend-It Game
Day 5	**Lesson 3:** More Syllables with Sammy
Day 6	**Lesson 3:** More Syllables with Sammy
Day 7	**Lesson 1:** Two-Syllable Blend-It Game
Day 8	**Lesson 2:** Sammy Syllable's Blend-It Game
Day 9	**Lesson 3:** More Syllables with Sammy
Day 10	**Lesson 4:** Syllable Blending Review

LESSON 1: Two-Syllable Blend-It Game

OBJECTIVES

Student will

- Learn how to listen carefully to the separate sounds of two-syllable words
- Learn how to blend the syllables together to say the entire word "the fast way"

Teacher will

- Model blending of two-syllable words and guide students to hear and blend separate word parts
- Teach children a game that practices two-syllable blending in an enjoyable format
- Watch each student's success and provide hand gestures and other multisensory supports as needed

RHYMES, SONGS, AND FINGERPLAYS

"Jack Be Nimble"

"Down by the Station"

MATERIALS

Large nursery rhyme book(s) with "Jack Be Nimble" and "Down by the Station"

10–15 large picture cards depicting two-syllable objects, including a candle and a pizza

Tokens for behavior/participation

Two-Syllable Blend-It Game

☑ Game cards (see Appendix D on the CD-ROM)

☑ Colored chips (up to three per child)

TASK 1   **Nursery rhyme to begin the lesson** (approximately 3 minutes)

INTRODUCE the big idea: syllable blending.

Say the following to the group after settling the children together at a table. You know how to listen and say short and long words. Starting today, you will learn how to listen to the word parts, or syllables, of long words and blend them together to say the long words. It is fun to blend syllables together and guess the word.

BEGIN the transition activity.

We are going to listen to words in a nursery rhyme about a funny boy who loves to jump. It's called "Jack Be Nimble." What's the name of the nursery rhyme?

▶ Children's response: "Jack Be Nimble."

Show the nursery rhyme picture and point to the words while reciting. My turn to say the rhyme.

Jack be nimble, Jack be quick,
Jack jump over the candlestick.

Your turn to say it with me.

▶ Children's response: Jack be nimble, Jack be quick, Jack jump over the candlestick.

Let's say it together again.

▶ Children's response: Jack be nimble, Jack be quick, Jack jump over the candlestick.

TASK 2   **Hearing and blending two-syllable words** (approximately 12–14 minutes)

LINK the transition rhyme to the big idea: syllable blending.

Good job saying the words in our nursery rhyme. Some of the words were short, such as *Jack,* and some of the words were long, such as *nimble.*

Listen: *Nimble* means lively and quick. Everyone, what does *nimble* mean?

▶ Children's response: Lively and quick.

Vocabulary

NIMBLE

Yes, *nimble* means lively and quick. So, when we say that Jack was nimble, we know that he is lively and quick, with lots of energy! That's why he can jump so well! Everyone, say *nimble*.

▶ Children's response: Nimble.

Nimble means lively and quick.

Hold up both hands, about a foot apart, palms toward children. When you say the first syllable, emphasize your right hand by spreading fingers and moving that hand slightly away from the other and closer to the children. Do the same with the second syllable on the left hand.

INTRODUCE hand gestures for syllable awareness and blending.

TEACHING TIP: Pause for 2 seconds between syllables to ensure that the children are blending the syllables on their own and increasing auditory memory skills.

Nimble has two word parts, or syllables. I have one syllable on each hand: nim-ble. Now, watch me blend them together and say both syllables the fast way. *Bring your hands together while saying the whole word smoothly.* Nimble. Say it with me.

▶ Children's response: Nimble.

CONDUCT group practice to blend two-syllable words.

Let's practice. I will say some longer words in two parts. Listen carefully to see if you can guess what word I am saying. Then say it the fast way. Listen. *Use the hand gestures described previously.* Can-dle. Say it the fast way.

▶ Children's response: Candle.

Turn On Your Ears

Yes, candle. *Show a picture of a candle.* You heard the two word parts in candle, and you said them the fast way to make the word *(point to picture)* candle. Our next word is piz-za. *Show a picture of a pizza.* Say it the fast way.

▶ Children's response: Pizza.

Yes, pizza. *Point to picture.*

Continue with six to eight more examples of two-syllable words, following the previous format. If students are successful after several examples, then discontinue using hand gestures but continue to show a picture after children blend the word correctly.

Use these additional examples of two-syllable words:

Compound words	Other words
baseball	basket
teapot	station
cowboy	morning
bookbag	handle
playroom	cookie
doghouse	flower
milkshake	dancer
rainbow	baby

*Correction procedure: If any child names only part of the word or gives an incorrect response, then show him or her the hand gestures. Watch my hands. Can-dle. *Bring hands together.* Candle. What is it?

▶ Child's response: Candle.

Say it again.

▶ Child's response: Candle.

If difficulty persists, then guide the child's hands in the blending motion while saying the syllables and then whole word together until he or she is successful. Practice the same word several times so that the child feels confident and positive.*

Vocabulary

SYLLABLE

You are doing a nice job of listening hard and blending two word parts together and saying them the fast way. Listen. I said that a word part is called a syllable. Say that word.

▶ Children's response: Syllable.

Yes, syllable. Say it again. *Repeat until all can say it.* A syllable is a word part. What is a syllable?

▶ **Children's response: A word part.**

Yes, a syllable is a word part. You are learning how to say syllables the fast way. That means you can hear how word parts go together to make words. Good learning!

 PLAY the game.

| **CD-ROM** | See Appendix D on the CD-ROM for the Two-Syllable Blend-It Game instructions and cards. |

 TASK 3   Nursery rhyme and exit task *(approximately 3 minutes)*

END the lesson with a transition nursery rhyme and exit task.

Do you know the nursery rhyme song called "Down by the Station"? It is about train cars lined up all in a row. In the front car, a person called the station master pulls a handle down to make the train go down the track.

Now let's sing the nursery rhyme. You may already know it. *Show the nursery rhyme and point to the words while singing.*

SING the song.

Down by the station, early in the morning.
See the little pufferbellies, all in a row.
See the station master turn the little handle.
Puff, puff, toot, toot, off we go.

Repeat the song.

DO the exit task to demonstrate skill mastery.

Excellent singing. Let's see if each of you can hear and blend syllables to guess a word from our song. _____ *(insert child's name)*, your turn. Listen. Morning. Say it fast.

▶ **Child's response: Morning.**

Do not use hand gestures unless child is unable to respond correctly. Yes, morning. We wake up early in the morning.

REINFORCE word meanings.

Let each child have one turn. Use the words below, following the previous format. After the child blends the two-syllable word successfully, repeat it in the suggested sentence or in a meaningful short sentence of your choice.

TEACHING TIP: Build in the 2-second pause when saying these words in syllables.

Sta-tion. (Yes, station. Let's walk to the train station.)

Ear-ly. (Yes, early. We eat breakfast early in the morning.)

Lit-tle. (Yes, little. My baby sister is so little.)

Han-dle. (Yes, handle. Pull the handle to open the drawer.)

Nim-ble. (Yes, nimble. Jack is clever and nimble.)

END Lesson 1.

You all did a good job today. Everyone now gets their winnings for blending syllables to say words the fast way and for working hard. *Give out token rewards to each child.*

LESSON 2: Sammy Syllable's Blend-It Game

OBJECTIVES

Student will

- Learn how to listen carefully to the separate sounds of two- and three-syllable words
- Blend two and three syllables together to say words "the fast way"

Teacher will

- Model blending of two- and three-syllable words
- Guide students to hear and blend separate word parts
- Teach children a board game that practices syllable blending in an enjoyable format
- Watch each student's success and provide multisensory supports as needed

RHYMES, SONGS, AND FINGERPLAYS

"Jack Be Nimble, with a Twist"

"Jack Be Nimble"

MATERIALS

10–15 two-syllable picture cards/objects

5–10 large picture cards depicting animals with three-syllable names, including a kangaroo and dinosaur

Tokens for behavior/participation

> ### Sammy Syllable's Blend-It Game
> ☑ Game board (see Appendix D on the CD-ROM) **CD-ROM**
> ☑ Game cards (see Appendix D on the CD-ROM)
> ☑ One game piece (see Appendix D on the CD-ROM)
> ☑ Word list (see Appendix D on the CD-ROM)

 TASK 1   **Nursery rhyme to begin the lesson** (approximately 5 minutes)

INTRODUCE the lesson and review the big idea: syllable blending.

BEGIN the transition activity.

 Turn On Your Ears

Say the following to the group after settling the children together at a table. You have been learning how to listen to the word parts, or syllables, of words and blend them together to say the word the fast way. Today we will blend syllables in some longer words and learn a new syllables game to play. First, I will say our nursery rhyme, "Jack Be Nimble."

Jack be nimble, Jack be quick,
Jack jump over the candlestick.

Now we will have fun by changing the word *candlestick* to some other things that Jack could jump over. Get your ears ready to hear the funny new words I will say. Turn on your ears and listen up.

Jack be nimble, Jack be quick,
Jack jump over the piz-za.

Pause and then look surprised as you say the unexpected word. What word did I just say?

▶ Children's response: Pizza.

Yes, pizza. *Show picture of pizza [optional].* Jack jumped over a pizza. I hope he didn't fall into it. Let's try another one.

Jack be nimble, Jack be quick,
Jack jump over the sta-tion.

What word did I just say?

▶ Children's response: Station.

Yes, station. *Show picture of a station [optional].* Jack jumped over the station. Wow. He must be a very nimble jumper to jump all the way over the roof of a station, like the train station.

7.1

CONTINUE to review two-syllable blending and listening in transition activity.

Use the previous format to repeat the nursery rhyme, with a twist, two or three more times. Choose comical two-syllable pictures from your syllable picture deck. Look surprised every time you segment one of the words and insert it in the rhyme, and comment on how the meaning changes from the original rhyme.

 TASK 2   Sammy Syllable's Blend-It Game (approximately 12 minutes)

LINK the transition rhyme to syllable blending.

INTRODUCE the skill of listening to three separate syllables that can be blended together.

Good job blending funny words in our nursery rhyme. You listened to words that have two word parts, or syllables. Now, let's listen to some words that have three syllables. Here's a clue—these words are the names of animals.

Listen. This animal likes to jump. It is a kang-a-roo. What word did I just say?

▶ **Children's response: Kangaroo.**

Yes, kangaroo. *Show picture of a kangaroo.* You heard three word parts in kangaroo, and you said them the fast way to make the word *(point to picture)* kangaroo.

Next word. This animal lived a long time ago. It is a di-no-saur. What word did I just say?

▶ **Children's response: Dinosaur.**

Yes, dinosaur. *Show picture of a dinosaur.* You heard three word parts in dinosaur, and you said them the fast way to make the word *(point to picture)* dinosaur.

Continue with three or four more examples of three-syllable animal names, following the previous format.

TEACHING TIP: Withdraw the visual (picture) supports to allow students to respond to auditory cues. This will deepen phonological awareness.

CONDUCT group practice in blending three-syllable words, without pictures.

Use these additional examples of three-syllable words:

elephant
hummingbird
crocodile
porcupine

Let's practice some more. I will say words in three parts. Listen carefully to see if you can guess what word I am saying. Then say it the fast way.

Com-pu-ter. Say it the fast way.

▶ **Children's response: Computer.**

Yes, computer.

Next word. Um-brel-la. Say it the fast way.

▶ **Children's response: Umbrella.**

Yes, umbrella. *Continue with six to eight more examples of three-syllable words, following the previous format.*

*Correction procedure: Guide the child to say it accurately and more quickly each time until he or she can hear the word and say it smoothly.

Listen. Mi-cro-wave. Say the word parts with me.

▶ **Child's response: Mi-cro-wave.** *Say it with the child.*

Say it again.

▶ **Child's response: Mi-cro-wave.** *Say it with the child.*

Now, let's say it faster.

▶ Child's response: Microwave.

Again.

▶ Child's response: Microwave.

*Practice several more times until firm.**

 PLAY the game.

 CD-ROM See Appendix D on the CD-ROM for the Sammy Syllable's Blend-It Game instructions, board, piece, cards, and word list.

 TASK 3 Nursery rhyme to end the lesson *(approximately 3 minutes)*

END the lesson with a transition nursery rhyme.

Now we're all going to say the nursery rhyme "Jack Be Nimble." This time, I will not change the last word. Let's say it together.

▶ **Children's response: Jack be nimble, Jack be quick, Jack jump over the candlestick.**

Repeat once or twice.

DO the exit task to demonstrate skill mastery.

Good job saying a nice nursery rhyme. Now, get ready to show me who can hear word parts and guess the word, all by yourself.

_____ *(insert child's name)*, your turn. Listen. Croc-o-dile. Say it fast.

▶ **Child's response: Crocodile.**

Yes, crocodile. A crocodile is like a big lizard.

TEACHING TIP: Build in the 2-second pause between syllables when saying these words.

REINFORCE word meanings.

Let each child have one turn. Use the words below, following the previous format. After the child blends the three-syllable word successfully, repeat it in the suggested sentence or in a meaningful short sentence of your choice.

Po-ta-to. (Yes, potato. A baked potato is good to eat.)

Um-brel-la. (Yes, umbrella. We use umbrellas when it rains.)

Ba-nan-a. (Yes, banana. The monkey ate a banana.)

Mi-cro-wave. (Yes, microwave. Put the food in the microwave.)

Gor-il-la. (Yes, gorilla. I saw a gorilla at the zoo.)

END Lesson 2.

You all did a good job today. Everyone now gets their winnings for blending syllables to say words the fast way and for working hard. *Give out token rewards to each child.*

LESSON 3: More Syllables with Sammy

OBJECTIVES

Student will

- Learn how to listen carefully to the separate sounds of two- to five-syllable words

- Blend two to five syllables together to say words "the fast way"

Teacher will

- Teach a new fingerplay that develops syllable awareness

- Model blending of syllables in longer words

- Lead children in an expanded game of multisyllabic blending

- Watch each student's success and provide multisensory supports as needed

RHYMES, SONGS, AND FINGERPLAYS

"There Was a Little Turtle"

MATERIALS

Optional: Small toy turtle

Optional: Insect pictures or objects—mosquito, dragonfly, bumblebee, grasshopper, ladybug, worm

Tokens for behavior/participation

Sammy Syllable's Blend-It Game   **CD-ROM**

- ☑ Game board (see Appendix D on the CD-ROM)

- ☑ Game cards (see Appendix D on the CD-ROM)

- ☑ One game piece (see Appendix D on the CD-ROM)

- ☑ Word list (see Appendix D on the CD-ROM)

 TASK 1   Fingerplay to begin the lesson (approximately 3 minutes)

INTRODUCE the lesson and review the big idea: syllable blending.	*Settle the group at a table and say the following.* You have been learning how to listen to the word parts, or syllables, of words and blend them together to say the word the fast way. Today we will blend syllables in some new long words. Then we will practice our words in Sammy Syllable's Blend-It Game.

MODEL the fingerplay.

 Model the Activity

This is a fingerplay about an animal. See if you can guess what kind of animal. It is small and walks very slowly. It has a hard shell on its back. It sometimes lives at a pond. Who thinks they know what it is? *Accept several answers, up to turtle.*

Yes, this fingerplay is about a turtle. *Optional: Show a small turtle figure.*

My turn to say the fingerplay. Watch my hands and try to do what I do during the rhyme.

Multisensory Reinforcement

There was a little turtle. *(Make a small circle with hand.)*

He lived in a box. *(Make a box with hands.)*

He swam in a puddle. *(Wiggle hands.)*

He climbed on the rocks. *(Stack hands, one on the other.)*

He snapped at a mosquito. *(Clap hands.)*

He snapped at a flea. *(Clap hands.)*

He snapped at a minnow. *(Clap hands.)*

And he snapped at me. *(Clap hands.)*

He caught the mosquito. *(Clap hands.)*

He caught the flea. *(Clap hands.)*

He caught the minnow. *(Clap hands.)*

But he didn't catch me. *(Shake index finger.)*

SCAFFOLD the rhyming production for rhyme reinforcement: If students cannot recall the missing word, then repeat that verse and provide the first sound.	I'll say the rhyme again. This time, see if you can help me say it by saying the rhyming words. Here we go. There was a little turtle. He lived in a box. He swam in a puddle. He climbed on the /r/_____. ▶ **Children's response: Rocks.**
PAUSE AND PUNCH.	He snapped at a mosquito. He snapped at a flea. He snapped at a minnow. And he snapped at /m/_____. ▶ **Children's response: Me.** He caught the mosquito. He caught the flea. He caught the minnow. But he didn't catch /m/_____. ▶ **Children's response: Me.**
DO skill review for Rhyme recognition.	Good job figuring out the missing words. When I said box, you said rocks. Box, rocks. Box, rocks. Hey, do they rhyme? ▶ **Children's response: Yes.**
SING the "Rhyming Exercise Song."	Yes. They rhyme! Let's sing our Rhyming Exercise Song. Get your rhyme muscles nice and firm so our rhymes are in great shape. Follow me. Put your hands in the sky. *On the word hands, stretch one arm up to the sky and then the other arm.* Do the rhyming exercise. *As you sing, switch and stretch arms one by one.* Box *(Stretch one arm up.)* Rocks *(Stretch the other arm up.)* Box *(Switch arms.)* Rocks *(Switch arms.)* Box *(Switch arms.)* Rocks *(Switch arms.)* Do they rhyme? *Pause here and allow them to show thumbs up or down before you respond. Look around at each student and make eye contact.* Yes. *Nod vigorously.* They rhyme. *Give two thumbs up.*

TASK 2　　**Sammy Syllable's Blend-It Game** (approximately 12 minutes)

LINK the transition rhyme to syllable blending.	Good job hearing rhymes. Your ears are working very well today. You know how to listen to word parts, or syllables, and guess the whole word. Get ready to listen to some new word parts and see if you can guess the word I'm saying. Here's a clue—these are insects. Some are from our nursery rhyme about the turtle.

TEACHING TIP: Pause for 2 seconds before pronouncing each syllable in the target words. This catches students' attention and signals for them to prepare to answer.

7.1

LESSON 3

REINFORCE three-syllable blending.

Listen. This is an insect that likes to fly around and bite people. It is a *(pause)* mos-qui-to. What word did I just say?

▶ **Children's response: Mosquito.**

Yes, mosquito. *Show picture of mosquito [optional].* Mosquitoes like to bite people, but in our nursery rhyme, it was the turtle who bit the . . .

▶ **Children's response: Mosquito.**

Yes, mosquito. Good job hearing and saying the word parts in mosquito.

Next word. This insect is green and likes to hop in the grass. It is a *(pause)* grass-hop-per. What word did I just say?

▶ **Children's response: Grasshopper.**

Yes, grasshopper. *Show picture of grasshopper [optional].* You heard three word parts in grasshopper and you said them the fast way to make the word *(point to picture)* grasshopper.

New word. Dra-gon-fly. Say it the fast way.

▶ **Children's response: Dragonfly.**

Yes, dragonfly.

INTRODUCE four- to five-syllable blending.

After the several practice items, do not give sentence clues in order to pick up the pace of the game. Continue with three or four more examples of three-syllable insect names, following the previous format. Let's listen to the parts of some really long words. Can you guess what word I'm saying? *(pause)* Al-li-ga-tor. Say it fast.

▶ **Children's response: Alligator.**

Yes, alligator. *Pictures are optional at this stage. Continue with the longest words you will use in Sammy Syllable's Blend-It Game.*

 PLAY the game.

 CD-ROM See Appendix D on the CD-ROM for the Sammy Syllable's Blend-It Game instructions, board, piece, cards, and word list.

Use the same game board as with Lesson 2, but use picture cards of longer multi-syllabic words. Begin with three-syllable words practiced on previous days. Then, proceed to longer words after the first round.

 TASK 3   **Fingerplay to end the lesson** *(approximately 3 minutes)*

END Lesson 3 with a transition fingerplay.

Let's review our new fingerplay about a snappy little tur-tle. Say it fast.

▶ **Children's response: Turtle.**

Yes, turtle. Do you remember that the turtle snaps at some things? Let's remember. He snaps at a *(pause)* mos-qui-to. Say it fast.

▶ **Children's response: Mosquito.**

Next, the turtle snapped at a *(pause)* min-now. Say it fast.

▶ **Children's response: Minnow.**

✦ **Vocabulary**

MINNOW

Yes, minnow. Who can tell me what a minnow is? Raise your hand. *Accept several answers.* A minnow is a small, silver fish. What is a minnow?

▶ **Children's response: A small, silver fish.**

Yes, a minnow is a small, silver fish that usually lives in a pond, river, or lake. So if the turtle snapped up a minnow, what did it catch?

▶ **Children's response: A small, silver fish.**

SCAFFOLD rhyming support for the fingerplay.

Let's say the fingerplay together. Watch my hands and try to do what I do during the rhyme. *Don't be surprised if students cannot recite most of the rhyme. Build their memories by having them fill in the rhyming word in every fourth line.*

There was a little turtle. *(Make a small circle with hand.)*
He lived in a box. *(Make a box with hands.)*
He swam in a puddle. *(Wiggle hands.)*
He climbed on the . . . *(Stack hands.)*

▶ **Children's response: Rocks.**

Multisensory Reinforcement

He snapped at a mosquito. *(Clap hands.)*
He snapped at a flea. *(Clap hands.)*
He snapped at a minnow. *(Clap hands.)*
And he snapped at . . . *(Clap hands.)*

▶ **Children's response: Me.**

He caught the mosquito. *(Clap hands.)*
He caught the flea. *(Clap hands.)*
He caught the minnow. *(Clap hands.)*
But he didn't catch . . . *(Shake index finger.)*

▶ **Children's response: Me.**

Aren't your fingers smart to learn our new fingerplay?

DO the exit task to demonstrate skill mastery.

Now, get ready to show me who can hear word parts and guess really long words all by yourself. _____ *(insert child's name)*, your turn. Listen. Ther-mo-met-er. Say it fast.

▶ **Child's response: Thermometer.**

Yes, thermometer. Good job saying such a long word the fast way!

Use these additional words for exit task blending:

buffalo
helicopter
porcupine
graduation
elephant

Let each child have one turn. The emphasis is now on blending syllables, so do not use the words in sentences.

You all did a good job today. Everyone now gets their winnings for blending syllables to say words the fast way and for working hard. *Give out token rewards to each child.*

END Lesson 3.

LESSON 4: Syllable Blending Review

OBJECTIVES

Student will

- Demonstrate the ability to listen carefully to the separate sounds of multisyllabic words
- Blend the syllables together to say the entire word "the fast way"

Teacher will

- Review blending of multisyllabic words
- Guide students to demonstrate syllable blending independently in two game formats
- Scaffold students' success with the choice of shorter or longer words

RHYMES, SONGS, AND FINGERPLAYS

"I Say—You Say"

MATERIALS

- ☑ DROPP 7 Skill Assessment Checkout (see Appendix B on the CD-ROM)
- ☑ Tokens for behavior/participation

Two-Syllable Blend-It Game

- ☑ Game cards (see Appendix D on the CD-ROM)
- ☑ Colored chips (up to three per child)

Sammy Syllable's Blend-It Game

- ☑ Game board (see Appendix D on the CD-ROM)
- ☑ Game cards (see Appendix D on the CD-ROM)
- ☑ One game piece (see Appendix D on the CD-ROM)
- ☑ Word list (see Appendix D on the CD-ROM)

TEACHING TIP: Intervention Task 2A is simpler than 2B. The items in Task 2A are limited to two- and three-syllable words, reinforced with pictures or objects. Task 2B has longer words and no pictures. As you deliver this lesson, note where students' individual comfort zones occur to aid in your assessment of their varying degrees of skill mastery.

 TASK 1 Rhyme to begin the lesson: "I Say—You Say" *(approximately 4 minutes)*

INTRODUCE the rhyme.

I know a tricky rhyming game that we can play. Listen and say the rhyming words! We will do the first one together. Watch where I point my finger, to help you find the rhyming answer: When I say *bed,* you say _____. *Point to your head.*

▶ Children's response: Head!

Yes, head! *Prompt the children to repeat rhyming the word pair twice.* Bed—head! Again, bed—head! *Rhyme reinforcement: If students cannot guess the missing word, then provide the first sound.*

New one: When I say *rose,* you say _____ . *Point to your nose.*

▶ Children's response: Nose!

Say the rhyming pair twice.

▶ Children's response: Rose—nose! Rose—nose!

Continue with 5–8 more rhymes, following the same format. Be sure to include several two-syllable options.

When I say *fly,* you say _____. *(Point to your eye.)*
When I say *week,* you say _____. *(Point to your cheek.)*
When I say *dear,* you say _____. *(Point to your ear.)*
When I say *chair,* you say _____. *(Point to your hair.)*
When I say *peck,* you say _____. *(Point to your neck.)*
When I say *linger,* you say _____. *(Point to your finger.)*

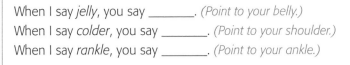

When I say *jelly*, you say _____. *(Point to your belly.)*
When I say *colder*, you say _____. *(Point to your shoulder.)*
When I say *rankle*, you say _____. *(Point to your ankle.)*

 TASK 2A Reviewing two- to three-word syllable blending with pictures *(approximately 8 minutes)*

 Turn On Your Ears

 Vocabulary

SYLLABLE

Wow, your ears are getting to be such good listeners! They can hear rhymes. They can hear sentences and compound words. Now, they know how to listen hard to word parts to help you blend them together and say them the fast way. Turn on your ears and give them a compliment: Good job, ears!

Listen. You know that a word part is called a syllable. Say that word.

▶ **Children's response: Syllable.**

Yes, syllable. Say it again. *Repeat until all can say it.* A syllable is a word part. What is a syllable?

▶ **Children's response: A word part.**

Yes, a syllable is a word part. You are learning how to say syllables the fast way. That means you can hear how word parts go together to make words.

 ♣ **PLAY** the game.

 CD-ROM See Appendix D on the CD-ROM for the Two-Syllable Blend-It Game instructions and cards.

This time, continue the game for three rounds. Students will, therefore, need three chips to win.

 TASK 2B Sammy Syllable's Blend-It Game *(approximately 8 minutes)*

 ♣ **PLAY** the game.

 CD-ROM See Appendix D on the CD-ROM for the Sammy Syllable's Blend-It Game instructions, board, piece, cards, and word list.

Use the same game board as with Lesson 2, but use picture cards of longer multi-syllabic words. Begin with three-syllable words. Advance to four- and five-syllable words after the first round.

Individual skill practice: Do not use picture cards for this task. Say multisyllabic words from the word list or from your class content.

END Lesson 4.

You all did a good job today. Everyone now gets their winnings for blending sylla-bles to say words the fast way and for working hard. *Give out token rewards to each child.*

 CD-ROM The DROPP 7 Skill Assessment Checkout will be completed for each student following this lesson.

ACTIVITY SET 7.2

Lesson Descriptions

Lessons	Sequence of daily activities	◇ Vocabulary
Lesson 1: Two Syllable Blend-It Game	Nursery rhyme: "Jack and Jill" Target: Game–Two-Syllable Blend-It Game Rhyme: "Twinkle, Twinkle, Little Star"	Nursery Syllable Twinkle
Lesson 2: Sammy Syllable's Blend-It Game	Nursery rhyme: "Milkman, Milkman" Target: Game—Blending two- and three-syllable words Rhyme: "I Say—You Say"	Minnow
Lesson 3: More Syllables with Sammy	Fingerplay: "Sleepy Caterpillars" Target: Game—Blending multisyllabic words Fingerplay: "There Was a Little Turtle"	Syllable
Lesson 4: Syllable Blending Review	"Milkman, Milkman" Review Task 2A: Blending two- and three-syllable words Review Task 2B: Sammy Syllable's Blend-It Game with multisyllabic words	

Materials Needed

- ☑ Large nursery rhyme book(s) with "Jack and Jill"; "Twinkle, Twinkle, Little Star"; and "Milkman, Milkman"
- ☑ 10–15 small picture cards of animals with two-syllable names, including a goldfish and a raccoon
- ☑ Five large picture cards depicting two- and three-syllable professionals, including a doctor and a firefighter
- ☑ Pictures of a caterpillar and a butterfly
- ☑ Optional: Pictures of clothing with two- and three-syllable names
- ☑ Syllable blending assessment checklist

> ☑ DROPP 7 Skill Assessment Checkout (see Appendix B on the CD-ROM)   **CD-ROM**
>
> ☑ Tokens for behavior/participation
>
> **Two-Syllable Blend-It Game**
>
> ☑ Game cards (see Appendix D on the CD-ROM)
>
> ☑ Colored chips (up to three per child)
>
> **Sammy Syllable's Blend-It Game**
>
> ☑ Game board (see Appendix D on the CD-ROM)
>
> ☑ Game cards (see Appendix D on the CD-ROM)
>
> ☑ One game piece (see Appendix D on the CD-ROM)
>
> ☑ Word list (see Appendix D on the CD-ROM)

ACTIVITY SET

7.2 ## 10-Day Planner

Day 1	**Lesson 1:** Two-Syllable Blend-It Game
Day 2	**Lesson 1:** Two-Syllable Blend-It Game
Day 3	**Lesson 2:** Sammy Syllable's Blend-It Game
Day 4	**Lesson 2:** Sammy Syllable's Blend-It Game
Day 5	**Lesson 3:** More Syllables with Sammy
Day 6	**Lesson 3:** More Syllables with Sammy
Day 7	**Lesson 1:** Two-Syllable Blend-It Game
Day 8	**Lesson 2:** Sammy Syllable's Blend-It Game
Day 9	**Lesson 3:** More Syllables with Sammy
Day 10	**Lesson 4:** Syllable Blending Review

LESSON 1: Two-Syllable Blend-It Game

OBJECTIVES

Student will

- Learn how to listen carefully to the separate sounds of two-syllable words and blend the syllables together to say the entire word "the fast way"

Teacher will

- Model blending of two-syllable words
- Guide students to hear and blend separate word parts
- Teach children a game that practices two-syllable blending in an enjoyable format
- Watch each student's success and scaffold with multisensory supports as needed

RHYMES, SONGS, AND FINGERPLAYS

"Jack and Jill"

"Twinkle, Twinkle, Little Star"

MATERIALS

- ☑ Large nursery rhyme book(s) with "Jack and Jill" and "Twinkle, Twinkle, Little Star"
- ☑ 10–15 small picture cards of animals with two-syllable names, including a goldfish and a raccoon
- ☑ Tokens for behavior/participation

Two-Syllable Blend-It Game CD-ROM

- ☑ Game cards (see Appendix D on the CD-ROM)
- ☑ Colored chips (up to three per child)

 **TASK 1** | **Nursery rhyme to begin the lesson** (approximately 3 minutes)

INTRODUCE the lesson and review the big idea: syllable blending.	*Say the following to the group after settling the children together at a table.* You know how to listen to word parts called syllables. Starting today, we are going to practice listening to a lot of new words to hear their syllables. It will be fun to blend the syllables together and guess the new word.

Let's start with a nursery rhyme you know. It's called "Jack and Jill."

What's the name of the nursery rhyme?

BEGIN the transition activity.

▶ **Children's response: "Jack and Jill."**

Who remembers what *nursery* means? Raise your hand if you know. *Call on one or two children.* A nursery is a place where a baby sleeps. What is a nursery?

 Vocabulary

NURSERY

▶ **Children's response: A place where a baby sleeps.**

What is the name of a place where a baby sleeps?

▶ **Children's response: A nursery.**

Yes, a nursery is a place where a baby sleeps.

Let's say our nursery rhyme together. It's called "Jack and Jill." *Show the nursery rhyme pictures and point to the words while reciting to reinforce beginning print awareness and word length awareness.*

▶ **Children's response:**
Jack and Jill went up the hill,
to fetch a pail of water.
Jack fell down and broke his crown,
and Jill came tumbling after.

 **TASK 2**   **Hearing and blending two syllable words** (approximately 12–14 minutes)

LINK the transition rhyme to syllable blending.	Good job saying the words in our nursery rhyme. Some of the words were short, such as *Jack* and *Jill,* but some of the words were longer and had two word parts, such as *water.*
	Water has two word parts, or syllables. I have one syllable on each hand. Wa-ter.

TEACHING TIP: Build in the 2-second pause between syllables when saying these words.

USE hand gestures for syllable awareness and blending.	*Hold up both hands, about a foot apart, palms toward children. When you say the first syllable, emphasize your right hand by spreading fingers and moving that hand slightly away from the other and closer to the children. Do the same with the second syllable on the left hand.*
Model the Activity	Now watch me blend them together and say both syllables the fast way. *Bring your hands together while saying the whole word smoothly.* Water. Say it with me.
	▶ Children's response: Water.
PRACTICE blending two-syllable words.	Let's practice. I will say some words in two parts. Turn on your ears so you can listen carefully to see if you can guess what word I am saying. Then say it the fast way. Here's a clue—these words are the names of animals.
Turn On Your Ears	First word: gold-fish. *Use hand gestures described previously.* Say it fast.
	▶ Children's response: Goldfish.

Use these additional examples of two-syllable names:

Compound words	Other words
sunfish	tiger
blackbird	lizard
bulldog	donkey
earthworm	penguin
hedgehog	giraffe
muskrat	hamster
polecat	puppy
seahorse	kitten
sheepdog	

Yes, goldfish. *Show a picture of a goldfish.* You heard the two word parts in gold-fish and you said them the fast way to make the word *(point to picture) goldfish.*

Next word: rac-coon. Say it fast.

▶ Children's response: Raccoon.

Yes, raccoon. *Show a picture of a raccoon. Point to picture.*

Continue with six to eight more examples of two-syllable animal names, following the previous format. If students are successful after several examples, then discontinue using the hand gestures but continue to show the picture after children blend the word correctly.

*Correction procedure: If difficulty persists, then guide the child's hands in the blending motion while saying the syllables and then whole word together until he or she meets with success.

Watch my hands. Gold-fish. Goldfish. What is it?

▶ Child's response: Goldfish.

Say it again.

▶ Child's response: Goldfish.

Practice the same word several times so that the child feels confident and positive.*
You are doing a nice job of listening hard and blending two word parts together and saying them the fast way. I said that a word part is called a syllable. Say that word.

 Vocabulary

SYLLABLE

▶ Children's response: Syllable.

Yes, syllable. Say it again. *Repeat until all can say it.* A syllable is a word part. What is a syllable?

▶ Children's response: A word part.

Yes, a syllable is a word part. You are learning how to say two syllables the fast way. That means you can hear how word parts go together to make words. Good learning!

 PLAY the game.

 CD-ROM See Appendix D on the CD-ROM for the Two-Syllable Blend-It Game instructions and cards.

 TASK 3 Nursery rhyme to end the lesson *(approximately 3 minutes)*

END the lesson with a transition nursery rhyme and exit task.

Do you know the nursery rhyme song called "Twinkle, Twinkle, Little Star?" It tells about the stars that twinkle in the sky at night. Who knows what twinkle means? Raise your hand. *Call on several children.* Twinkle means to give out light or shine. Everyone, what does twinkle mean?

 Vocabulary

TWINKLE

▶ Children's response: Shine.

Yes, twinkle means to shine. So we want the little star to twinkle, or shine. Now let's sing the nursery rhyme "Twinkle, Twinkle, Little Star." You already know it. *Sing the song and point to the words in the nursery rhyme book while singing.*

Twinkle, twinkle, little star,
How I wonder what you are.
Up above the world so high,
like a diamond in the sky.
Twinkle, twinkle, little star,
How I wonder what you are.

DO the exit task to demonstrate skill mastery.

Repeat the song. Excellent singing! Let's see if each of you can hear and blend syllables to guess a word from our song. _____ *(insert child's name)*, your turn. Listen. Won-der. Say it fast.

 TEACHING TIP: Build in the 2-second pause when saying words in syllables.

Multisensory Reinforcement

▶ Child's response: Wonder.

Use multisensory hand gestures if any child is unable to respond correctly. Yes, wonder. When we wonder about something, it means that we think about it and try to figure it out.

REINFORCE word meanings.

Let each child have one turn. Use the words below, following the previous format. After the child blends the two-syllable word successfully, repeat it in the suggested sentence or in a meaningful short sentence of your choice.

Twin-kle. (Yes, twinkle. The stars will twinkle and shine tonight.)
Lit-tle. (Yes, little. The baby is very little.)
A-bove. (Yes, above. The ceiling is above our heads.)
Dia-mond. (Yes, diamond. The diamond in Mother's ring is twinkling and shining.)
Won-der. (Yes, wonder. I wonder what's for lunch.)

END Lesson 1.

You all did a good job today. Everyone now gets their winnings for blending syllables to say words the fast way and for working hard. *Give out token rewards to each child.*

LESSON 2: Sammy Syllable's Blend-It Game

OBJECTIVES

Student will

- Learn how to listen carefully to the separate sounds of two- to three-syllable words
- Blend two to three syllables together to say words "the fast way"

Teacher will

- Model blending of two- to three-syllable words
- Guide students to hear and blend separate word parts
- Teach children a board game that practices syllable blending in an enjoyable format
- Watch each student's success and provide multisensory supports as needed

RHYMES, SONGS, AND FINGERPLAYS

"Milkman, Milkman"
"I Say—You Say"

MATERIALS

Large nursery rhyme book with "Milkman, Milkman"
Five large picture cards depicting two- and three-syllable professionals, including a doctor and a firefighter
Tokens for behavior/participation

Sammy Syllable's Blend-It Game CD-ROM

- ☑ Game board (see Appendix D on the CD-ROM)
- ☑ Game cards (see Appendix D on the CD-ROM)
- ☑ One game piece (see Appendix D on the CD-ROM)
- ☑ Word list (see Appendix D on the CD-ROM)

 TASK 1   Nursery rhyme to begin the lesson (approximately 3 minutes)

INTRODUCE the lesson and review the big idea: syllable blending.

 Turn On Your Ears

SAY the rhyme and point to the words in nursery rhyme book while reciting the rhyme.

Say the following to the group after settling the children together at a table. You have been learning how to listen to the word parts, or syllables, of words and blend them together to say the word the fast way. Today we will blend syllables in some longer words and learn a new syllables game to play.

First, I will say a nursery rhyme called "Milkman, Milkman." It is about a man who delivers bottles of milk, like the milk we get delivered to the cafeteria. But this milkman fell into the river. Let's see if he got cold in the river. Listen up.

Milkman, milkman, where have you been?
In Buttermilk Channel up to my chin.
I spilled my milk and I spoiled my clothes.
And I got a long icicle hung from my nose. *Repeat rhyme once.*

Oh, the poor milkman got something on his nose. Listen while I say the name of what was on his nose. I will say the word in three parts and see if you can guess the word.

Listen. I-ci-cle. Say it fast.

▶ Children's response: Icicle.

Yes, icicle. He got a long icicle, made of ice, on his nose. Do you think he was cold?

▶ Children's response: Yes.

Yes, he must have been very cold if he had a frozen icicle on his nose. Good job hearing the syllables in a word from our nursery rhyme. Let's see if you can guess another word from the nursery rhyme. Listen. But-ter-milk. Say it fast.

▶ **Children's response: Buttermilk.**

Yes, buttermilk. The milkman fell into a channel, or river, of buttermilk. I'll say the rhyme once more. You can try to say it with me. *Repeat the nursery rhyme, encouraging the children to say it too.*

TASK 2   **Sammy Syllable's Blend-It Game** (approximately 12–14 minutes)

LINK the transition rhyme to syllable blending.

Good job blending words in our nursery rhyme. You listened to words that have two or three word parts, or syllables. Now, let's listen to some more words that have two or three syllables. Here's a clue: these words tell about jobs that people have.

Listen. This person works in a hospital. She is a doc-tor. What word did I just say?

▶ **Children's response: Doctor.**

Yes, doctor. *Show a picture of a doctor.* You heard two word parts in doctor and you said them the fast way to make the word *(point to picture)* doctor.

INTRODUCE the skill of listening to three separate syllables that can be blended together.

Next word. This person helps to put out fires. He is a fire-fight-er. What word did I just say?

▶ **Children's response: Firefighter.**

Yes, firefighter. *Show a picture of a firefighter.* You heard three word parts in fire-fighter and you said them the fast way to make the word *(point to picture)* fire-fighter.

PRACTICE blending three-syllable words, without pictures.

Continue with three or four more examples of two- and three-syllable professions, following the previous format. However, withdraw visual supports. Let's practice some more. I will say words in three parts. Listen carefully to see if you can guess what word I am saying. Bull-do-zer. Say it the fast way.

▶ **Children's response: Bulldozer.**

Yes, bulldozer.

Next word: bi-cy-cle. Say it the fast way.

▶ **Children's response: Bicycle.**

Yes, bicycle. *Continue with six to eight more examples of three-syllable words, following the previous format.*

Use these optional examples:

president   farmer
dentist   hairdresser
carpenter

***Correction procedure: Guide the child to say it accurately and more quickly each time until he or she can hear the word and say it smoothly.*

Listen. Tel-e-phone. Say the word parts with me.

▶ **Child's response: Tel-e-phone.**

Say it again.

▶ **Child's response: Tel-e-phone.** *Say it with the child.*

Now, let's say it faster.

▶ **Child's response: Tel-e-phone.**

Again.

▶ **Child's response: Tel-e-phone.** *Practice several more times until firm.**

7.2

TASK 2 *(continued)*

♣ **PLAY** the game.

 CD-ROM See Appendix D on the CD-ROM for the Sammy Syllable's Blend-It Game instructions, board, cards, and word list.

 TASK 3 | Rhyme to end the lesson: "I Say—You Say" *(approximately 3 minutes)*

END the lesson with a transition rhyming activity.

INTRODUCE the rhyme.

Now we are going to say our rhyme called "I Say—You Say." Get ready to guess what my rhyme will be! Listen to my rhymes and you can figure out what body parts I'm talking about. You can point to them. We will do the first one together. Watch where I point my finger, to help you find the rhyming answer:

When I say *bed,* you say _____. *Point to your head.*

▶ Children's response: Head!

Say the rhyme; wait for children to respond. Yes, head! Bed—head! Again, bed—head! *Rhyme reinforcement: If students cannot guess the missing word, then provide the first sound.*

New one: When I say *rose,* you say _____. *Point to your nose.*

▶ Children's response: Nose!

Say the rhyming pair twice.

▶ Children's response: Rose—nose! Rose—nose!

Continue with 5–8 more rhymes, following the same format. Be sure to include several two-syllable options. Be sure to build in the 2-second pause.

When I say *fly,* you say _____. *(Point to your eye.)*
When I say *week,* you say _____. *(Point to your cheek.)*
When I say *dear,* you say _____. *(Point to your ear.)*
When I say *chair,* you say _____. *(Point to your hair.)*
When I say *peck,* you say _____. *(Point to your neck.)*
When I say *linger,* you say _____. *(Point to your finger.)*
When I say *jelly,* you say _____. *(Point to your belly.)*
When I say *colder,* you say _____. *(Point to your shoulder.)*
When I say *rankle,* you say _____. *(Point to your ankle.)*

DO the exit task to demonstrate skill mastery.

Good job saying some rhyming pairs of words! Now get ready to show me who can hear word parts and guess the word all by yourself.

_____ *(insert child's name),* your turn. Listen. Spa-ghet-ti. Say it fast.

▶ Child's response: Spaghetti.

REINFORCE word meanings.

Yes, spaghetti. Let's have spaghetti for dinner. *Let each child have one turn. Use the following words, following the previous format. After the child blends a three-syllable word successfully, use the word in a meaningful short sentence.*

Straw-ber-ry. (Yes, strawberry. A strawberry is good to eat.)
Prin-ci-pal. (Yes, principal. The principal is in charge of the school.)
Wall-pa-per. (Yes, wallpaper. There is pretty wallpaper on the wall.)
Pa-jam-as. (Yes, pajamas. Put on your pajamas and go to bed.)
O-ver-coat. (Yes, overcoat. I wear my overcoat when it's cold out.)

END Lesson 2.

You all did a good job today. Everyone now gets their winnings for blending syllables to say words the fast way and for working hard. *Give out token rewards to each child.*

LESSON 3: More Syllables with Sammy

OBJECTIVES

Student will

- Learn how to listen carefully to the separate sounds of two- to four-syllable words
- Blend two to four syllables together to say words "the fast way"

Teacher will

- Model blending of two- to four-syllable words
- Guide students to hear and blend separate word parts
- Lead children in an expanded game of multisyllabic blending
- Watch each student's success and provide multisensory supports as needed

RHYMES, SONGS, AND FINGERPLAYS

"Sleepy Caterpillars"
"Little Turtle"

MATERIALS

Pictures of a caterpillar and a butterfly
Optional: Pictures of clothing with two- and three-syllable names
Tokens for behavior/participation

> ### Sammy Syllable's Blend-It Game   **CD-ROM**
>
> ☑ Game board (see Appendix D on the CD-ROM)
> ☑ Game cards (see Appendix D on the CD-ROM)
> ☑ One game piece (see Appendix D on the CD-ROM)
> ☑ Word list (see Appendix D on the CD-ROM)

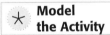 **TASK 1**   Fingerplay to begin the lesson (approximately 3 minutes)

INTRODUCE the lesson.

Review the big idea. Settle the group at a table and say the following. You have been learning how to listen to the word parts, or syllables, of words and blend them together to say the word the fast way. Today we will blend syllables in some new long words. Then we will practice our words in Sammy Syllable's Blend-It Game.

★ Model the Activity

Show caterpillar picture. Who knows what this is? Raise your hand. *Accept several answers, such as worm, caterpillar.* Yes, this insect is called a caterpillar. Everybody, what is this insect called?

▶ Children's response: A caterpillar.

Yes, a caterpillar. *Optional: Show a caterpillar and/or a butterfly figure.* A caterpillar is an insect that starts out like a worm and then turns into a butterfly. *Show butterfly picture.* What does a caterpillar turn into?

▶ Children's response: A butterfly.

Yes, a caterpillar turns into a butterfly. Let's practice a fingerplay about sleepy caterpillars. Watch my fingers and do what I do to tell a story about caterpillars turning into butterflies. Listen. Say it with me, watch, and move your fingers like me.

Let's go to sleep, the caterpillars said. *(Wiggle pointer finger.)*
As they tuck themselves into their beds. *(Close fist around finger, then rock closed hand like a cradle.)*
They will awaken by and by. *(Open hand, one finger at a time.)*
And each one will be a lovely butterfly. *(Make your hand "fly" away while flapping thumb and little finger as wings.)*

Let's say it again.

7.2

TASK 1 *(continued)*

Repeat each line of the fingerplay slowly, leading them in the words and movements. Good job doing our fingerplay. Let's do it one more time.

 TASK 2   Sammy Syllable's Blend-It Game *(approximately 12 minutes)*

LINK the transition finger-play to syllable blending.

You did a nice job listening to and saying our fingerplay. Your ears are working very well today! You know how to listen to word parts, or syllables, and guess the whole word. Let's listen to some words and word parts from our fingerplay, and see if you can guess the word I'm saying.

Listen. A-wa-ken. What word did I just say?

REINFORCE three-syllable blending.

▶ **Children's response: Awaken.**

Yes, awaken. When the caterpillars awaken from their nap, they will be butterflies. Next word: but-ter-fly. What word did I just say?

▶ **Children's response: Butterfly.**

Yes, butterfly. *Show picture of butterfly [optional].*

Good listening. Now, let's listen to some new words. Here's a clue—the words all tell about clothing that you might wear. Get ready. First word: rain-coat. Say it fast.

▶ **Children's response: Raincoat.**

Yes, raincoat. Next word: sweat-shirt. Say it fast.

▶ **Children's response: Sweatshirt.**

Yes, sweatshirt.

Use these optional examples:

snowsuit   jacket

sweater   undershirt

Continue with at least four more examples of clothing names, following the previous format. For students who continue to be challenged by hearing the word parts, begin with two-syllable compound word options. When all students are meeting with success, add three-syllable words.

 PLAY the game.

CD-ROM See Appendix D on the CD-ROM for the Sammy Syllable's Blend-It Game instructions, board, piece, cards, and word list.

Use the same game board as with Lesson 2. Begin with two-syllable words practiced on previous days, then proceed to a mix of multisyllabic words after the first round.

 TASK 3   Fingerplay to end the lesson *(approximately 3 minutes)*

END Lesson 3 with a transition fingerplay.

We said a fingerplay about a but-ter-fly. Say it fast. *Continue to use the 2-second pause.*

▶ **Children's response: Butterfly.**

Yes, butterfly. And about a cat-er-pil-lar. Say it fast.

▶ **Children's response: Caterpillar.**

Yes, caterpillar. We know that a caterpillar and a butterfly can live out-side. Say it fast.

▶ **Children's response: Outside.**

Yes, outside. Let's do another fingerplay we know about something that lives out-side. It is a snappy little *(pause)* tur-tle. Say it fast.

▶ Children's response: Turtle.

Yes, turtle. Do you remember that the turtle snaps at some things? Let's remember. He snaps at a *(pause)* mos-qui-to. Say it fast.

▶ Children's response: Mosquito.

Next, the turtle snapped at a *(pause)* min-now. Say it fast.

▶ Children's response: Minnow.

Vocabulary

MINNOW

Yes, minnow. Who remembers what a minnow is? Raise your hand. *Accept several answers.* A minnow is a small, silver fish. What is a minnow?

▶ Children's response: A small, silver fish.

Yes, a minnow is a small, silver fish that usually lives in a pond, river, or lake. So if the turtle snapped up a minnow, what did it catch?

▶ Children's response: A small, silver fish.

SCAFFOLD rhyming support for the fingerplay.

Let's say the fingerplay together. Watch my hands and try to do what I do during the rhyme. *Do not be surprised if students do not remember most of the rhyme. Build their memories by having them fill in the rhyming word in each fourth line.*

There was a little turtle. *(Make a small circle with hand.)*
He lived in a box. *(Make a box with hands.)*
He swam in a puddle. *(Wiggle hands.)*
He climbed on the . . . *(Stack hands.)*

Multisensory Reinforcement

▶ Children's response: Rocks.

He snapped at a mosquito. *(Clap hands.)*
He snapped at a flea. *(Clap hands.)*
He snapped at a minnow. *(Clap hands.)*
And he snapped at . . . *(Clap hands.)*

▶ Children's response: Me.

He caught the mosquito. *(Clap hands.)*
He caught the flea. *(Clap hands.)*
He caught the minnow. *(Clap hands.)*
But he didn't catch . . . *(Shake index finger.)*

▶ Children's response: Me.

DO the exit task to demonstrate skill mastery.

Great job on our fingerplay. Now get ready to show me who can hear word parts and guess really long words all by yourself.

_____ *(insert child's name)*, your turn. Listen. Mos-qui-to. Say it fast.

▶ Child's response: Mosquito.

Yes, mosquito. Good job saying such a long word the fast way.

Use these additional words for exit task blending:

microwave   calculator
television   potato
crocodile

Let each child have one turn. The emphasis is now on blending syllables, so do not use the words in sentences.

You all did a good job today. Everyone now gets their winnings for blending syllables to say words the fast way and for working hard. *Give out token rewards to each child.*

END Lesson 3.

LESSON 4: Syllable Blending Review

OBJECTIVES

Student will

- Demonstrate the ability to listen carefully to the separate sounds of multisyllabic words
- Blend the syllables together to say the entire word "the fast way"

Teacher will

- Review blending of multisyllabic words
- Guide students to demonstrate syllable blending independently in two game formats
- Scaffold students' success with the choice of shorter or longer words

RHYMES, SONGS, AND FINGERPLAYS

"Milkman, Milkman"

MATERIALS

Large nursery rhyme book with "Milkman, Milkman"

DROPP 7 Skill Assessment Checkout

Tokens for behavior/participation

Two-Syllable Blend-It Game

☑ Game cards (see Appendix D on the CD-ROM)

☑ Colored chips (up to three per child)

Sammy Syllable's Blend-It Game

☑ Game board (see Appendix D on the CD-ROM)

☑ Game cards (see Appendix D on the CD-ROM)

☑ One game piece (see Appendix D on the CD-ROM)

☑ Word list (see Appendix D on the CD-ROM)

TEACHING TIP: Intervention Task 2A is simpler than 2B. The items in Task 2A are limited to two-syllable words, reinforced with pictures or objects. Task 2B has longer words and no pictorial referents. As you deliver this lesson, note where students' individual comfort zones occur to aid in your assessment of their varying degrees of skill mastery.

 TASK 1   Nursery rhyme to begin the lesson (approximately 4 minutes)

INTRODUCE the lesson and review the big idea: syllable blending.

Settle the group at a table and say the following. You have been learning how to listen to the word parts, or syllables, of words and blend them together to say the word the fast way. Today we will blend syllables in all of the ways that you have learned.

First, we will say our nursery rhyme about the man who delivers bottles of milk. He is called a *(pause)* milk-man. Say it fast.

▶ Children's response: Milkman.

Yes, milkman. Our nursery rhyme is "Milkman, Milkman." Do you remember that this milkman fell down into a river of *(pause)* but-ter-milk? Say it fast.

▶ Children's response: Buttermilk.

Yes, buttermilk. Let's see if he got cold in the river. You can say the parts that you remember with me. Here we go.

Milkman, milkman, where have you been?
In Buttermilk Channel up to my chin.
I spilled my milk and I spoiled my clothes.
And I got a long icicle hung from my nose. *Repeat rhyme once.*

🔈 **Turn On Your Ears**

Oh, the poor milkman got something on his nose. Listen while I say the name of what was on his nose. I will say the word in three parts and see if you can guess the word. Turn on your ears.

SAY the rhyme and point to the words in nursery rhyme book.	Listen. I-ci-cle. Say it fast. ▶ Children's response: Icicle. Yes, icicle. He got a long icicle, made of ice, on his nose. Do you think he was cold? ▶ Children's response: Yes. Yes, he must have been very cold if he had a frozen icicle on his nose. Good job hearing the syllables in icicle.

 **TASK 2A**   Reviewing two- and three-syllable blending with pictures (approximately 8 minutes)

Turn On Your Ears	Your ears are helping you to become such good listeners. They can hear rhymes. They can hear sentences and compound words. Now they know how to listen hard to word parts to help you blend them together and say them the fast way. Turn on your ears and give them a compliment: Good job, ears! Listen. You know that a word part is called a syllable. Say that word. ▶ Children's response: Syllable.
◇ **Vocabulary** **SYLLABLE**	Yes, syllable. Say it again. *Repeat until all can say it.* A syllable is a word part. What is a syllable? ▶ Children's response: A word part. Yes, a syllable is a word part. You are learning how to say syllables the fast way. That means you can hear how word parts go together to make words.
PLAY the game.	**CD-ROM** See Appendix D on the CD-ROM for the Two-Syllable Blend-It Game instructions and cards. *This time, continue the game for three rounds. (Students will, therefore, need three chips to win.)*

 **TASK 2B**   Sammy Syllable's Game (approximately 8 minutes)

PLAY the game.	**CD-ROM** See Appendix D on the CD-ROM for the Sammy Syllable's Blend-It Game instructions, board, piece, cards, and word list. *Use the same game board as with Lesson 2, but use picture cards of longer multi-syllabic words. Begin with three-syllable words. Advance to four-syllable words after the first round. Individual skill practice: Do not use picture cards for this task. Say multisyllabic words from the word list or from your class content.*
END Lesson 4.	You all did a good job today. Everyone now gets their winnings for blending sylla-bles to say words the fast way and for working hard. *Give out token rewards to each child.*

 CD-ROM   The DROPP 7 Skill Assessment Checkout will be completed for each student following this lesson.

Syllable Segmentation

Overview

WHY SYLLABLE SEGMENTATION IS IMPORTANT

Segmenting words into syllables helps children begin to grasp the alphabetic principle—the basic understanding that words are composed of individual sounds that can be represented by letter symbols. Before young learners can detect individual sounds in words, they must become familiar with more holistic units of speech, such as syllables and onset-rime. In time, this will lead to individual phoneme awareness, and the child will be ready to learn how to read and write.

HOW DROPP 8 IS STRUCTURED

DROPP 8 has two Activity Sets—8.1 and 8.2. Each Activity Set consists of four scripted lessons (Teacher Talk) that are used on 10 sequential learning days (the four lessons are repeated over the 10-day span). DROPP 8 has 20 days of intervention lessons designed to develop and practice students' syllable awareness and segmenting skills. During the first 9 days of each set, students are given guidance and practice in hearing, saying, and segmenting multisyllabic words through songs, nursery rhymes, and multisensory games. On the 10th day, the children practice all of the skills to prepare for a short skill assessment checkout. (See the CD-ROM for the DROPP 8 Skill Assessment Checkout.)

Length of Activity Sets and Lessons

Each Activity Set is designed to be delivered across 10 sequential learning days. Each day's intervention lesson, including the transition activities, takes about 20 minutes to complete.

Goal and Emphasis of the Syllable Segmentation Lessons

The goal of Activity Sets 8.1 and 8.2 is to develop students' syllable awareness and their ability to segment spoken words into separate syllables. The emphasis of these lessons is syllable play through interesting songs, nursery rhymes, and multisensory games that will guide children to recognize and manipulate the syllables in spoken words. As your students learn to tap out and count syllables, they are progressing toward the important skill of hearing individual phonemes in words.

Student Objectives

Students will be able to demonstrate syllable segmentation by doing the following activities:

- Listening carefully to, saying, and sorting short and long words

- Stomping or hopping once for each syllable in three- and four-syllable words

- Tapping once for each syllable in words containing up to five syllables

- Counting up to three syllables in a word

Teacher Objectives

- Develop students' syllable awareness and segmentation skills through scaffolded, multisensory activities.

- Model how to stomp or hop out the syllables in words.

- Provide explicit, guided practice in segmenting and counting the syllables in two- and three-syllable words.

How the Syllable Segmenting Activity Sets Develop Early Literacy

Multisensory Techniques

Activity Sets 8.1 and 8.2 provide great opportunities for visual, auditory, kinesthetic, and tactile stimulation in every lesson. Each day's activities incorporate both large and small motor movements in entertaining, noncompetitive games that will deepen students' understanding and memory of the skills being addressed. In Lesson 1, students use the hand gestures for syllable awareness that were introduced in Activity Set 6.1 and incorporate that awareness into the new activity of sorting short and long words and tapping out their syllables using syllable sticks. In Syllable Stomp, students use their whole bodies to stomp or hop once for each syllable in spoken words. In Lesson 3, students learn to tap and count the syllables in words while hearing and saying new, longer words in Sue's Syllable Slide. Even the songs and fingerplays use multiple senses. On each day of these Activity Sets, the students will use multiple learning channels to deepen their understanding of the segments of sounds in words.

Making Meaning and Building Vocabulary

To further your students' thinking skills, the songs, fingerplays, and word lists in Activity Sets 8.1 and 8.2 are organized around the themes of animals, insects, and things at home. This appeals to children's natural inclination to categorize objects and activates background knowledge in ways that make learning more meaningful while enriching oral vocabulary. New vocabulary words are found at the beginning of the Activity Set and are presented in the two-step approach described in Chapter 2. We recommend that you use the new words throughout the day to reinforce student vocabulary growth. The emphasized words in these sets are *syllable, stomp, flick, awaken, speckled, goose,* and *down*.

Print Awareness

In the syllable awareness hand gestures described in Lesson 1, students see the left-to-right progression of word reading as the syllables are spoken. They also experience the printed word awareness that comes from the teacher saying and pointing to words while reading the nursery rhyme "Cackle, Cackle, Mother Goose." Here, students will see that some words look and sound longer than others. This supports their emerging understanding that words are composed of individual segments. Later, they will learn to analyze these word parts as they learn to read.

GENERAL TIPS FOR IMPLEMENTING ACTIVITY SETS 8.1 AND 8.2

- Syllable Play—"Thumbalina": In both Activity Sets, you will sing the popular counting song "Thumbalina" several times as a transition activity. This song has a wealth of learning opportunities, from counting to rhyming and, best of all, explicit syllable play. Each verse takes the long name of Thumbalina and adds unexpected syllable changes that the children love to hear and say.

- Rhyming Reinforcement: In these sets, the word pairs *flea, me* and *pool, cool* are selected from the transition activities for rhyming practice with the "Rhyming Exercise Song." In nursery rhymes such as "Cackle, Cackle, Mother Goose" you have additional opportunities to reinforce rhymes by pausing to prompt students to fill in the missing rhyming word. If students cannot guess the missing rhyme, repeat the verse while providing the first sound of the rhyme. Be alert for other chances throughout your day to reinforce the skill of rhyming, which is always a fun and important way to build phonological awareness.

TEACHING TIP: **Check for Success**

During every activity, maintain eye contact with the students, and ensure they are responding correctly and on cue. In this way, you are doing a mini assessment for each child to see who may need additional help at every step of the way.

Syllable Sort

- Prepare a Syllable Sort Chart ahead of time. Draw a short line at the top of the left column, and draw a long line at the top of the right column. Make rows under each column for pictures.

- Assemble 10 picture cards (5 with one-syllable names and 5 with three-syllable names). Give each child a short and a long stick, such as short popsicle sticks and 7-inch craft sticks.

- Procedure:

  Show and say a picture name.

  Children repeat the name, then hold up a long or short stick to sort words by length.

  Place the picture in the correct column.

  Continue until all 10 picture cards/words are sorted.

  Collect the short sticks. The long sticks become syllable tapping sticks.

  Follow the lesson's scripted instructions to guide students to repeat and tap out the syllables in each column's words, beginning with the short words.

  Provide individual practice by having each student tap out several words from the Syllable Sort Chart in the Syllable Stick Tap-It-Out Game.

Syllable Stomp

- Refer to Appendix D on the accompanying CD-ROM to prepare a stomping board ahead of time.

- Procedure: Model how to stomp out a three-syllable word.

  - Jump with both feet in two boxes, side by side, saying the whole word smoothly: *Mosquito*.

  - Hop on one foot into box A while saying the first syllable: *mos*.

- Hop on one foot into box B while saying the second syllable: *qui*.

- Hop on one foot into box C while saying the third syllable: *to*.

- Jump with both feet into final two boxes, repeating whole word: *Mosquito*.

- Show children how to stomp out a two-syllable word, such as *spider*, following the same procedure but skipping box C as you jump into the final two boxes.

- Day 1: Give students several turns to stomp out words, beginning with two-syllable compound words and progressing only to two-syllable words. Before each student takes a turn, have the whole group say the word and tap out the syllables to ensure the stomper's success.

- Subsequent days: Reduce the scaffolded supports as students become more capable of stomping out words successfully. With practice, students will be able to stomp out up to three syllables independently. Stomping more than three syllables is not recommended for pre-K students.

Sue's Syllable Slide

- Prepare the game materials in advance. Print the game cards and board from Appendix D on the CD-ROM. A game piece also appears on the right side of the game board. This game piece represents "Sue" and is for the whole group.

- Procedure: Call on one child at a time. Say the picture name slowly with distinct space between the syllables to assist the children in counting correctly. After a child counts the syllables in the word, he or she may move the Sue game piece ahead that many spaces. As children become more skilled and confident, say the words more smoothly and quickly as in everyday speech. When Sue reaches the final square, everyone wins.

Skill Assessment Checkouts

After your review lesson is completed, set aside a few minutes during that day to give each child an individual sentence segmentation checkout. These take about 2 minutes per child to administer and provide useful information to guide your small-group placements. Based on the checkout and collaborative conversations with all teachers, you will determine which students should continue in Tier 2 small-group intervention and which students can successfully return to Tier 1 whole-class instruction.

Assessment Outcome: The student can segment syllables in spoken words by tapping out and counting the number of syllables.

ACTIVITY SET 8.1

Lesson Descriptions

Lessons	Sequence of daily activities	◇ Vocabulary
Lesson 1: Syllable Sticks	Song: "Thumbalina" Target: Tap to segment one- to three-syllable words Song: "Little Peter Rabbit"	Syllable Flick
Lesson 2: Syllable Stomp	Song: "Little Peter Rabbit" Target: Game—Hop to segment syllables Fingerplay: "There Was a Little Turtle"	Flick Stomp
Lesson 3: Sue's Syllable Slide	Rhyme: "I Say—You Say" Target: Board game—Syllable segmentation Song: "Thumbalina"	Finger
Lesson 4: Syllable Segmentation Review	Song: "Three Green and Speckled Frogs" Review Task 2A: Syllable Stomp Game Review Task 2B: Sue's Syllable Slide Game with multisyllabic words	Syllable

Materials Needed

☑ 10 food picture cards (5 with one-syllable words, including cake, and 5 with three-syllable words, including hamburger)

☑ 6–10 picture cards with one- to three-syllable words, including dog, duck, dolphin, and bicycle

☑ One short stick (e.g., popsicle stick) and one long stick (e.g., tongue depressor) for each child and teacher

☑ Syllable Sort Chart (prepared ahead of time; see directions in text)

☑ DROPP 8 Skill Assessment Checkout (see Appendix B on the CD-ROM) **CD-ROM**

☑ Tokens for behavior/participation

Syllable Stick Tap-It-Out Game

☑ Syllable stick   ☑ Sample syllable sort chart

☑ Colored chips (up to three per child)

☑ Game cards (see Appendix D on the CD-ROM)

☑ Word list (see Appendix D on the CD-ROM)

Syllable Stomp Game

☑ Stomping board (see Appendix D on the CD-ROM)

☑ Game cards (see Appendix D on the CD-ROM)

☑ Word list (see Appendix D on the CD-ROM)

Sue's Syllable Slide Game

☑ Game board (see Appendix D on the CD-ROM)

☑ Game cards (see Appendix D on the CD-ROM)

☑ Game piece (see Appendix D on the CD-ROM)

☑ Word list (see Appendix D on the CD-ROM)

ACTIVITY SET 8.1   10-Day Planner

Day 1	**Lesson 1:** Syllable Sticks
Day 2	**Lesson 1:** Syllable Sticks
Day 3	**Lesson 2:** Syllable Stomp
Day 4	**Lesson 2:** Syllable Stomp
Day 5	**Lesson 3:** Sue's Syllable Slide
Day 6	**Lesson 3:** Sue's Syllable Slide
Day 7	**Lesson 1:** Syllable Sticks
Day 8	**Lesson 2:** Syllable Stomp
Day 9	**Lesson 3:** Sue's Syllable Slide
Day 10	**Lesson 4:** Syllable Segmentation Review

LESSON 1: Syllable Sticks

OBJECTIVES

Student will

- Learn how to separate (segment) two- to three-syllable words by tapping out each syllable

Teacher will

- Review long and short words
- Model how to segment two- to three-syllable words
- Guide students to hear and segment word parts

RHYMES, SONGS, AND FINGERPLAYS

"Thumbalina"

"Little Peter Rabbit"

MATERIALS

10 food picture cards (5 with one-syllable names, including cake, and 5 with three-syllable names, including hamburger)

One short stick (e.g., popsicle stick) and one long stick (e.g., tongue depressor) for each child

Syllable sort chart (prepared ahead of time; see directions in lesson)

Tokens for behavior/participation

Syllable Stick Tap-It-Out Game CD-ROM

☑ Game cards (see Appendix D on the CD-ROM)

☑ Word list (see Appendix D on the CD-ROM)

☑ Syllable stick

☑ Colored chips (up to three per child)

 TASK 1   Song to begin the lesson (approximately 3 minutes)

INTRODUCE the big idea of syllable segmentation.	*Settle the children into their seats and say the following.* You know how to listen to short words and long words. Long words have more word parts, called syllables. Today we will listen to some new words and tap out their syllables.
	Listen. I said that a word part is called a syllable. Say that word.
 **Vocabulary** **SYLLABLE**	▶ Children's response: Syllable. Yes, syllable. Say it again. *Repeat until all say it clearly.* A syllable is a word part. What is a syllable? ▶ Children's response: A word part. Yes, a syllable is a word part. You are learning how to hear and tap out syllables in words. That means you will hear how words are made up of word parts. Good learning!
BEGIN the transition activity.	I have a funny new song for you. It is about a little boy named Johnny Boy. Everybody, what is the boy's name? ▶ Children's response: Johnny Boy. Yes, Johnny Boy. Listen while I sing you the song.
SING the song.	When Johnny Boy was one, he learned to suck his thumb. Thumbalina, Thumbalina, half past one. When Johnny Boy was two, he learned to tie his shoe. Shoebalina, Shoebalina, half past two. When Johnny Boy was three, he learned to climb a tree. Treebalina, Treebalina, half past three. When Johnny Boy was four, he learned to shut the door. Doorbalina, Doorbalina, half past four. When Johnny Boy was five, he learned to take a dive. Divealina, Divealina, half past five.

| **SING** the song again, showing one to five on your fingers. | Let's sing our silly song again. You can help me count how old Johnny Boy was, from one to five. |

 TASK 2   Hearing and segmenting syllables in words *(approximately 12–14 minutes)*

LINK the song to syllable awareness.	Good job helping me count in our silly song. Some of the words were short, such as *dive* and *door.* But some of the words were longer and had a lot of word parts, such as *Thumbalina. Gesture with your hands to show short and longer words: Use your hands, palms facing each other as if measuring length. As you say the longer words, extend the distance between your hands about 1 foot with each syllable until your hands are wide apart.*
INTRODUCE hand gestures for syllable awareness.	
Model the Activity	Let's say some more short words with only one syllable. Say each of these words after me.
	Shoe. Say it.
REVIEW syllable awareness using short words.	▶ Children's response: Shoe.
	Yes, shoe.
	Tree. Say it.
	▶ Children's response: Tree.
	Yes, tree. *Continue in the same format and gestures, practicing five to six more words.*
REVIEW syllable awareness for longer words.	Now let's say some longer words with more syllables. Say these words.
	Thum-ba-li-na. Say it.
	▶ Children's response: Thumbalina.
Use these longer words:	Yes, thumbalina.
watermelon	Ball-er-i-na. Say it.
macaroni	▶ Children's response: Ballerina.
television	Yes, ballerina. *Continue in the same format, practicing five to six more words.*

TEACHING TIP: Whenever possible, insert vocabulary words you are studying from other content areas.

SORT pictures of short and long words, using sticks for visual demonstration.	*Assemble 10 picture cards (5 with one-syllable names and 5 with three-syllable names) and prepare a Syllable Sort Chart ahead of time. Draw a short line at the top of the left column, draw a long line at the top of the right column, and make rows under each column for pictures. Give each child a short and a long stick.*
Model the Activity	Good job saying short and long words! Now I want you to help me measure some short and long words.
Turn On Your Ears	I will say some picture names. One will be short and one will be long. I wonder if my ears can hear which is short *(measure a short distance with your hands)* and which is long *(measure longer distance).* Let's turn on our ears.
	Cake. *Show a picture of a cake.* That is a short little word.

Hamburger. *Show a picture of a hamburger.* Ham-bur-ger. I can hear that this is a long word.

Point to the short line at the top of the left column. Put the cake picture in the left column and the hamburger picture in the right column. This is a short line, so I will put the cake in this column because *cake* is a short word. I will put the hamburger in the other column where the line is longer because *hamburger* is a longer word.

PRACTICE the skill.

Let's sort some more words together. First we will say the words. Listen hard to see if the word is short, with one syllable, or long, with more syllables. Hold up your short stick if the word is short and your long stick if the word is long.

First word: ball. Say it.

▶ **Children's response: Ball.**

Yes, ball. Hold up a stick to show me if you heard a short word or a long word.

▶ **Children's response is to hold up a short stick.**

Yes, *ball* is a short word, so I will put the picture under the short line.

Next word: banana. Say it.

▶ **Children's response: Banana.**

CONTINUE until all 10 pictures are sorted.

Yes, banana. *Show and say the word.*

▶ **Children repeat word. Children hold up long or short stick to sort words by length.**

Place the picture in correct column. When all pictures have been sorted on the chart, collect the short sticks. Great job sorting long and short words! Let's check our work by saying the words. Short words first. *Say each short word with the children. Then, hold up the longer stick.*

INTRODUCE syllable sticks.

I call the long stick my syllable stick. I can use it to tap out each syllable in the long words. Watch me. Ham-bur-ger. *Tap out syllables using the longer stick. Tap three times.* I tapped out each syllable in *hamburger.* Let's see if you can do it with me. Ham-bur-ger. Say it.

▶ **Children's response is to tap their sticks three times while saying the word hamburger.**

Wonderful! You are listening so well that you can hear all of the syllables in a long word and tap them out with your syllable stick. Let's practice tapping out the syllables in some more long words. Say each word after me, and tap once for each syllable.

ENGAGE in group practice in tapping out syllables.

First word: pineapple. Say it and tap it.

▶ **Children's response is to tap three times while saying the word pineapple.**

Yes, pineapple. We tapped for each syllable in pineapple.

Here are examples of one-and three-syllable words for sorting and tapping:

Tap all of the remaining three-syllable words in the long column on the syllable chart.
*Use a correction procedure if a child does not tap the correct number of times.

One-syllable words	Three-syllable words
rake	ladybug
ring	potato
crib	computer
bear	tornado
book	barbecue
eggs	dragonfly

Tor-na-do. *Spread hands wider with each syllable.*

Watch me tap for each syllable. Tor-na-do. *Tap distinctly three times.*

Let's tap it out together. Tornado. Say it with me.

▶ **Child's response: Tornado.**

Let's say it slowly while we tap it out.

*Work with the child until he or she meets with success. If confusion persists, then try a two-syllable word. Practice the same word several times so that the child feels confident and positive.***

 PLAY the game.

> **CD-ROM**   See Appendix D on the CD-ROM for the Syllable Stick Tap-It-Out Game instructions, cards, and word list.

 TASK 3   **Song to end the lesson** (approximately 3 minutes)

END the lesson with a transition song and exit task.

Now I am going to sing you another new song. This song is about a nice little rabbit named Peter Rabbit. One day while Peter was eating his carrot, a little bug landed on him. Listen to see what Peter Rabbit does.

SING the song to the tune of "Battle Hymn of the Republic."

Little Peter Rabbit had a fly upon his tail.
Little Peter Rabbit had a fly upon his tail.
Little Peter Rabbit had a fly upon his tail.
And he flicked it till it flew away.
Repeat the song.

Did you like that song? Tell me about it. What kind of bug landed on Peter Rabbit?

▶ **Children's response: A fly.**

◇ **Vocabulary**

FLICK

Yes, a fly landed on Peter Rabbit, and he flicked it. What do you think flick means? *Accept several answers.*

Flick means to give something a quick tap. Let's all pretend a fly landed on our knee. Let's flick it off. *Have all the children pretend to brush a fly away.* Flick, flick, flick. Go away, you little fly.

REPEAT the song.

I'll sing the song one more time. You can sing it with me. We'll each pretend to be Peter Rabbit and flick that fly away. *Sing the song and act out "flicking" the fly away.*

DO the exit task to demonstrate skill mastery.

Excellent singing. Let's see if each of you can tap out the syllables in a word from our song.

_____ *(insert child's name)*, your turn. Listen. Lit-tle. Say it and tap it.

▶ **Child's response: Little (two taps).**

Yes, little. Good job tapping out the word parts in little.

Let each child have one turn. Use the following words, following the previous format, so that each child can tap out a word successfully: Peter, rabbit, away, *and* upon.

END Lesson 1.

You all did a good job today. Everyone now gets their winnings for hearing the syllables in words and for working hard. *Give out token rewards to each child.*

LESSON 2: Syllable Stomp

OBJECTIVES

Student will

- Learn how to segment syllables in words by jumping to show how many syllables are heard

Teacher will

- Model how to segment two- and three-syllable words
- Guide students to hear and segment word parts
- Teach children an action game that uses multi-sensory learning to reinforce the segmenting of syllables
- Watch each student's success and provide supports as needed

RHYMES, SONGS, AND FINGERPLAYS

"Little Peter Rabbit"

"There Was a Little Turtle"

MATERIALS

One syllable stick (e.g., tongue depressor) for each child

6–10 picture cards with one- to three-syllable names, including dog, duck, dolphin, and bicycle

Tokens for behavior/participation

Syllable Stomp Game

☑ Stomping board (see Appendix D on the CD-ROM)

☑ Game cards (see Appendix D on the CD-ROM)

 TASK 1   **Song to begin the lesson** (approximately 3 minutes)

INTRODUCE the lesson; review the big idea: syllable segmentation.

Say the following to the group after settling the children together at a table. You know how to listen to short words and long words and to tap out their word parts, called syllables. Today we will say and tap out the syllables in some new words and then learn a game called Syllable Stomp.

SING the song, with some new verses.

First, I will sing you our song called "Little Peter Rabbit." Do you remember what happened to Peter one day while he was eating his carrot? Raise your hand. *Accept several answers.* Yes, a little fly landed on him and he flicked it off.

Today, I know some new parts to the song. Listen to see what else lands on Peter Rabbit.

Little Peter Rabbit had a fly upon his tail.
Little Peter Rabbit had a fly upon his tail.
Little Peter Rabbit had a fly upon his tail.
And he flicked it till it flew away. *(Make flicking motion.)*
Little Peter Rabbit had mosquitoes on his ear. *(Sing three times.)*
And he flicked them till they buzzed away. *(Make flicking motion.)*
Little Peter Rabbit had a grasshopper on his knee. *(Sing three times.)*
And he flicked it till it hopped away. *(Make flicking motion.)*
Little Peter Rabbit had a ladybug on his nose. *(Sing three times.)*
And she gave him a nice little kiss. *(Blow a big kiss.)*

REVIEW syllable blending and segmenting with words from the song.

Gee, Peter Rabbit certainly has a lot of insects who like to sit on his nice soft fur. See if you can guess which insect's name I am saying. Listen.

Mos--qui--toes. Say it fast. *(Use the 2-second pause in these practice words.)*

▶ Children's response: Mosquitoes.

Yes, mosquitoes. Peter had mosquitoes buzzing in his ear.

Grass-hop-per. Say it fast.

▶ **Children's response: Grasshopper.**

Yes, grasshopper. It hopped on Peter Rabbit's knee.

La-dy-bug. Say it fast.

▶ **Children's response: Ladybug.**

Yes, ladybug. She gave Peter Rabbit a nice little . . .

▶ **Children's response: Kiss.**

Good job remembering who was in the story! Now, let's practice tapping out the syllables in those words. *Give each child a syllable stick.* Say each word after me, and tap once for each syllable.

First word: mosquito. Say it and tap it.

▶ **Children's response is to tap three times while saying the word mosquito.**

Yes, mosquito. We tapped for each syllable in mosquito.

Follow the same format for remaining words (grasshopper, ladybug). Good job tapping out the syllables and saying the name of some insects.

 Vocabulary

FLICK

Think about this. Peter Rabbit flicked most of those bugs to make them fly away. What does that mean, he flicked them? *Accept several responses.* Yes, *flicked* means that he gave them a quick tap or a shake. Let's pretend a mosquito is on our shoulder. Let's flick it off. *Have everyone motion as if flicking a fly away.* Now, let's flick water off our fingers. *Shake fingers.* Flick, flick, flick. Who can tell me a sentence using the word *flick? Encourage several examples.* Good job using our new word *flick.*

SING the first verse of the song again.

Now let's sing the first verse of the song together. When the fly lands on Peter's tail, be sure to flick it away.

 TASK 2   Syllable Stomp *(approximately 12–14 minutes)*

LINK the transition song to segmenting syllables.

I like the Peter Rabbit song. I like the way you listened to the word parts, or syllables, in the longer words.

Practice tapping out several short words. Let's tap out some more words to show how well we can hear syllables. We'll start with short words that only have one syllable. They only need one tap.

First word *(show picture)*: dog. Say it and tap it.

Multisensory Reinforcement

▶ **Children's response: Dog (one tap).**

Yes, dog. Next word *(show picture)*: duck. Say it and tap it.

▶ **Children's response: Duck (one tap).**

Yes, duck. *Continue in the same format. Choose three to four more examples of one-syllable words from your prepared deck of syllable pictures.*

ENGAGE in group practice using one- to three-syllable words.

Now I will add some longer words. Listen carefully. Some words will have two or three syllables, and some will be short with only one syllable.

First word *(show picture)*: dol-phin. Say it and tap it.

▶ **Children's response: Dolphin (two taps).**

Yes, dol-phin.

New word *(show picture)*: bi-cy-cle. Say it and tap it.

▶ **Children's response: Bicycle (three taps).**

Yes, bicycle. *Continue in the same format. Choose six to eight more examples of one- to three-syllable words from your deck.*

*Correction procedure if the child does not tap the correct number of times: Watch my hands. Bi-cy-cle. *Spread hands wider with each syllable.* Bi-cy-cle. Watch me tap for each syllable. Bi-cy-cle. *Tap distinctly three times.* Let's tap it out together. Bicycle. Say it with me.

▶ **Child's response: Bicycle.**

Let's say it slowly while we tap it out. *Work with the child until he or she meets with success. If confusion persists, then try a two-syllable word. Practice the same word several times so that the child feels confident and positive.******

 Vocabulary

STOMP

Model the Activity

Today we will have fun hearing syllables and then stomping them out on a stomping board. Listen, I said the word *stomp.* Who knows what *stomp* means? *Accept several answers.*

Stomp means to bring your foot down with a heavy step. *Stomp.*

If a bad bug comes in our classroom, we will stomp on it. Everybody, stand up and stomp your foot on that bad bug. *Model action. Guide children to stomp their feet a few times.* We had to stomp our feet. What did we do?

▶ **Children's response: Stomp our feet.**

Yes. We stomped our feet on that bad bug. Sometimes it is fun to stomp our feet at a sports game. Let's see who can stomp for our team while we're sitting down. *Guide all children to stomp alternate feet a few times.* Good stomping. What do you call it when you bring your foot down hard?

▶ **Children's response: Stomp.**

Yes, when we want to stomp, we bring our foot down hard.

 PLAY the game.

CD-ROM See Appendix D on the CD-ROM for the Syllable Stomp Game instructions, stomping board, cards, and word list.

 **TASK 3**

Fingerplay to end the lesson *(approximately 3 minutes)*

END the lesson with a transition fingerplay and exit task.

We already sang about Little Peter Rabbit who flicked off the insects that landed on him. Let's end today's work with a fingerplay about the little turtle who snapped at some insects and other things. If you know it, then you can say it with me. Remember to do the movements with your fingers.

RECITE the fingerplay and perform the motions.

There was a little turtle. *(Make a small circle with hand.)*
He lived in a box. *(Make a box with hands.)*
He swam in a puddle. *(Wiggle hands.)*
He climbed on the rocks. *(Stack hands, one on the other.)*

Multisensory Reinforcement

He snapped at a mosquito. *(Clap hands.)*
He snapped at a flea. *(Clap hands.)*
He snapped at a minnow. *(Clap hands.)*
And he snapped at me. *(Clap hands.)*

8.1

LESSON 2

He caught the mosquito. *(Clap hands.)*
He caught the flea. *(Clap hands.)*
He caught the minnow. *(Clap hands.)*
But he didn't catch me. *(Shake index finger.)*

DO skill review of rhyme recognition.

Good job remembering that fingerplay about the turtle who snapped at the flea and who snapped at me. Listen. Flea, me. Flea, me. Hey, do they rhyme? *Look around at each student.*

▶ **Children's response: Yes.**

SING the "Rhyming Exercise Song."

Yes. They rhyme! Let's sing our Rhyming Exercise Song. Get your rhyme muscles nice and firm so our rhymes are in great shape. Follow me.

Put your hands in the sky. *On the word hands, stretch one arm up to the sky and then the other arm.* Do the rhyming exercise. *As you sing, switch and stretch arms one by one.*

🖐 **Multisensory Reinforcement**

Flea *(Stretch one arm up.)*
Me *(Stretch the other arm up.)*
Flea *(Switch arms.)*
Me *(Switch arms.)*
Flea *(Switch arms.)*
Me *(Switch arms.)*

Do they rhyme? *Pause here and allow them to show thumbs up or down before you respond. Look around at each student and make eye contact.* Yes. *Nod vigorously.* They rhyme! *Give two thumbs up.*

DO the exit task to demonstrate skill mastery.

Excellent singing! Now, let's see if each of you can tap out the syllables in a word from our fingerplay.

_____ *(insert child's name)*, your turn. Listen. Tur-tle. Say it and tap it.

▶ **Child's response: Turtle (two taps).**

Yes, turtle. Good job tapping out the word parts in *turtle*.

Let each child have one turn. Use the following words, following the previous format so that each can tap out a word successfully: mosquito, minnow, little, puddle.

END Lesson 2.

You all did a good job today. Everyone now gets their winnings for hearing, tapping, and stomping the syllables in words and for working hard. *Give out token rewards to each child.*

LESSON 3: Sue's Syllable Slide

OBJECTIVES

Student will

- Reinforce the ability to segment syllables in words by practicing the skill in a new game
- Be introduced to the concept of counting the number of syllables

Teacher will

- Provide explicit, guided practice in segmenting and counting the syllables in two- and three-syllable words
- Teach children a new game of syllable segmentation

RHYMES, SONGS, AND FINGERPLAYS

"I Say—You Say"

"Thumbalina"

MATERIALS

Syllable sticks (one for teacher and one for each child)

Tokens for behavior/participation

Sue's Syllable Slide Game

☑ Game board (see Appendix D on the CD-ROM)

☑ Game cards (see Appendix D on the CD-ROM)

☑ One game piece (see Appendix D on the CD-ROM)

☑ Word list (see Appendix D on the CD-ROM)

CD-ROM

 TASK 1   **Song to begin the lesson** (approximately 3 minutes)

INTRODUCE the lesson.

REVIEW the big idea: syllable segmentation.

SAY the rhyme.

Settle the group at a table and say the following. You know how to listen to short words and long words and to tap out and stomp out their word parts, called syllables. Today we will hear and tap out syllables in a game called Sue's Syllable Slide. We'll start with a rhyming game called "I Say—You Say." Get ready to guess what my rhyme will be!

Listen to my rhymes and you will know what body parts I'm singing about. You can point to them. We will do the first one together. Watch where I point my finger, to help you find the rhyming answer: When I say *bed*, you say _____. *Point to your head. Rhyme reinforcement: If students cannot guess the missing word, then provide the first sound.*

▶ Children's response: Head!

Yes, head! Say it with me. *(Wait for children to respond.)* Bed—head! Again, bed—head!

New one: When I say *rose*, you say _____. *Point to your nose.*

▶ Children's response: Nose!

Yes, nose! Say it.

▶ Children's response: Rose—nose! Rose—nose!

Continue with 5–8 more rhymes, following the same format. Be sure to include several from the two-syllable options. If students cannot guess the missing word, then provide the first sound.

When I say *fly,* you say _____. *(Point to your eye.)*

When I say *week,* you say _____. *(Point to your cheek.)*

When I say *dear,* you say _____. *(Point to your ear.)*

When I say chair, you say _____. *(Point to your hair.)*

When I say *peck,* you say _____. *(Point to your neck.)*

When I say *linger,* you say _____. *(Point to your finger.)*

When I say *jelly,* you say _____. *(Point to your belly.)*

When I say *colder,* you say _____. *(Point to your shoulder.)*

When I say rankle, you say _____. *(Point to your ankle.)*

TASK 2   **Sue's Syllable Slide Game** (approximately 12 minutes)

LINK the transition rhyme to syllable segmentation.

Great job saying those rhymes so well! Let's tap out the syllables in one of our rhyming words—*finger. Distribute syllable sticks.* Say it and tap it.

▶ **Children's response: Fing–er. (Two taps).**

Yes, finger.

INTRODUCE syllable counting.

When I tap out the syllables in a word, I can count how many there are. In a short word, such as *head,* there is only one syllable. Watch me as I hear and count one syllable. *Demonstrate the skill.* Head. *Tap with one hand while holding up one finger on the other hand.* One syllable. I heard one syllable so I put up one finger.

Now watch me as I hear and count two syllables. Fing–er. *Tap twice with one hand while raising two fingers on the other hand, one at a time.* Finger has two syllables, so I put up two fingers. Count with me.

▶ **Children's response: One. Two. Two syllables.**

Now watch me hear and count three syllables. Um–brell–a. *Tap three times while raising three fingers, one at a time.* Umbrella has three syllables, so I put up three fingers. Count with me.

▶ **Children's response: One. Two. Three. Three syllables.**

Great job helping me count syllables on my fingers.

ENGAGE in group practice in syllable counting.

Let's practice counting some more syllables. This time, you will put up your fingers to count syllables, and I will tap them out. Get ready to listen hard. Turn on your ears. *Begin with two-syllable compound words to make it easier for students to count the word parts without tapping.*

🦻 **Turn On Your Ears**

First word: skate-board. Say it and count it. *Tap twice while students raise two fingers.*

▶ **Children's response: Skateboard (raising two fingers, one at a time).**

Yes, skateboard. How many syllables did you count? Count with me.

▶ **Children's response: One. Two. Two syllables.**

Yes. You heard two syllables and you counted them on two fingers. Great job hearing syllables and counting them on your fingers. Let's do another word. Get ready. Play-ground. Say it and count it. *Tap twice while students raise two fingers.*

▶ **Children's response: Playground (raising two fingers, one at a time).**

Yes, playground. How many syllables did you count? Count with me.

▶ **Children's response: One. Two. Two syllables.**

Practice with the whole group until the counting skill is firm. Be sure that every child repeats the words and counts on fingers. Do not be tempted to count four or more syllable words at this point. Stop tapping the syllable stick as soon as students are able to hear and count the syllables without it.

Examples of sequence of words to practice include goldfish, dragonfly, raincoat, dishwasher, tiger, fox, spider, cat, monkey, crocodile, donkey, dinosaur, turkey, *and* elephant.

*Correction procedure if a child does not put up the correct number of fingers: My turn. Watch me. *Say each word part slowly, pausing much longer than usual between syllables. Tap with one hand while raising fingers on the other. Repeat entire process.* Wall-pa-per. How many syllables did I count? Count with me.

▶ **Child's response: One. Two. Three. Three syllables.**

Yes. Wallpaper has three syllables. Let's count them again together. Wall-pa-per. Say it and count it.

▶ **Child's response: Wall-pa-per (raising three fingers).**

Yes, wall-pa-per. How many syllables did you count? *Touch each of the child's fingers as he or she counts.*

▶ **Child's response: One. Two. Three. Three syllables.**

Work with the child until he or she meets with success. If confusion persists, then try a two-syllable word. Practice the same word several times so that the child feels confident and positive. *

TEACHING TIP: It is essential to determine the child's problem—whether he or she cannot hear the separate syllables or cannot count on fingers. If counting is the problem, then provide individual practice with counting concrete objects after the lesson is over.

 PLAY the game.

CD-ROM See Appendix D on the CD-ROM for the Sue's Syllable Slide Game instructions, board, piece, cards, and word list.

 TASK 3 Silly song to end the lesson *(approximately 3 minutes)*

END Lesson 3 with a transition song.

We know a funny counting song about a boy named Johnny Boy. Everybody, what is the boy's name?

▶ **Children's response: Johnny Boy.**

Yes, Johnny Boy. Let's sing that song. We can count how old Johnny Boy was on our fingers, from one to five.

SING the song with the children, showing one to five on your fingers.

When Johnny Boy was one, he learned to suck his thumb.
Thumbalina, Thumbalina, half past one.
When Johnny Boy was two, he learned to tie his shoe.
Shoebalina, Shoebalina, half past two.
When Johnny Boy was three, he learned to climb a tree.
Treebalina, Treebalina, half past three.
When Johnny Boy was four, he learned to shut the door.
Doorbalina, Doorbalina, half past four.
When Johnny Boy was five, he learned to take a dive.
Divealina, Divealina, half past five.

Repeat the song once or twice, as time permits. Nice job singing about Johnny Boy. Now, get ready to show me who can count word parts on your fingers all by yourself.

DO the exit task to demonstrate skill mastery.

_____ *(insert child's name)*, your turn. Listen. Mos–qui–to. Say it and count it.

▶ **Child's response: Mosquito (raising three fingers).**

Yes, mosquito. Let me check your fingers. Count with me.

▶ **Child: One. Two. Three. Three syllables.**

Let each child have one turn. Use words from today's lesson. You all did a good job today. Everyone now gets their winnings for learning how to hear and count syllables on your fingers and for working hard. *Give out token rewards to each child.*

END Lesson 3.

LESSON 4: Syllable Segmentation Review

OBJECTIVES

Student will

- Demonstrate the ability to listen carefully to the separate sounds of multisyllabic words
- Tap and stomp multisyllablic words out in multi-sensory practice
- Count syllables on fingers

Teacher will

- Review segmenting of multisyllabic words
- Guide students to demonstrate the skill independently in two game formats

RHYMES, SONGS, AND FINGERPLAYS

"Three Green and Speckled Frogs"

MATERIALS

One syllable stick for each child

- ☑ DROPP 8 Skill Assessment Checkout (see Appendix B on the CD-ROM)
- ☑ Tokens for behavior/participation

Syllable Stomp Game

- ☑ Stomping board (see Appendix D on the CD-ROM)
- ☑ Game cards (see Appendix D on the CD-ROM)

Sue's Syllable Slide Game

- ☑ Game board (see Appendix D on the CD-ROM)
- ☑ Game cards (see Appendix D on the CD-ROM)
- ☑ Game piece (see Appendix D on the CD-ROM)
- ☑ Word list (see Appendix D on the CD-ROM)

TEACHING TIP: Some children may be able to segment two-syllable compound words but may struggle with longer, noncompound words. As you deliver this lesson, note where students' individual comfort zones occur to aid in your assessment of their varying degrees of skill mastery.

 TASK 1   Song to begin the lesson (approximately 3 minutes)

INTRODUCE the lesson.	*Settle the group at a table and say the following.* You have been learning how to listen, tap, and stomp out the word parts, or syllables, of words and count them on your fingers. Today we will count syllables in all of the ways that you have learned.
INTRODUCE the new song with motions.	First, I will sing you a new counting song about some green frogs. Watch my fingers and see what happens as the frogs hop away. Do what I do and sing along if you know the song. *See http://www.youtube.com/watch?v=FPxZLtXK8Yw for demonstration of music and song motions.*

Three green and speckled frogs *(Show three fingers on one hand)*
Sat on a speckled log *("Sit" that hand on opposite arm)*
Eating some most delicious bugs *(Gesture as if eating)*
Yum. Yum. *(Rub your stomach and smile).*
One jumped into the pool *("Jump" your hand downward)*
Where it was nice and cool
Now there were *(pause, put down one finger and emphasize two remaining fingers)*

▶ Children's response: Two.

Two green speckled frogs.

Second verse; same hand motions. Two green and speckled frogs
Sat on a speckled log
Eating some most delicious bugs
Yum. Yum.
One jumped into the pool
Where it was nice and cool

Now there was *(pause, put down one finger and emphasize last remaining finger)*

▶ Children's response: One.

One green speckled frog.

Third verse; same hand motions. One green and speckled frog
Sat on a speckled log
Eating some most delicious bugs
Yum. Yum.
He jumped into the pool
Where it was nice and cool
Now there were *(pause, put down last finger and emphasize none remaining)*

▶ Children's response: None.

No green speckled frogs.

 TASK 2A   Reviewing syllable segmentation with Syllable Stomp *(approximately 9 minutes)*

 Turn On Your Ears

 Vocabulary

SYLLABLE

You are learning how to be such careful listeners. You know how to use your ears to hear rhymes. You can hear short words and long words. Now you know how to blend together the word parts, called syl-la-bles. What word did I just say?

▶ Children's response: Syllables.

Yes. Good job saying that word the fast way. You know a big word, called syllables, that means word parts. A syllable is a word part. What is a syllable?

▶ Children's response: A word part.

Yes, a syllable is a word part. You are learning how to tap out, stomp out, and count syllables on your fingers. That means you can hear the word parts that go together to make words. You are smart learners who are learning about words.

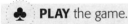 **PLAY** the game.

> **CD-ROM** See Appendix D on the CD-ROM for the Syllable Stomp Game instructions, stomping board, and game cards.

A suggested mix of multisyllabic words from more to less difficult: skateboard, dragonfly, bathtub, dishwasher, tiger, spider, monkey, crocodile, donkey, dinosaur, turkey, elephant

---

 TASK 2B   Sue's Syllable Slide Game *(approximately 8 minutes)*

 PLAY the game.

> **CD-ROM** See Appendix D on the CD-ROM for the Sue's Syllable Slide game instructions, board, piece, cards, and word list.

END Lesson 4.

You all did a good job today. Everyone now gets their winnings for hearing, tapping, and stomping the syllables in words and for working hard. *Give out token rewards to each child.*

> **CD-ROM** The DROPP 8 Skill Assessment Checkout will be completed for each student following this lesson.

ACTIVITY SET 8.2

Lesson Descriptions

Lessons	Sequence of daily activities	◇ Vocabulary
Lesson 1: Syllable Sticks	Song: "Three Green and Speckled Frogs" Target: Tap to segment one- to three-syllable words Song: "Thumbalina"	Syllable
Lesson 2: Syllable Stomp	Fingerplay: "Sleepy Caterpillars" Target: Game—Hopping to segment syllables Fingerplay: "There Was a Little Turtle"	Awaken Stomp
Lesson 3: Sue's Syllable Slide	Nursery rhyme: "Cackle, Cackle, Mother Goose" Target: Syllable Segmentation Board Song: "Three Green and Speckled Frogs"	Down (Goose) down Speckled
Lesson 4: Syllable Segmentation Review	Nursery rhyme: "Cackle, Cackle, Mother Goose" Review Task 2A: Syllable Stomp Game Review Task 2B: Sue's Syllable Slide Game with multisyllabic words	Down (Goose) down Syllable

Materials Needed

☑ 10 animal picture cards (5 with one-syllable words, including frog, and 5 with three-syllable names, including elephant)

☑ 6–10 picture cards with one- to three-syllable words, including bug, bee, horsefly, and butterfly

☑ One short stick (e.g., popsicle stick) and one long stick (e.g., tongue depressor) for each child and teacher

☑ Syllable Sort Chart (prepared ahead of time; see directions in text)

☑ Optional: Picture of goose; goose or duck feather; nursery rhyme book with "Cackle, Cackle, Mother Goose"

☑ Picture of a caterpillar

> ☑ DROPP 8 Skill Assessment Checkout (see Appendix B on the CD-ROM)
> ☑ Tokens for behavior/participation
>
> **Syllable Stick Tap-It-Out Game**
>
> ☑ Syllable stick   ☑ Sample syllable sort chart
> ☑ Colored chips (up to three per child)
> ☑ Game cards (see Appendix D on the CD-ROM)
> ☑ Word list (see Appendix D on the CD-ROM)
>
> **Syllable Stomp Game**
>
> ☑ Stomping board (see Appendix D on the CD-ROM)
> ☑ Game cards (see Appendix D on the CD-ROM)
> ☑ Word list (see Appendix D on the CD-ROM)
>
> **Sue's Syllable Slide Game**
>
> ☑ Game board (see Appendix D on the CD-ROM)
> ☑ Game cards (see Appendix D on the CD-ROM)
> ☑ Game piece (see Appendix D on the CD-ROM)
> ☑ Word list (see Appendix D on the CD-ROM)

CD-ROM

ACTIVITY SET 8.2 10-Day Planner

Day 1	**Lesson 1:** Syllable Sticks
Day 2	**Lesson 1:** Syllable Sticks
Day 3	**Lesson 2:** Syllable Stomp
Day 4	**Lesson 2:** Syllable Stomp
Day 5	**Lesson 3:** Sue's Syllable Slide
Day 6	**Lesson 3:** Sue's Syllable Slide
Day 7	**Lesson 1:** Syllable Sticks
Day 8	**Lesson 2:** Syllable Stomp
Day 9	**Lesson 3:** Sue's Syllable Slide
Day 10	**Lesson 4:** Syllable Segmentation Review

LESSON 1: Syllable Sticks

OBJECTIVES

Student will

- Learn how to separate (segment) two- to three-syllable words by tapping out each syllable

Teacher will

- Review long and short words
- Model how to segment two- to three-syllable words
- Guide students to hear and segment word parts

RHYMES, SONGS, AND FINGERPLAYS

"Three Green and Speckled Frogs"

"Thumbalina"

MATERIALS

10 animal picture cards (5 with one-syllable names, including frog, and 5 with three-syllable names, including elephant)

One short stick (e.g., popsicle stick) and one long stick (e.g., tongue depressor) for each child

Syllable sort chart (prepared ahead of time; see directions in lesson)

Tokens for behavior/participation

Syllable Stick Tap-It-Out Game

- ☑ Game cards (see Appendix D on the CD-ROM)
- ☑ Word list (see Appendix D on the CD-ROM)
- ☑ Syllable stick
- ☑ Colored chips (up to three per child)

 TASK 1   **Song to begin the lesson** (approximately 3 minutes)

INTRODUCE the big idea of syllable segmentation.	*Settle the children into their seats and say the following.* You know how to listen to the word parts, or syllables, in short words and long words. Today we will listen to some short words and tap out their syllables.
	Listen. I said that a word part is called a syllable. Say that word.
	▶ Children's response: Syllable.
 **Vocabulary** **SYLLABLE**	Yes, syllable. Say it again. *Repeat until all say it clearly.* A syllable is a word part. What is a syllable?
	▶ Children's response: A word part.
	Yes, a syllable is a word part. You are learning how to hear and tap out syllables in words. That means you will hear how words are made up of word parts. Good learning.
BEGIN the transition activity.	I have a funny new song for you. It is about some little spotted and speckled frogs that live in a pond of water. Listen while I sing you the song. Watch my fingers and do what I do to make the song more fun.
SING the song.	Three green and speckled frogs *(Show three fingers on one hand)* Sat on a speckled log *("Sit" that hand on opposite arm)* Eating some most delicious bugs *(Gesture as if eating)* Yum. Yum. *(Rub your stomach and smile)* One jumped into the pool *("Jump" your hand downward)* Where it was nice and cool Now there are two green speckled frogs. *(Hold up two fingers)*
SING the second verse.	*Continue singing with the same hand gestures. Encourage children to chime in where possible, with "yum yum" and the numbers, as follows.*
	One jumped into the pool *(Hold up one pointer finger, then make a jumping down motion with your hand)*

8.2

END with the third verse.	Where it was nice and cool Now there is *(pause with one finger up; children say "one")* one green speckled frog. *Repeat gestures, drawing children into song and gestures as much as possible.* Now there are no green speckled frogs.

 **TASK 2**   Hearing and segmenting syllables in words *(approximately 12–14 minutes)*

LINK the song to syllable awareness.	Good job helping me count in our silly song. Listen. Some of the words were short, such as *green* and *frog,* but some of the words were longer and had more word parts, such as *delicious. Gesture with your hands to show short and longer words.*
REVIEW syllable awareness: Short words.	Let's say those short, little words with only one syllable. Say each word after me. Green. Say it. ▶ **Children's response: Green.** Yes, green. Frog. Say it. ▶ **Children's response: Frog.** Yes, frog. *Continue in the same format, practicing five to six more words. Additional one-syllable words: sat, log, one, bugs, pool, and cool.*
SKILL review: Rhyme recognition—pool, cool.	Good job saying short words with one syllable. You said pool and cool. Hey, do they rhyme? *Look around at each student.* ▶ **Children's response: Yes.** Yes. They rhyme. Let's sing our rhyming song. Follow me.
SING the "Rhyming Exercise Song."	Put your hands in the sky. *On the word hands, stretch one arm up to the sky and then the other arm.* Do the rhyming exercise. *As you sing, switch and stretch arms one by one.*
🖐 **Multisensory Reinforcement**	Pool *(Stretch one arm up.)* Cool *(Stretch the other arm up.)* Pool *(Switch arms.)* Cool *(Switch arms.)* Pool *(Switch arms.)* Cool *(Switch arms.)* Do they rhyme? *Pause here and allow them to show thumbs up or down before you respond. Look around at each student and make eye contact.* Yes. *Nod vigorously.* They rhyme! *Give two thumbs up.*
INTRODUCE hand gestures for syllable awareness.	*In the following activity, use your hands, palms facing each other as if measuring length. As you say the longer words, extend the distance between your hands about 1 foot with each syllable, until hands are wide apart.*
REVIEW syllable awareness: Longer words.	Now let's say some longer words with more syllables. Say these words. De-li-cious. Say it. *Be sure to use a 2-second pause between syllables.* ▶ **Children's response: Delicious.** Yes, delicious. Speck-led. Say it.

▶ **Children's response: Speckled.**

Yes, speckled.

Continue in the same format, practicing five to six more words. Use these additional longer words: helicopter, watermelon, rhinoceros, dinosaur, crocodile, *and* porcupine.

TEACHING TIP: When possible, insert vocabulary words you are studying from other content areas.

SORT pictures of short and long words, using sticks for visual demonstration.	*Assemble 10 picture cards (5 with one-syllable names and 5 with three-syllable names) and prepare a Syllable Sort Chart ahead of time. Draw a short line at the top of the left column, draw a long line at the top of the right column, and make rows under each column for pictures. Give each child a short and a long stick.*

Good job saying short and long words! Now I want you to help me measure some short and long words. My turn. I will say some picture names. One will be short and one will be long. I wonder if my ears can hear which is short *(measure a short distance with your hands)* and which is long *(measure a longer distance).* Let's turn on our best listening ears.

Turn On Your Ears

Frog. Frog. *Show a picture of a frog.* That is a short little word.

Elephant. El-e-phant. *Show a picture of an elephant.* I can hear that this is a long word.

Look. *Point to the short line at the top of the left column. Put frog picture in the left column and elephant picture in right column.* This is a short line, so I will put the frog in this row because *frog* is a short little word. I will put the elephant in the other row where the line is longer because *elephant* is a longer word.

PRACTICE the skill.

Let's sort some more words together. First we will say the words. Listen hard to see if the word is short, with one syllable, or long, with more syllables. Hold up your short stick if the word is short and your long stick if the word is long.

First word: bug. *Show picture.* Say it.

▶ **Children's response: Bug.**

Yes, bug. Hold up a stick to show me if you heard a short word or a long word.

▶ **Children's response is to hold up a short stick.**

Yes, *bug* is a short word. So I will put the picture under the short line.

Next word: porcupine. Say it.

▶ **Children's response: Porcupine.**

Yes, porcupine. *Show the picture and say the word.*

CONTINUE until all 10 pictures are sorted.

▶ **Children repeat word. Children hold up long or short stick to sort words by length.**

Place picture in correct column. When all pictures have been sorted on the chart, collect the short sticks.

INTRODUCE syllable sticks.

Great job sorting long and short words. Let's check our work by saying the words. Short words first. *Say each short word with the children. Then hold up the longer stick.*

I call the long stick my syllable stick. I can use it to tap out each syllable in the long words. Watch me. El-e-phant. *Tap out syllables using the longer stick. Tap three times.* I tapped out each syllable in *elephant.* Let's see if you can do it with me. El-e-phant. Say it.

8.2

▶ **(Children respond by tapping three times.)**

Wonderful. You are listening so well that you can hear all of the syllables in a long word and tap them out with your syllable stick. Let's practice tapping out the syllables in some more long words. Say each word after me, and tap once for each syllable. First word: dinosaur. Say it and tap it.

▶ **Children's response is to tap three times.**

Yes, dinosaur. We tapped for each syllable in dinosaur. *Tap all of the remaining three-syllable words in the long column on the syllable chart. Use a correction procedure if a child does not tap the correct number of times.*

***Correction procedure (if a child does not tap the correct number of times):** Jel-ly-fish. Spread hands wider with each syllable.* Watch me tap for each syllable. Jel-ly-fish. *Tap distinctly three times.* Let's tap it out together. Jellyfish. Say it with me.

▶ **Child's response: Jellyfish.**

Let's say it slowly while we tap it out.

*Work with the child until he or she meets with success. If confusion persists, then try a two-syllable word. Practice the same word several times so that the child feels confident and positive.**

ENGAGE in group practice in tapping out syllables.

Examples of one- and three-syllable words for sorting and tapping:

One-syllable words	Three-syllable words
pig	ladybug
goat	buffalo
dog	gorilla
bear	crocodile
bird	kangaroo
duck	dragonfly

 PLAY the game.

 CD-ROM   See Appendix D on the CD-ROM for the Syllable Stick Tap-It-Out Game instructions, cards, and word list.

 TASK 3   **Song to end the lesson** *(approximately 3 minutes)*

END the lesson with a transition song.

I know a funny counting song about a boy named Johnny Boy. Everybody, what is the boy's name?

▶ **Children's response: Johnny Boy.**

Yes, Johnny Boy. I am going to sing that song. If you know this song, then sing it with me. We can count how old Johnny Boy was on our fingers, from one to five.

SING the song with the children, showing one to five on your fingers.

When Johnny Boy was one, he learned to suck his thumb.
Thumbalina, Thumbalina, half past one.
When Johnny Boy was two, he learned to tie his shoe.
Shoebalina, Shoebalina, half past two.
When Johnny Boy was three, he learned to climb a tree.
Treebalina, Treebalina, half past three.
When Johnny Boy was four, he learned to shut the door.
Doorbalina, Doorbalina, half past four.
When Johnny Boy was five, he learned to take a dive.
Divealina, Divealina, half past five.

DO the exit task to demonstrate skill mastery.

Repeat the song once or twice, as time permits. Nice job singing about Johnny Boy. Now get ready to show me who can tap out the syllables in a word all by yourself.

_____ *(insert child's name)*, your turn. Listen. El-e-phant. Say it and tap it.

▶ **Child's response: Elephant (three taps).**

Yes, elephant. Good job tapping out the word parts in elephant.

Let each child have one turn. Use words from today's lesson.

END Lesson 1.

You all did a good job today! Everyone now gets their winnings for hearing the syllables in words and for working hard. *Give out token rewards to each child.*

LESSON 2: Syllable Stomp

OBJECTIVES

Student will

- Learn how to segment syllables in words by jumping to show how many syllables are heard

Teacher will

- Model how to segment two- and three-syllable words
- Guide students to hear and segment word parts
- Teach children an action game that uses multi-sensory learning to reinforce the segmenting of syllables
- Watch each student's success and provide supports as needed

RHYMES, SONGS, AND FINGERPLAYS

"Sleepy Caterpillars"

"There Was a Little Turtle"

MATERIALS

One syllable stick (e.g., tongue depressor) for each child

6–10 picture cards with one- to three-syllable names, including bug, bee, horsefly, and butterfly

Picture of a caterpillar

Tokens for behavior/participation

Syllable Stomp Game

☑ Stomping board (see Appendix D on the CD-ROM)

☑ Game cards (see Appendix D on the CD-ROM)

 **TASK 1**   **Fingerplay to begin the lesson** (approximately 3 minutes)

INTRODUCE the lesson; review the big idea: syllable segmentation.

Say the following to the group after settling the children together at a table. You know how to listen to short words and long words and to tap out their word parts, called syllables. Today we will say and tap out the syllables in some new words and then play a game called Syllable Stomp.

⭐ **Model the Activity**

This insect is called a caterpillar. *Show caterpillar picture.* Everybody, what is this insect called?

▶ Children's response: A caterpillar.

Yes, a caterpillar. We learned that a caterpillar is an insect that starts out like a worm and then turns into a butterfly. *Show butterfly picture.* What does a caterpillar turn into?

▶ Children's response: A butterfly.

Yes, a caterpillar turns into a butterfly.

 Turn On Your Ears

Let's practice our fingerplay about sleepy caterpillars. Watch my fingers and do what I do to tell a story about caterpillars turning into butterflies. Listen up; turn on your ears! Say it with me, watch, and move your fingers like me.

8.2

Let's go to sleep, the caterpillars said. *(Wiggle pointer finger.)*
As they tuck themselves into their beds. *(Close fist around finger.)*
They will awaken by and by *(Rock closed hand like a cradle.)*
And each one will be a lovely butterfly. *(Open hand, one finger at a time; make your hand "fly" away while flapping thumb and little finger as wings.)*

Let's say it again. *Repeat each line of the fingerplay slowly, leading them in the words and movements.* Good job remembering our fingerplay.

REVIEW syllable blending and segmenting, including words from the song.

Now I am going to say some insect names. See if you can guess which insect's name I am saying. Listen. But-ter-fly. Say it fast.

▶ **Children's response: Butterfly.**

Yes, butterfly.

New word: cat-er-pil-lar. Say it fast.

▶ **Children's response: Caterpillar.**

Yes, caterpillar.

Grass-hop-per. Say it fast.

▶ **Children's response: Grasshopper.**

Yes, grasshopper.

New word: bum-ble-bee. Say it fast.

▶ **Children's response: Bumblebee.**

Yes, bumblebee.

Good job blending word parts to hear words. Now, let's practice tapping out the syllables in those words. *Give each child a syllable stick.* Say each word after me, and tap once for each syllable.

First word: butterfly. Say it and tap it.

▶ **Children's response is to tap three times.**

Yes, but-ter-fly. We tapped for each syllable in butterfly. *Follow same format for remaining words (caterpillar, grasshopper, bumblebee).* Good job tapping out the syllables and saying the names of some insects.

 Vocabulary

AWAKEN

Think about this—the caterpillars tucked themselves into bed and fell asleep. Then they awakened. What does awaken mean? *Accept several responses.* Awaken means to wake up. Let's pretend that we are asleep and then we will awaken. What will we do after we sleep?

▶ **Children's response: Awaken.**

Yes, awaken. Show me awaken. *Have everyone act out being asleep and waking up.* Let's stretch our arms as we awaken. *Stretch arms overhead.* There, we are all awake. We awakened. Who can tell me a sentence about awaken? *Encourage several examples.* Good job using our new word *awaken.*

PERFORM the fingerplay again.

Now let's say our fingerplay again. When the caterpillar awakens, we will make our fingers fly like a butterfly.

 **TASK 2** | Syllable Stomp *(approximately 12–14 minutes)*

LINK the transition fingerplay to segmenting syllables.

Multisensory Reinforcement

ENGAGE in group practice using one- to three-syllable words.

I like the "Sleepy Caterpillars" fingerplay. I like the way you listened to the word parts, or syllables, in the longer words. *Practice tapping out several short words.*

Let's tap out some more words to show how well we can hear syllables. We'll start with short words that only have one syllable. They only need one tap.

First word *(show picture)*: bug. Say it and tap it.

▶ **Children's response: Bug (one tap).**

Yes, bug. Next word: bee. Say it and tap it.

▶ **Children's response: Bee (one tap).**

Yes, bee. *Continue in the same format. Choose three to four more examples of one-syllable words from your deck.*

Now I will add some longer words. Listen carefully. Some words will have two or three syllables, and some will be short with only one syllable.

First word *(show picture)*: horse-fly. Say it and tap it.

▶ **Children's response: Horsefly (two taps).**

Yes, horsefly. New word: hon-ey-bee. Say it and tap it.

▶ **Children's response: Honeybee (three taps).**

Yes, honeybee. *Continue in the same format. Choose six to eight more examples of one- to three-syllable words from your deck.*

*Correction procedure if a child does not tap the correct number of times: Watch my hands: hon-ey-bee. *Spread hands wider with each syllable.* Watch me tap for each syllable. Hon-ey-bee. *Tap distinctly three times.* Let's tap it out together. Say it with me.

▶ **Child's response: Honeybee.**

Let's say it slowly while we tap it out. *Work with the child until he or she meets with success. If confusion persists, then try a two-syllable word. Practice the same word several times so that the child feels confident and positive.**

◇ Vocabulary

STOMP

Today we will have fun hearing syllables and then stomping them out on a stomping board. Listen. I said the word stomp. Who remembers what stomp means? *Accept several answers. Stomp* means to bring your foot down with a heavy step. *Model action.* Let's pretend that we are at a ball game and everyone is stomping their feet to cheer for the team. Everybody, stomp your feet on the bleachers at the ball game. We stomped our feet. What did we do?

▶ **Children's response: Stomped our feet.**

Yes. We stomped our feet at the ball game. It's fun to stomp our feet at a sports game, like baseball. Good stomping! Everybody, what do you call it when you bring your foot down hard?

▶ **Children's response: Stomp.**

Yes, when we stomp, we bring our foot down hard.

♣ PLAY the game.

CD-ROM See Appendix D on the CD-ROM for the Syllable Stomp Game instructions, stomping board, cards, and word list.

TASK 3 | Fingerplay to end the lesson (approximately 3 minutes)

END the lesson with a transition fingerplay and exit task.

We already did a fingerplay about caterpillars turning into butterflies. Let's end today's work with our fingerplay about the little turtle who snapped at some insects and other things. If you remember it, then you can say it with me. Remember to show the fingerplay on your fingers.

RECITE the fingerplay and perform the motions.

There was a little turtle. *(Make a small circle with hand.)*
He lived in a box. *(Make a box with hands.)*
He swam in a puddle. *(Wiggle hands.)*
He climbed on the rocks. *(Stack hands, one on the other.)*

He snapped at a mosquito. *(Clap hands.)*
He snapped at a flea. *(Clap hands.)*
He snapped at a minnow. *(Clap hands.)*
And he snapped at me. *(Clap hands.)*

He caught the mosquito. *(Clap hands.)*
He caught the flea. *(Clap hands.)*
He caught the minnow. *(Clap hands.)*
But he didn't catch me. *(Shake index finger.)*

DO the exit task to demonstrate skill mastery.

Use the following words, following the previous format so that each child can tap out a word successfully: little, puddle, minnow, and flea.

Nice job on our fingerplay. Now, let's see if each of you can tap out the syllables in a word from our fingerplay:

_____ *(insert child's name)*, your turn. Listen. Tur-tle. Say it and tap it.

▶ **Child's response: Turtle (two taps).**

Yes, turtle. Good job tapping out the word parts in turtle. *Let each child have one turn.*

END Lesson 2.

You all did a good job today! Everyone now gets their winnings for hearing, tapping, and stomping the syllables in words and for working hard. *Give out token rewards to each child.*

LESSON 3: Sue's Syllable Slide

OBJECTIVES

Student will

- Strengthen the ability to segment syllables in words by practicing the skill in a new game
- Be introduced to the concept of counting the number of syllables

Teacher will

- Provide explicit, guided practice in segmenting and counting the syllables in two- and three-syllable words
- Teach children a new game of syllable segmentation

RHYMES, SONGS, AND FINGERPLAYS

"Cackle, Cackle, Mother Goose"
"Three Green and Speckled Frogs"

MATERIALS

Syllable sticks (one for teacher and one for each child)

Optional: Picture of goose; goose or duck feather; nursery rhyme book with "Cackle, Cackle, Mother Goose"

Tokens for behavior/participation

Sue's Syllable Slide Game

☑ Game board (see Appendix D on the CD-ROM)

☑ Game cards (see Appendix D on the CD-ROM)

☑ Game piece (see Appendix D on the CD-ROM)

☑ Word list (see Appendix D on the CD-ROM)

TASK 1   Nursery rhyme to begin the lesson (approximately 3 minutes)

INTRODUCE the lesson. Review the big idea of syllable segmentation.

Settle the group at a table and say the following. You know how to listen to short words and long words and to tap out and stomp out their word parts, called syllables. Today we will practice hearing and tapping out syllables in our game called Sue's Syllable Slide.

INTRODUCE the rhyme.

We'll start with a nursery rhyme about a goose named Mother Goose, who has nice soft goose feathers called down. *(Optional: Show students a picture of a goose, a toy goose, and/or a feather.)* Everyone, what are the goose feathers called?

◇ **Vocabulary**

▶ **Children's response: Down.**

(GOOSE) DOWN

Yes, down. Goose feathers are called goose down or just down. Sometimes our pillows are filled with nice, soft, goose down.

Listen to the nursery rhyme. *You can wave a feather while you chant.*

SAY the nursery rhyme.

Cackle, cackle, Mother Goose.
Have you any feathers loose?
Truly have I, pretty fellow.
I have enough to fill a pillow.
Here are quills, take one or two.
And down to make a bed for you.

REINFORCE the rhyme.

I'm going to say it again. This time, see if you can help me remember the rhymes in our nursery rhyme. *Guide children to say the missing rhyme. If necessary, give them the first sound: /l/ . . . oose.*

PAUSE AND PUNCH.

Cackle, cackle, Mother Goose.
Have you any feathers . . .

▶ **Children's response: Loose.**

Truly have I, pretty fellow.
I have enough to fill a . . .

▶ **Children's response: Pillow.**

Here are quills; take one or two
And down to make a bed for . . .

▶ **Children's response: You.**

 TASK 2   Sue's Syllable Slide Game (approximately 12 minutes)

LINK the transition rhyme to syllable segmentation.

Nice job listening to our new nursery rhyme and helping me say the rhymes. Now let's tap out the syllables in some words from the rhyme. *Distribute syllable sticks.*

First word: mother. Say it and tap it.

▶ **Children's response: Mother (two taps).**

 **Multisensory Reinforcement**

Yes, mother. *Practice at least five words at a brisk pace. Switch between one- and two-syllable words.*

Next word: feather. Say it and tap it.

▶ **Children's response: Feather (two taps).**

Yes, feather.

Next word: goose. Say it and tap it.

▶ **Children's response: Goose (one tap).**

Yes, goose. Next word: fellow. Say it and tap it.

▶ **Children's response: Fellow (two taps).**

Yes, fellow. Next word: loose. Say it and tap it.

▶ **Children's response: Loose (one tap).**

Yes, loose.

When I tap out the syllables in a word, I can count how many there are. In a short word, such as *goose,* there is only one syllable. Watch me as I hear and count one syllable. Goose. *Tap with one hand while holding up one finger on the other hand.* One syllable. I heard one syllable, so I put up one finger.

Now watch me as I hear and count two syllables. Fel-low. *Tap twice with one hand while raising two fingers on the other hand, one at a time.* Fellow has two syllables, so I put up two fingers. Count with me.

▶ **Children's response: One. Two. Two syllables.**

Now watch me hear and count three syllables. Nur-ser-y. *Tap three times while raising three fingers, one at a time.* Nursery has three syllables, so I put up three fingers. Count with me.

▶ **Children's response: One. Two. Three. Three syllables.**

Great job helping me count syllables on my fingers.

Let's practice counting some more syllables. This time, you will put up your fingers to count syllables, and I will tap them out. Turn on your ears and get ready to listen hard. Get ready. *Begin with two-syllable compound words to make it easier for students to count the word parts without tapping.*

First word: dog-house. Say it and count it. *Tap twice while students raise two fingers.*

▶ **Children's response: Doghouse (raising two fingers, one at a time).**

Yes, doghouse. How many syllables did you count? Count with me.

▶ **Children's response: One. Two. Two syllables.**

Yes. You heard two syllables and you counted them on two fingers. Great job hearing syllables and counting them on your fingers. Let's do another word. Get ready. Play sta-tion. Say it and count it. *Tap three times while students raise three fingers.*

▶ **Children's response: Play station (raising three fingers, one at a time).**

Yes, play station. How many syllables did you count? Count with me.

▶ **Children's response: One. Two. Three. Three syllables.**

Practice with the whole group until the counting skill is firm. Be sure that every child repeats the words and counts on one to three fingers. Do not be tempted to count four or more syllable words at this point. Stop tapping the syllable stick as soon as students are able to hear and count the syllables without it. Examples of the sequence of words to practice include monkey, butterfly, rainbow, microwave, lion, pig, housefly, bug, turkey, crocodile, donkey, doghouse, *and* turkey.

*****Correction procedure if a child does not put up the correct number of fingers:** My turn. Watch me. Croc-o-dile. *Say each word part slowly, pausing much longer than*

Sidebar

PRACTICE syllable counting.

  Model the Activity

ENGAGE in group practice in syllable counting.

  Turn On Your Ears

ADVANCE to a mix of noncompound words with one to three syllables.

usual between syllables. Tap with one hand while raising fingers on the other. Repeat the entire process.

How many syllables did I count? Count with me.

▶ **Child's response: One. Two. Three. Three syllables.**

Yes. Crocodile has three syllables. Let's count them again together. Croc-o-dile. Say it and count it.

▶ **Child's response: Croc-o-dile (raising three fingers).**

Yes, Crocodile. How many syllables did you count? *Touch each of the child's fingers as he or she counts.*

▶ **Child's response: One. Two. Three. Three syllables.**

Work with the child until he or she meets with success. If confusion persists, then try a two-syllable word. Practice the same word several times so that the child feels confident and positive. *

♣ **PLAY** the game.

CD-ROM | See Appendix D on the CD-ROM for the Sue's Syllable Slide Game instructions, board, piece, cards, and word list.

 TASK 3   **Song to end the lesson** *(approximately 3 minutes)*

END Lesson 3 with a transition song.

We know a counting song about some green and speckled frogs. Let's sing that song. We can count the frogs on our fingers, from one to three.

SING the song.

Three green and speckled frogs *(Show three fingers on one hand)*
Sat on a speckled log *("Sit" that hand on opposite arm)*
Eating some most delicious bugs *(Gesture as if eating)*
Yum. Yum. *(Rub your stomach and smile)*
One jumped into the pool *("Jump" your hand downward)*
Where it was nice and cool
Now there are two green speckled frogs. *(Hold up two fingers)*

SING the second verse.

Continue singing with the same hand gestures. Encourage children to chime in where possible, with "yum yum" and the numbers, as follows.

One jumped into the pool *(Hold up one pointer finger, then make a jumping down motion with your hand)*
Where it was nice and cool
Now there is *(pause with one finger up; children say "one")* one green speckled frog.

END with the third verse.

Repeat gestures, drawing children into song and gestures as much as possible.

Now there are no green speckled frogs.

 Vocabulary

SPECKLED

Nice job singing about our three green and speckled frogs. Listen. I said that the frogs were speckled. Who knows what *speckled* means? *Accept one or two responses.* Speckled means spotted. Everyone, what does speckled mean?

▶ Children's response: Spotted.

Yes, speckled means spotted. Everyone, what is another word for spotted?

▶ Children's response: Speckled.

Yes, speckled. So our three frogs were green and spotted. They had spots, called speckles, on them. Did you ever see something that was speckled? *Accept several responses.*

DO the exit task to demonstrate skill mastery.	Now get ready to show me who can count word parts on your fingers all by yourself.
	_____ (insert child's name), your turn. Listen. Speck-led. Say it and count it.
	▶ **Child's response:** Speckled (raising two fingers).
	Yes, speckled. Let me check your fingers. Count with me.
	▶ **Child:** One. Two. Two syllables.
	Let each child have one turn. Use words from today's lesson.
END Lesson 3.	You all did a good job today! Everyone now gets their winnings for learning how to hear and count syllables on your fingers and for working hard. *Give out token rewards to each child.*

LESSON 4: Syllable Segmentation Review

OBJECTIVES

Student will

- Demonstrate the ability to listen carefully to the separate sounds of multisyllabic words
- Tap and stomp multisyllabic words out in multi-sensory practice
- Count syllables on fingers

Teacher will

- Review segmenting of multisyllabic words
- Guide students to demonstrate the skill independently in two game formats

RHYMES, SONGS, AND FINGERPLAYS

"Cackle, Cackle, Mother Goose"

MATERIALS

One syllable stick for each child
DROPP 8 Skill Assessment Checkout
Tokens for behavior/participation

Syllable Stomp Game
☑ Stomping board (see Appendix D on the CD-ROM)
☑ Deck of small picture cards with two- and three-syllable names

Sue's Syllable Slide Game
☑ Game board (see Appendix D on the CD-ROM)
☑ Game cards (see Appendix D on the CD-ROM)
☑ One game piece (see Appendix D on the CD-ROM)

TEACHING TIP: Some children may be able to segment two-syllable compound words but may struggle with longer, noncompound words. As you deliver this lesson, note where students' individual comfort zones occur to aid in your assessment of their varying degrees of skill mastery.

 TASK 1 | **Nursery rhyme to begin the lesson** (approximately 3 minutes)

INTRODUCE the lesson.	*Settle the group at a table and say the following.* You have been learning how to listen, tap, and stomp out the word parts, or syllables, of words and count them on your fingers. Today we will count syllables in all of the ways that you have learned.
INTRODUCE the rhyme.	We'll start with our nursery rhyme called "Cackle, Cackle, Mother Goose" about Mother Goose and her nice soft goose feathers called down. *(Optional: Show students a picture of a goose, a toy goose, and/or a feather.)* Who remembers what the goose feathers are called?

 **Vocabulary** **(GOOSE) DOWN**	▶ Children's response: Down. Yes, down. Goose feathers are called goose down or just down. Sometimes our pillows are filled with nice, soft, goose down.
SAY the nursery rhyme.	Listen to the nursery rhyme. If you remember it, you can say it with me. *You can wave a feather while you chant.* Cackle, cackle, Mother Goose. Have you any feathers loose? Truly have I, pretty fellow. I have enough to fill a pillow. Here are quills; take one or two And down to make a bed for you.
REINFORCE the rhyme.	I'm going to say it again. This time, see if you can help me remember the rhymes in our nursery rhyme. *Guide children to say the missing rhyme. If necessary, give them the first sound: /l/ . . . oose.*
PAUSE AND PUNCH.	Cackle, cackle, Mother Goose. Have you any feathers . . . ▶ Children's response: Loose. Truly have I, pretty fellow. I have enough to fill a . . . ▶ Children's response: Pillow. Here are quills, take one or two. And down to make a bed for . . . ▶ Children's response: You.

 TASK 2A Syllable Stomp *(approximately 9 minutes)*

Turn On Your Ears	You are learning how to be such careful listeners. You know how to use your ears to hear rhymes. You can hear short words and long words. Now you know how to blend together the word parts. A word part is called a syl-la-ble. What word did I just say?
Vocabulary **SYLLABLE**	▶ Children's response: Syllable. Yes, syllable. A syllable is a word part. What is a syllable? ▶ Children's response: A word part. Yes, a syllable is a word part. You are learning how to hear and tap out syllables in words. That means you will hear how words are made up of word parts. Good learning!
PLAY the game.	**CD-ROM** See Appendix D on the CD-ROM for the Syllable Stomp Game instructions, stomping board, cards, and word list.

TASK 2B Sue's Syllable Slide Game (approximately 8 minutes)

♣ **PLAY** the game.

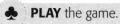 See Appendix D on the CD-ROM for the Sue's Syllable Slide Game instructions, board, piece, cards, and word list.

END Lesson 4.

You all did a good job today! Everyone now gets their winnings for hearing, tapping, and stomping the syllables in words and for working hard. *Give out token rewards to each child.*

 The DROPP 8 Skill Assessment Checkout will be completed for each student following this lesson.

Blending Awareness

Overview

WHY BLENDING AWARENESS IS IMPORTANT

Exposing pre-K students to auditory blending awareness through listening to onset-rimes (word families) and smaller speech sounds (phonemes) and orally blending them into words lays an important foundation for learning to read. Children build their understanding of the alphabet and phonics when they manipulate the sounds of phonemes and translate these sounds into symbols.

HOW DROPP 9 IS STRUCTURED

DROPP 9 has two Activity Sets—9.1 and 9.2. Each Activity Set consists of four scripted lessons (Teacher Talk) that are used on 10 sequential learning days (the four lessons are repeated over the 10-day span). DROPP 9 has a total of 20 days of intervention lessons designed to develop and practice students' blending skills. During the first 9 days of each set, students are learning to "say it the fast way" and blend sounds together by playing games specifically targeted to this skill. On the 10th day, the children practice all of the skills to prepare for a short skill assessment checkout. (See the CD-ROM for the DROPP 9 Skill Assessment Checkout.)

Length of Activity Sets and Lessons

Each Activity Set is designed to be delivered across 10 sequential learning days. Each day's intervention lesson, including the transition activities, takes about 20 minutes to complete.

Goal and Emphasis of the Blending Awareness Lessons

The goal of Activity Sets 9.1 and 9.2 is to help students feel comfortable and successful at hearing sounds and blending them together to make words. The first 2 days of Activity Sets 9.1 and 9.2 emphasize onset-rimes. Onset-rimes are smaller than syllables but larger than phonemes, so it is appropriate that young learners begin to practice hearing sounds and blending them into known words. A teaching technique called "say it the fast way," which helps them understand that sounds that are said quickly become words, is also emphasized. Once the students learn this method, present words with two and three phonemes and ask them to be "word hunters" as they hunt for pictures of the new words they made by saying them the fast way. We observed that the students who were blending sounds into words had an easier time later on with phoneme segmentation and phonics—the key to decoding.

> TEACHING TIP: **Check for Success**
>
> During every activity, maintain eye contact with the students, and ensure they are responding correctly and on cue. In this way, you are doing a mini assessment for each child to see who may need additional help at every step of the way.

Student Objectives

Students will know how to blend sounds to form words by doing the following activities:

- Orally blending onset-rimes (word families) into a whole word by saying them the fast way

- Orally blending two phonemes into one-syllable words by saying them the fast way and using a picture stimulus in the Word Hunter Game

- Orally blending two to three phonemes into one-syllable words by saying them the fast way and using a picture stimulus in the Blending Card Game

Teacher Objectives

The teacher will expose students to blending awareness by having them listen to onset-rimes (word families) and smaller speech sounds (phonemes) and orally blend them into words.

The teacher will accomplish this by doing the following activities:

- Emphasizing onset-rimes so students can clearly hear that the endings of words from the same word family sound the same

- Emphasizing two or three phoneme sounds so students can clearly hear them, and at the same time, stretching out the phoneme sounds for auditory ease of blending

- Associating the term *say it the fast way* with blending the sounds together to make a new word

- Checking that all students are fully focused on the target sounds and pictures

> TEACHING TIP: **Positive Teaching Approach**
>
> Continually smile and nod affirmations to your students, even when they make mistakes or find the lesson difficult. Your time with them is clearly instructional, but the content is fun and the goal is always success for all students.

HOW BLENDING AWARENESS ACTIVITY SETS DEVELOP EARLY LITERACY

Multisensory Techniques

In Activity Sets 9.1 and 9.2, children continue to use both fine motor skills and large muscle movements to emphasize rhyming words in songs and fingerplays. They are becoming so attuned to hearing rhyming words that they can anticipate the rhyme mentally and make a verbal prediction of what the rhyming word will be. The students are also beginning to employ visual, auditory, and verbal clues as they view selected picture cards, listen for small sounds that make up spoken words, and then blend the sounds together by saying them "the fast way" to form words. Children who are having additional trouble with blending onsets and rimes will use blending blocks as a concrete way to see how different onset sounds are blended with a stationary rime.

Making Meaning and Building Vocabulary

As students go through Activity Sets 9.1 and 9.2, they are exposed to new vocabulary words associated with songs, fingerplays, and games.

- Activity Set 9.1: *blend, hunt*

- Activity Set 9.2: *pufferbelllies*

These new words are listed at the beginning of each Activity Set and are presented in a two-step approach (see Chapter 2). Although some of these words are not common ones that children hear often in everyday speech, we recommend using these words throughout the day and in a variety of ways (e.g., meaningful conversation, dramatic play, storytelling) to reinforce student vocabulary and oral language growth. Encourage students to use the words when talking to each other. Set time aside to give them the opportunity to engage in meaningful conversation with their peers.

Children also are producing many words through auditory blending that they may or may not have heard before. One way of reinforcing either known or new words is through visual images so that all blending activities have pictures associated with the target words. Choose one or two of these words daily and discuss meaning and context. Scaffold student use by giving children as much time and opportunity as possible to create connections with words.

Print Awareness

Students will have the opportunity to take part in the read-aloud during the Literature Link in Lesson 1 of Activity Set 9.1, thereby experiencing the left-to-right progression of word reading and reviewing their familiarity with the overall framework of using a book. One rhyming book (*Hop on Pop*; LeSieg, 1963) is used in DROPP 9 for students to hear onsets and rimes in the context of a story. Students will then use those and build on the onset-rime concept as they blend sounds to make new words. They also will be blending sounds into words and choosing one picture from a set of three on each card that matches the target word. The students will be identifying the pictures from top to bottom on the card, which helps to reinforce concepts about how print is read.

GENERAL TIPS FOR IMPLEMENTING ACTIVITY SETS 9.1 AND 9.2

In Activity Sets 9.1 and 9.2, your students will learn the words and hand movements to a hunting song, practice fingerplays, and listen to a story to begin the onset-rime lesson. Many games are introduced in these Activity Sets: the Say It the Fast Way, Word Hunter, Hunt the Rhymes, and Blending Card games.

Before teaching these Activity Sets, please check the following word lists in Appendix E: Resources on the CD-ROM for the correct method the teacher must use to train students to telescope sounds. Telescoping begins with the teacher holding a series of blended sounds for a fraction of a second (e.g., /mmaaann/). Students then translate the string of slowly blended sounds by saying it the fast way to make a familiar word (i.e., *man*). Telescoping sounds directly demonstrates that words are formed by saying strings of sounds together (Carnine, Silbert, & Kame'enui, 1997). For successful lessons, teachers must be able to slowly blend sounds for students to hear the phonemes in this way. Please see the lists on the CD-ROM for the letter sounds that are held (e.g., /fff/) and for stop sounds (e.g., /b/).

In Activity Set 9.1, students listen for onsets and rimes as they play Say It the Fast Way. Use any book on word families to give you ideas. This game uses an effective technique called Say It the Fast Way to help students learn to blend sounds into words (i.e., telescoping). The teacher says a series of blended sounds, meaning that he or she holds those sounds for a fraction of a second. The students listen to these slower blended sounds to give them the auditory opportunity to hear every phoneme. Then, they take the slow-blended sounds and say them the fast way—at the normal conversational rate of speaking or reading aloud—and make a word they know. In Lessons 2 and 3, students are shown pictures to help guide their responses. Here is an example.

Everyone, close your eyes and blend these slow sounds together in your brain. Get ready to listen! *(Pause.)* /Sshhooe/. *(Say the two sounds clearly but hold the sounds.)* /Sshhooe/. Open your eyes, everyone, and say it the fast way!

▶ Children's response: Shoe.

Hunt for the picture of the word you just made.

▶ (Children respond by touching the picture of the shoe.)

In Activity Set 9.2, we used three colored blending blocks for onset and rime auditory blending as additional multisensory support. When working with the blending blocks, we found that it made more sense to the students if we stood or stooped behind students so they could see the left-to-right progression of blending sounds into words. Otherwise, it will be necessary to work backward (if you are sitting at a table) so that students are not blending the sounds opposite from the way they will later decode words. This skill lays the foundation for phoneme segmentation, so using the correct direction is very important. After working with blocks for awhile, it may be possible to work backward or upside down, but one must always be vigilant of directionality.

TEACHING TIP: **Using Visual Cues**

Try to find pictures of as many two-phoneme words as possible to cue students for blending sounds into known words to enhance their phonological awareness. This can be introduced as part of a pre-K program because it is an auditory activity and does not require students to know letter names or read any words. Auditory blending awareness is an important skill to grasp as it is directly related to sounding out words when students move into phonics. Research recommends that children learn to blend sounds together first and then segment later on in kindergarten (Carnine et al., 1997). Pictures help students focus on the sounds and make sense of them. You may choose to write the words on the back for any adult who may play with the students.

Word Hunter Game

Activity Set 9.1 introduces the Word Hunter Game, which targets auditory blending awareness for our struggling students by working with sound segmentation pictures. We had the students blend together sounds using auditory clues and matching pictures. Prepare the game cards in advance. After printing and cutting out the cards, fold them in half. The picture sides of the cards should face students during the game. The names of the pictures will be on the back of the cards so everyone working with or helping out in the classroom uses the same words.

Blending Card Game

Activity Set 9.1 also introduces the Blending Card Game. We used syllable and sound blending cards with three pictures per card to target auditory blending awareness for our students. Prepare the game cards in advance. Print the pages and attach each pair of word and picture card pages so that both the word and picture sides are facing out. The pictures will be on one side for the students to see; the card backs will have the names of the pictures as a series of blended sounds for the teacher to say. The students listen to the sounds, say the sounds the fast way to blend them into words, look at the pictures, and then choose the picture that matches the target word.

Skill Assessment Checkouts

After your review lesson is completed, set aside a few minutes during that day to give each child an individual blending checkout. These take about 2 minutes per child to administer and provide useful information to guide your future small-group placements. Based on the checkout and collaborative conversations with all teachers, you will determine which students should continue on in Tier 2 small-group intervention and which students can successfully return to Tier 1 whole-class instruction (see Chapter 2).

Assessment Outcome: The student can blend sounds into words using onset-rimes and words with two to three sounds.

ACTIVITY SET 9.1

Lesson Descriptions

Lessons	Sequence of daily activities	⬦ Vocabulary
Lesson 1: Say It the Fast Way	Rhyming song: "John Jacob Jingleheimer Schmidt" Target: Rhyming book—*Hop on Pop* (LeSieg, 1963) Target: Blending sounds: Say It the Fast Way Game Rhyming song: "John Jacob Jingleheimer Schmidt"	
Lesson 2: Word Hunters	Fingerplay: "A Family Fingerplay" Target: Blending sounds: Word Hunter Game Rhyming song: "One, Two, Buckle My Shoe"	Blend Hunt
Lesson 3: Blending Card Game	Rhyming song: "A Hunting We Will Go" Target: Blending sounds: Blending Card Game Fingerplay: "A Family Fingerplay"	
Lesson 4: Blending Awareness Review	Fingerplay: "A Family Fingerplay" Target: Blending sounds: "A Hunting We Will Go" Word Hunter Game, Blending Card Game	

Materials Needed

☑ Book: *Hop on Pop* (LeSieg, 1963)

☑ A book containing "One, Two, Buckle My Shoe" with pictures (e.g., Baker, 1994)

☑ DROPP 9 Skill Assessment Checkout

☑ Tokens for behavior/participation

Say It the Fast Way Game

☑ Word list (see Appendix D on the CD-ROM)

☑ Two colored chips per child

Word Hunter Game

☑ Game cards (see Appendix D on the CD-ROM)

☑ Two colored chips per child

Blending Card Game

☑ Game cards (see Appendix D on the CD-ROM)

☑ Two colored chips per child

ACTIVITY SET

9.1 10-Day Planner

Day 1	**Lesson 1:** Say It the Fast Way
Day 2	**Lesson 1:** Say It the Fast Way
Day 3	**Lesson 2:** Word Hunters
Day 4	**Lesson 2:** Word Hunters
Day 5	**Lesson 3:** Blending Card Game
Day 6	**Lesson 3:** Blending Card Game
Day 7	**Lesson 1:** Say It the Fast Way
Day 8	**Lesson 2:** Word Hunters
Day 9	**Lesson 3:** Blending Card Game
Day 10	**Lesson 4:** Blending Awareness Review

LESSON 1: Say It the Fast Way

OBJECTIVES

Students will

- Know how to blend sounds to form words and be able to orally blend onset-rimes (word families) into a whole word by saying them the fast way

Teacher will

- Emphasize the onset-rimes so students can clearly hear that the endings of words from the same word family sound the same

- Associate the term *say it the fast way* with blending the two sound parts together to make a new word

- Closely observe each student for focus and full participation

- Smile and ensure success for all children

- Ensure that all children win the game

RHYMES, SONGS, AND FINGERPLAYS

"John Jacob Jingleheimer Schmidt"

MATERIALS

Book: *Hop on Pop* (LeSieg, 1963)

Tokens for behavior/participation

Say It the Fast Way Game
- ☑ Word list (see Appendix D on the CD-ROM)
- ☑ Two colored chips per child

 TASK 1   Transition song to begin the lesson (approximately 3 minutes)

INTRODUCE the big idea.

Call the group together, settle them at a table, and say the following. We are going to listen for the little sounds we hear in words and blend them together to make words. We will say words the fast way. Everyone, how will we say words?

▶ Children's response: The fast way.

Yes, the fast way. Kiss your brain before we start. Do it with me. *Kiss your palm and place it on your head.*

BEGIN the transition.

You are going to sing a rhyming song today called "John Jacob Jingleheimer Schmidt." It's about a little boy with a very long name. What's the name of our rhyming song? *Prompt for response.*

▶ Children's response: "John Jacob Jingleheimer Schmidt."

Yes, our song is called "John Jacob Jingleheimer Schmidt." My turn to sing. Listen.

Turn On Your Ears

John Jacob Jingleheimer Schmidt,
His name is my name too.
Whenever we go out,
The people always shout,
There goes John Jacob Jingleheimer Schmidt. *(Sing slowly.)*
La, la, la, la, la, la, la.

Model the Activity

Your turn to sing it with me.

▶ (Children respond by singing the song with you.)

Nice singing. We'll sing it again at the end of our lesson with a little surprise.

TASK 2A   Rhyming book (approximately 5–7 minutes)

INTRODUCE the lesson.

You are going to read a book with me and listen for the sounds of rhyming words. The title is *Hop on Pop* and you probably already know this book. *Hold up the book and point to the title as you read.* What do you think the story is about? Take a look at the picture on the cover. Two thumbs up if you know. *Call on one child.*

▶ (Child responds with appropriate responses.)

Let's read *Hop on Pop* and listen to the sounds of rhyming words. *Read the book aloud.*

TEACHING TIP: Overemphasize the rhymes as you read.

 TASK 2B   Say It the Fast Way Game (approximately 5–7 minutes)

 PLAY the game.

 CD-ROM   See Appendix D on the CD-ROM for the Say It the Fast Way Game instructions and word list.

 TASK 3   Transition song to end the lesson (approximately 3 minutes)

MAKE the transition to end the lesson.

Everyone, let's say the name of the rhyming song we learned earlier. Say it with me.

▶ Children's response: "John Jacob Jingleheimer Schmidt."

Yes, "John Jacob Jingleheimer Schmidt." Let's sing together.

John Jacob Jingleheimer Schmidt, *(Use a conversational voice.)*
His name is my name too.
Whenever we go out,
The people always shout,
There goes John Jacob Jingleheimer Schmidt.
La, la, la, la, la, la, la. *(Use a softer voice.)*
John Jacob Jingleheimer Schmidt,
His name is my name too.
Whenever we go out,
The people always shout,
There goes John Jacob Jingleheimer Schmidt.
La, la, la, la, la, la, la. *(Whisper.)*
John Jacob Jingleheimer Schmidt,
His name is my name too.
Whenever we go out,
The people always shout,
There goes John Jacob Jingleheimer Schmidt.
La, la, la, la, la, la, la. *(Use a conversational voice.)*

Excellent singing. That was fun. Blow the train whistle if you liked hearing rhymes and blending words.

▶ (Students pull an imaginary train whistle and say "Whoo, whoo.")

| **END** Lesson 1. | You all did a good job today. Everyone now gets their winnings for blending words and for working hard. *Give out token rewards to each child.* |

LESSON 2: Word Hunters

OBJECTIVES

Student will

- Know how to blend sounds to form words and be able to orally blend two phonemes into one-syllable words by saying them the fast way and using a picture stimulus in the Word Hunter Game

Teacher will

- Emphasize the two-phoneme sounds so students can clearly hear them, and at the same time, stretch out the phoneme sounds for auditory ease of blending

- Associate the term *say it the fast way* with blending sounds together to make a new word

- Check that all students are fully focused on the target sounds and pictures

RHYMES, SONGS, AND FINGERPLAYS

"A Family Fingerplay"

"A Hunting We Will Go"

"One, Two, Buckle My Shoe"

MATERIALS

A book containing "One, Two, Buckle My Shoe" with pictures (e.g., Baker, 1994)

Tokens for behavior/participation

Word Hunter Game

☑ Game cards (see Appendix D on the CD-ROM)

☑ Two colored chips per child

 **TASK 1** Transition song to begin the lesson (approximately 3 minutes)

INTRODUCE the big idea.

Call the group together, settle the children at a table, and say the following. We are going to listen for the little sounds we hear in words and blend them together to make words. We will say words the fast way. Everyone, how will we say words?

▶ **Children's response: The fast way.**

Yes, we will say words the fast way.

 Vocabulary

BLEND

Explain vocabulary in a simple way, and have the students repeat back the new word. Follow a two-step approach. What do we do when we blend things together? Touch your left sleeve if you know. *Call on one child.*

▶ **(Child responds appropriately.)**

Step 1: Ask children to describe the new word.

When we blend things together, we put them all together to make something new. I might blend milk and chocolate syrup together. What new thing would I make? Who knows? Touch your right sleeve if you know. *Call on one child. Prompt for the correct response.*

▶ **Child's response: Chocolate milk.**

Step 2: Give students the description and have them supply the word.

 Model the Activity

Yes, chocolate milk. What's another way of saying I can mix milk with chocolate syrup to get chocolate milk? I can blend milk with chocolate syrup to get chocolate milk. Say it with me.

▶ **Children's response: I can blend milk with chocolate syrup to get chocolate milk.**

Yes, I can blend milk with chocolate syrup to get chocolate milk. If Terrence blends together soil or dirt from outside in the yard with water, what new something will he get? Touch your right eyebrow if you know. *Call on one child.*

▶ **Child's response: Terrence will get mud.**

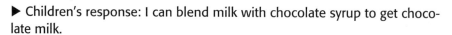

TEACHING TIP: Use the new word with a student's name. This will get students' attention.

Yes, if Terrence blends together dirt from outside in the yard with water, he will get mud. What's another way of saying Terrence can put dirt from the yard together with water to get mud? My turn *(point to yourself)*. Terrence can blend dirt from the yard with water to get mud. Your turn *(point to the children)*. What's another way of saying Terrence can put dirt from the yard together with water to get mud?

▶ **Children's response: Terrence can blend dirt from the yard with water to get mud.**

Yes, Terrence can blend dirt from the yard with water to get mud. We are going to blend together sounds to get new words. Everyone, what are we going to do with our sounds?

▶ **Children's response: Blend them together to get new words.**

Yes, blend together sounds to get new words. Great job learning the word *blend*.

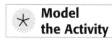 **Model the Activity**

Let's get ready for rhymes, songs, and saying words the fast way. Now it's time to put your hand in your pocket and take out your magic wand. *Reach across your body in a very exaggerated manner, put your hand in your pocket, and pull out your magic wand.* Hocus, pocus. *Wave your wand back and forth in the air.* Time to focus. *Take index fingers and thumbs of both hands and make eyeglasses on your face.* Let's do it one more time. *Repeat.*

BEGIN the transition.

You are going to say a rhyme today about a family. It's called "A Family Fingerplay." What's the name of our fingerplay? *Prompt the students for the correct response.*

▶ **Children's response: "A Family Fingerplay."**

 Model the Activity

Yes, "A Family Fingerplay." My turn. Watch what I do with my fingers.

This is the family. *(Hold up one hand with fingers spread and wiggling.)*
Let's count them and see.
How many are there?
And who can they be?
1, 2, 3, 4, 5 *(Count off on your fingers.)*

This is the mother *(Raise your pointer finger and use a kindly voice.)*
Who loves everyone.
And this is the father *(Raise your tall finger and use a deep voice.)*
Who is lots of fun.
This is the sister *(Raise your ring finger and use a high-pitched voice.)*
She helps and she plays.
And this is the baby *(Raise your little finger and use a baby voice.)*
He's growing each day.
But who is this one? *(Wiggle your thumb and use a questioning voice.)*

She's out there alone.
Why it's Lulu, the dog.
And she's chewing a bone.
Ruff. Ruff. *(Wiggle thumb and make dog sounds.)*

TEACHING TIP: Use drama to increase memory. Use different voices for the family members.

Your turn to do it with me. Take out your family. Get ready. *Repeat the fingerplay and do it with the students.*

Very nice work singing about this wonderful family. Touch your ears if you love your family.

 TASK 2   A Hunting We Will Go *(approximately 12–14 minutes)*

 Vocabulary

HUNT

Explain vocabulary in a simple way, and have the students repeat back the new word. Follow a two-step approach. Today we are going to be word hunters. We will listen for sounds and then say them the fast way to make words. Then you will hunt for the pictures of the words. You will have to be good hunters to win the game. Who knows what a hunter is? Touch your right hand if you know. *Call on one child.*

▶ **(Child responds appropriately.)**

A hunter looks for something and then finds it. *Pretend to look around.* Everyone, what does a hunter do?

▶ **Children's response: A hunter looks for something and then finds it.**

Step 1: Ask children to describe or act out the new word.

Yes, a hunter looks for something and then finds it. Good job knowing what a hunter does. I want to hunt for my board markers. *Pretend to look around and then find them.* Oh, there they are. I hunted for my board markers and then I found them. I am a hunter. What's another way of saying I looked for my board markers and then I found them?

▶ **Children's response: I hunted for my board markers and then I found them.**

Yes, I hunted for my board markers and then I found them. Everyone, am I a hunter?

▶ **Children's response: Yes.**

TEACHING TIP: Use the new word with a student's name. This will get students' attention.

Harris, will you look for your pencil? *Prompt for the correct response.*

▶ **(Child responds appropriately.)**

Step 2: Give students the description and have them supply the word.

Everyone, what's another way of saying that Harris looked for his pencil and then found it?

▶ **Children's response: Harris hunted for his pencil and then found it.**

Yes, Harris hunted for his pencil and then found it. Harris is a hunter. Everyone, what is Harris?

▶ **Children's response: Harris is a hunter.**

Is someone else a hunter? Sit up tall and proud if you can tell us that you hunted for something and then found it. *Call on one student.*

▶ **(Child responds appropriately.)**

Nice job knowing about the word *hunter.* We will all be hunters today.

INTRODUCE the lesson.

Everyone, we will sing our hunting song so we can hunt for words and find them. It's called "A Hunting We Will Go." Everyone, what's the name of our hunting song? *Guide for the correct response.*

▶ **Children's response: "A Hunting We Will Go."**

 Multisensory Reinforcement

Yes. Get ready to sing with me. *Sing to the tune of "The Farmer in the Dell."*

A hunting we will go. *(Make eyeglasses with fingers around eyes.)*
A hunting we will go.
Hear the sounds *(Put both hands behind each ear.)*
For words I found.
We'll make words that we know. *(Hold palms out in front and nod.)*

Okay, let's sing it one more time. *Repeat the song.*

Nice job singing our hunting song. Now it's time for us to be word hunters.

♣ **PLAY** the game.

CD-ROM See Appendix D on the CD-ROM for the Word Hunter Game instructions and cards.

Nice job being word hunters and blending sounds into words. You said words the fast way. Give yourselves a few clam claps. *Students make small clam-like shapes with their hands and "clap" their fingers to their palms.*

 TASK 3 Transition song to end the lesson *(approximately 3 minutes)*

MAKE the transition to end the lesson.

You are going to practice another rhyme. You know this one. It's called "One, Two, Buckle My Shoe." Everyone, what's the name of our rhyme?

▶ **Children's response: "One, Two, Buckle My Shoe."**

Yes, "One, Two, Buckle My Shoe." Let's look at the pictures as we say the rhyme together. We will practice saying our numbers, too.

Get ready. *Sing with them. Show each picture as you say that part of the rhyme. As some books use different rhyme patterns, adjust your words accordingly.*

One, two,
Buckle my shoe.
Three, four,
Shut the door.
Five, six,
Pick up sticks.
Seven, eight,

Lay them straight.
Nine, ten,
A big fat hen.

Let's say our rhyme again without the pictures to see if we can make rhyming words. I think you can do it. *Sing with them, and pause for a few moments so they can say the rhyme.*

My turn to say the rhyme.

One, two,
Buckle my . . .

▶ **Children's response: Shoe.**

Three, four,
Shut the . . .

▶ **Children's response: Door.**

Five, six,
Pick up . . .

▶ **Children's response: Sticks.**

Seven, eight,
Lay them . . .

▶ **Children's response: Straight.**

Nine, ten,
A big fat . . .

▶ **Children's response: Hen.**

Your rhyming and blending work was so good today. Let's give ourselves the old cowboy and cowgirl cheer. Do it with me. *Put one finger in the air. Circle it like a lasso.* Yee-haw.

END Lesson 2.

You all did a good job today. Everyone now gets their winnings for blending words and for working hard. *Give out token rewards to each child.*

LESSON 3: Blending Card Game

OBJECTIVES

Student will

- Know how to blend sounds to form words and be able to orally blend two to three phonemes into one-syllable words by saying them the fast way and using a picture stimulus in the Blending Card Game

Teacher will

- Emphasize the two or three phoneme sounds so students can clearly hear them, and at the same time, stretch out the phoneme sounds for auditory ease of blending

- Associate the term *say it the fast way* with blending sounds together to make a new word

- Check that all students are fully focused on the target sounds and pictures

- Smile and ensure success for all children

- Ensure that all children win the game

RHYMES, SONGS, AND FINGERPLAYS

"A Hunting We Will Go."

MATERIALS

Tokens for behavior/participation

Blending Card Game

☑ Game cards (see Appendix D on the CD-ROM)

☑ Two colored chips per child

 TASK 1 | Transition song to begin the lesson (approximately 3 minutes)

INTRODUCE the big idea. | We are going to listen for the sounds we hear in words, say them the fast way, and blend them together to make words. We will say words the fast way. Everyone, how will we say words?

▶ **Children's response: The fast way.**

Yes, the fast way. Let's put on our special headsets *(pretend you are putting on a headset)* and glasses *(make circles with your fingers)* so we can hear our sounds and hunt for the pictures.

▶ **(Children respond by doing it with you.)**

Nice job getting ready to hunt.

BEGIN the transition. | Everyone, we will sing our hunting song so we can hunt for words and find them. It's called "A Hunting We Will Go." Everyone, what's the name of our hunting song? *Guide for the correct response.*

▶ **Children's response: "A Hunting We Will Go."**

Yes, Get ready to sing with me. *Sing to the tune of "The Farmer in the Dell."*

A hunting we will go. *(Make eyeglasses with fingers around eyes.)*
A hunting we will go.
Hear the sounds *(Put both hands behind each ear.)*
For words I found.
We'll make words that we know. *(Hold palms out in front and nod.)*
Okay, let's sing it one more time. *(Repeat the song.)*

Nice job singing our hunting song. Now we're going to be word hunters again.

TASK 2 | Blending Card Game (approximately 12–14 minutes)

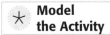 **PLAY** the game.

 CD-ROM See Appendix D on the CD-ROM for the Blending Card Game instructions and cards.

 TASK 3 | Transition fingerplay to end the lesson (approximately 3 minutes)

MAKE the transition to end the lesson.

You are going to say a fingerplay called "A Family Fingerplay." What's the name of our fingerplay?

▶ **Children's response: "A Family Fingerplay."**

✳ Model the Activity

Yes, "A Family Fingerplay." Let's do it together. Take out your family and get ready.

This is the family. *(Hold up one hand with the fingers spread and wiggling.)*
Let's count them and see.
How many are there?
And who can they be?
1, 2, 3, 4, 5 *(Count off on your fingers.)*

🖐 Multisensory Reinforcement

This is the mother *(Raise your pointer finger and use a kindly voice.)*
Who loves everyone.
And this is the father *(Raise your tall finger and use a deep voice.)*
Who is lots of fun.
This is the sister *(Raise your ring finger and use a high-pitched voice.)*
She helps and she plays.
And this is the baby *(Raise your little finger and use a baby voice.)*
He's growing each day.
But who is this one? *(Wiggle your thumb and use a questioning voice.)*
She's out there alone.
Why it's Lulu, the dog.
And she's chewing a bone.
Ruff. Ruff. *(Wiggle thumb and make dog sounds.)*

TEACHING TIP: Use drama to increase memory. Use different voices for the family members.

Let's do it one more time. Get your family ready. *Repeat the fingerplay and do it with the students.*

Nice work telling us about this wonderful family. Touch your forehead if you love your family.

Excellent job today being word hunters and word blenders. Let's give ourselves a snap, crackle, pop. Do it with me.

Snap! *Snap fingers once.*
Crackle! *Rub hands together quickly.*
Pop! *Clap hands once hard and quickly jet out hands with palms forward and fingers splayed.*

END Lesson 3.

You all did a good job today. Everyone now gets their winnings for blending words and for working hard. *Give out token rewards to each child.*

LESSON 4: Review

OBJECTIVES

Student will

- Know how to blend sounds to form words and be able to orally blend two phonemes into one-syllable words by saying them the fast way and using a picture stimulus in the Word Hunter Game

Teacher will

- Emphasize the two phoneme sounds so students can clearly hear them, and at the same time, stretch out the phoneme sounds for auditory ease of blending
- Associate the term *say it the fast way* with blending sounds together to make a new word
- Check that all students are fully focused on the target sounds and pictures

RHYMES, SONGS, AND FINGERPLAYS

"A Family Fingerplay"
"A Hunting We Will Go"

MATERIALS

- ☑ DROPP 9 Skill Assessment Checkout (see Appendix B on the CD-ROM)
- ☑ Tokens for behavior/participation

Word Hunter Game

- ☑ Game cards (see Appendix D on the CD-ROM)
- ☑ Two colored chips per child

Blending Card Game

- ☑ Game cards (see Appendix D on the CD-ROM)
- ☑ Two colored chips per child

 TASK 1   Transition fingerplay to begin the lesson (approximately 2 minutes)

INTRODUCE the big idea.	*Call the group together and settle the children at a table.* We are going to listen for the little sounds we hear in words and blend them together to make words. We will say words the fast way. Everyone, how will we say words?

▶ Children's response: The fast way.

Yes, we will say words the fast way. You are going to sing "A Family Fingerplay." What's the name of our fingerplay?

▶ Children's response: "A Family Fingerplay."

BEGIN the transition.

Yes, "A Family Fingerplay." Take out your family. Get ready.

This is the family. *(Hold up one hand with the fingers spread and wiggling.)*
Let's count them and see.
How many are there?
And who can they be?

Multisensory Reinforcement

1, 2, 3, 4, 5 *(Count off on your fingers.)*

This is the mother *(Raise your pointer finger and use a kindly voice.)*
Who loves everyone.
And this is the father *(Raise your tall finger and use a deep voice.)*
Who is lots of fun.
This is the sister *(Raise your ring finger and use a high-pitched voice.)*
She helps and she plays.
And this is the baby *(Raise your little finger and use a baby voice.)*
He's growing each day.
But who is this one? *(Wiggle your thumb and use a questioning voice.)*
She's out there alone.
Why it's Lulu, the dog.

And she's chewing a bone.
Ruff. Ruff. *(Wiggle thumb and make dog sounds.)*

TEACHING TIP: Use drama to increase memory. Use different voices for the family members.

Let's do it again. *Repeat the fingerplay.*

Nice work singing about this wonderful family. Touch your ears if you love your family.

 TASK 2A Word Hunter Game *(approximately 9 minutes)*

INTRODUCE the lesson.

Everyone, we will sing our hunting song so we can hunt for words and find them. It's called "A Hunting We Will Go." Everyone, what's the name of our hunting song? *Guide for the correct response.*

▶ Children's response: "A Hunting We Will Go."

Yes. Get ready to sing with me. *(Sing to the tune of "The Farmer in the Dell.")*
A hunting we will go. *(Make eyeglasses with fingers around eyes.)*
A hunting we will go.
Hear the sounds *(Put both hands behind each ear.)*
For words I found.
We'll make words that we know. *(Hold palms out in front and nod.)*

Okay, let's sing it one more time. Nice job singing our hunting song. Now it's time for us to be word hunters.

 PLAY the game.

 CD-ROM See Appendix D on the CD-ROM for the Word Hunter Game instructions and cards.

 TASK 2B Blending Card Game *(approximately 9 minutes)*

 PLAY the game.

CD-ROM See Appendix D on the CD-ROM for the Blending Card Game instructions and cards.

Let's do our good job dance.

Sing to the tune of "Stayin' Alive," and substitute the words "we did a good job, we did a good job." Extend your right index finger in the air to the right of your body. With your left hand on your hip, move your right finger from the air to your side as you sing.

END Lesson 4.

You all did a good job today. Everyone now gets their winnings for blending words and for working hard. *Give out token rewards to each child.*

 CD-ROM The DROPP 9 Skill Assessment Checkout will be completed for each student following this lesson.

ACTIVITY SET 9.2

Lesson Descriptions

Lessons	Sequence of daily activities	◇ Vocabulary
Lesson 1: Blending Blocks	Fingerplay: "Two Little Blackbirds" Target: Blending Blocks Rhyming song: "Down By the Station"	Pufferbellies
Lesson 2: Hunt the Rhymes	Fingerplay: "Here Is the Beehive" Target: Blending sounds: Hunt the Rhymes Rhyming song: "Here Is the Beehive"	
Lesson 3: Blending Card Game	Rhyming song: "A Hunting We Will Go" Target: Blending sounds: Blending Card Game Fingerplay: "Down By the Station"	
Lesson 4: Blending Awareness Review	Rhyming song: Blending sounds: "A Hunting We Will Go" Target: Hunt the Rhymes, Blending Card Game	

Materials Needed

☑ Large nursery rhyme picture book with "Down By the Station"

- ☑ DROPP 9 Skill Assessment Checkout (see Appendix B on the CD-ROM)
- ☑ Tokens for behavior/participation

Blending Blocks Game

- ☑ Word list (see Appendix D on the CD-ROM)
- ☑ Three colored blocks per child

Hunt the Rhymes Game

- ☑ Game board (see Appendix D on the CD-ROM)
- ☑ Game die (see Appendix D on the CD-ROM)
- ☑ Game cards (see Appendix D on the CD-ROM)

Blending Card Game

- ☑ Game cards (see Appendix D on the CD-ROM)
- ☑ Two colored chips per child

Day 1	**Lesson 1:** Blending Blocks
Day 2	**Lesson 1:** Blending Blocks
Day 3	**Lesson 2:** Hunt the Rhymes
Day 4	**Lesson 2:** Hunt the Rhymes
Day 5	**Lesson 3:** Blending Card Game
Day 6	**Lesson 3:** Blending Card Game
Day 7	**Lesson 1:** Blending Blocks
Day 8	**Lesson 2:** Hunt the Rhymes
Day 9	**Lesson 3:** Blending Card Game
Day 10	**Lesson 4:** Blending Awareness Review

LESSON 1: Blending Blocks

OBJECTIVES

Student will

- Develop an awareness of blending, know how to blend sounds to form words, and orally blend onset-rimes (word families) into a whole word by saying them the fast way

Teacher will

- Emphasize the onset-rimes so students can clearly hear that the endings of words from the same word family sound the same
- Associate the term *say it the fast way* with blending the two sound parts together to make a new word
- Closely observe each student for focus and full participation
- Smile and ensure success for all children
- Ensure that all children win the game

RHYMES, SONGS, AND FINGERPLAYS

"Two Little Blackbirds"
"Down by the Station"

MATERIALS

Large nursery rhyme picture book with "Down By the Station"

Tokens for behavior/participation

Blending Blocks Game

☑ Word list (see Appendix D on the CD-ROM)

☑ Three colored blocks per child

 **TASK 1**   Transition fingerplay to begin the lesson (approximately 3 minutes)

INTRODUCE the big idea.

Call the group together, settle them at a table, and say the following. We are going to listen for the little sounds we hear in words and blend them together to make words. We will say words the fast way. Everyone, how will we say words?

▶ Children's response: The fast way.

Yes, the fast way. Give yourselves a big thumbs up before we start. Do it with me. *Give a big thumbs up.*

▶ (Children respond by giving a big thumbs up.)

You are going to learn a fingerplay called "Two Little Blackbirds." Everyone, what's the name of our new fingerplay? *Prompt for response.*

▶ Children's response: "Two Little Blackbirds."

BEGIN the transition.

Yes, "Two Little Blackbirds." My turn. Listen and watch first and then we will do it together. *Say the words slowly.*

 **Turn On Your Ears**

Two little blackbirds
Sitting on the wall.
One named Peter. *(Hold up one finger.)*
One named Paul. *(Hold up one finger on the other hand.)*
Fly away, Peter. *(Put one hand behind your back.)*
Fly away, Paul. *(Put the other hand behind your back.)*
Come back, Peter. *(Bring the first hand from behind your back.)*
Come back, Paul. *(Bring the other hand from behind your back.)*

Multisensory Reinforcement

Your turn. Let's say it together. *Repeat fingerplay and prompt for hand motions.*

Nice job saying "Two Little Blackbirds." You are remembering your rhymes.

TASK 2   Blending Blocks (approximately 5–7 minutes)

 PLAY the game.

 CD-ROM   See Appendix D on the CD-ROM for the Blending Blocks Game instructions and word list.

 Vocabulary

PUFFERBELLIES

Explain vocabulary in a simple way, and have the students repeat back the new word. Follow a two-step approach. Remember our nursery rhyme song called "Down by the Station?" It is about trains. Have you ever seen train cars lined up all in a row? Touch your nose if you have seen train cars lined up in a row.

▶ **(Children respond by touching their noses.)**

In the front car, a person called the station master pulls a handle down to make the engine go down the track. Then it can pull the whole row of train cars behind it.

In this nursery rhyme, the train cars are called *pufferbellies.* Who can explain why they have that funny name? Touch your forehead if you know.

Step 1: Ask children to describe or act out the new word. Call on one child.

▶ **(Child responds appropriately.)**

Step 2: Give students the description and have them supply the word Yes, because when the train starts to go, it puffs out . . .

▶ **Children's response: Smoke.**

Yes, smoke. *Pufferbellies* is an old-fashioned name for train cars. Everyone, what is an old-fashioned name for train cars?

▶ **Children's response: Pufferbellies.**

Yes, pufferbellies.

 TASK 3   Transition song to end the lesson (approximately 3 minutes)

MAKE the transition to end the lesson.

Now let's sing this nursery rhyme. You already know it. *Show children the book and point to each word while singing.*

Down by the station, early in the morning.
See the little pufferbellies, all in a row.
See the station master turn the little handle.
Puff, puff, toot, toot, off we go.

TEACHING TIP: Use drama to increase memory.

Let's sing this song one more time, and we will line up like trains and move our arms like trains while we sing.

 Multisensory Reinforcement

▶ **(Children respond by lining up one behind the other, moving their arms like choo-choos, and pulling the whistle. They "toot toot" loudly when they pull the whistle.)**

Excellent singing. That was fun. Blow the whistle if you liked hearing rhymes and blending words.

END Lesson 1.

▶ **(Students pull an imaginary train whistle and say "Whoo, whoo.")**

You all did a good job today. Everyone now gets their winnings for blending words and for working hard. *Give out token rewards to each child.*

LESSON 2: Hunt the Rhymes

OBJECTIVES

Student will

- Know how to blend sounds to form words, orally blend two phonemes into one-syllable words by saying them the fast way, and use a picture stimulus in the Hunt the Rhymes Game

Teacher will

- Emphasize the two phoneme sounds so students can clearly hear them, and at the same time, stretch out the phoneme sounds for auditory ease of blending

- Associate the term *say it the fast way* with blending sounds together to make a new word

- Check that all students are fully focused on the target sounds and pictures

RHYMES, SONGS, AND FINGERPLAYS

"Here Is the Beehive"

"A Hunting We Will Go"

MATERIALS

Tokens for behavior/participation

Hunt the Rhymes Game   CD-ROM
- ☑ Game board (see Appendix D on the CD-ROM)
- ☑ Game die (see Appendix D on the CD-ROM)
- ☑ Game cards (see Appendix D on the CD-ROM)

 TASK 1   Transition fingerplay to begin the lesson *(approximately 3 minutes)*

INTRODUCE the big idea.

Call the group together, settle them at a table, and say the following. We are going to listen for the little sounds we hear in words and blend them together to make words. We will say words the fast way. Everyone, how will we say words?

▶ **Children's response: The fast way.**

Yes, we will say words the fast way.

 Vocabulary

BEEHIVE

Explain vocabulary in a simple way, and have the students repeat back the new word. Follow a two-step approach. Does anyone know what a beehive is? Touch your nose if you do. *Call on one child.*

▶ **(Child responds appropriately.)**

Step 1: Ask children to describe the new word.

A beehive is a home for bees. Everyone, what is a beehive? *Prompt for the correct response.*

▶ **Children's response: A home for bees.**

Step 2: Give students the description and have them supply the word.

Yes. A beehive is a home for bees. It is shaped like this. *Put both hands together to make a hive shape.*

Now, you make a beehive with your hands.

▶ **(Children respond by making a beehive with their hands.)**

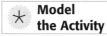

9.2

LESSON 2

TEACHING TIP: Use the new word with a student's name. This will get students' attention.

Everyone, what's another way of saying Jalen has a home for bees in his backyard?

▶ **Children's response: Jalen has a beehive in his backyard.**

Yes, Jalen has a beehive in his backyard. Good job knowing the word *beehive*.

BEGIN the transition.

You will work hard today hearing sounds and saying them the fast way to blend them into words. You will be just like a hive of busy bees. Now we will do a finger-play about bees that you all know. Do it with me and see if you all remember.

Everyone, take out your beehive. *Close one hand on top of the other.*

Model the Activity

▶ **(Children respond by taking out their beehive and mimicking you.)**

Here is the beehive
But where are the bees? *(Act puzzled; look back and forth.)*
Hidden inside where nobody sees. *(Look in the hole made by your finger and thumb.)*

Multisensory Reinforcement

Watch them closely come out of the hive. *(Look at children's faces with excitement.)*
1, 2, 3, 4, 5 *(Pop one finger up for each number until you have five fingers up and your palm forward. Make a buzzing sound.)*

Nice job with our beehives. Let's do it one more time. Take out your beehives again. *Repeat the fingerplay and do it with the students. Hold up one hand with your fingers spread and wiggling.*

Great job with your beehive. Touch your knees if you are ready to hunt for words.

TASK 2   A Hunting We Will Go *(approximately 12–14 minutes)*

INTRODUCE the lesson.

Everyone, we will sing our hunting song so we can hunt for words and find them. It's called "A Hunting We Will Go." Everyone, what's the name of our hunting song? *Guide for the correct response.*

▶ **Children's response: "A Hunting We Will Go."**

Multisensory Reinforcement

Yes. Get ready to sing with me. *Sing to the tune of "Farmer in the Dell."*

A hunting we will go. *(Make eyeglasses with fingers around eyes.)*
A hunting we will go.
Hear the sounds *(Put both hands behind each ear.)*
For words I found.
We'll make words that we know. *(Hold palms out in front and nod.)*

Okay, let's sing it one more time. *Repeat the song.*

Nice job singing our hunting song. Now it's time for us to be word hunters.

PLAY the game.

CD-ROM See Appendix D on the CD-ROM for the Hunt the Rhymes Game instructions, board, cards, and die.

| **TASK 3** | Transition fingerplay to end the lesson (approximately 3 minutes) |

MAKE the transition to end the lesson.	You worked hard today hearing sounds and saying them the fast way to blend them into words. You worked just like a hive of busy bees. Let's do our fingerplay about bees that you all know. Do it with me and see if you all remember.

Everyone, take out your beehive. *Close one hand on top of the other.*

▶ **(Children respond by taking out their beehive and mimicking you.)**

Here is the beehive
But where are the bees? *(Act puzzled; look back and forth.)*
Hidden inside where nobody sees. *(Look in the hole made by your finger and thumb.)* |
| **Multisensory Reinforcement** | Watch them closely come out of the hive. *(Look at children's faces with excitement.)*
1, 2, 3, 4, 5 *(Pop one finger up for each number until you have five fingers up, palm forward. Make a buzzing sound.)*

Nice job with our beehives. Let's do it one more time. Take out your beehives again. *Repeat the fingerplay and do it with the students.* Great job with your bee-hive. Touch your knees if you like your bees. Great job playing the Hunt the Rhymes Game.

You are a gold star class. You know what that means.
Take out your star box. *(Cup one hand.)*
Get your star. *(Pretend to get a star on the pointer finger of the other hand, lick it, and put it on your forehead.)*
You are all gold star kids. |
| **END** Lesson 2. | You all did a good job today. Everyone now gets their winnings for blending words and for working hard. *Give out token rewards to each child.* |

LESSON 3: Blending Card Game

OBJECTIVES

Student will

- Know how to blend sounds to form words, orally blend two to three phonemes into one-syllable words by saying them the fast way, and use a picture stimulus in the Blending Card Game

Teacher will

- Emphasize the two or three phoneme sounds so students can clearly hear them, and at the same time, stretch out the phoneme sounds for auditory ease of blending
- Associate the term *say it the fast way* with blending sounds together to make a new word
- Check that all students are fully focused on the target sounds and pictures
- Smile and ensure success for all children
- Ensure that all children win the game

RHYMES, SONGS, AND FINGERPLAYS

"A Hunting We Will Go"
"Down By the Station"

MATERIALS

Large nursery rhyme picture book with "Down By the Station"
Tokens for behavior/participation

Blending Card Game

☑ Game cards (see Appendix D on the CD-ROM)

☑ Two colored chips per child

TASK 1 | **Transition song to begin the lesson** (approximately 3 minutes)

INTRODUCE the big idea. | We are going to listen for the sounds we hear in words, say them the fast way, and blend them together to make words. We will say words the fast way. Everyone, how will we say words?

▶ **Children's response: The fast way.**

Yes, the fast way. Let's put on our special headsets *(pretend you are putting on a headset)* and glasses *(make circles with your fingers)* so we can hear our sounds and hunt for the pictures.

▶ **(Children respond by doing it with you.)**

Nice job getting ready to hunt.

BEGIN the transition. | Everyone, we will sing our hunting song so we can hunt for words and find them. It's called "A Hunting We Will Go." Everyone, what's the name of our hunting song? *Guide for the correct response.*

▶ **Children's response: "A Hunting We Will Go."**

Yes, get ready to sing with me. *Sing to the tune of "Farmer in the Dell."*

A hunting we will go. *(Make eyeglasses with fingers around eyes.)*
A hunting we will go.
Hear the sounds *(Put both hands behind each ear.)*
For words I found.
We'll make words that we know. *(Hold palms out in front and nod.)*

Okay, let's sing it one more time. *Repeat the song.*

Nice job singing our hunting song. Now we're going to be word hunters again.

 TASK 2 | **Blending Card Game** (approximately 13–15 minutes)

 PLAY the game. | **CD-ROM** See Appendix D on the CD-ROM for the Blending Card Game instructions and cards.

 TASK 3 | **Transition song to end the lesson** (approximately 1–2 minutes)

MAKE the transition to end the lesson. | Now let's sing this nursery rhyme. You already know it. *Show children the book and point to each word while singing.*

Down by the station, early in the morning.
See the little pufferbellies, all in a row.
See the station master turn the little handle.
Puff, puff, toot, toot, off we go.

TEACHING TIP: Use drama to increase memory.

Let's sing this song one more time and we will line up like trains and move our arms like trains while we sing.

Multisensory Reinforcement	▶ *(Children respond by lining up one behind the other, moving their arms like choo-choos, and pulling the whistle. They "toot toot" loudly when they pull the whistle.)*
	Excellent singing. Nice job, everyone. Let's get out our cameras.
	Click. Click. Click. *(Make a camera with your hands and make a "click, click" with your tongue as your reposition the camera and take some pictures of your students. They do the same.)*
	Lookin' good. *(Thumbs up. Big smile. Nod.)*
END Lesson 3.	You all did a good job today. Everyone now gets their winnings for blending words and for working hard. *Give out token rewards to each child.*

LESSON 4: Blending Awareness Review

OBJECTIVES

Student will

- Know how to blend sounds to form words, orally blend two phonemes into one-syllable words by saying them the fast way, and use a picture stimulus in the Hunt the Rhymes Game

- Know how to blend sounds to form words and be able to orally blend two to three phonemes into one-syllable words by saying them the fast way and using a picture stimulus in the Blending Card Game

Teacher will

- Emphasize the two phoneme sounds so students can clearly hear them, and at the same time, stretch out the phoneme sounds for auditory ease of blending

- Associate the term *say it the fast way* with blending sounds together to make a new word

- Check that all students are fully focused on the target sounds and pictures

RHYMES, SONGS, AND FINGERPLAYS

"A Hunting We Will Go"

MATERIALS

☑ DROPP 9 Skill Assessment Checkout (see Appendix B on the CD-ROM)

☑ Tokens for behavior/participation

Hunt the Rhymes Game

☑ Game board (see Appendix D on the CD-ROM)

☑ Game die (see Appendix D on the CD-ROM)

☑ Game cards (see Appendix D on the CD-ROM)

Blending Card Game

☑ Game cards (see Appendix D on the CD-ROM)

☑ Two colored chips per child

🪐 TASK 1 | Transition song to begin the lesson *(approximately 1–2 minutes)*

INTRODUCE the big idea.	*Call the group together, settle them at a table, and say the following.* We are going to listen for the little sounds we hear in words and blend them together to make words. We will say words the fast way. Everyone, how will we say words?
	▶ **Children's response: The fast way.**
	Yes, we will say words the fast way.
BEGIN the transition.	Everyone, we will sing our hunting song so we can hunt for words and find them. It's called "A Hunting We Will Go." Everyone, what's the name of our hunting song? *Guide for the correct response.*

▶ Children's response: "A Hunting We Will Go."

Yes, get ready to sing with me. *Sing to the tune of "Farmer in the Dell."*

A hunting we will go. *(Make eyeglasses with fingers around eyes.)*
A hunting we will go.
Hear the sounds *(Put both hands behind each ear.)*
For words I found.
We'll make words that we know. *(Hold palms out in front and nod.)*

Okay let's sing it one more time. *Repeat the song.*

Nice job singing our hunting song. Now we're going to be word hunters again.

 TASK 2A | Hunt the Rhymes Game *(approximately 9 minutes)*

 PLAY the game.

 CD-ROM | See Appendix D on the CD-ROM for the Hunt the Rhymes Game instructions, board, cards, and die.

 TASK 2B | Blending Card Game *(approximately 9 minutes)*

 PLAY the game.

 CD-ROM | See Appendix D on the CD-ROM for the Blending Card Game instructions and cards.

Your rhyming work was so good today. We are going to sing the "Give Me a Snap" song. *Sing to the tune of* The Addams Family *theme song.*

Give me a snap. *(Snap twice.)*
Give me a snap. *(Snap twice.)*
Give me a snap, give me a snap,
Give me a snap. *(Snap twice.)*

Repeat the tune but say, "Give me a cheer."

Give me a cheer. "Hooray!" *Say "Hooray!" once instead of snapping twice.*

END Lesson 4.

You all did a good job today. Everyone now gets their winnings for blending words and for working hard. *Give out token rewards to each child.*

 CD-ROM | The DROPP 9 Skill Assessment Checkout will be completed for each student following this lesson.

Beginning Sound Alliteration

Overview

WHY BEGINNING SOUND ALLITERATION IS IMPORTANT

In DROPP 10, children continue to broaden their scope of emergent skills by listening and identifying beginning sounds in words. They also begin to identify words that have the same initial sound—and we term this awareness as *beginning sound alliteration*. For instance, students who are aware of beginning sound alliteration will know that *sad* starts with the same sound as *sick*. This is an early phonemic awareness skill that students usually develop during pre-K. Listening for beginning sounds is easier and less taxing than sound segmentation, which is also a phonemic awareness skill, but one that is saved for kindergarten.

Phonological and phonemic awareness skills do not always progress as a linear process—some develop concurrently as the child grows developmentally and is exposed to early skills and a rich literacy environment. Because rhyme awareness and beginning sound awareness develop at about the same time (National Reading Panel, 2000), it makes sense that students should spend some time at the beginning of pre-K enjoying rhyme and the sounds of words. As the year progresses, they continue to manipulate the language by becoming more phonologically sensitive, and they learn some letter names and their associated sounds as part of the pre-K core literacy curriculum. Understanding that words begin with a particular sound and other words start the same way gently shifts the child into perceiving phonemes—the smallest sounds of language (e.g., /b/). This builds on the auditory blending awareness of DROPP 9, in which students learn to say words *the fast way*.

HOW DROPP 10 IS STRUCTURED

DROPP 10 is made up of three complete Activity Sets—10.1, 10.2, and 10.3. Each Activity Set consists of four scripted lessons (Teacher Talk) that are used on 10 sequential learning days (the four lessons are repeated over the 10-day span). DROPP 10 has 30 days of intervention lessons in all (three Activity Sets of 10 days each). During the first 9 days of each set, students learn the words to alliterative songs and nursery rhymes, learn dance movements and fingerplays, and take part in interactive alliterative stories. On the 10th day, students review the skills to prepare for a short skill assessment checkout. (See the CD-ROM for the DROPP 10 Skill Assessment Checkout.)

Length of Activity Sets and Lessons

Each Activity Set is designed to be delivered across 10 sequential learning days. Each day's intervention lesson, including the transition activities, takes about 20 minutes to complete.

Goal and Emphasis of the Beginning Sound Alliteration Lessons

The goal of DROPP 10 is to support classroom instruction and saturate your students in beginning sound alliteration. It is important to remember that pre-K students who are in Tier 2 are emphasizing and strengthening their sound awareness—their ability to hear that *sad* starts with the same sound as *sick*—not to say that both words start with the letter *s* or to try to read the words. In the core literacy curriculum, students will learn to recognize several letters and their respective sounds (sound–symbol relationship), but in the intervention group, the students are working on their phonological and phonemic awareness of the sounds of letters and how to manipulate those sounds.

TEACHING TIP: **Check for Success**

Maintain eye contact with all students in your group, and ensure they are responding correctly and on cue. By doing this, you are conducting a mini assessment for each child to see who may need additional help.

Student Objective

- Know how to discriminate sounds and words and be able to categorize words as same or different by initial sounds

Teacher Objectives

The teacher will expose students to awareness of beginning sound alliteration by using targeted sounds from the core curriculum and providing students with practice opportunities to hear initial sounds and match pictures of words that begin the same way. The teacher will accomplish this by

- Emphasizing the beginning sounds in words so students can clearly hear that two words begin with the same initial sound

- Prompting the students to identify two words that begin with the same sound by exaggerating and holding the initial sound

- Checking that all students are fully focused on the target sounds and pictures

TEACHING TIP: **Check for Success**

Always have a mirror available so the students can look at their own mouth and tongue placements at the same time they look at yours. Although it is helpful for you to exaggerate your mouthing of the sounds and encourage the students to watch your mouth, a mirror allows them to mimic your movements directly.

TEACHING TIP: **Positive Teaching Approach**

Continually smile and nod affirmations to your students even when they make mistakes or find the lesson difficult. Your time with them is clearly instructional, but the content is fun and the goal is always success for all students.

HOW THE BEGINNING SOUND ALLITERATION ACTIVITY SETS DEVELOP EARLY LITERACY

Multisensory Techniques

In Activity Sets 10.1–10.3, students learn the words and hand movements to alliterative fingerplays and songs, sing "The Name Game," and use stories and pictures to enhance their understanding of words that start with the same sound. New games are introduced for added multisensory benefit: the Beginning Sound Game, Beginning Sound Card Sort, Beginning Sounds Pictures Game, and Sound Riddles. Although all of the songs and fingerplays still rhyme at this point, the children use fine motor skills and large muscle movements to add to their growing arsenal of early literacy experiences— that of emphasizing words that have like beginning sounds. The students see the beginning sound picture cards, sing songs with words that have the same beginning sounds while participating in dance motions, hear others sing them, and play board and card games to practice initial sound alliteration. They maintain their focus on like beginning sounds.

Making Meaning and Building Vocabulary

As students go through Activity Sets 10.1–10.3, they review vocabulary from prior lessons and are introduced to a few new words. The new words appear at the beginning of each Activity Set and are presented in a two-step approach (see Chapter 2). The children are also learning that some words can begin with the same sound; most of these alliterative words are well known and associated with visual cues. Continue to use new vocabulary in creative ways throughout the day while emphasizing beginning sounds. This will reinforce the students' daily use of new words and increase oral language growth. We also recommend setting aside time for students to engage in meaningful conversation with their peers.

- Activity Set 10.1: *beginning*, *skidoo*

- Activity Set 10.2: *sort*

- Activity Set 10.3: *silly*

Print Awareness

Students will have the opportunity to take part in read-alouds during the literature links, to review the left-to-right progression of word reading, and to reinforce their familiarity with the framework with using a book. In the book *Alphabet Zoo* (Holmes, 2003), children will learn the significance of looking carefully at the pictures on each page to discern important information (the book has no words, only letters of the alphabet). Learning this skill is a valuable precursor to reading comprehension. Students also will use a game board and practice following the natural progression of playing a game.

GENERAL TIPS FOR IMPLEMENTING ACTIVITY SETS 10.1–10.3

For students to clearly pinpoint like initial sounds, you must exaggerate the beginning sounds of words. It is important that you know the difference between held sounds and stop sounds to produce them correctly for precise modeling (see Appendix E on the CD-ROM for the Held Letters and Sounds and Stop Letters and Sounds reference charts). For example, the letter s is a held sound (/sss/) and the letter b is a stop sound (/b/). A stop sound cannot be held, but it can be repeated (e.g., /b/, /b/, /b/) as a teaching tool for beginning sound alliteration only—not for phoneme building. This is an important distinction between teaching phoneme blending and beginning sound alliteration, and we highly recommend that you review held and stop sounds before teaching DROPP 10.

TIPS FOR SPECIFIC ASPECTS OF ACTIVITY SETS 10.1–10.3

Beginning Sounds Game and Same Sounds Game

The Beginning Sounds Game is introduced in Activity Set 10.1. Related skill work continues in Activity Set 10.2 in the Same Sounds Game. The games use a picture deck with a picture of the targeted sound on one side and a blank on the other side, and the goal is to choose the sounds that coincide with instruction. Use the card decks from Appendix D: Games on the accompanying CD-ROM. The Beginning Sounds Game and Same Sounds Game are easy, straightforward games. The teacher does the following:

- Chooses a targeted sound that coincides with instruction

- Picks eight picture cards and lays them face down (five cards begin with targeted sound, three do not)

- Tells the student the targeted sound (e.g., /sss/), and the student picks a card and determines if the picture begins with the targeted sound

- Collects all picture cards that start with the targeted sound so the students can experience alliteration of picture clues and sounds (e.g., *sick, sad, snow*).

Initially, we used cards that had picture names printed on the bottom to help other adult volunteers identify the targeted sound. We found, however, that by the middle of pre-K, many of our students learned to recognize their letters and relied on knowing the letter names by sight rather than the letter sounds. A better idea is to use picture cards without names and supply a chart with the picture names to the small-group instructors. Then the students build their knowledge of targeted sounds, which, of course, is the point of the lesson (see the card decks from Appendix D: Games on the accompanying CD-ROM).

Beginning Sounds Card Sort Game

The Beginning Sounds Card Sort Game is also introduced in Activity Set 10.1. A four-step approach is used in this game, and it is important to speak slowly, clearly, and exaggerate the initial sounds.

Standard Teacher Talk for the Beginning Sounds Card Sort Game

For the following example, use *Matt, man,* and *foot* from the Beginning Sounds Card Sort Game card deck from Appendix D: Games on the accompanying CD-ROM.

Lay out three cards face up in a triangle formation, saying each card, one by one.

Matt *is on the first card at the top.*

Man *is on the second card, which is placed beneath the first card.*

Foot *is on the third card, which is placed next to the second card.*

Does *Matt* start with the same sound as *man? (Touch the man card.)*

Or, does *Matt (touch the Matt card)* start with the same sound as *foot (touch the foot card)?*

Mmmatt, mmman? *(Touch them as you say their names.)*

Or, Mmmatt, foot? *(Touch them as you say their names.)*

Mmmatt *(touch it)* starts with the same sound as . . . ? Who can touch the same beginning sound? *(Call on a student to touch the card and say the word.)*

▶ Child's response: Man.

Yes, *Mmmatt* starts with the same sound as *mmman.* You earn a point. *(Give a chip to the student.)*

Instructional Tips for Playing the Beginning Sounds Card Sort Game

Mix up the alliterative pair. Sometimes place the same sound card on the left and other times place it on the right; otherwise, the students rely on the placement of the card rather than identifying the sound.

- Whenever you begin a new lesson that includes the Beginning Sounds Card Sort Game, mix in some new pairs with the old ones. Eventually, you will rotate the whole deck and the students will become familiar with many beginning sounds.

- Once your students learn to play this game, make a student game (using sounds they know and feel comfortable with) and keep it in a center or workstation for independent play.

Game Management Tips

Make a chart of the beginning sound words and keep your deck in this order (see the Beginning Sound Card Sort Game Word List in Appendix D: Games on the accompanying CD-ROM) in order to minimize your time finding new alliterative matches for the students. Put all of your alliterative pairs together. As you play, use a continual pattern of two alliterative pair and one card from the subsequent pair. Here are some tips on how to work with your card deck.

- Keep your deck face up and in the same order as the Beginning Sound Card Sort Game Word List in Appendix D: Games on the accompanying CD-ROM.

- Complete the three-card sort with the first student. Pick up the alliterative pair and turn these cards over in a discard pile (students won't be distracted by past cards).

- Leave the unmatched card on the table for the next round; take the next two cards from your deck.

- At the end of the game, pick up your discard pile, turn it over, and put it at the bottom of your deck.

- At the start of the next lesson, take a few of the cards already used from the bottom and put them in the front of the deck. The students find success quickly with the previous beginning sound matches and then move to new ones.

Beginning Sounds Picture Game

The Beginning Sounds Picture Game is introduced in Activity Set 10.2. Students are shown one card with three pictures—pictures that have the same beginning sound and one picture that does not—and asked which two pictures begin with the same sound. The cards have the pictures on the front for the students and the words on the back for the teacher.

Standard Teacher Talk for the Beginning Sounds Picture Game

You will note in the intervention lessons how students are growing developmentally and are able to hear that two words start with the same beginning sound and a third word does not. All children develop differently, and they need to say the beginning sounds at their own pace. Beginning sounds are emphasized as much as possible.

It is important for the teacher to observe and note how the students are growing in their sounds. Many students will already know the letter name associated with the sound. But, at the pre-K intervention level, we are working on awareness of beginning sounds. While reviewing the following Teacher Talk, it is important to observe that some students can answer at *A* with only one prompt; some answer at *C* with two prompts; others may need three prompts to answer at *E*; and some may not be hearing the beginning sound "sameness" as yet and will actually be given the correct answer at *F*. This is scaffolded instruction. It is important to speak slowly and clearly and exaggerate the beginning sounds. For the following example, use *bell* (top), *book* (middle), and *towel* (bottom) from the Beginning Sounds Picture Game Word List in Appendix D: Games on the accompanying CD-ROM.

Hold up the first card to the first student, say all three pictures, and point to each one.

Bell. *(Touch it.)*

Book. *(Touch it.)*

Towel. *(Touch it.)*

Bell starts with the same sound as _____. *(Give the student a chance to process the cards and answer.)*

▶ Child's response: Book. (A)

Yes, *bell* starts with the same sound as *book*. You get a point. *(Give a chip and move to the next student.)*

▶ Child responds incorrectly or does not respond. (B)

Listen again. Does *bbbell* *(touch it)* start with the same sound as *bbbook* *(touch it)*?

Or, does *bbbell* *(touch it again)* start with the same sound as *towel* *(touch it)*?

▶ Child's response: Book. (C)

Yes, *bbbell* starts with the same sound as *bbbook*. You get a point. *(Give a chip and move to the next student.)*

▶ Child responds incorrectly or does not respond. (D)

Keep listening.

Bbbell, bbbook? *(Touch the pictures as you say them.)* Or, bbbell, towel? *(Touch the pictures as you say them.)*

Bbbell starts with the same sound as . . .? *(Touch bell.)*

▶ Child's response: Book. (E)

Yes, *bbbell* starts with the same sound as *bbbook*. You get a point. *(Give a chip and move to the next student.)*

▶ (Child cannot respond correctly.) (F)

Bbbell starts with the same sound as *bbbook*. Say it with me.

▶ Child's response: Bbbell starts with the same sound as bbbook.

Instructional Tips for Playing the Beginning Sounds Picture Game

Mix in some new cards with the old ones whenever you begin a new lesson that includes the Beginning Sounds Picture Game. Eventually, you will rotate the deck, and the students will become familiar with many new sounds. Once your students learn to play this game, make a student game and keep it in a center or workstation for independent play.

Sound Riddles

The Sound Riddles Game is introduced in Activity Set 10.3. Prepare the game cards in advance by printing the pages and attaching each pair of word and picture card pages so that both the word and picture sides are facing out. This way, the cards have a riddle on one side and a picture of the target word on the other. The riddle gives a rhyming word clue and then changes the beginning sound. After hearing the riddle, students are given some "think time" to process the clue before seeing the picture. The cards allow students to review their rhyming skills and couple them with beginning sounds. The target pictures help students focus in on both the rhyme and the sounds together to experience success. Note that all students must see all of the cards and remain fully focused on every riddle.

Standard Teacher Talk for Sound Riddles

You will pick a card and hand it to me. I will give you the riddle and you will try to guess it. When you get it right, you roll the die and take your turn. Let's start and then we'll go around the table. *(The first player picks a card and hands it to you. He or she does not look at the picture.)*

My word rhymes with *kick*, but begins with /sssss/. *(Give him or her some think time.)* Listen again. My word rhymes with *kick*, but begins with /sssss/. Look at the picture. *(Show the picture.)*

▶ Child's response: Sick.

Yes, kick, sick. Kick rhymes with . . . *(Keep showing the picture.)*

▶ Child's response: Sick.

Sick starts with /ssss/. Everyone, say it with me.

▶ Children's response: Sick starts with /ssss/.

Good job. Spin the spinner and take your turn. *(Hand child the die.)*

Instructional Tips for Sound Riddles

Use the game board provided in Appendix D on the CD-ROM. It is important to note that we planned this game in a way that did not have the students lose turns, switch places, or go backward at this level. Before each game, we reviewed the following rules.

- Determine who goes first. (Go around the table, but don't choose the same child to begin each time.)

- The student who goes first is the last to pick his or her play marker for the board.

- The first player picks a card and produces a response.

- If the student is correct, then he or she takes his or her turn by rolling the die. Hand the child the die and take it back after use; otherwise, it becomes a distraction to the students.

- If the student is incorrect, then you make the correction and move on to the next person. (Tell the student he or she will have to wait until the next turn.)

- Important: Keep playing until everyone wins.

Do not place the only copy of the game board in a student center for independent use because the pieces get lost too easily. Print several copies on different-colored card stock, laminate them, and put one in a student center. Use colored cubes from the math center for play markers and keep the die in your desk until students want to play.

Literature Link

There are three alliterative books used in DROPP 10 in order for our students to hear alliteration of beginning sounds in the context of stories. They are all presented in Lesson 3.

- Activity Set 10.1: *Silly Sally* (Wood, 1992)

- Activity Set 10.2: *Alphabet Zoo* (Holmes, 2003)

- Activity Set 10.3: *Tikki, Tikki, Tembo* (Mosel, 2007)

While reading, continue to encourage students to anticipate and predict any rhyming words at the end of the sentences. Read the words with the same beginning sounds in an overemphasized voice and stretch out the beginning sounds for easy identification by the students.

10

Read-Aloud Tip

Always preview the book privately before reading aloud to the students to become familiar with the story and the alliterative words. Once you are comfortable with the storyline and the words that have the same beginning sounds, you will be able to read the book "from the side" and hold it open for the children to see the pictures. Using this approach will keep the students actively engaged in the story. *Alphabet Zoo* (Holmes, 2003) is a great book for beginning sounds, as every letter has a page or two with pictures of animals and props that begin with that specific sound. There are no words (only the alphabet letter). The students have a terrific time trying to guess animal names and other related words that begin with the targeted sound.

Skill Assessment Checkouts

After your review lesson is completed, set aside a few minutes during that same day to give each child an individual sound alliteration checkout. These take about 2 minutes per child to administer and provide useful information to guide your future small-group placements. Based on the checkout and collaborative conversations with all teachers, you will determine which students should continue on in Tier 2 small-group intervention and which students can successfully return to Tier 1 whole-class instruction (see Chapter 2).

Assessment Outcome: The student can identify that two words start with the same beginning sound (alliteration).

ACTIVITY SET 10.1

Lesson Descriptions

Lessons	Sequence of daily activities	◇ Vocabulary
Lesson 1: Beginning Sounds Game	Rhyming song and dance: "Teddy Bear, Teddy Bear" Target: Beginning sounds: Beginning Sounds Game Alliterative fingerplay: "Tiny Tim the Turtle"	Beginning Skidoo
Lesson 2: Beginning Sounds Card Sort Game	Alliterative fingerplay: "A Sailor" Target: Beginning sounds: Beginning Sounds Card Sort Game Alliterative fingerplay: "The Muffin Man"	Sort
Lesson 3: Silly Sally	Alliterative fingerplay: "A Sailor" Alliterative book: *Silly Sally* (Wood, 1992) Alliterative fingerplay: "Tiny Tim the Turtle"	Silly
Lesson 4: Beginning Sound Alliteration Review	Alliterative song: "The Muffin Man" Target: Beginning sounds: Beginning Sounds Card Sort Game; rhyming book: *Silly Sally* (Wood, 1992)	

Materials Needed

☑ Book: *Silly Sally* (Wood, 1992)

☑ Optional: Stuffed bears

> ☑ DROPP 10 Skill Assessment Checkout (see Appendix B on the CD-ROM)   **CD-ROM**
>
> ☑ Tokens for behavior/participation
>
> **Beginning Sounds Game**
>
> ☑ Game cards (see Appendix D on the CD-ROM)
>
> ☑ Word list (see Appendix D on the CD-ROM)
>
> ☑ Three colored chips per child
>
> **Beginning Sounds Card Sort Game**
>
> ☑ Game cards (see Appendix D on the CD-ROM)
>
> ☑ Beginning Sounds Word List (see Appendix D on the CD-ROM)
>
> ☑ Three colored chips per child

ACTIVITY SET
10.1   10-Day Planner

Day 1	**Lesson 1:** Beginning Sounds Game
Day 2	**Lesson 1:** Beginning Sounds Game
Day 3	**Lesson 2:** Beginning Sounds Card Sort Game
Day 4	**Lesson 2:** Beginning Sounds Card Sort Game
Day 5	**Lesson 3:** Silly Sally
Day 6	**Lesson 3:** Silly Sally
Day 7	**Lesson 1:** Beginning Sounds Game
Day 8	**Lesson 2:** Beginning Sounds Card Sort Game
Day 9	**Lesson 3:** Silly Sally
Day 10	**Lesson 4:** Beginning Sound Alliteration Review

LESSON 1: Beginning Sounds Game

OBJECTIVES

Student will

- Know how to discriminate sounds and words and be able to categorize words as same or different by initial sounds

Teacher will

- Emphasize the beginning sounds in words so students can clearly hear that two words begin with the same initial sound
- Prompt for students to identify two words that begin with the same sound by exaggerating and holding the initial sound
- Check that all students are fully focused on the target sounds and pictures
- Smile and ensure success for all children
- Ensure that all children win the game

RHYMES, SONGS, AND FINGERPLAYS

"Teddy Bear, Teddy Bear"

"Tiny Tim the Turtle"

MATERIALS

Optional: Stuffed bears

Tokens for behavior/participation

Beginning Sounds Game

☑ Game cards (see Appendix D on the CD-ROM

☑ Word list (see Appendix D on the CD-ROM

☑ Three colored chips per child

 TASK 1   Transition song to begin the lesson (approximately 3 minutes)

INTRODUCE the big idea.

Call the group together, settle the children at a table, and say the following. We are going to listen for beginning sounds in words. Everyone, what are we going to listen for? *Prompt for a response.*

▶ **Children's response: The beginning sounds in words.**

Yes, we are going to listen for beginning sounds in words. Touch your nose if you are ready to listen for beginning sounds.

▶ **(Children respond by touching their noses.)**

We are listening for beginning sounds in words. Who knows where the beginning sounds are? Put your pinkie finger in the air if you know. *Call on one child.*

 Vocabulary

BEGINNING

▶ **(Child responds.)**

Explain vocabulary in a simple way. Follow a two-step approach. Step 1: Show an example and give a brief description of the word.

The beginning sound is the first sound you hear in a word. Like in the word *Malik. (Use your students' names.)* /Mmmm/ is the first sound you hear in *Malik.* Everyone, what's the first sound you hear in *Malik?*

▶ **Children's response: /Mmmm/.**

Step 2: Give students the description and have them supply the word. Guide children to use a complete sentence.

Yes, /Mmmmm/. Another way of saying *the very first sound in a word* is to say *the beginning sound in a word.* What's another way of saying *the very first sound in a word? Prompt for response.*

▶ **Children's response: The beginning sound in the word.**

Yes, the beginning sound is the very first sound. Now, we will all stand up and get in line, but Malik will be first in line. *Vocabulary memory tip: Act it out. Use movement with the students.*

▶ **(Children respond by getting line.)**

Malik is the first person you see in our line. Another way of saying that Malik is the first person in line is that Malik is at the beginning of the line. Everyone, what's another way of saying that Malik is the first person in line? *Prompt for response.*

▶ **Children's response: Malik is at the beginning of the line.**

Yes, Malik is at the beginning of the line. Everyone, what's another way of saying *the very first sound in a word? Prompt for response.*

▶ **Children's response: The beginning sound in the word.**

Yes, the beginning sound is the very first sound. Nice job learning that the word *beginning* means first.

BEGIN the transition.

You will sing a rhyming song and dance called "Teddy Bear, Teddy Bear." I know you'll remember this terrific song. What's the name of the song and dance?

▶ **Children's response: "Teddy Bear, Teddy Bear."**

 Model the Activity

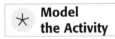 **Multisensory Reinforcement**

My turn to sing. Watch me dance. Stay in your seats now but sing with me. *Stand up and do dance movements that mimic the song.*

Teddy bear, teddy bear turn around.
Teddy bear, teddy bear touch the ground.
Teddy bear, teddy bear go upstairs.
Teddy bear, teddy bear say your prayers.

Teddy bear, teddy bear turn out your light.
Teddy bear, teddy bear say good night.
Teddy bear, teddy bear time to wake up.
Teddy bear, teddy bear drink from your cup.
Teddy bear, teddy bear shine your shoe.
Teddy bear, teddy bear skidoo, skidoo.

When you sing skidoo, *do two sideways slides—not a big movement but a fun one to do with young children, as they should learn to do this developmental movement.* Let's talk about the word *skidoo*. Some of you may already know this word.

Explain vocabulary in a simple way. Follow a two-step approach. Step 1: Show an example and give a brief description of the word.

Skidoo is a funny way of saying good-bye and then leaving the room. Watch me. *Do two sideway slides that get you close to an exit.*

 **Vocabulary**

SKIDOO

Step 2: Give students the description and have them supply the word. Guide children to use a complete sentence. Everyone, what's a funny way of saying good-bye and leaving the room?

▶ **Children's response: Skidoo is a funny way of saying good-bye and leaving the room.**

Yes, *skidoo* is a funny way of saying good-bye and leaving. Let's all stand up and skidoo. *Vocabulary memory tip: Act it out. Use exaggerated movements with the students. If you keep stuffed bears in your classroom, then let each student do the song and dance movements with a bear.*

10.1

Your turn to sing and dance with me. Everyone stand up. *Each child should have their own space. Sing with them and lead them in their dance movements.*

▶ **(Children respond by following you.)**

Teddy bear, teddy bear turn around.
Teddy bear, teddy bear touch the ground.
Teddy bear, teddy bear go upstairs.
Teddy bear, teddy bear say your prayers.

Teddy bear, teddy bear turn out your light.
Teddy bear, teddy bear say good night.
Teddy bear, teddy bear time to wake up.
Teddy bear, teddy bear drink from your cup.
Teddy bear, teddy bear shine your shoe.
Teddy bear, teddy bear skidoo, skidoo.

Good job singing and dancing. Let's go back and sit in our seats.

 TASK 2   **Beginning Sounds Game** (approximately 5–7 minutes)

 PLAY the game.   **CD-ROM** See Appendix D on the CD-ROM for the Beginning Sounds Game instructions, cards, and word list.

 TASK 3   **Transition fingerplay to end the lesson** (approximately 3 minutes)

MAKE the transition to end the lesson.   Today we'll say a rhyme about a turtle named Tiny Tim. You might already know a lizard named Tiny Tim, but now we have a turtle with the same name. Everyone, what sound do you hear at the beginning of *ttturtle, tttiny,* and *TTTim*?

▶ **Children's response:** /tttt/.

Yes, *Tiny Tim the turtle* begins with /tttt/. My turn to say the rhyme.

TEACHING TIP: Use drama to increase memory. Exaggerate the turtle moves.

 **Model the Activity**

I had a little turtle, his name was Tiny Tim.
I put him in the bathtub, to teach him how to swim. *(Move fingers in a swimming motion.)*
He drank up all the water. *(Pretend to drink.)*
He ate up all the soap. *(Pretend to eat.)*
And now when he talks, there is a bubble in his throat. *(Exaggerate the /tttt/ sound.)*

Your turn to say it with me. *Repeat the song, leading children in the song and movements.* Good job saying our funny rhyme. Let's do it one more time.

Excellent singing. Let's give ourselves a snap, crackle, pop. Do it with me.

Snap! *(Snap fingers once.)*
Crackle! *(Rub hands together quickly.)*
Pop! *(Clap hands once hard and quickly jet out hands with palms forward and fingers splayed.)*

END Lesson 1.	You all did a good job today. Everyone now gets their winnings for knowing words with the same beginning sounds and for working hard. *Give out token rewards to each child.*

LESSON 2: Beginning Sounds Card Sort Game

OBJECTIVES

Student

- Know how to discriminate sounds and words and be able to categorize words as the same or different by initial sounds

Teacher will

- Emphasize the beginning sounds in words so students can clearly hear that two words begin with the same initial sound
- Prompt for students to identify two words that begin with the same sound by exaggerating and holding the initial sound
- Check that all students are fully focused on the target sounds and pictures

- Smile and ensure success for all children
- Ensure that all children win the game

RHYMES, SONGS, AND FINGERPLAYS

"A Sailor"

"The Muffin Man"

MATERIALS

Tokens for behavior/participation

Beginning Sounds Card Sort Game

☑ Game cards

☑ Beginning Sounds Card Sort word list

☑ Three colored chips per child

 TASK 1   Transition fingerplay to begin the lesson *(approximately 3 minutes)*

INTRODUCE the big idea.

Call the group together, settle the children at a table, and say the following. We are going to listen for beginning sounds in words. Everyone, what are we going to listen for? *Prompt for a response.*

▶ Children's response: The beginning sounds in words.

Yes, we are going to listen for beginning sounds in words. Touch your nose if you are ready to listen for beginning sounds.

▶ (Children respond by touching their noses.)

BEGIN the transition.

Now we'll say a rhyme called "A Sailor" and use our hands to help us remember the words.

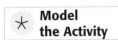 **Model the Activity**

Aaaaaaaa

sailor went to *(Tap table with both hands two times, then clap hands two times.)*

sea, sea, sea *(Salute with right hand over right eyebrow three times.)*

 Multisensory Reinforcement

To see what he could *(Repeat tap, tap, clap, clap pattern on the word see.)*

see, see, see. *(Repeat salute three times.)*

And all that he could *(Repeat tap, tap, clap, clap pattern on the word all.)*

see, see, see *(Repeat salute three times.)*

Was the bottom of the dark blue *(Repeat tap, tap, clap, clap pattern on the word bottom.)*

sea, sea, sea. *(Repeat salute three times.)*

Let's sing "A Sailor" together. *Repeat the fingerplay and do it with the students.*

Aaaaaaaa

sailor went to *(Tap table with both hands two times, then clap hands two times.)*

sea, sea, sea *(Salute with right hand over right eyebrow three times.)*

To see what he could *(Repeat tap, tap, clap, clap pattern on the word see.)*

see, see, see. *(Repeat salute three times.)*

And all that he could *(Repeat tap, tap, clap, clap pattern on the word all.)*

see, see, see *(Repeat salute three times.)*

Was the bottom of the dark blue *(Repeat tap, tap, clap, clap pattern on the word bottom.)*

sea, sea, sea. *(Repeat salute three times.)*

Let's change it up a little. This time, instead of saluting, let's chop our elbow. *Chop inside of elbow. Repeat the rhyme with new movements.*

Aaaaaaaa

sailor went to *(Tap table with both hands two times, then clap hands two times.)*

sea, sea, sea *(Right hand chops to inside of left elbow three times.)*

To see what he could *(Repeat tap, clap movement two times on the word see.)*

see, see, see. *(Repeat elbow chop three times.)*

And all that he could *(Repeat tap, tap, clap, clap pattern on the word all.)*

see, see, see *(Repeat elbow chop three times.)*

Was the bottom of the dark blue *(Repeat tap, tap, clap, clap pattern on the word bottom.)*

sea, sea, sea. (Repeat elbow chop two times.)

Let's change it up again. Now, instead of chopping inside our elbows, let's chop behind our knee. *Repeat the rhyme but have the right hand chop gently behind right knee.*

Excellent job with "A Sailor."

TASK 2 | Beginning Sounds Card Sort Game (approximately 12–14 minutes)

 Vocabulary

SORT

Who remembers what *sort out the beginning sounds cards* means? Touch your cheek if you remember. *Call on one child.*

▶ **Child responds appropriately.**

Yes, *sort out the beginning sounds cards* means to put the pictures that have the same beginning sounds together. Everyone, what's another way of saying you put the pictures that have the same beginning sounds together? *Prompt the students throughout the game.*

TEACHING TIP: Use a game format to practice the word. Students love anything in a game format.

▶ **Children's response: Sort out the cards that have the same beginning sounds.**

Yes, sort out the cards that have the same beginning sounds. Sherrod can sort out the cards with the same beginning sounds or the cards that start the same way. Let's say that again.

▶ **Children's response: Sherrod can sort out the cards that have the same beginning sounds.**

Great job using the word *sort*.

 PLAY the game.

CD-ROM | See Appendix D on the CD-ROM for the Beginning Sounds Card Sort Game instructions, cards, and word list.

 TASK 3 | Transition song to end the lesson (approximately 3 minutes)

MAKE the transition to the next lesson.

 Turn On Your Ears

We are going to sing a song called "The Muffin Man." You probably know it. Everyone, what is the name of our song?

▶ **Children's response: "The Muffin Man."**

What sound do the words *muffin* and *man* start with? Listen. Mmmmuffin mmman.

▶ **Children's response: /mmmm/.**

Yes, /mmmm/. My turn. Listen.
Do you know the muffin man, the muffin man, the muffin man?
Do you know the muffin man
Who lives on Drury Lane?
Oh yes, I know the muffin man, the muffin man, the muffin man.
Oh yes, I know the muffin man
Who lives on Drury Lane.

Your turn. Let's sing together. *Repeat the song with the students.*

Terrific work singing about the mmmmuffin mmman *(hold beginning sounds)*. Does *muffin* start with the same sound as *man*?

▶ **Children's response: Yes.**

Muffin starts with the same sound as . . .? *Prompt for response.*

▶ Children's response: Man.

Yes, man. Nice work with /mmmm/.

Your beginning sound work was so good today. Let's give ourselves the trucker cheer. Do it with me.

Grab your steering wheel. *(Put your hands on the "wheel" and "steer" it.)*
Rrrrrrr. *(Make the sound of a truck.)*
Honk, honk. *(Put your fist in the air and pull the horn.)*
Grab your CB radio and say, "Good job, good buddy." *(Talk into your fist.)*

END Lesson 2.

You all did a good job today. Everyone now gets their winnings for knowing words with the same beginning sounds and for working hard. *Give out token rewards to each child.*

LESSON 3: Silly Sally

OBJECTIVES

Student will

- Know how to discriminate sounds and words and be able to categorize words as the same or different by initial sounds

Teacher will

- Emphasize the beginning sounds in words so students can clearly hear that two words begin with the same initial sound

- Prompt for students to identify two words that begin with the same sound by exaggerating and holding the initial sound

- Closely observe each student for focus and full participation

- Smile and ensure success for all children

RHYMES, SONGS, AND FINGERPLAYS

"A Sailor"
"Tiny Tim the Turtle"

MATERIALS

Book: *Silly Sally* (Wood, 1992)
Tokens for behavior/participation

 TASK 1   Transition fingerplay to begin the lesson *(approximately 3 minutes)*

INTRODUCE the big idea.

Call the group together, settle the children at a table, and say the following. We are going to listen for beginning sounds in words. Everyone, what are we going to listen for? *Prompt for response.*

▶ Children's response: The beginning sounds in words.

Yes, we are going to listen for beginning sounds in words. Touch your nose if you are ready to listen for beginning sounds.

▶ (Children respond by touching their noses.)

BEGIN the transition.

Now we'll say a rhyme called "A Sailor" and use our hands to help us remember the words. Let's say "A Sailor" together. *Do the rhyme with the students.*

Aaaaaaaa

sailor went to *(Tap table with both hands two times, then clap hands two times.)*

sea, sea, sea *(Salute with right hand over right eyebrow three times.)*

To see what he could *(Repeat tap, tap, clap, clap pattern on the word see.)*

see, see, see. *(Repeat salute three times.)*

And all that he could *(Repeat tap, tap, clap, clap pattern on the word all.)*

see, see, see *(Repeat salute three times.)*

Was the bottom of the dark blue *(Repeat tap, tap, clap, clap pattern on the word bottom.)*

sea, sea, sea. *(Repeat salute three times.)*

Let's change it up a little. This time, instead of saluting, let's chop our elbow. *Chop inside of elbow. Repeat the rhyme.*

Aaaaaaaa

sailor went to *(Tap table with both hands two times, then clap hands two times.)*

sea, sea, sea *(Right hand chops to inside of left elbow three times.)*

To see what he could *(Repeat tap, tap, clap, clap pattern on the word see.)*

see, see, see. *(Repeat elbow chop three times.)*

And all that he could *(Repeat tap, tap, clap, clap pattern on the word all.)*

see, see, see *(Repeat elbow chop three times.)*

Was the bottom of the dark blue *(Repeat tap, tap, clap, clap pattern on the word bottom.)*

sea, sea, sea. *(Repeat elbow chop three times.)*

Let's change it up again. Now, instead of chopping inside our elbows, let's chop behind our knee. *Repeat the rhyme but have the right hand chop gently behind right knee.*

Excellent job with "A Sailor."

 Multisensory Reinforcement

🪐 **TASK 2**   **Alliterative and rhyming book** *(approximately 13–15 minutes)*

INTRODUCE the lesson.

👂 **Turn On Your Ears**

You are going to read a rhyming story with me today and listen for rhymes and beginning sounds. This book is called *Silly Sally. Hold up the book and point to the title as you read.* Listen to the title again. Sssssilly Sssssally *Hold beginning sounds.* What sound do you hear at the beginning of Sssssilly?

▶ Children's response: /ssss/.

Yes, /sssss/. What sound do you hear at the beginning of Sssssally?

▶ Children's response: /ssss/.

Yes, /sssss/. Everyone, *silly* starts with the same sound as . . .? *Prompt for response.*

▶ Children's response: Sally.

Yes. Let's say it. Silly Sally.

▶ Children's response: Silly Sally.

10.1

LESSON 3

◇ **Vocabulary**

SILLY

Good job. What do you think it means to be silly? Touch your nose if you know. *Call on one child.*

▶ **(Child responds appropriately.)**

Explain vocabulary in a simple way, and have the students repeat back the new word. Follow a two-step approach. Focus tip: Use the new word with a student's name. This will get their attention. Step 1: Ask children to describe (or act out) the new word.

Yes, silly is when we do things that are funny. Everyone, what's another way of saying Deverlyn is a funny boy?

▶ **Children's response: Deverlyn is a silly boy.**

Yes, Deverlyn is a silly boy. Let's all make silly faces.

▶ **(Children respond by making silly faces.)**

Step 2: Give students the description and have them supply the word.

Everyone, what's another way of saying we are all making funny faces?

▶ **Children's response: We are all making silly faces.**

Yes, we are all making silly faces. Great job knowing the word *silly.*

Look at the cover of the book. Everyone, what's another way of saying that Silly Sally is acting funny?

▶ **Children's response: Silly Sally is silly.**

Yes, Silly Sally is silly. What is Silly Sally doing? Touch your hair if you know. *Call on one student.*

▶ **(Child responds appropriately.)**

Let's read to find out all about Silly Sally. I just love this silly book. *Read the book aloud.*

TEACHING TIP: Overemphasize the rhymes and beginning sounds as you read.

Read the book again, if possible. Encourage and prompt for students to rhyme and say beginning sounds with you.

 TASK 3   **Transition fingerplay to end the lesson** (approximately 1–2 minutes)

MAKE the transition to end the lesson.

Today we'll say a rhyme about a turtle named Tiny Tim. You might already know a lizard named Tiny Tim, but now we have a turtle with the same name. Everyone, what sound do you hear at the beginning of *ttturtle, tttiny,* and *TTTim*?

▶ **Children's response: /tttt/.**

Yes, *Tiny Tim the turtle* begins with /tttt/. My turn to say the rhyme.

TEACHING TIP: Use drama to increase memory. Exaggerate the turtle moves.

I had a little turtle, his name was Tiny Tim.
I put him in the bathtub, to teach him how to swim. *(Move fingers in a swimming motion.)*

Multisensory Reinforcement	He drank up all the water. *(Pretend to drink.)*
	He ate up all the soap. *(Pretend to eat.)*
	And now when he talks, there is a bubble in his throat. *(Exaggerate the /tttt/ sound.)*
	Your turn to say it with me. *Repeat the song, leading children in the song and movements.*
	Good job saying our funny rhyme. Let's do it one more time.
	Let's do our good job dance. *Extend your right index finger in the air to the right of your body. With your left hand on your hip, move your right finger from the air to your side as you sing. Sing to the tune of "Stayin' Alive," and substitute the words "we did a good job, we did a good job."*
END Lesson 3.	You all did a good job today. Everyone now gets their winnings for knowing words with the same beginning sounds and for working hard. *Give out token rewards to each child.*

LESSON 4: Beginning Sound Alliteration Review

OBJECTIVES

Student will

- Know how to discriminate sounds and words and be able to categorize words as the same or different by initial sounds

Teacher will

- Emphasize the beginning sounds in words so students can clearly hear that two words begin with the same initial sound

- Prompt for students to identify two words that begin with the same sound by exaggerating and holding the initial sound

- Closely observe each student for focus and full participation

- Smile and ensure success for all children

RHYMES, SONGS, AND FINGERPLAYS

"The Muffin Man"

MATERIALS

Book: Silly Sally (Wood, 1992)

- ☑ DROPP 10 Skill Assessment Checkout (see Appendix B on the CD-ROM)

- ☑ Tokens for behavior/participation

Beginning Sounds Card Sort Game

- ☑ Game cards (see Appendix D on the CD-ROM)

- ☑ Beginning Sounds Card Sort word list (see Appendix D on the CD-ROM)

- ☑ Three colored chips per child

TASK 1   Transition song to begin the lesson *(approximately 1–2 minutes)*

INTRODUCE the big idea.

Call the group together, settle the children at a table, and say the following. We are going to listen for beginning sounds in words. Everyone, what are we going to listen for? *Prompt for response.*

▶ **Children's response: The beginning sounds in words.**

Yes, we are going to listen for beginning sounds in words. Touch your nose if you are ready to listen for beginning sounds.

BEGIN the transition.

▶ (Children respond by touching their noses.)

We are going to sing a song called "The Muffin Man." You know it from an earlier lesson. Everyone, what is the name of our song?

▶ Children's response: "The Muffin Man."

What sound do the words *muffin* and *man* start with? Listen. Mmmmuffin mmman.

▶ Children's response: /mmmm/.

 **Turn On Your Ears**

Yes, /mmmm/. My turn. Listen.

Do you know the muffin man, the muffin man, the muffin man?
Do you know the muffin man
Who lives on Drury Lane?
Oh yes, I know the muffin man, the muffin man, the muffin man.
Oh yes, I know the muffin man
Who lives on Drury Lane.

Your turn. Let's sing together. *Repeat the song and do it with the students.*

Terrific work singing about the mmmmuffin mmman. Does *muffin* start with the same sound as *man*?

▶ Children's response: Yes.

Muffin starts with the same sound as . . . ? *Prompt for response.*

▶ Children's response: Man.

Yes, *man*. Nice work with /mmmm/.

 TASK 2A   Beginning Sounds Card Sort Game *(approximately 9 minutes)*

 PLAY the game.

CD-ROM   See Appendix D on the CD-ROM for the Beginning Sounds Card Sort Game instructions, cards, and word list.

 TASK 2B   Alliterative and rhyming book *(approximately 9 minutes)*

INTRODUCE the lesson.

You are going to read a rhyming story with me today and listen for rhymes and beginning sounds. This book is called *Silly Sally. Hold up the book and point to the title as you read.* Listen to the title again. Ssssilly Sssssally. What sound do you hear at the beginning of Sssssilly?

▶ Children's response: /ssss/.

Yes, /ssss/. What sound do you hear at the beginning of Ssssally?

▶ Children's response: /ssss/.

Yes, /ssss/. Everyone, silly starts with the same sound as . . .? *Prompt for response.*

▶ Children's response: Sally.

Yes. Let's say it. Silly Sally.

▶ **Children's response: Silly Sally.**

Good job. Look at the cover of the book. Everyone, what's another way of saying that Silly Sally is acting funny?

▶ **Children's response: Silly Sally is silly.**

Yes, Silly Sally is silly. What is Silly Sally doing?

Let's read to find out all about Silly Sally. *Read the book aloud. Tip: Overemphasize the rhymes and beginning sounds as you read.*

Read the book again, if possible. Encourage and prompt for students to rhyme and say beginning sounds with you.

That was fun. Pull the train whistle if you liked hearing and saying the words with the same beginning sound. *Put your hand in the air and mime pulling a train whistle.*

▶ **(Children respond with a Whoo! Whoo! as they pull the whistle.)**

END Lesson 4.

You all did a good job today. Everyone now gets their winnings for knowing words with the same beginning sounds and for working hard. *Give out token rewards to each child.*

CD-ROM

The DROPP 10 Skill Assessment Checkout will be completed for each student following this lesson.

ACTIVITY SET 10.2

Lesson Descriptions

Lessons	Sequence of daily activities	◇ Vocabulary
Lesson 1: Same Sounds Game	Rhyming song and dance: "I'm a Fish" Target: Beginning sound alliteration: Same Sounds Game Alliterative song: "John Jacob Jingleheimer Schmidt"	
Lesson 2: Beginning Sounds Picture Game	Alliterative fingerplay: "It Is Raining" Target: Beginning sound alliteration: Beginning Sounds Picture Game Alliterative song and dance: "I'm a Fish"	
Lesson 3: Alphabet Zoo	Alliterative fingerplay: "Family Fingerplay" Alliterative book: *Alphabet Zoo* (Holmes, 2003) Alliterative fingerplay: "It Is Raining"	
Lesson 4: Beginning Sound Alliteration Review	Alliterative fingerplay: "Family Fingerplay" Target: Beginning Sounds Picture Game; alliterative book—*Alphabet Zoo* (2003)	

Materials Needed

☑ Book: *Alphabet Zoo* (Holmes, 2003)

☑ DROPP 10 Skill Assessment Checkout (see Appendix B on the CD-ROM)   **CD-ROM**

☑ Tokens for behavior/participation

Same Sounds Game

☑ Game cards (see Appendix D on the CD-ROM)

☑ Word list (see Appendix D on the CD-ROM)

☑ Three colored chips per child

Beginning Sounds Picture Game

☑ Game cards (see Appendix D on the CD-ROM)

☑ Three colored chips per child

ACTIVITY SET

10.2 **10-Day Planner**

Day 1	**Lesson 1:** Same Sounds Game
Day 2	**Lesson 1:** Same Sounds Game
Day 3	**Lesson 2:** Beginning Sounds Picture Game
Day 4	**Lesson 2:** Beginning Sounds Picture Game
Day 5	**Lesson 3:** Alphabet Zoo
Day 6	**Lesson 3:** Alphabet Zoo
Day 7	**Lesson 1:** Same Sounds Game
Day 8	**Lesson 2:** Beginning Sounds Picture Game
Day 9	**Lesson 3:** Alphabet Zoo
Day 10	**Lesson 4:** Beginning Sound Alliteration Review

LESSON 1: Same Sounds Game

OBJECTIVES

Student will

- Know how to discriminate sounds and words and be able to categorize words as the same or different by initial sounds

Teacher will

- Emphasize the beginning sounds in words so students can clearly hear that two words begin with the same initial sound
- Prompt for students to identify two words that begin with the same sound by exaggerating and holding the initial sound
- Check that all students are fully focused on the target sounds and pictures
- Smile and ensure success for all children
- Ensure that all children win the game

RHYMES, SONGS, AND FINGERPLAYS

"I'm a Fish"

"John Jacob Jingleheimer Schmidt"

MATERIALS

Tokens for behavior/participation

Same Sounds Game

- ☑ Game cards (see Appendix D on the CD-ROM)
- ☑ Word list (see Appendix D on the CD-ROM)
- ☑ Three colored chips per child

 TASK 1 | Transition song to begin the lesson (approximately 3 minutes)

INTRODUCE the big idea.

 Turn On Your Ears

Call the group together, settle the children at a table, and say the following. We are going to listen for beginning sounds in words. Everyone, what are we going to listen for? *Prompt for a response.*

▶ Children's response: The beginning sounds in words.

Yes, we are going to listen for beginning sounds in words. Touch your nose if you are ready to listen for beginning sounds.

▶ (Children respond by touching their noses.)

You are going to sing a rhyming song and do some movements. The song is called "I'm a Fish." Everyone, what's the name of the song and dance?

▶ Children's response: "I'm a Fish."

BEGIN the transition.

★ **Model the Activity**

I know you'll like this new rhyming song. Listen to the name again. "I'm a FFFish." What sound does *fish* start with?

▶ Children's response: /fff/.

Yes, *fish* starts with /fff/. My turn. Listen first and try to follow with your hands. *Sing to the tune of "I'm a Little Teapot." Do movements that mimic the song.*

I'm a little fishy, I can swim. (*Palms closed in front with thumbs crossed; "swim" them like a fish.*)
Here is my tail and here is my fin. (*Point to your "tail" and to your back.*)
When I want to have fun with my friend,
I wiggle my tail and dive right in. (*Wiggle tail and mimic diving with your arms.*)

 Turn On Your Ears

Great job. Listen up. I have some words for you. *Fish. Fin. Fun. Friend. Say words slowly and emphasize the beginning sound.* What sound do you hear at the beginning of *FFFFFish. FFFFFin. FFFFun. FFFFriend?*

▶ Children's response: /fff/.

10.2

Yes, /ffff/. Now it's your turn to sing. *Repeat the song with the students and model the movements.*

Very nice work singing about the fish, fin, fun, and friend. Pat yourselves on the back and each of you say, "I'm good stuff."

▶ **Children's response: I'm good stuff.**

 TASK 2   **Same Sounds Game** (approximately 5–7 minutes)

♣ **PLAY** the game.

 CD-ROM   **See Appendix D on the CD-ROM for the Same Sounds Game instructions, cards, and word list.**

Good work playing the Same Sounds Game. Your beginning sounds were so good today.

We will do a sit down cheer for everyone's terrific work today. *Sing the cheer to the tune of "Kiss Him Goodbye." Substitute the words "good job."*

TASK 3   **Transition song to end the lesson** (approximately 3 minutes)

MAKE the transition to end the lesson.

Everyone, let's say the name of our rhyming song. It's called "John Jacob Jingleheimer Schmidt." Say it with me.

▶ **Children's response: "John Jacob Jingleheimer Schmidt."**

Yes, "John Jacob Jingleheimer Schmidt." Let's sing together.

Use a conversational voice.
John Jacob Jingleheimer Schmidt,
His name is my name too.
Whenever we go out,
The people always shout,
There goes John Jacob Jingleheimer Schmidt.
La, la, la, la, la, la, la. *(Use a softer voice.)*

John Jacob Jingleheimer Schmidt,
His name is my name too.
Whenever we go out,
The people always shout,
There goes John Jacob Jingleheimer Schmidt.
La, la, la, la, la, la, la. *(Whisper.)*

John Jacob Jingleheimer Schmidt,
His name is my name too.
Whenever we go out,
The people always shout,
There goes John Jacob Jingleheimer Schmidt.
La, la, la, la, la, la, la. *(Use a conversational voice.)*

END the transition.

Excellent singing.

END Lesson 1.

You all did a good job today. Everyone now gets their winnings for knowing words with the same beginning sounds and for working hard.

Give out token rewards to each child.

LESSON 2: Beginning Sounds Picture Game

OBJECTIVES

Student will

- Know how to discriminate sounds and words and be able to categorize words as the same or different by initial sounds

Teacher will

- Emphasize the beginning sounds in words so students can clearly hear that two words begin with the same initial sound

- Prompt for students to identify two words that begin with the same sound by exaggerating and holding the initial sound

- Check that all students are fully focused on the target sounds and pictures

- Smile and ensure success for all children

- Ensure that all children win the game

RHYMES, SONGS, AND FINGERPLAYS

"It Is Raining"

"I'm a Fish"

MATERIALS

Tokens for behavior/participation

Beginning Sounds Picture Game

- ☑ Game cards (see Appendix D on the CD-ROM)

- ☑ Three colored chips per child

 TASK 1   Transition fingerplay to begin the lesson *(approximately 3 minutes)*

INTRODUCE the big idea.

Call the group together, settle them at a table, and say the following. We are going to listen for beginning sounds in words. Everyone, what are we going to listen for? *Prompt for a response.*

▶ **Children's response: The beginning sounds in words.**

Yes, we are going to listen for beginning sounds in words. Touch your nose if you are ready to listen for beginning sounds.

▶ **(Children respond by touching their noses.)**

BEGIN the transition.

You are going to sing a rhyme called "It Is Raining." Everyone, what's the name of our rhyming song?

▶ **Children's response: "It Is Raining."**

★ **Model the Activity**

My turn. Watch me. *Sing to the tune of "Frère Jacques."*

It is raining, it is raining. *(Wiggle fingers to the side of your head to make rain.)*

On my head, on my head. *(Pat head.)*

Pitter, patter rain drops, pitter patter rain drops. *(Wiggle fingers again making rain.)*

I'm all wet, I'm all wet. *(Hands down at side, looking sad.)*

LESSON 2

 Multisensory Reinforcement

Everyone, before you get your turn to sing, what sound do you hear at the beginning of *pppitter, ppppatter*.

▶ **Children's response: /ppp/.**

Yes, /ppp/. Does *pitter* start with the same sound as *patter*? Listen, pppitter, ppppatter. *Prompt for a response.*

▶ **Children's response: Yes.**

Say it with me. Ppppitter, ppppatter.

Your turn to sing. I'll do it with you. *Repeat the fingerplay and do it with the students.*

Nice work singing about the pitter patter of the rain.

 TASK 2 **Beginning Sounds Picture Game** (approximately 12–14 minutes)

 PLAY the game.

> **CD-ROM** See Appendix D on the CD-ROM for the Beginning Sounds Picture Game instructions and cards.

TASK 3 **Transition song to end the lesson** (approximately 3 minutes)

MAKE the transition to end the lesson.

You are going to sing a rhyming song and do some movements. The song is called "I'm a Fish." Everyone, what's the name of the song and dance?

▶ **Children's response: "I'm a Fish."**

I know you'll like this new rhyming song. Listen to the name again. I'm a fffish. What sound does *fffish* start with?

▶ **Children's response: /fff/.**

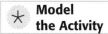 **Model the Activity**

Yes, *fish* starts with /fff/. My turn. Listen first and try to follow with your hands. *Do the movements that mimic the song. Sing to the tune of "I'm a Little Teapot."*

I'm a little fishy, I can swim. *(Palms closed in front with thumbs crossed; "swim" them like a fish.)*
Here is my tail and here is my fin. *(Point to your "tail" and to your back.)*
When I want to have fun with my friend,
I wiggle my tail and dive right in. *(Wiggle tail and mimic diving with your arms.)*

Great job. Listen up. I have some words for you. Fish. Fin. Fun. Friend. *Say the words slowly and emphasize the beginning sound.* What sound do you hear at the beginning of *fffish, fffin, fffun, fffriend*? *Prompt for the sound.*

▶ **Children's response: /fff/.**

Yes, /fff/. Now it's your turn to sing. *Repeat the song and model the movements.*

END the transition.

Nice work singing. Nice job, everyone. Let's get out our cameras. *Make a camera with your hands and make a "click, click" with your tongue as you reposition the camera and take some pictures of the students. They do the same.*

Click. Click. Click.

END Lesson 2.	Lookin' good. *(Thumbs up. Big smile. Nod.)*
	You all did a good job today. Everyone now gets their winnings for knowing words with the same beginning sounds and for working hard. *Give out token rewards to each child.*

LESSON 3: Alphabet Zoo

OBJECTIVES

Student will

- Know how to discriminate sounds and words and be able to categorize words as the same or different by initial sounds

Teacher will

- Emphasize the beginning sounds in words so students can clearly hear that two words begin with the same initial sound

- Prompt for students to identify two words that begin with the same sound by exaggerating and holding the initial sound

- Closely observe each student for focus and full participation

- Smile and ensure success for all children

RHYMES, SONGS, AND FINGERPLAYS

"Family Fingerplay"

"It Is Raining"

MATERIALS

Book: *Alphabet Zoo* (Holmes, 2003)

Tokens for behavior/participation

 TASK 1   **Transition fingerplay to begin the lesson** (approximately 3 minutes)

INTRODUCE the big idea.	*Call the group together, settle the children at a table, and say the following.* We are going to listen for beginning sounds in words. Everyone, what are we going to listen for? *Prompt for a response.*
	▶ **Children's response: The beginning sounds in words.**
	Yes, we are going to listen for beginning sounds in words. Touch your nose if you are ready to listen for beginning sounds.
	▶ **(Children respond by touching their noses.)**
BEGIN the transition.	You are going to sing a rhyme today about a family. It's called "A Family Fingerplay." What's the name of our fingerplay? *Prompt the students for the correct response.*
	▶ **Children's response: "A Family Fingerplay."**
	Yes, "A Family Fingerplay." My turn. Watch what I do with my fingers. Sing with me if you remember it.
✳ **Model the Activity**	This is the family. *(Hold up one hand with the fingers spread and wiggling.)*
	Let's count them and see.
	How many are there?
	And who can they be?
	1, 2, 3, 4, 5 *(Count off on your fingers.)*

TEACHING TIP: Use drama to increase memory. Use different voices for the family members.

10.2

LESSON 3

Multisensory Reinforcement	This is the mother *(Raise your pointer finger and use a kindly voice.)* Who loves everyone. And this is the father *(Raise your tall finger and use a deep voice.)* Who is lots of fun. This is the sister *(Raise your ring finger and use a high-pitched voice.)* She helps and she plays. And this is the baby *(Raise your little finger and use a baby voice.)* He's growing each day. But who is this one? *(Wiggle your thumb and use a questioning voice.)* She's out there alone. Why it's Lulu, the dog. And she's chewing a bone. Ruff. Ruff. *(Wiggle thumb and make dog sounds.)*
	Your turn to do it with me. Take out your family. Get ready. *Repeat the fingerplay and do it with the students.*
END the transition.	Nice work singing about this wonderful family. Touch your ears if you love your family.

🪐 **TASK 2**   **Alliterative book** *(approximately 13–15 minutes)*

	We are going to use a book that has many terrific pictures for us to look at and tell the beginning sounds. All set? *Snap two times.*
	▶ **Children's response: You bet. *(Snap two times.)***
	You are ready to look and listen and learn. Everyone, what sound do you hear at the beginning of *lllook, lllisten,* and *lllearn*? *Guide students to respond.*
	▶ **Children's response: /lll/.**
	Yes, *lllook, lllisten,* and *lllearn* start or begin with /llll/. You are really lllooking, lllistening, and lllearning.
INTRODUCE the lesson.	Here is an alphabet book that has the best pictures. This book is called *Alphabet Zoo. Hold up the book and point to the title as you read. All students must be able to see all of the pages.* Look at the cover of the book. What do you think the book is about? Hold up your index finger if you know. *Call on one child.*
	▶ **(Child responds appropriately.)**
	The first thing we are going to do is think of the sound at the beginning of the word fox. Everyone, what sound does *ffffox* start with?
	▶ **Children's response: /ffff/.**
	Yes, *ffffox* starts with /ffff/. Everyone, say it with me.
	▶ **Children's response: Ffffox starts with /ffff/.**
	Let's take a look inside at the /ffff/ page. *Open to the F page.* Tell me everything you see that begins with the /ffff/ sound. We will go around the table. You will earn one point if you find a picture that begins with /ffff/. You need five points to win.
	This is a great book for beginning sounds as every letter has a page or two with pictures of animals and props that begin with that specific sound. There are no words (only the alphabet letter). The students have a terrific time trying

to guess animal names and other related words that begin with the targeted sound. Choose three to four sounds and work with those pages until time runs out.

TEACHING TIP: Overemphasize the beginning sounds as you say the names of the pictures.

Great job saying beginning sounds.

 TASK 3   Transition fingerplay to end the lesson *(approximately 1–2 minutes)*

MAKE the transition to end the lesson.	You are going to sing a rhyme called "It Is Raining." Everyone, what's the name of our rhyming song?
	▶ **Children's response: "It Is Raining."**
✳ **Model the Activity**	My turn. Watch me. *Sing to the tune of "Frère Jacques."*
	It is raining, it is raining. *(Wiggle fingers to the side of your head to make rain.)* On my head, on my head. *(Pat head.)* Pitter, patter rain drops, pitter patter rain drops. *(Wiggle fingers again, making rain.)* I'm all wet, I'm all wet. *(Hands down at side, looking sad.)*
 **Multisensory Reinforcement**	Everyone, before you get your turn to sing, what sound do you hear at the beginning of *ppppitter, ppppatter.*
	▶ **Children's response: /ppp/.**
	Yes, /ppp/. Does *pitter* start with the same sound as *patter*? Listen, ppppitter, ppppatter. *Prompt for a response.*
	▶ **Children's response: Yes.**
	Say it with me. Ppppitter, ppppatter. Your turn to sing. I'll do it with you. *Repeat the song and do it with the students.*
END the transition.	Nice work singing about the pitter patter of the rain.
	Excellent singing. Let's give ourselves a snap, crackle, pop. Do it with me.
	Snap! *(Snap fingers once.)* Crackle! *(Rub hands together quickly.)* Pop! *(Clap hands once hard and quickly jet out hands with palms forward and fingers splayed.)*
END Lesson 3.	You all did a good job today. Everyone now gets their winnings for knowing words with the same beginning sounds and for working hard. *Give out token rewards to each child.*

LESSON 4: Beginning Sound Alliteration Review

OBJECTIVES

Student will

- Know how to discriminate sounds and words and be able to categorize words as the same or different by initial sounds

Teacher will

- Emphasize the beginning sounds in words so students can clearly hear that two words begin with the same initial sound

- Prompt for students to identify two words that begin with the same sound by exaggerating and holding the initial sound

- Check that all students are fully focused on the target sounds and pictures

- Smile and ensure success for all children

- Ensure that all children win the game

RHYMES, SONGS, AND FINGERPLAYS

"Family Fingerplay"

MATERIALS

Book: *Alphabet Zoo* (Holmes, 2003)

☑ DROPP 10 Skill Assessment Checkout (see Appendix B on the CD-ROM)

☑ Tokens for behavior/participation

Beginning Sounds Picture Game

☑ Game cards (see Appendix D on the CD-ROM)

☑ Three colored chips per child

 TASK 1 Transition fingerplay to begin the lesson (approximately 1–2 minutes)

INTRODUCE the big idea.	*Call the group together, settle them at a table, and say the following.* We are going to listen for beginning sounds in words. Everyone, what are we going to listen for? *Prompt for a response.*
	▶ Children's response: The beginning sounds in words.
Turn On Your Ears	Yes, we are going to listen for beginning sounds in words. Touch your nose if you are ready to listen for beginning sounds.
	▶ (Children respond by touching their noses.)
BEGIN the transition.	You are going to sing a rhyme today about a family. It's called "A Family Fingerplay." What's the name of our fingerplay? *Prompt the students for the correct response.*
	▶ Children's response: "A Family Fingerplay."
	Yes, "A Family Fingerplay." Sing with me and take out your "family" if you remember our fingerplay.
	This is the family. *(Hold up one hand with the fingers spread and wiggling.)* Let's count them and see. How many are there? And who can they be? 1, 2, 3, 4, 5 *(Count off on your fingers.)*

TEACHING TIP: Use drama to increase memory. Use different voices for the family members.

Multisensory Reinforcement	This is the mother *(Raise your pointer finger and use a kindly voice.)* Who loves everyone.

And this is the father *(Raise your tall finger and use a deep voice.)*

Who is lots of fun.

This is the sister *(Raise your ring finger and use a high-pitched voice.)*

She helps and she plays.

And this is the baby *(Raise your little finger and use a baby voice.)*

He's growing each day.

But who is this one? *(Wiggle your thumb and use a questioning voice.)*

She's out there alone.

Why it's Lulu, the dog.

And she's chewing a bone.

Ruff. Ruff. *(Wiggle thumb and make dog sounds.)*

Let's do it again. Get ready. *Repeat the fingerplay.*

END the transition. | Nice work singing about this wonderful family. Touch your ears if you love your family.

 **TASK 2A**   **Beginning Sounds Picture Game** (approximately 9 minutes)

 PLAY the game.

 CD-ROM   See Appendix D on the CD-ROM for the Beginning Sounds Picture Game instructions and cards.

 TASK 2B   **Alliterative and rhyming book** (approximately 9 minutes)

We are going to use a book that has many terrific pictures for us to look at and tell the beginning sounds. All set? *Snap two times.*

▶ **Children's response: You bet. *(Snap two times.)***

You are ready to look and listen and learn. Everyone, what sound do you hear at the beginning of *lllook, lllisten,* and *lllearn*? *Guide students to respond.*

▶ **Children's response: /lll/.**

Yes, *lllook, lllisten,* and *lllearn* start or begin with /llll/. You are really lllooking, lllistening, and lllearning.

INTRODUCE the lesson.   Here is an alphabet book that has the best pictures. This book is called *Alphabet Zoo. Hold up the book and point to the title as you read. All students must be able to see all of the pages.*

The first thing we are going to do is think of the sound at the beginning of the word *fox*. Everyone, what sound does *ffffox* start with?

▶ **Children's response: /ffff/.**

Yes, *ffffox* starts with /ffff/. Everyone, say it with me.

▶ **Children's response: *Ffffox* starts with /ffff/.**

Let's take a look inside at the /ffff/ page. *(Open to the F page.)* Tell me everything you see that begins with the /ffff/ sound. We will go around the table. You will earn one point if you find a picture that begins with /ffff/. You need five points to win.

This is a great book for beginning sounds, as every letter has a page or two with pictures of animals and props that begin with that specific sound. There are no words (only the alphabet letters). The students have a terrific time trying to guess animal names and other related words that begin with the targeted sound. Choose three to four sounds and work with those pages until time runs out.

TEACHING TIP: Overemphasize the beginning sounds as you say the names of the pictures.

Great job saying beginning sounds. *Sing to the tune of* The Addams Family *theme song. Clap twice after the words.*

Give me a clap. *(Clap twice.)*
Give me a clap. *(Clap twice.)*
Give me a clap, give me a clap, give me a clap. *(Clap twice.)*
I listen for sounds. *(Clap twice.)*
I listen for sounds. *(Clap twice.)*
Listen for sounds, listen for sounds, listen for sounds. *(Clap twice.)*

END Lesson 4.

You all did a good job today. Everyone now gets their winnings for knowing words with the same beginning sounds and for working hard. *Give out token rewards to each child.*

> **CD-ROM**   **The DROPP 10 Skill Assessment Checkout will be completed for each student following this lesson.**

ACTIVITY SET 10.3

Lesson Descriptions

Lessons	Sequence of daily activities	◇ Vocabulary
Lesson 1: The Name Game	Alliterative fingerplay: "It Is Raining" Target: Beginning sound alliteration: "The Name Game" Rhyming song: "Muffin Man"	
Lesson 2: Sound Riddles Game	Alliterative fingerplay: "John Jacob Jingleheimer Schmidt" Target: Beginning sound alliteration: Sound Riddles Alliterative song and dance: "I'm a Fish"	
Lesson 3: Tikki, Tikki, Tembo	Alliterative fingerplay: "Tiny Tim" Alliterative book: *Tikki, Tikki, Tembo* (Mosel, 2007) Alliterative fingerplay: "A Sailor"	
Lesson 4: Beginning Sound Alliteration Review	Rhyming song: "I'm a Fish" Target: Beginning sounds and rhyming words: Sound Riddles Game; alliterative book: *Tikki, Tikki, Tembo* (Mosel, 2007)	

Materials Needed

☑ Book: *Tikki, Tikki, Tembo* (Mosel, 2007)

☑ DROPP 10 Skill Assessment Checkout (see Appendix B on the CD-ROM)

 CD-ROM

☑ Tokens for behavior/participation

Sound Riddles Game

☑ Game board (see Appendix D on the CD-ROM)

☑ Game die (see Appendix D on the CD-ROM)

☑ Game cards (see Appendix D on the CD-ROM)

☑ Word list (see Appendix D on the CD-ROM)

ACTIVITY SET

10.3 **10-Day Planner**

Day 1	**Lesson 1:** The Name Game
Day 2	**Lesson 1:** The Name Game
Day 3	**Lesson 2:** Sound Riddles Game
Day 4	**Lesson 2:** Sound Riddles Game
Day 5	**Lesson 3:** Tikki, Tikki, Tembo
Day 6	**Lesson 3:** Tikki, Tikki, Tembo
Day 7	**Lesson 1:** The Name Game
Day 8	**Lesson 2:** Sound Riddles Game
Day 9	**Lesson 3:** Tikki, Tikki, Tembo
Day 10	**Lesson 4:** Beginning Sound Alliteration Review

LESSON 1: The Name Game

OBJECTIVES

Student will

- Know how to discriminate sounds and words and be able to categorize words as the same or different by initial sounds

Teacher will

- Emphasize the beginning sounds in words so students can clearly hear that two words begin with the same initial sound

- Prompt for students to identify two words that begin with the same sound by exaggerating and holding the initial sound

- Check that all students are fully focused on the target sounds and pictures

- Smile and ensure success for all children

- Ensure that all children win the game

RHYMES, SONGS, AND FINGERPLAYS

"I'm a Fish"

"John Jacob Jingleheimer Schmidt"

MATERIALS

Tokens for behavior/participation

  TASK 1   Transition fingerplay to begin the lesson (approximately 3 minutes)

INTRODUCE the big idea.	*Call the group together, settle the children at a table, and say the following.* We are going to listen for beginning sounds in words. Everyone, what are we going to listen for? *Prompt for a response.*

▶ Children's response: **The beginning sounds in words.**

Yes, we are going to listen for beginning sounds in words. Touch your nose if you are ready to listen for beginning sounds.

▶ **(Children respond by touching their noses.)**

BEGIN the transition.	You are going to sing a fingerplay called "It Is Raining." Everyone, what's the name of our rhyming song?

▶ Children's response: **"It Is Raining."**

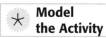 **Model the Activity**

My turn. Watch me. *Sing to the tune of "Frère Jacques."*

It is raining, it is raining. *(Wiggle fingers to the side of your head to make rain.)*
On my head, on my head. *(Pat head.)*
Pitter, patter rain drops, pitter patter rain drops. *(Wiggle fingers again, making rain.)*
I'm all wet, I'm all wet. *(Hands down at side, looking sad.)*

Everyone, before you get your turn to sing, what sound do you hear at the beginning of *pppitter, ppppatter.*

▶ Children's response: **/ppp/.**

 Turn On Your Ears

Yes, /ppp/. Does *pitter* start with the same sound as *patter*? Listen, ppppitter, pppatter. *Prompt for a response.*

▶ Children's response: **Yes.**

Say it with me. Pppitter, pppatter.

Your turn to sing. I'll do it with you. *Repeat the fingerplay and do it with the students.*

TASK 2   The Name Game *(approximately 5–7 minutes)*

INTRODUCE "The Name Game," by Shirley Ellis (commonly referred to as "The Bananafana Song").

 Turn On Your Ears

Today we are going to play "The Name Game." It's easy, and we get to do beginning sounds with our own names. Listen carefully. We'll try _____'s *(insert student's name)* name first. *Sing song with student's name.*

Isn't that silly? *Pick the next student's name to sing.* **Your turn.** *Walk the children through the game by eliciting each line of the chorus. Then, ask the children to repeat whose name was used in the song. Prompt for the entire song.*

Let's do it again. Listen first. *Sing the song with another child's name.*

Your turn. We'll sing together. *Follow the preceding steps for prompting the entire song.*

Continue singing with everyone's name, and your own, until time runs out. Prompt for the beginning sounds and the rhyme at the end.

Terrific job singing your names. I think we should take our picture. Do it with me. Let's get out our cameras. *Make a camera with your hands and make a "click, click" with your tongue as you reposition the camera and take some pictures of your students. They do the same.*

Click. Click. Click. Lookin' good. *Thumbs up. Big smile. Nod.*

TASK 3   Transition song to end the lesson *(approximately 3 minutes)*

BEGIN the transition.

We are going to sing a song called "The Muffin Man." You probably know it. Everyone, what is the name of our song?

▶ **Children's response: "The Muffin Man."**

What sound does *muffin man* start with? Listen again. Mmmmuffin mmman.

▶ **Children's response: /mmmm/.**

Yes, /mmmm/. My turn. Listen.

Do you know the muffin man, the muffin man, the muffin man?
Do you know the muffin man
Who lives on Drury Lane?
Oh yes, I know the muffin man, the muffin man, the muffin man.
Oh yes, I know the muffin man
Who lives on Drury Lane.

Your turn. Let's sing together. *Repeat the song and do it with the students.*

Terrific work singing about the mmmmuffin mmman. Does *muffin* start with the same sound as *man*?

▶ **Children's response: Yes.**

Muffin starts with the same sound as . . . ? *Prompt for a response.*

▶ **Children's response: Man.**

END the transition.	Yes, *man*. Nice work with /mmmm/.
	You all did a good job today. Everyone now gets their winnings for knowing words with the same beginning sounds and for working hard. *Give out token rewards to each child.*
END Lesson 1.	

LESSON 2: Sound Riddles Game

OBJECTIVES

Student will

- Know how to discriminate sounds and words and be able to categorize words as the same or different by initial sounds

Teacher will

- Emphasize the beginning sounds in words so students can clearly hear that two words begin with the same initial sound

- Prompt for students to identify two words that begin with the same sound by exaggerating and holding the initial sound

- Check that all students are fully focused on the target sounds and pictures

- Smile and ensure success for all children

- Ensure that all children win the game

RHYMES, SONGS, AND FINGERPLAYS

"It Is Raining"
"I'm a Fish"

MATERIALS

Tokens for behavior/participation

Sound Riddles Game

☑ Game board (see Appendix D on the CD-ROM)

☑ Game die (see Appendix D on the CD-ROM)

☑ Game cards (see Appendix D on the CD-ROM)

☑ Word list (see Appendix D on the CD-ROM)

 TASK 1   Transition song to begin the lesson *(approximately 3 minutes)*

INTRODUCE the big idea.	*Call the group together, settle the children at a table, and say the following.* We are going to listen for beginning sounds in words. Everyone, what are we going to listen for? *Prompt for a response.*
	▶ **Children's response: The beginning sounds in words.**
	Yes, we are going to listen for beginning sounds in words. Touch your nose if you are ready to listen for beginning sounds.
	▶ **(Children respond by touching their noses.)**
	Everyone, let's say the name of our rhyming song. It's "John Jacob Jingleheimer Schmidt." Say it with me.
BEGIN the transition.	▶ **Children's response: "John Jacob Jingleheimer Schmidt."**
	Yes, "John Jacob Jingleheimer Schmidt." Let's sing together.
	Use a conversational voice.
	John Jacob Jingleheimer Schmidt,
	His name is my name too.
	Whenever we go out,
	The people always shout,

There goes John Jacob Jingleheimer Schmidt.

La, la, la, la, la, la, la. *(Use a softer voice.)*

John Jacob Jingleheimer Schmidt,

His name is my name too.

Whenever we go out,

The people always shout,

There goes John Jacob Jingleheimer Schmidt.

La, la, la, la, la, la, la. *(Whisper).*

John Jacob Jingleheimer Schmidt,

His name is my name too.

Whenever we go out,

The people always shout,

There goes John Jacob Jingleheimer Schmidt.

La, la, la, la, la, la, la. *(Use a conversational voice.)*

 TASK 2 **Sound Riddles Game** (approximately 12–14 minutes)

 PLAY the game.

CD-ROM See Appendix D on the CD-ROM for the Sound Riddles Game instructions, board, die, cards, and word list.

TASK 3 **Transition song to end the lesson** (approximately 3 minutes)

MAKE the transition to end the lesson.

You are going to sing a rhyming song and do some movements. The song is called "I'm a Fish." Everyone, what's the name of the song and dance?

▶ **Children's response: "I'm a Fish."**

I know you'll like this new rhyming song. Listen to the name again. I'm a fffish. What sound does *fffish* start with.

▶ **Children's response: /fff/.**

Yes, fish starts with /fff/. My turn. Listen first and try to follow with your hands. *Sing to the tune of "I'm a Little Teapot." Do the movements that mimic the song.*

I'm a little fishy, I can swim. *(Palms closed in front with thumbs crossed; "swim" them like a fish.)*

Here is my tail and here is my fin. *(Point to your "tail" and to your back.)*

When I want to have fun with my friend,

I wiggle my tail and dive right in. *(Wiggle tail and mimic diving with your arms.)*

 Turn On Your Ears

Great job. Listen up. I have some words for you. *Say the words slowly and emphasize the beginning sound.* **Fish. Fin. Fun. Friend.** What sound do you hear at

TASK 3 *(continued)*

the beginning of *ffffish, fffin, fffun, ffffriend*? *Prompt for the sound.*

▶ Children's response: /fff/.

Yes, /fff/. Now it's your turn to sing. *Repeat the song and model the movements.*

END the transition.

Nice work singing.

Your beginning sound work was so good today. Nice job everyone. Let's get out our cameras. *Make a camera with your hands and make a "click, click" with your tongue as you reposition the camera and take some pictures of your students. They do the same.*

Click. Click. Click. Lookin' good. *Thumbs up. Big smile. Nod.*

END Lesson 2.

You all did a good job today. Everyone now gets their winnings for knowing words with the same beginning sounds and for working hard. *Give out token rewards to each child.*

LESSON 3: Tikki, Tikki, Tembo

OBJECTIVES

Student will

- Know how to discriminate sounds and words and be able to categorize words as the same or different by initial sounds

Teacher will

- Emphasize the beginning sounds in words so students can clearly hear that two words begin with the same initial sound

- Prompt for students to identify two words that begin with the same sound by exaggerating and holding the initial sound

- Check that all students are fully focused on the target sounds and pictures

- Smile and ensure success for all children

- Ensure that all children win the game

RHYMES, SONGS, AND FINGERPLAYS

"Family Fingerplay"

"It Is Raining"

MATERIALS

Book: *Tikki, Tikki, Tembo* (Mosel, 2007)

Tokens for behavior/participation

 TASK 1   Transition fingerplay to begin the lesson *(approximately 3 minutes)*

INTRODUCE the big idea.

Call the group together, settle the children at a table, and say the following. We are going to listen for beginning sounds in words. Everyone, what are we going to listen for? *Prompt for a response.*

▶ Children's response: The beginning sounds in words.

Yes, we are going to listen for beginning sounds in words. Touch your nose if you are ready to listen for beginning sounds.

▶ (Children respond by touching their noses.)

BEGIN the transition.

Today we'll say a rhyme about a turtle named Tiny Tim. You might already know a lizard named Tiny Tim, but now we have a turtle with the same name. Everyone, what sound do you hear at the beginning of *ttturtle, tttiny,* and *TTTim*?

▶ Children's response: /tttt/.

Yes, *Tiny Tim the turtle* begins with /tttt/. My turn to say the rhyme.

TEACHING TIP: Use drama to increase memory. Exaggerate the turtle moves.

Multisensory Reinforcement

I had a little turtle, his name was Tiny Tim.

I put him in the bathtub, to teach him how to swim. *(Move fingers in a swimming motion.)*

He drank up all the water. *(Pretend to drink.)*

He ate up all the soap. *(Pretend to eat.)*

And now when he talks, there is a bubble in his throat. *(Exaggerate the /tttt/ sound.)*

Your turn to say it with me. *Repeat the rhyme, leading children in the song and movements.*

Good job saying our funny rhyme. Let's do it one more time.

 TASK 2 **Alliterative book** *(approximately 13–15 minutes)*

We are going to use a book that has many terrific sounds for us to hear. All set? *Snap two times.*

▶ **Children's response: You bet.** *Snap two times.*

Turn On Your Ears

You are ready to look and listen and learn. Everyone, what sound do you hear at the beginning of *lllook, lllisten,* and *lllearn*? *Guide students to respond.*

▶ **Children's response: /lll/.**

Yes, *lllook, lllisten,* and *lllearn* start or begin with /llll/. You are really lllooking, lllistening, and lllearning.

INTRODUCE the lesson.

You are going to read a great book called *Tikki, Tikki, Tembo. Hold up the book and point to the title as you read. All students must be able to see all of the pages.* What sound does *Ttttiikki, Ttttembo* start with?

▶ **Children's response: /ttt/.**

Yes, /ttt/. Today you are going to listen to a story about a little boy who has a very long name. Listen for the sounds at the beginning of the words. Part of his name is Tikki, Tikki, Tembo and that is the name of our book. What is the name of our book?

▶ **Children's response: Tikki, Tikki, Tembo.**

Who has a long name here? Gently pull your ear lobe if you have a long name. *Call on one or two children to respond.*

▶ **(Children respond with appropriate answers.)**

Let's get ready to hear all of the long names in our story. Think of sounds as we read. *Read the book aloud.*

TEACHING TIP: Overemphasize the beginning sound alliteration as you read and prompt for beginning sounds.

 **TASK 3**   Transition fingerplay to end the lesson (approximately 1–2 minutes)

MAKE the transition to end the lesson.

Aaaaaaaa

sailor went to *(Tap table with both hands two times, then clap hands two times.)*

sea, sea, sea *(Salute with right hand over right eyebrow three times.)*

To see what he could *(Repeat tap, tap, clap, clap pattern on the word see.)*

see, see, see. *(Repeat salute three times.)*

And all that he could *(Repeat tap, tap, clap, clap pattern on the word all.)*

see, see, see *(Repeat salute three times.)*

Was the bottom of the dark blue *(Repeat tap, tap, clap, clap pattern on the word bottom.)*

sea, sea, sea. *(Repeat salute three times.)*

Let's sing "A Sailor" together. *Do it with the students.*

 **Model the Activity**

Multisensory Reinforcement

Aaaaaaaa

sailor went to *(Tap table with both hands two times, then clap hands two times.)*

sea, sea, sea *(Salute with right hand over right eyebrow three times.)*

To see what he could *(Repeat tap, tap, clap, clap pattern on the word see.)*

see, see, see. *(Repeat salute three times.)*

And all that he could *(Repeat tap, tap, clap, clap pattern on the word all.)*

see, see, see *(Repeat salute three times.)*

Was the bottom of the dark blue *(Repeat tap, tap, clap, clap pattern on the word bottom.)*

sea, sea, sea. *(Repeat salute three times.)*

Let's change it up a little. This time, instead of saluting, let's chop our elbow. *Chop inside of elbow. Repeat the rhyme.*

Aaaaaaaa

sailor went to *(Tap table with both hands, then clap hands; repeat.)*

sea, sea, sea *(Right hand chops to inside of left elbow three times.)*

To see what he could *(Repeat tap, tap, clap, clap pattern on the word see.)*

see, see, see. *(Repeat elbow chop three times.)*

And all that he could *(Repeat tap, tap, clap, clap pattern on the word all.)*

see, see, see *(Repeat elbow chop three times.)*

Was the bottom of the dark blue *(Repeat tap, tap, clap, clap pattern on the word bottom.)*

sea, sea, sea. *(Repeat elbow chop three times.)*

Let's change it up again. Now, instead of chopping inside our elbows, let's chop behind our knee. *Repeat the rhyme but have the right hand chop gently behind right knee.*

END the transition.

Excellent job with "A Sailor."

	Excellent singing. Let's give ourselves a snap, crackle, pop. Do it with me.
	Snap! *(Snap fingers once.)*
	Crackle! *(Rub hands together quickly.)*
	Pop! *(Clap hands once hard and quickly jet out hands with palms forward and fingers splayed.)*
END Lesson 3.	You all did a good job today. Everyone now gets their winnings for knowing words with the same beginning sounds and for working hard. *Give out token rewards to each child.*

LESSON 4: Beginning Sound Alliteration Review

OBJECTIVES

Student will

- Know how to discriminate sounds and words and be able to categorize words as the same or different by initial sounds

Teacher will

- Emphasize the beginning sounds in words so students can clearly hear that two words begin with the same initial sound
- Prompt for students to identify two words that begin with the same sound by exaggerating and holding the initial sound
- Check that all students are fully focused on the target sounds and pictures
- Smile and ensure success for all children
- Ensure that all children win the game

RHYMES, SONGS, AND FINGERPLAYS

"Family Fingerplay"

MATERIALS

Book: *Tikki, Tikki, Tembo* (Mosel, 2007)

☑ DROPP 10 Skill Assessment Checkout (see Appendix B on the CD-ROM)   **CD-ROM**

☑ Tokens for behavior/participation

Sound Riddles Game

☑ Game board (see Appendix D on the CD-ROM)

☑ Game die (see Appendix D on the CD-ROM)

☑ Game cards (see Appendix D on the CD-ROM)

☑ Word list (see Appendix D on the CD-ROM)

 **TASK 1**   Transition song to begin the lesson *(approximately 1–2 minutes)*

INTRODUCE the big idea.	*Call the group together, settle them at a table, and say the following.* We are going to listen for beginning sounds in words. Everyone, what are we going to listen for? *Prompt for a response.*
	▶ Children's response: The beginning sounds in words.
	Yes, we are going to listen for beginning sounds in words. Touch your nose if you are ready to listen for beginning sounds.
	▶ (Children respond by touching their noses.)
BEGIN the transition.	You are going to sing a rhyming song and do some movements. The song is called "I'm a Fish." Everyone, what's the name of the song and dance?
	▶ Children's response: "I'm a Fish."

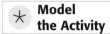

I know you'll like this new rhyming song. Listen to the name again. I'm a fffish. What sound does *fffish* start with.

▶ **Children's response: /fff/.**

★ **Model the Activity**

Yes, *fish* starts with /fff/. My turn. Listen first and try to follow with your hands. *Sing to the tune of "I'm a Little Teapot." Do the movements that mimic the song.*

I'm a little fishy, I can swim. *(Palms closed in front with thumbs crossed; "swim" them like a fish.)*
Here is my tail and here is my fin. *(Point to your "tail" and to your back.)*
When I want to have fun with my friend,
I wiggle my tail and dive right in. *(Wiggle tail and mimic diving with your arms.)*

👂 **Turn On Your Ears**

★ **Model the Activity**

Great job. Listen up. I have some words for you. *Say the words slowly and emphasize the beginning sound. Fish. Fin. Fun. Friend.* What sound do you hear at the beginning of *fffish, fffin, fffun, ffffriend*? *Prompt for the sound.*

▶ **Children's response: /fff/.**

Yes, /fff/. Now it's your turn to sing. *Repeat the song and model the movements.*

END the transition.

Nice work singing.

 TASK 2A   Sound Riddles Game *(approximately 9 minutes)*

♣ **PLAY** the game.

CD-ROM   See Appendix D on the CD-ROM for the Sound Riddles Game instructions, board, die, cards, and word list.

 TASK 2B   Alliterative book *(approximately 9 minutes)*

We are going to use a book that has many terrific sounds for us to hear. All set? *Snap two times.*

▶ **Children's response: You bet.** *Snap two times.*

You are ready to look and listen and learn. Everyone, what sound do you hear at the beginning of *lllook, lllisten,* and *lllearn*? *Guide students to respond.*

▶ **Children's response: /lll/.**

Yes, *lllook, lllisten,* and *lllearn* start or begin with /llll/. You are really lllooking, lllistening, and lllearning.

INTRODUCE the lesson.

You are going to read a great book called *Tikki, Tikki, Tembo. Hold up the book and point to the title as you read. All students must be able to see all of the pages.* What sound does *Ttttiikki, Ttttembo* start with?

▶ **Children's response: /ttt/.**

Yes, /ttt/. Today you are going to listen to a story about a little boy who has a very long name. Listen for the sounds at the beginning of the words. Part of his name is Tikki, Tikki, Tembo and that is the name of our book. What is the name of our book?

▶ Children's response: Tikki, Tikki, Tembo.

Who has a long name here? Gently pull your ear lobe if you have a long name. *Call on one or two children to respond.)*

▶ **(Children respond with appropriate answers.)**

Let's get ready to hear all of the long names in our story. Think of sounds as we read. *Read the book aloud.*

TEACHING TIP: Overemphasize the beginning sound alliteration as you read and prompt for beginning sounds.

You are a gold star class. You know what that means.

Take out your star box. *(Cup one hand.)*
Get your star. *(Pretend to get a star on the pointer finger of the other hand, lick it, and put it on your forehead.)*
You are all gold star kids.

END Lesson 4.

You all did a good job today. Everyone now gets their winnings for knowing words with the same beginning sounds and for working hard. *Give out token rewards to each child.*

CD-ROM The DROPP 10 Skill Assessment Checkout will be completed for each student following this lesson.

References

Adams, M.J. (1990). *Beginning to read: Thinking and learning about print.* Cambridge, MA: MIT Press.

Adams, M.J., Foorman, B.R., Lundberg, I., & Beeler, T. (1998). *Phonemic awareness in young children: A classroom curriculum.* Baltimore: Paul H. Brookes Publishing Co.

Armbruster, B.B., Lehr, F., & Osborn, J. (2001). *Put reading first: The research building blocks for teaching children to read: Kindergarten through grade 1.* Jessup, MD: National Institute for Literacy.

Baker, L. (2006). *An evaluation of the Baltimore Public School Early Identification and Intervention Project.* Baltimore: University of Maryland, Baltimore County, and The Abell Foundation.

Baker, L. (2007). *An evaluation of the Baltimore Public School Early Identification and Intervention Project.* Baltimore: University of Maryland, Baltimore County, and The Abell Foundation.

Baker, L. (2008). *An evaluation of the Baltimore Public School Early Identification and Intervention Project.* Baltimore: University of Maryland, Baltimore County, and The Abell Foundation.

Blachman, B.A., Tangel, D.M., Ball, W.B., Black, R., & McGraw, C.K. (1999). Developing phonological awareness and word recognition skills: A two-year intervention with low-income, inner-city children. *Reading and Writing: An Interdisciplinary Journal, 11,* 239–273.

Bowman, B., Donovan, M.S., & Burns, M.S. (Eds.). (2000). *Eager to learn: Educating our preschoolers.* Washington, DC: National Academies Press.

Brabeck, M. (2008, May 20). *Why we need "translational" research.* Retrieved May 22, 2008, from http://www.edweek.org/ew/articles/2008/05/21/38brabeck.h27.html

Carnine, D.W., Silbert, J., & Kame'enui, E.J. (1997). *Direct instruction reading* (3rd edition). Upper Saddle River, NJ: Prentice-Hall.

Carta, J.J., Greenwood, C., Walker, D., & Buzhardt, J. (2010). *Using IGDIs: Monitoring progress and improving intervention for infants and young children.* Baltimore: Paul H. Brookes Publishing Co.

Causton-Theoharis, J., Giangreco, M., Doyle, M., & Vadasy, P. (2007). The "sous-chefs" of literacy instruction. *Teaching Exceptional Children, 40*(1), 56–63.

Chandler, L., et al. (2007). Promoting early literacy skills within daily activities and routines in preschool classrooms. *Young Exceptional Children, 11*(2), 2–16.

Children of the Code. (2010). *Dr. Grover (Russ) Whitehurst: Evidence based education science and the challenge of learning to read.* Retrieved July 22, 2010, from http://www.childrenofthecode.org/interviews/whitehurst.htm#ReadingSchool

Cobb, C. (2007). Training paraprofessionals to effectively work with all students. *The Reading Teacher, 60,* 686–690.

Coleman, M.R., Buysse, V., & Neitzel, J. (2006). *Recognition and response: An early intervening system for young children at risk for learning disabilities.* Chapel Hill: University of North Carolina, FPG Child Development Institute.

Dickinson, D.K., & Tabors, P.O. (2001). *Beginning literacy with language: Young children learning at home and school.* Baltimore: Paul H. Brookes Publishing Co.

Feldman, J. (1995). *Transition time: Let's do something different!* Beltsville, MD: Gryphon House.

Foorman, B.R., Francis, D.J., Fletcher, J.M., Schatschneider, C., & Mehta, P. (1998). The role of instruction in learning to read: Preventing reading failure in at-risk children. *Journal of Educational Psychology, 90,* 37–55.

Fowler, A.E. (1991). How early phonological development might set the stage for phoneme awareness. In S.A. Brady & D.A. Shankweiler (Eds.), *Phonological processes in literacy* (pp. 97–117). Mahwah, NJ: Lawrence Erlbaum Associates.

Francis, D.J., Shaywitz, S.E., Stuebing, K.K., Shaywitz, B.A., & Fletcher, J.M. (1996). Developmental lag versus deficit models of reading disability: A longitudinal, individual growth curves analysis. *Journal of Educational Psychology, 88,* 3–17.

Giangreco, M., & Broer, S. (2003). Paraprofessionals: No perfect solution. *CEC Today, 9,* 5–12.

Granger, J., & Grek, M. (2005). Struggling readers stretch their skills. *Journal of Staff Development, 26*(3), 32–36, 70.

Haager, D., Klingner, J., & Vaughn, S. (2007). *Evidence-based reading practices for response to intervention.* Baltimore: Paul H. Brookes Publishing Co.

Hall, S. (2007). *Implementing Response to Intervention: A principal's guide.* Thousand Oaks, CA: Corwin Press.

Hall, S.L., & Moats, L.C. (2002). *Parenting a struggling reader.* New York: Broadway.

Harcourt Educational Measurement. (2002). *Stanford Achievement Test, Tenth Edition (Stanford 10).* Upper Saddle River, NJ: Pearson Education.

Hart, B., & Risley, T.R. (1995). *Meaningful differences in the everyday experience of young American children.* Baltimore: Paul H. Brookes Publishing Co.

Hiebert, E.H., & Taylor, B.M. (1994). Early literacy interventions: Answers and issues. In E.H. Hiebert & B.M. Taylor (Eds.), *Getting ready right from the start: Effective early literacy interventions.* Boston: Allyn & Bacon.

Hiebert, E.H., & Taylor, B.M. (2003). Beginning reading instruction: Research on early interventions. In M.L. Kamil & P.B. Mosenthal (Eds.), *Handbook of reading research* (pp. 455–482.) Mahwah, NJ: Lawrence Erlbaum Associates.

Individuals with Disabilities Education Improvement Act (IDEA) of 2004, PL 108-446, 20 U.S.C. §§ 1400 *et seq.*

International Reading Association. (1998). *Phonemic awareness and the teaching of reading: A position statement from the Board of Directors of the International Reading Association.* http://www.reading .org/Libraries/Position_Statements_and_Resolutions/ps1025_phonemic.sflb.ashx

Juel, C. (1991). Beginning reading. In R. Barr, M.L. Kamil, P.B. Mosenthal, & P.D. Pearson (Eds.), *Handbook of reading research* (pp. 759–788). New York: Longman.

Juel, C. (1994). *Learning to read and write in one elementary school.* New York: Springer-Verlag.

Kame'enui, E., & Carnine, D.W. (1998). *Effective teaching strategies that accommodate diverse learners.* Upper Saddle River, NJ: Prentice Hall.

Keller, C., Bucholz, J., & Brady, M. (2007). Yes, I can! Empowering paraprofessionals to teach learning strategies. *Teaching Exceptional Children, 39,* 18–32.

Lane, K., Fletcher, T., Carter, E., Dejud, C., & DeLorenzo, J. (2007). Paraprofessional-led phonological awareness training with youngsters at risk for reading and behavioral concerns. *Journal of Remedial and Special Education, 28,* 266–276.

Leslie, L., & Allen, L. (1999). Factors that predict success in an early literacy intervention program. *Reading Research Quarterly, 26,* 404–424.

Lewis, J.J. (2001). *Maria Montessori quotes.* Retrieved May 13, 2011, from http://womenshistory.about.com/od/quotes/a/montessori.htm

Likins, M. (2003). NCLB implications for paraprofessionals. *Principal Leadership, 3,* 10–13.

Lundberg, I., Frost, J., & Peterson, O. (1988). Effects of an extensive program for stimulating phonological awareness in pre-school children. *Reading Research Quarterly, 23,* 263–284.

Lyon, G.R., (1996, Oct. 27). Why Johnny can't decode. *Washington Post,* p. E1.

McClurkin, M.G. (2004). *Developing tutor expertise in an early reading intervention program.* Dekalb: Northern Illinois University Press.

McConnell, S. (2001). *Get It! Got It! Go! The preschool individual growth and development indicator.* St. Paul: University of Minnesota, Center for Early Education Development.

McCormick, C., Throneburg, R., & Smitley, J. (2002). *A sound start: Phonemic awareness lessons for reading success.* New York: Guilford Press.

Moats, L.C. (2001). Overcoming the language gap. *American Educator, 25*(5), 8–9.

National Center for Education Statistics. (2001). *The nation's report card: Fourth-grade reading highlights 2000.* Washington, DC: U.S. Department of Education.

National Early Learning Panel (NELP). (2009). *Developing early literacy: Report of the National Early Learning Panel.* Washington, DC: National Institute for Literacy.

National Reading Panel. (2001). *Teaching children to read: An evidence-based assessment of the scientific research literature on reading and its implications for reading instruction.* Bethesda, MD: National Institutes of Health.

No Child Left Behind Act of 2001, PL 107-110, 115 Stat. 1425, 20 U.S.C. §§ 6301 *et seq.*

Scarborough, H.S. (1998). Early identification of children at risk for reading disabilities: Phonological awareness and some other promising predictors. In B.K. Shapiro, P.J. Accardo, & A.J. Capute (Eds.), *Specific reading disability: A view of the spectrum* (pp. 75–120). Timonium, MD: York Press.

SEDL. (2010). *Reading and literacy.* Retrieved October 13, 2010, from http://www.sedl.org/expertise/reading_literacy.html

Serpell, R., Baker, L., & Sonnenschein, S. (2005). *Becoming literate in the city: The Baltimore Early Childhood Project.* New York: Cambridge University Press.

Shaywitz, S. (2003). *Overcoming dyslexia: A new and complete science-based program for overcoming reading problems at any level.* New York: Knopf.

Shonkoff, J.P., & Phillips, D.A. (Eds.). (2000). *From neurons to neighborhoods: The science of early childhood development.* Washington, DC: National Academies Press.

Siegel, L.S. (1989). IQ is irrelevant to the definition of learning disabilities. *Journal of Learning Disabilities, 22,* 469-479.

Slavin, R., Karweit, N., & Wasik, B. (1993). Preventing early school failure: What works. *Educational Leadership, 50*(4), 10–18.

Snow, C.E., Burns, M.S., & Griffin, P. (Eds.). (1998). *Preventing reading difficulties in young children.* Washington, DC: National Academies Press.

Torgesen, J.K. (2002). The prevention of reading difficulties. *Journal of School Psychology, 40,* 7–26.

Torgesen, J.K. (2004). Lessons learned from research on interventions for students who experience difficulty learning to read. In P. McCardle & V. Chhabra (Eds.), *The voice of evidence in reading research* (pp. 355–382). Baltimore: Paul H. Brookes Publishing Co.

Torgesen, J.K., & Burgess, S.R. (1998). Consistency of reading-related phonological processes throughout early childhood: Evidence from longitudinal-correlational and instructional studies. In J. Metsala & L. Ehri (Eds.), *Word recognition in beginning reading.* Mahwah, NJ: Lawrence Erlbaum Associates.

U.S. Department of Education. (2011). *Race to the Top fund.* Retrieved May 19, 2011, from http://www2.ed.gov/programs/racetothetop/index.html

Vaughn Gross Center for Reading and Language Arts. (2005). *Implementing the 3-tier reading model: Reducing reading difficulties for kindergarten through third grade students* (4th ed.). Austin, TX: Author.

Refer also to the Children's Book Bibliography in Appendix E on the accompanying CD-ROM.

Index

Page numbers followed by *t* indicate tables; page numbers followed by *f* indicate figures.